An Amos Yong Reader

An Amos Yong Reader

The Pentecostal Spirit

EDITED AND INTRODUCED BY

CHRISTOPHER A. STEPHENSON

CASCADE *Books* • Eugene, Oregon

AN AMOS YONG READER
The Pentecostal Spirit

Copyright © 2020 Wipf and Stock Publishers. All rights reserved. Except for brief quotations in critical publications or reviews, no part of this book may be reproduced in any manner without prior written permission from the publisher. Write: Permissions, Wipf and Stock Publishers, 199 W. 8th Ave., Suite 3, Eugene, OR 97401.

Cascade Books
An Imprint of Wipf and Stock Publishers
199 W. 8th Ave., Suite 3
Eugene, OR 97401

www.wipfandstock.com

PAPERBACK ISBN: 978-1-7252-5089-5
HARDCOVER ISBN: 978-1-7252-5090-1
EBOOK ISBN: 978-1-7252-5091-8

Cataloguing-in-Publication data:

Names: Yong, Amos, author. | Stephenson, Christopher A., editor.

Title: Book title : An Amos Yong reader : the pentecostal spirit / Amos Yong, author; Christopher A. Stephenson, editor.

Description: Eugene, OR: Cascade Books, 2020 | Includes bibliographical references and index.

Identifiers: ISBN 978-1-7252-5089-5 (paperback) | ISBN 978-1-7252-5090-1 (hardcover) | ISBN 978-1-7252-5091-8 (ebook)

Subjects: LCSH: Theology—Doctrinal. | Pentecostalism. | Religion and science. | Theology—Methodology. | Political Theology. | People with disabilities—Religious aspects—Christianity.

Classification: BR1644 .Y74 2020 (print) | BR1644 (ebook)

Manufactured in the U.S.A. APRIL 27, 2020

Front cover image, "Receive the Holy Spirit" by Hanna Varghese, 2000, 16" x 16" Batik, used by permission of the Overseas Ministries Study Center.

Dedicated to
Cheryl Bridges Johns
and
Jackie David Johns,
whose imaginative shared journey
has blazed trails
in the academy and the church.

Contents

Preface | xi

Introduction—Amos Yong: Pentecostalism's Premier Theologian | 1

PART ONE   Theology of Religions and Interreligious Dialogue
- 1.1 Discerning the Spirit(s) | 23
- 1.2 Beyond the Impasse | 32
- 1.3 The Spirit Bears Witness | 38
- 1.4 Toward a Pneumatological Theology of Religions | 46
- 1.5 Pneumatological Performance—Many Tongues, Many Practices | 53
- 1.6 Salvation—Pneumatological and Buddhological Comparisons and Contrasts | 57
- 1.7 Starting with the Spirit—Pneumatology and the Christian-Buddhist-Science Trialogue | 63

PART TWO   Religion and Science
- 2.1 The Spirit and the Orders of Creation | 75
- 2.2 The Emergence of Interdisciplinarity | 79
- 2.3 The Books of Scripture and of Nature—The Hermeneutics of Science | 85
- 2.4 Faith and Science—Friend or Foe? | 91
- 2.5 Speaking in Scientific Tongues | 98
- 2.6 Toward a Pneumato-Ecological Ethic—Christian-Buddhist Convergences | 104
- 2.7 A Trinitarian Theology of Creation | 112

PART THREE   Theology and Disability

   3.1   Theology and Down Syndrome | 119

   3.2   Honoring the "Weaker" Member—A Disability Ecclesiology and Charismology | 123

   3.3   The Spirit Meets the Ethiopian Eunuch—Redeeming Disability | 129

   3.4   Zacchaeus—Short and Unseen | 132

   3.5   Disability Theology of the Resurrection | 139

   3.6   Disability in the Christian Tradition | 147

   3.7   Be Healed! Saving the Church, Redeeming the World | 155

PART FOUR   Political Theology

   4.1   The Multidimensionality of Salvation | 163

   4.2   Poured Out on All Flesh—The Spirit, World Pentecostalism, and the Performance of Renewal Theology | 170

   4.3   Many Tongues, Many Political Practices | 175

   4.4   The Spirit's New Economy of Salvation | 178

   4.5   Empowered Witness—The Reconciling Movement of Love | 181

   4.6   Toward a Pent-Evangelical Theology of Migration | 187

   4.7   Toward a Pentecostal-Political-Theology | 192

PART FIVE   Luke-Acts

   5.1   Spirit Christology and Spirit Soteriology | 199

   5.2   Luke-Acts and the Trinitarian Shape of Hospitality | 204

   5.3   "Times of Refreshing" from the Lord—A Lukan Glimpse of the Universal Restoration | 209

   5.4   Promising to Restore the Kingdom of Israel, and the Spirit Came! | 214

   5.5   The Gift of Pentecost—Intimations of a Pneumatological Theology of Love | 218

   5.6   Pentecost and a New Theology of Diverse Dis/Abilities | 225

   5.7   The Early Church in Jerusalem as a Migrant Community | 231

PART SIX Theological Method
- 6.1 Spirit-Word-Community | 237
- 6.2 The Hermeneutical Trialectic | 244
- 6.3 Theology and/as Performance | 253
- 6.4 Method in Political Theology—A Pentecostal Perspective | 260
- 6.5 Pneumatology and Interreligious Engagement | 267
- 6.6 Evangelical Theology in the Twenty-First Century—Hybrid Soundings from the Asian American Diaspora | 271
- 6.7 The Dialogical Spirit | 282

Bibliography | 293
Index of Scripture | 319
Index of Subjects and Names | 3##

Preface

AMOS YONG IS THE most prolific pentecostal theologian to date. He is author of more than twenty books and more than 200 essays and editor of more than thirty books. He is an accomplished teacher and administrator, his most recent appointment being Dean of the School of Theology and of the School of Intercultural Studies at Fuller Theological Seminary. An Assemblies of God minister and a past president of the Society for Pentecostal Studies and former co-editor of its journal, *Pneuma*, Yong is also recognized in academic circles outside pentecostalism, especially in the fields of Christian theology of religions and theology of disability. Yong's published works are so voluminous that it is difficult to find an amiable entry point into his thought. This *Reader* is the first one-volume introduction to Yong's theology in his own words.

Several people helped bring this project to completion. I thank Amos Yong for fully supporting the idea for this *Reader* from the beginning. He also assisted me to such a great degree—including attaining permissions for republication and giving input on the reading selections—that I once joked with him that this would be "the *Amos Yong Reader* edited by Amos Yong"! Amos's patience when the timetable for this project extended due to no fault of his own demonstrated anew his collegiality and friendship to me.

This *Reader* would not have been completed without the tireless aid of Nok Kam and Jeremy Bone, Yong's research assistants. Kam compiled into one place the selections that I chose and made sure that each one begins and ends where I specified; he also reformatted the footnotes to Cascade's short citation style and created the table of contents. Later, Bone helped to generate the scripture index.

Richard Gamble, my own former student assistant, and his spouse, Courtney, took on the arduous task of verifying that the text for the *Reader* selections match their original publication versions verbatim. Richard also created bibliography entries for sources that Yong originally cited parenthetically.

Drenda N. Butler, fellow reader of Amos Yong and budding pentecostal theologian in her own right, read the entire manuscript and saved me from many careless errors and minor inconsistencies. She also prepared the index.

I thank Lisa, my wife, for supporting my vision for this *Reader*. She must have thought "Still?" more than once when I told her the project on which I was working. I also thank my daughters, Abigail and Bella, for their patience with me during the copyediting that they described as "grading papers." May they, too, one day take up and benefit from Yong's writings.

It remains only to thank the many publishers who granted permissions for the reproduction of the selections collected here. Special appreciation goes to Oxford University Press for allowing the use of a portion of an essay that is not yet in print. The first footnote in each selection gives the title of the original source, the full citation of which is in the bibliography.

Thanks to Tom Hastings at the Overseas Ministries Study Center for facilitating the permissions for use of "Receive the Holy Spirit" by Malaysian artist Hanna Varghese (1938–2009) on the front cover. We were looking for a Pentecost image by an Asian artist and were delighted to find one from Malaysia, Amos Yong's country of birth.

Amos Yong joins me in dedicating this collection to Jackie David Johns and Cheryl Bridges Johns, educators, colleagues, and friends who have modeled mutual support, shared leadership, and dialogue for many who have come after them, including the author and editor of this volume. Thank you, Cheryl and Jackie, for your sustained efforts, and may your example continue to point ways forward for all who learn from you.

—CHRISTOPHER A. STEPHENSON
  Memorial of St. Ignatius of Loyola, 2019

Introduction

Amos Yong: Pentecostalism's Premier Theologian

THE ARRIVAL OF THE twentieth anniversary (2020) of the publication of Amos Yong's first book is an occasion especially ripe for assessing his voluminous theological contributions. That first book, *Discerning the Spirit(s): A Pentecostal-Charismatic Contribution to Christian Theology of Religions*, became the first installment in Yong's sustained engagement with the relationships among Christianity and other religions. It also gave readers the first substantive insight into the methodological engine of not only Yong's theology of religions but also of his investigation of all of the major topics that have surfaced in his work since then—including religion and science, theology and disability studies, political theology, and theological interpretation of and in light of Luke-Acts.

In this opening chapter, I do not give an exhaustive introduction to the whole of Yong's theology.[1] Instead, I advance and support this claim: Yong's theological method as developed most explicitly in his *Spirit-Word-Community* is the key to understanding the whole of his theology. Yong engages in philosophical and fundamental theology from a pentecostal perspective by developing a pneumatological metaphysic, ontology, and epistemology. In so doing, he gives accounts of the God-world relationship (foundational pneumatology), the processes of human knowing (pneumatological imagination), and hermeneutics (communal interpretation). The major points of Yong's theology derive from this methodological basis. Thus, to prepare for the selections from Yong that follow, I (1) describe Yong's theological method in *Spirit-Word-Community*; (2) situate aspects of his methodology in relation to some classical liberal and postliberal methodological concerns; (3)

---

1. For this, see Stephenson, *Types of Pentecostal Theology*, 82–110; Stephenson, "Reality, Knowledge, and Life in Community."

give a brief overview of how this methodology informs other major theological topics; and (4) offer some observations about the style and format of the selections gathered here and how to use them most efficiently.

THEOLOGICAL METHOD

Metaphysics and Foundational Pneumatology

In its most basic sense, Yong's foundational pneumatology is an account of the relationship between God and the world from a pneumatological perspective. The primacy of pneumatology owes to Yong's contention that "Holy Spirit" is the most fundamental symbol of, and therefore, most appropriate category for referring to God's agency in the world.[2] The respective ideas of God and the world are correlated in such a manner that God is capable of acting in the world and the world is capable of receiving God's presence and activity.[3] While it is in part a theology of the Holy Spirit, one should not confuse foundational pneumatology with pneumatology as merely a locus of systematic theology. According to Yong, the latter is a coherent theological account of the Holy Spirit, constructed primarily in light of Scripture and tradition and directed primarily within the confines of the Christian church. Foundational pneumatology, however, addresses questions of fundamental theology and engages all interlocutors in the public domain who pursue questions concerning divine presence and agency in the world, including persons outside the church. This difference between systematic and foundational pneumatology implies that truth claims about pneumatology meet not only the criterion of coherence (inasmuch as they are elements of a single system of thought) but also the criterion of correspondence (inasmuch as they are claims about reality that are believed to maintain universally, not simply within a single—in this case, ecclesial—context).[4] The criterion of correspondence invites an engagement of truth claims between competing ideological frameworks, not only a consideration of them within a single system of thought.[5] Yong bases his desire for such engagement on a "cautious optimism regarding the possibility of a universal rationality and grammar."[6] The qualifier "foundational" does not imply epistemic foundations in the hard sense of incorrigible beliefs. Rather, foundational

2. Yong, "On Divine Presence and Divine Agency," 175.
3. Yong, *Discerning the Spirit(s)*, 99.
4. Yong, "On Divine Presence and Divine Agency," 178–80.
5. Yong, *Spirit-Word-Community*, 164–75.
6. Yong, "On Divine Presence and Divine Agency," 175.

pneumatology invites inquiry from any community of interpreters that wishes to address its tenets. Because it does not draw heavily on *a priori* necessity in its quest for universal truth claims, foundational pneumatology is subject to correction by empirically driven processes of verification and falsification.[7]

Yong's foundational pneumatology includes the construction of a metaphysic and ontology characterized by relationality. Yong predicates both constructs on a doctrine of the Trinity that pursues the integration of an Irenaean model of Spirit and Word as the two hands of God with an Augustinian model of the Spirit as the bond of love between Father and Son. In his discussion of these two trinitarian models, Yong poignantly establishes from a pneumatological perspective the relationality of all reality and being. For Yong, the two-hands model suggests a mutuality of Spirit and Word that leads to the notion of the coinherence of the divine persons. Coinherence, which is an affirmation of the reciprocity and interrelationality of the divine persons and a denial of any degree of ontological subordination or division among them, creates the conceptual space for three subsistent relations indwelling each other as one God.[8] Relationality is even more prominent in Yong's appropriation of the Augustinian model of the Spirit as the mutual love between Father and Son. As mutual love, the Spirit relates the Father to the Son and the Son to the Father, eternally in the immanent Trinity and temporally in the economic Trinity.[9] In addition to the relations of the divine persons, both the two-hands model and the mutual-love model provide accounts of God's relationship to the world and of the relationships of the plurality of things in the world to each other. From the perspective of the two-hands model, everything in the world exists by virtue of being created by God through Spirit and Word; therefore, things are what they are because they are instantiated as such by both Spirit and Word.[10] From the perspective of the mutual-love model, the Spirit not only relates Father and Son to each other but also relates God to the world, inasmuch as the Father loves the Son by bestowing the Spirit on him in the economy of salvation, that is, in the world. Likewise, the Spirit relates the world to God, inasmuch as the Son—from within the economy of salvation—returns that love to the Father.[11] All of reality, then, is inherently relational, and the idea "spirit" itself refers to the quality of relationality that holds together various things

---

7. Yong, *Spirit-Word-Community*, 100.
8. Yong, *Spirit-Word-Community*, 52–59.
9. Yong, *Spirit-Word-Community*, 67–72.
10. Yong, *Discerning the Spirit(s)*, 116–17.
11. Yong, *Spirit-Word-Community*, 69–70.

in their integrity without the dissolution of their individual identities.[12] Crucial to Yong's claim that reality is inherently relational is his insistence that relations are part of the real identities of things, rather than mere categories that human minds employ when interpreting reality. In short, things in the world exist as such because they are products of the creative activities of Spirit and Word and because their relationships to other things constitute them as such.

In addition to relationality, Yong's metaphysic and ontology are also characterized by rationality, as supported by the biblical witness to the Spirit as both source and communicator of rationality. According to Yong, the Spirit's hovering over the waters at creation suggests the Spirit's role in bringing order out of chaos through God's spoken words.[13] In fact, human beings are rational creatures precisely because the Spirit creates them in the image of God. Further, Wisdom of Solomon associates the Spirit with attributes such as intelligence and particularity. Also, the New Testament relates the Spirit to the divine mind. In 1 Corinthians 1, specifically, the Spirit searches the depths of God, solely comprehends what is God's, and enables humans to understand the gifts they have received from God. Similarly, in John 14, the Spirit is the one who will lead Jesus' followers into all truth. Just as the Spirit relates created things to each other, the Spirit also makes all created things intelligible. Finally, in addition to relationality and rationality, Yong's metaphysic and ontology are characterized by dynamism, understood as the Spirit's life-giving activity in the world. From creation to consummation, the Spirit spawns life, heals the fractures stemming from finitude and fallenness, and sustains God's creative act. The Spirit also directs the flow of history to its end and fulfillment and will ultimately triumph over sin and death.[14]

Epistemology and Pneumatological Imagination

Only implicit in the discussion so far is the fact that Yong's metaphysic and ontology are realist, meaning that things exist apart from being known by human minds and that the order of being is distinct from, although related to, the order of knowing. For Yong, the gap between the two is spanned by the pneumatological imagination, which is an orientation to God and the world that the pentecostal-charismatic life in the Spirit continually nurtures

---

12. Yong, *Spirit-Word-Community*, 84–86.
13. Yong, *Spirit-Word-Community*, 35–41.
14. Yong, *Spirit-Word-Community*, 43–48.

and shapes.[15] As the divine mind, the Spirit illuminates the rationality of the world and makes it intelligible to human minds.[16] The pneumatological imagination observes the phenomena of the world and, rather than assessing only their plurality and individuality, attempts to discern reality. The Spirit, then, both instantiates the world as rational and makes its rationality accessible to human knowing.

According to Yong, the pneumatological imagination understands truth as pragmatic, correspondence, and coherence. On the pragmatic score, the truth of a proposition depends in part on its meaningfulness and is judged by its ability to predict the behavior of a thing. Correct predictions over time lead to the establishment of habits concerning a thing and, therefore, connections between human knowing and things in the world, that is, between the orders of being and knowing. Truth as correspondence refers to the real distinction and representational connection between things in the world and human knowing. While external realities exist apart from human minds, propositions can reflect those realities accurately, in the sense of approximate correlation rather than exact congruence. Truth as coherence refers to a proposition's dependence on consistency with other statements within the same thought system. The coherence criterion presumes comprehensive investigation of all relevant data. Yong states that rather than choosing one of these criteria of truth over the other, the pneumatological imagination strives to meet all three criteria in its accounts of reality.[17]

One of the most significant characteristics of the pneumatological imagination is epistemic fallibilism. While the orders of knowing and being are correlated, one must make truth claims with great humility because all human knowledge is fallible.[18] It is because of the pneumatological imagination's fallibilism that foundational pneumatology exhibits a chastised optimism about the possibility of a universal rationality and grammar.[19] Summarizing the basic contours of foundational pneumatology and the pneumatological imagination, Yong writes that the object of interpretation is ultimately reality itself, that which measures and corrects our interpretations. Although reality is discerned hermeneutically and all knowledge is fallible, epistemological skepticism and relativism are warded off by the fact that "we do engage reality, our engagement is more or less truthful, and

---

15. Yong, *Spirit-Word-Community*, 123.
16. Yong, *Spirit-Word-Community*, 133–35.
17. Yong, *Spirit-Word-Community*, 164–75.
18. Yong, *Spirit-Word-Community*, 176–83.
19. Yong, "On Divine Presence and Divine Agency," 175.

it is normed by reality itself."[20] According to Yong, hermeneutics neither displaces nor nullifies the possibilities of metaphysics or epistemology as legitimate enterprises, but rather augments and complements them. The combination of metaphysical realism and epistemic fallibilism both makes interpretation possible (inasmuch as there is a world apart from human minds to interpret in the first place) and requires interpretation to continue until the eschaton (inasmuch as incomplete knowledge invites ongoing attempts to account for reality).

Hermeneutics and Communal Interpretation

Within Yong's triadic construct of Spirit-Word-Community, community is the context within which Spirit and Word come together. Metaphysics and epistemology are necessarily hermeneutical, inasmuch as all human attempts to know reality arise within interpretive communities.[21] The dynamic of communal discernment is an avoidance of two extremes: naïve realism and epistemological pluralism. That is, communal discernment both grants the perspectival nature of all human knowing and denies that interpretive communities are insulated intellectual ghettos that could somehow be normed only by their own parochial concerns.

In the broadest sense, community refers to the global human community, which is neither monolithic nor separated by clearly delineated, impenetrable borders. According to Yong, an informed theology of culture is characterized by the understanding that the borders among communities of participation are not entirely insulated. Each person participates in multiple communities of discourse to a greater extent, while also participating in other such communities to a lesser extent. Concerning theological interpretation, he writes that "each theological interpreter negotiates membership in multiple intellectual, national, socio-political and cultural-religious communities, each of which have identities that are shaped by specific canons, narratives rituals, and the like."[22] The ongoing process of interpretation, Yong believes, can theoretically lead to consensus. When we encounter others who participate primarily in traditions different than our own, we do not encounter pure alterity—at least not hermeneutically speaking. After all, we live in the same world and attempt to give account of the same mind-independent reality. Although we do so from within our respective interpretive communities, it is ultimately the same Spirit that enables human minds to

---

20. Yong, *Spirit-Word-Community*, 184.
21. Yong, *Spirit-Word-Community*, 275–76.
22. Yong, *Spirit-Word-Community*, 303–04.

understand the one world in which we all live and that drives the discourse, exchange, and dialogue necessary to pursue consensus.

CONCERNING THE LIBERAL AND THE POSTLIBERAL

Yong's theological method holds together qualified elements of classical liberal and postliberal methodologies that are often thought to be at odds with each other, especially his commitments to aspects of both universality and particularity. One way to see the tensions that Yong holds together is to situate part of his methodology with parts of the methodologies of David Tracy and George Lindbeck, both of whom Yong engages explicitly.[23] Although both Tracy and Lindbeck recognize the hermeneutical nature of theology and both write in light of the linguistic turn, they differ significantly on whether (at least some) experiences precede linguistic and symbolic structures (Tracy) or whether linguistic and symbolic structures precede and therefore help to create (all) experiences (Lindbeck). This difference leads Tracy to affirm the existence of universal human experiences that may come to expression in the form of different linguistic and symbolic structures and leads Lindbeck to conclude that different linguistic and symbolic structures—in the context of theology, doctrines functioning as regulative grammars—in fact produce different experiences. These notions, in turn, lead to different ideas about the nature of theological truth claims. Tracy sees them as public, in part because one can correlate them with the experiences of persons in the public sphere who are not part of the community of discourse out of which theological truth claims arise, that is, those who have a different linguistic and symbolic structure. Thus, those in the public sphere may understand, evaluate, and correct theological truth claims. Lindbeck sees theological truth claims as statements whose primary meaning is for those internal to the community of discourse from which the theological truth claims arise, that is, those who share the same linguistic and symbolic structure. Thus, those in the public sphere are likely to find theological truth claims largely, if not entirely, unintelligible and are in no position to evaluate whether or not they are true—understood first and foremost as being internally coherent with other theological truth claims.

Therefore, Tracy describes the nature of fundamental, systematic, and practical theology as follows:

---

23. See especially Tracy, *Blessed Rage for Order*; idem, *The Analogical Imagination*; idem, *Plurality and Ambiguity*; Lindbeck, *The Nature of Doctrine*.

In terms of primary reference groups, *fundamental* theologies are related primarily to the public represented but not exhausted by the academy. *Systematic* theologies are related primarily to the public represented but not exhausted in the church, here understood as a community of moral and religious discourse and action. *Practical* theologies are related primarily to the public of society, more exactly to the concerns of some particular social, political, cultural or pastoral movement or problematic which is argued or assumed to possess major religious import.[24]

Based in part on Tracy's account of these three distinctions within theology, Yong concludes that theology must address the academy (fundamental), ecclesial self-understanding (systematic), and ecclesial praxis (practical), each of which Yong correlates with the three criteria of truth—correspondence, coherence, and pragmatic, respectively.[25] The acceptance of these distinctions also forms the basis of Yong's commitment to formulate a foundational pneumatology for debate in the public arenas outside the Christian church, not merely pneumatology as a locus of systematic theology. Yong's adoption of Tracy's various "publics" is a significant driving force in his decision to include world religions, the sciences, North American philosophical traditions, persons with intellectual disabilities, and so on in his quest for truth wherever one may find it.

And yet, Yong is motivated less by belief in universal pre-categorial human experiences (as is Tracy) and more by the universal presence and potential universal activity of the Holy Spirit—as described in his foundational pneumatology—and the potential of universal discourse led by the pneumatological imagination. Yong's affirmation of actual and potential universality operates at the creational level, since things are what they are to some extent because of the universal work of the Spirit at the ontological level and because created things demonstrate the activity of the Spirit to the extent that they function precisely as what they were created to be. The same affirmation operates also at the hermeneutical level, since the same Spirit transcends different linguistic and symbolic structures and may help those who follow the pneumatological imagination to render discourse internal to a community with one linguistic and symbolic structure intelligible to a community with a different linguistic and symbolic structure. Similarly, created things themselves transcend different linguistic and symbolic structures because the Holy Spirit instantiates them as such independently of the always hermeneutical interpretation of them by human minds. None of

---

24. Tracy, *The Analogical Imagination*, 56–57.
25. Yong, *Spirit-Word-Community*, 275–310.

Yong's ideas on this score require belief in universal pre-categorial human experience per se, only in the universal work of the Spirit.

With respect to particularity, Yong qualifies and accepts some aspects of Lindbeck's cultural-linguistic theory. Yong affirms that truth claims, theological and otherwise, arise from particular, finite contexts with limited perspectives. These contexts, or communities of discourse, constitute truth claims from the ground up, and make all human knowing perspectival and partial. Truth claims must cohere not only with the other truth claims internal to a particular system of thought, but with an entire way of life manifested in part through concrete practices and behaviors. Lindbeck's famous illustration of *incoherence* between an action and a truth claim is that of the act of "cleaving the skull of the infidel" rendering false in the immediate intratextual context the accompanying truth claim "Christ if Lord."[26] Perhaps the strongest point of continuity between Yong and Lindbeck is on the inseparability of beliefs and practices, such that one must speak of beliefs to a certain extent as being performed. This point is crucial for Yong, because of its implications for interreligious dialogue. For example, one's understanding of the beliefs of a non-Christian religion will be limited necessarily if one does not engage in—to whatever extent Christian conscience allows and, even then, perhaps only temporarily—any of the practices or rituals of that religion, because such practices and rituals are in part performative beliefs to adherents of that religion. Furthermore, according to Yong, the practice of hospitality is an important gesture in interreligious dialogue. Both giving hospitality to and receiving hospitality from practitioners of non-Christian religions can bring greater understanding of beliefs held in both religious dialogue partners.

Nevertheless, Yong tries to guard against the insularity and incommensurability to which cultural-linguistic theory may be susceptible. He denies that communities of discourse are hermetically sealed and observes that most of us are simultaneously both "insider" and "outsider" to multiple such communities and traditions. He also insists that truth is pragmatic in the sense that all of us—even when we participate in different communities of discourse with different linguistic and symbolic structures—continually bump up against reality, which exists independently of human minds. Discerning reality is itself part and parcel of the pneumatological imagination, and the Holy Spirit—in all of its universality—can guide members of different communities of discourse to truths about reality, which exists externally to the perceptions of those communities. Thus, it is possible for new insights to unsettle or render invalid part or all of one's current linguistic or

---

26. Lindbeck, *The Nature of Doctrine*, 64.

symbolic structure, and new insight may come from others who are very different than we but in fact live in the same singular world.

Yong, then, holds specific kinds of commitments to universality—often associated with classical liberal theology—and particularity—often associated with postliberal theology. The universality has less to do with universal human experience than with the universal outpouring of the Holy Spirit "on all flesh" (Acts 2:17). The particularity acknowledges the endless complexity of local contexts, concerns, and perspectives but resists retreat into intellectual ghettos. These features alone make Yong's theological method worthy of attention in and of itself; they are also indispensable for understanding all of the many topics that his theology treats.

METHOD MEETS CONTENT

I now wish to outline how foundational pneumatology, pneumatological imagination, and communal interpretation shape the content of Yong's theology, as we keep in mind the fact that the most thorough statement of these methodological features occurs in *Spirit-Word-Community*. I focus on his contributions in the areas of theology of religions, global pentecostal theology, theology of disability, political theology, and the relationship between religion and science.

Theology of Religions

Integral to Yong's theology of religions is his account of discerning the presence, activity, and absence of both the Holy Spirit and other spirits in various religious traditions. Two factors drive Yong's efforts towards a theology of discernment: 1) his desire to cultivate a pneumatological orientation in theology of religions and 2) foundational pneumatology's assumptions about the Spirit's relationship to the created order. Concerning the first, Yong states that the respective economies of Spirit and Word in the world are distinct, although intimately related.[27] This distinction affords the potential of affirming the Spirit's presence and activity in arenas in which Christ is not explicitly professed, inasmuch as the Spirit's economy is not restricted to the Word's economy. The result for interreligious dialogue is that participants can temporarily postpone the christological questions of Jesus' identity and significance in order to pursue pneumatological questions first. This choice

---

27. Yong, *Discerning the Spirit(s)*, 133. For a map to subsequent developments on this issue in Yong's thought, see Yong, *The Spirit Poured Out on All Flesh*.

allows participants to establish greater mutual understanding between the two religious traditions before arriving at the debate over Jesus' particularity, a possible impasse that threatens to terminate dialogue.[28]

As a second driving force behind the determination to discern the Holy Spirit within other religions, Yong connects his theology of religions directly to foundational pneumatology. Building on the premises that the Holy Spirit is God's way of being present to and active within the world and that the norms and values of all created things are instantiated by the Spirit in relation to all other created things, Yong suggests that Christians should assess the Spirit's presence within non-Christian religions both ontologically and concretely.[29] On the ontological level, the elements within world religions such as texts, myths, rituals, and moral codes are what they are precisely as creations of the Spirit. On the concrete level, the degree to which these elements represent themselves authentically and are situated coherently within their respective religious traditions attests to the Spirit's presence within those religious traditions to a greater or lesser degree. However, not all symbols and rituals convey divine presence to practitioners. Instead, those symbols that destroy rather than promote social relationships and human authenticity indicate divine absence, or, the demonic.[30]

While Christians may legitimately expect to find the Spirit at work in various religious beliefs and practices, the possibility that the demonic may also be at work requires Christians to develop a theology of discernment for interpreting religious symbols.[31] For Yong, discerning spirits is a two-part process involving both interpretation and comparison. First, practitioners of the religious tradition in question offer interpretations of their own symbols and rituals by articulating their value and utility. As long as the symbols and rituals accomplish what they are supposed to accomplish without deviating significantly from their habits and norms, one can affirm the Spirit's presence and activity in those symbols and rituals to a limited degree. After all, it is the Spirit who enables a thing's authentic representation relative to other constituent things in a given symbol system. Second, one devises comparative categories for judging claims within the religion in question and then between religious traditions. To a certain extent, then, discerning the spirits is an exercise in comparative theology, the hermeneutical process of classifying and interpreting similarities and differences in symbols between Christianity and the beliefs of another religious tradition. In a

---

28. Yong, *Discerning the Spirit(s)*, 57–58.
29. Yong, *Discerning the Spirit(s)*, 133.
30. Yong, *Discerning the Spirit(s)*, 136.
31. Yong, *Discerning the Spirit(s)*, 137.

pneumatologically guided theology of religions, Yong states, discernment's comparative dimension involves finding within the non-Christian tradition analogies to a Christian account of the Holy Spirit. If such analogies are found, one can then engage the comparative task in attempt to discern the Spirit's presence (or absence) in the non-Christian religion. In respect to symbols and rituals specifically, the comparative task might involve determining whether or not they accomplish in the practitioners of the non-Christian religion goals similar to what the Holy Spirit accomplishes in practitioners of Christian rituals. The importance that practitioners ascribe to rituals becomes a measure by which one can discern the Spirit.[32]

Yong proposes that the two-part process of interpretation and comparison should be carried out on three different levels: the phenomenological-experiential, the moral-ethical, and the theological-soteriological.[33] The phenomenological-experiential pertains primarily to the realm of religious experience and all of the phenomena of accompanying symbols and rituals. At this level, discernment is concerned less with the symbols and rituals themselves than with how practitioners interpret and respond to certain symbols and rituals. While discernment at this level might be sufficient to lead to the initial conclusion that the Spirit is present and active in a non-Christian religion, Yong insists that discernment must proceed to the moral-ethical realm, which pertains to questions of religious utility and outcome. At this next level, discernment is concerned with whether and how the symbols and rituals achieve in religious practitioners the effects that they desire. While one can attribute similarities between Christianity and another religion on the moral-ethical front to the work of the Spirit, Yong argues that discernment at this level should not be determinative on its own. One still has to discern the referents of the symbols and rituals and render judgment on their relationship to the transcendent. At the level of the theological-soteriological, then, one must still determine whether the transcendent realities behind symbols and rituals are the Holy Spirit or another, perhaps demonic, spirit.[34] All three levels of discernment are ultimately predicated on empirical investigation, to which I now turn.

Towards a "World Theology"

A central component of Yong's foundational pneumatology is its alliance with fundamental theology and the need to engage truth claims in the

32. Yong, *Discerning the Spirit(s)*, 141–44.
33. Yong, *Discerning the Spirit(s)*, 250–55.
34. Yong, *Discerning the Spirit(s)*, 253–54.

public domain outside the immediate confines of ecclesial contexts. In keeping with this premise, Yong takes up the question of the possibility of constructing a truly global theology on the basis that the Holy Spirit is being poured out on all flesh, not merely within the confines of the church. He contends that Christian theology has much to contribute amid the endless complexities and pluralities of the global context that characterize the late modern world, and that theology should not shy away from making global claims. At the same time, by remaining attuned to and informed by those very pluralities, Yong wishes to avoid the oversimplified ideas of homogenization that often accompany ideas of globalization. In order to accentuate the sensitivity that he gives to various global contexts, Yong prefers the term "world theology" to describe his theological aims.[35]

Yong offers two accounts of several of systematic theology's traditional *loci*, each informed by foundational pneumatology and driven by pneumatological imagination. The first envisions systematic theology from a pentecostal perspective; the second takes the form of systematic *loci* informed by a theology of disability. The first exercise yields a pneumatological soteriology and ecclesiology, and the second addresses creation and resurrection.

Pentecostal Theology and Systematic Loci: Pneumatological Soteriology and Ecclesiology

Because pentecostalism spans the globe, Yong claims that it provides unique resources for shaping a Christian theology that can address all people groups without minimizing the differences among the various cultural instantiations of Christianity.[36] In order to establish the complexities of the various cultures in which pentecostalism flourishes, he surveys pentecostal traditions in Latin America, Asia, and Africa.[37] Guided by the pneumatological imagination's concerns for the empirical investigation of concrete religious expressions, Yong acknowledges the vast differences among the many pentecostal traditions while arguing for a reoccurring theological theme, namely, an emphasis on the concrete nature of salvation as attested by the Spirit's works in physical, social, and political dimensions. Yong makes soteriology the thematic starting point of his exploration of pentecostal systematic *loci*. At the same time, his efforts are ultimately oriented towards pneumatology, for salvation comes precisely as the *Spirit* is poured out on all flesh. The pneumatological imagination is the driving force behind Yong's soteriology

35. Yong, *The Spirit Poured Out on All Flesh*, 18.
36. Yong, *The Spirit Poured Out on All Flesh*, 17–30.
37. Yong, *The Spirit Poured Out on All Flesh*, 31–80.

and ecclesiology. It makes possible his phenomenology of implicit soteriologies in global pentecostalism and provides his pneumatological perspective on the constructive components of each of these two *loci*.

According to Yong, the contours of salvation include at least the following seven dimensions: 1) *personal*, the transformation of an individual into the image of Christ marked customarily by repentance, baptism, and reception of the Holy Spirit; 2) *familial*, the conversion of entire households, clans, or tribes; 3) *ecclesial*, baptism into the body of Christ and, thus, into a new communal way of living; 4) *material*, healing of body, soul, and mind; 5) *social*, deliverance from structural evils resulting in race, class, and gender reconciliation; 6) *cosmic*, redemption of the entire creation; and 7) *eschatological*, the final consummation of the other six dimensions.[38] Yong offers these seven aspects of salvation as an expansion of the tenets of the fivefold gospel that traditionally represents classical pentecostalism.[39] He writes, "[W]e can give preliminary articulation to the pentecostal intuition of the fivefold gospel: Jesus is Savior precisely as healer, sanctifier, and baptizer, all in anticipation of the full salvation to be brought with the coming kingdom."[40]

Yong observes that pentecostals have not historically discussed ecclesiology in detail and that, when they have, they have not usually done so in explicit connection with soteriology. He argues, however, that pentecostal soteriology and ecclesiology are intimately related, inasmuch as pentecostalism has always been a missiological movement. As Yong states, questions about what it means to be saved necessarily raise questions about the church's nature.[41] Before proposing how pentecostals might begin to explore ecclesiology more explicitly in connection with soteriology, Yong rehearses some of the different ways that the Christian tradition has articulated the relationship between soteriology and ecclesiology.[42] In conversation with church models ranging from those that define entrance into the church in terms of baptism, confession of Christ's lordship, or spiritual union with Christ, to those that describe the church as an alternative community distinguished by its core practices, he proposes elements of a pneumatological ecclesiology on the fronts of baptism and Eucharist.

---

38. Yong, *The Spirit Poured Out on All Flesh*, 91–98.
39. Yong, *The Spirit Poured Out on All Flesh*, 91.
40. Yong, *The Spirit Poured Out on All Flesh*, 120.
41. Yong, *The Spirit Poured Out on All Flesh*, 121–22, 127.
42. Yong, *The Spirit Poured Out on All Flesh*, 127–31.

INTRODUCTION

Theology of Disability and Systematic Loci: Creation and Resurrection

The same foundational pneumatology and pneumatological imagination that directs Yong's theology of religions and quest for a world theology also guides his theology of disability, resulting in a Christian theology informed by disabilities perspectives.[43] Inasmuch as the Spirit holds together disparate things without compromising each thing's identity and integrity, the pneumatological imagination is attuned to the many contextual voices in our pluralistic world in order to be informed by them without silencing one voice by conflating it to another. Just as Yong wishes to interpret the "many tongues" of the various cultural manifestations of global pentecostalism, he also wishes to be attentive to the "diverse tongues" of persons with disabilities (intellectual and otherwise), both in allowing them to articulate their own self-understandings and in allowing their insights to shape Christian theology.

Yong's investigations of the impact of experiences of intellectual disabilities on a theology of creation yield notable results for theological anthropology. He focuses particularly on how such experiences both complicate traditional Christian accounts of human creation in the image of God and invite their reformulation.[44] Yong states that the difficulty with the substantive view, which locates the *imago Dei* in the human's analogical reflection of God's rational and moral capacities, is its implication that persons with intellectual disabilities bear the *imago Dei* to a lesser degree. Moreover, Yong claims that the functional view, which locates the *imago Dei* in the human's ability to exercise authority and dominion over the rest of creation, implies similar problems as the substantive view, because persons with intellectual disabilities frequently exhibit diminished capacities for making decisions and taking responsibility for themselves and others. Most promising, according to Yong, is the relational view, which locates the *imago Dei* in the human's capacity for relationships with God and with fellow humans, something that intellectual disabilities do not necessarily diminish.[45]

Since a theology of embodiment highlights the significance of one's physical body for identity, it raises poignant questions about the continuity of human persons in relation to eschatology, especially from the perspective of the resurrection of the body as the removal of all deformity. As Yong points out, a purely physical disability with no intellectual defects might

---

43. Yong, *Theology and Down Syndrome*, 10–14.
44. Yong, *Theology and Down Syndrome*, 157–65.
45. Yong, *Theology and Down Syndrome*, 169–74.

not be obviously constitutive of the person in any meaningful sense, but an intellectual disability like Down Syndrome is more likely to shape one's being in the world. The question then arises, if the resurrected body were to be transformed to a state that did not include Down Syndrome, would the human self in question truly have endured such transformation? Yong states that the challenges concerning personal continuity from a disabilities perspective warn against quickly accepting the notion that all deformity will be removed from resurrected bodies as well as invite a more dynamic eschatology than has typically been conceived in the Christian tradition. He suggests that the Holy Spirit is the force of continuity between the embodied life of the present and the life of the resurrected body. Thus, Yong calls for a dynamic eschatology that takes disability perspectives seriously, in light of the pneumatological imagination's initiatives to draw on disparate voices.[46]

Political Theology

Yong addresses political theology in light of the basic logic of foundational pneumatology's commitment to address all concerned interlocutors. Engaging persons in the public square that are outside the church directly raises the issue of political theology inasmuch as it invites questions about the societal implications of a Christian theology that is fully public. Yong examines both the dominant paradigms in political theology and the political logic implicit in certain pentecostal practices. In *In the Days of Caesar*, Yong's lengthiest treatment of political theology, his extensive phenomenology of current global pentecostal practices in the public sphere silences once for all the dismissive criticism that pentecostals are preoccupied with individual salvation to the exclusion of social concern.

In ways that intersect with political theology, Yong adopts a pentecostal perspective on a pneumatological theology of love, including considerations of God as love and creation as participating in divine love. Conceding that the pentecostal tradition has associated the Holy Spirit far more frequently with "power" than with "love," he attempts to make pentecostal pneumatology's implications for a theology of love explicit. Building in part on recent social-scientific investigations of benevolence among certain pentecostal faith communities, Yong argues that pentecostal practices of divine *power*, such as spiritual gifts, can also be seen as encounters with divine *love*. After exploring Lukan, Pauline, and Johannine texts, he concludes that Spirit, gift, and love come together to suggest that God's gift of the Spirit at Pentecost

---

46. Yong, *Theology and Down Syndrome*, 271–92.

is a gift of both power and love and, in turn, that manifestations of divine power through spiritual gifts are God's gift of love through the Spirit.[47]

Religion and Science

Yong's proposals in science and religion also stem from the logic of Spirit-Word-Community. In this case, among the "many tongues" to which theology must listen are the natural, social, and human sciences. The plurality of methodologies in religious discourse, the sciences themselves, and approaches to conversations between the two are both consonant with and able to be explicated by the "many tongues" metaphor.[48]

Foundational pneumatology's tenets about the role of the Spirit in the God-world relationship leads to a pneumatological view of nature that avoids reductionistic accounts of the world. Yong's foray into religion and science is in part an explication of underlying themes of divine agency in foundational pneumatology, but with direct engagement of the claims and technical vocabularies of the natural sciences.[49] The pneumatological imagination's commitment to epistemic fallibilism also surfaces in the conversation between religion and science. Yong brings to the table a pneumatological perspective shaped by pentecostal ethos that in turn attempts to shape the conversation by giving an account of topics such as creation, divine action in the world, and emergence theory. Yet, this attempt does not proceed along the line of *a priori* necessities that may unduly privilege a particular kind of theological reasoning over scientific methodologies. Rather, it is open to be corrected by reliable scientific data, all of which must be hermeneutically discerned as theologians and scientists give their respective accounts of the one world in which they live.[50]

Yong's contributions to the religion and science dialogue intersects with other areas of his work. In fact, he incorporates aspects of the dialogue into his abiding interest in theology of religions and into a new exploration into a theology of love in pneumatological perspective. Concerning theology of religions, Yong focuses on Christian accounts of *pneuma* and Buddhist accounts of *shunyata* (emptying) in connection with the neurosciences. With respect to *pneuma*, he interfaces an emergence model of mind-brain relations with a pneumatological reading of the creation accounts in Genesis to suggest that 1) inasmuch as mental processes are dependent on

---

47. Yong, *Spirit of Love*.
48. Yong, *The Spirit of Creation*, 27–29.
49. Yong, *The Spirit of Creation*, 34–47, 102–32.
50. Yong, *The Spirit of Creation*, 25–33.

brain activity, humans are truly dependent on "the dust of the earth"; 2) the mind is affectively and emotively constituted by the body, and these dimensions manifest in the emergent self that the Spirit constitutes as irreducibly particular according to its unique fields of activity; 3) the mind also exhibits "top-down" influence on the body that is consonant with the interactivity attested between the Spirit and creation; and 4) humans are intersubjective selves who interact with other persons and other aspects of creation that are equally dependent on the divine Spirit.[51] With respect to *shunyata*, Yong observes that emptying occurs through empirical particularities in such a way that objects are empty precisely in their interdependence with other objects. Further, subject-object relations are transformed as each emerges together through an encounter or experience.[52]

NOTES ON THE SELECTIONS IN THIS *READER*

The order of selections in this *Reader* moves from the particular to the general. That is, it follows an inductive path from specific topics—theology of religions and interreligious dialogue, religion and science, theology and disability, political theology, and Luke-Acts—to theological method. Those who wish to follow a deductive path that moves from the general to the particular, like this Introduction, might consider reading first the selections on theological method before returning to theology of religions and interreligious dialogue and so on. Any section of interest can be read on its own, as can any individual selection.

Some of the selections bear minor stylistic changes from their original publications, such as the conversion of parenthetical citations to footnotes, the correction of a couple of typographical errors, the occasional insertion of an Oxford comma, and some Editor's Notes. All Scripture quotations are from the New Revised Standard Version or based on it with only minor variation. All of Yong's allusions to other sections of his writings refer to the texts from which I took the selections compiled here, not to any of the selections themselves. I made no updates to the content of Yong's ideas. All of the selections carry the same claims as they did at the time of their publications. Most of the selections come from Yong's books, and a few come from articles. The selections attempt to encapsulate Yong's theology over the first two decades of his academic career. At the same time, those chosen for inclusion represent themes that have remained most important for Yong up to the present.

51. Yong, *Pneumatology and the Christian-Buddhist Dialogue*, 43–51.
52. Yong, *Pneumatology and the Christian-Buddhist Dialogue*, 67–74.

Since this *Reader* is a manageably sized, representative collection of selections from Yong's own writings rather than a secondary source analysis of his theology, I hope that it will be an accessible entry point into the thought of one of pentecostalism's most accomplished scholars. Of course, it is in no way a substitute for a more extensive reading of his works, and I trust that the primary source selections that follow will whet readers' appetites for just that.

—Christopher A. Stephenson

PART ONE

Theology of Religions and Interreligious Dialogue

1.1

Discerning the Spirit(s)[1]

INTRODUCTION

THE INTERRELIGIOUS DIALOGUE HAS only just begun. We have, however, completed the opening exchange between two traditions and are at a rest area along our own road to Emmaus.[2] It is therefore a good place to stop and chart the gains that have been made. I begin with ten theses that have emerged so far in this quest for a pentecostal-charismatic theology of religions. The implications of these theses will then be explored. This project concludes by outlining the many directions that this study has opened up for further research and dialogue.

A PENTECOSTAL-CHARISMATIC *THEOLOGIA RELIGIONUM*: SOME EXPLORATORY THESES

Thesis One: A pentecostal-charismatic theology of religions should complement rather than displace other Christian theological efforts to comprehend the non-Christian faiths.

---

1. Yong, *Discerning the Spirit(s)*, 310–19.
2. This reference is, of course, to the city Cleopas and another disciple were on their way to when they were joined by the risen Christ. It is interesting to note, however, that modern scholarship has been unable to confirm the historicity of this city even though Luke clearly states that it was "about seven miles from Jerusalem" (Luke 24:13; cf. Liefeld, *Luke,* 1054–55). My reference to this "mystery city" is therefore an apt metaphor for our own contemporary interreligious journey: we may not know exactly where we are headed, but we sense the presence and leading of the Spirit who raised Jesus from the dead.

Thesis Two: A pentecostal-charismatic theology of religions should be founded on a robust trinitarianism that recognizes the Son and the Spirit as the two hands of the Father even while it avoids the popular and lay-level tripersonalistic understanding of the Trinity rejected by Oneness Pentecostals. Such a trinitarian theology allows for both christological and pneumatological approaches to the phenomenon of human religiosity, albeit in different respects.

Thesis Three: A pentecostal-charismatic theology of religions should be capable of establishing the relationship between the economy of the Holy Spirit and the religions not only at a theological level, but also at a philosophical or metaphysical level of generality. At the former level, the religions can be understood as created by God through Word and Spirit. At the latter level, the religions can be understood to be dynamic historical realities that are in processes of transformation, and through which human beings potentially experience ultimate transformation.

Thesis Four: A pentecostal-charismatic theology of religions should be able to provide a pneumatological account for the transformative character of human experience in general and the experience of ultimate salvation in particular. This is retrieved from the pentecostal-charismatic encounter with the Holy Spirit which in turn shapes their engagement with the world. Such a way of looking at the world—a pneumatological imagination—enables the instantiation of the divine symbol of the Holy Spirit in the human experience of the world. This is to acknowledge the divine presence and activity in creation. The former relates to the constitution of the harmonies of things in their own authenticity and integrity, and the latter relates to the constitution of things in their networks of relationships with others. Divine presence is evidenced by a thing's fulfilling its created purpose while divine activity can be said to occur when greater and greater degrees of harmony are realized in the processes of history. Non-Christian faiths can be regarded as salvific in the Christian sense when the Spirit's presence and activity in and through them are evident as hereby defined.

Thesis Five: A pentecostal-charismatic theology of religions should also be able to account for processes that are not transformative but rather destructive. This it does by way of combining pneumatology and anthropology: it recognizes that human beings are free and that their lives are influenced not only by the Holy Spirit but also by other spiritually destructive fields of force symbolized by divine absence or the demonic. The pneumatological imagination enables the recognition of religions as a complex welter of spiritual forces, all of which are ambiguous in and of themselves but tend either toward the divine or the demonic, although never fully so in either case.

Thesis Six: A pentecostal-charismatic theology of religions should therefore provide a means by which to discern the divine from the demonic in the religions. The modality of the pneumatological imagination—from divine presence to divine activity to divine absence—provides *a* normative measure by which such discernment is exercised. The religious symbols, practices, and doctrines of other faiths can be assessed as modalities which lead either to divine blessedness or to demonic condemnation and destruction.

Thesis Seven: A pentecostal-charismatic theology of religions should be open to learning more about the world and the religions from the Spirit. Such epistemological openness is intrinsic to a genuine pneumatological orientation. This reflects both the fact that the Spirit leads fallible human beings into a greater and greater grasp of the truth and the fact that the Spirit is continuously at work in the world of religions and transforming them. Discerning the Spirit(s) in the religions is therefore always provisional, subject to both the enlargement of epistemological horizons and to the facts as revealed by the transformative work of the Spirit.

Thesis Eight: A pentecostal-charismatic theology of religions should therefore free human beings for participation in the interreligious dialogue. The goal of such dialogues is not a mere agreement on similarities that ignores serious differences. Rather, the activity of apologetics needs to be included in acknowledging such conversations to be in the service of the righteousness, peace, and truth that characterize the Kingdom of God. Dialogue is thus ultimately about providing the kind of self-criticism that leads to the mutual and, ultimately, eschatological transformation of religious traditions, including the Christian faith.

Thesis Nine: A pentecostal-charismatic theology of religions should also free human beings to follow the leading of the Spirit into the world, to work with all those who bear the marks of the Spirit for the transformation of the world and for the counteraction of demonic forces in anticipation of the impending Kingdom of God. To the extent that the religions are discerned to be working toward these objectives, they can be acknowledged to be fulfilling their divine mandate for being.

Thesis Ten: A pentecostal-charismatic theology of religions should, finally, invigorate the proclamation of the Christian gospel even as it recognizes the eschatological horizon of the Holy Spirit's presence and activity. Dialogue as truth-seeking-encounters, service as labors-of-Christian-love, and proclamation of the redemption of the world from the forces of the demonic and of the reconciliation of the creation to the creator through Jesus Christ, all need to be combined. In this way, Christian faith in Christ is put to public test whereby the power of the Holy Spirit can be demonstrated throughout the course of human history. Ultimately, however, no empirical evidence suffices to establish the validity of Christian truth claims beyond doubt vis-à-vis that of other religious traditions beyond doubt since such confirmation can only be obtained at the eschaton. A pneumatological orientation to this reality is therefore able to embrace the ambiguities of history without succumbing to a nihilistic relativism. Instead, it allows itself to be led by the Spirit who is believed to have raised Christ from the dead and will do so also for the religions now and in the end.

IMPLICATIONS OF THIS STUDY

The above theses report the provisional findings of this study. Allow me to briefly tease out three implications emerging from them.

First, recall the statement at the conclusion of Chapter 1 regarding this being a "pneumatology of quest." Such a pneumatology allows only a provisional certitude at every turn, beginning with the theological and metaphysical presuppositions and hypotheses, continuing with the interpretation of empirical data, and including (but not terminating at) the discernment of Spirit(s). Needless to say, nothing can be prejudged. This is not so much because our subject is pneumatology as it is that the creation of the world through Word and Spirit provides the open context within which human beings live and know.

Such provisional certitude pertains also to our knowledge and discernment of the non-Christian faiths.[3] It may be that the Spirit's presence is evident only on Christian terms; but it may also be that the Spirit's presence and activity can be confirmed on grounds delineated by both traditions. Alternatively, it may be that the Spirit is here present in this religious symbol but not in that one, here active in this ritual but not in that one, here at work in this religious process but not in that one. Or perhaps the comparative process or conversation will reveal areas under the control of the demonic within either tradition. This of course, requires repentance and the righting of wrongs, much more so if Christians discover themselves to be guilty as has been the case in so many instances previously. But it also may be that there is a relative void of the Spirit's presence and activity in other traditions. Even in this case, however, who is to say that the Spirit's entrance into these traditions has not been providentially arranged through a genuine interreligious dialogical interchange?

Because of human fallibility, understanding the ways of the Spirit can never be an individualistic effort. A pneumatology of quest requires

---

3. Cf. Volf, "A Study in Provisional Certitude."

that discernment be subject to public examination, either for ratification or for correction. This is the reason for the interim nature of my concluding theses. They are hereby submitted to the review of my peers, colleagues and partners in Christian ministry generally, and pentecostal-charismatic ministry specifically. As Lederle and Clark say,

> in the final event it is the Spirit himself who grants the people of God the ability to recognise in the lives of others the working of God (cf. Acts 10). Pentecostal theology may thus attempt to pinpoint criteria for doctrine and experience—but in the long run it will be that discernment which is given the community of Spirit-filled believers at large which will approve or disprove the matter.[4]

A second theological implication of the foregoing study relates to the proposed criteria for discernment. According to the metaphysical hypothesis developed here, all things and events can and should be evaluated both pneumatologically and christologically. In fact, a more thorough understanding of any thing or event cannot be attained apart from the acknowledgment and assessment of the contributions of both hands of the Father. In this work, I have developed some criteria to test the Spirit(s) by focusing on the character and nature of pneumatology. All pneumatological criteria, however, have their corresponding christological dimension. The latter has not been seriously examined in this project for two reasons. First, as previously noted, the dialogue between Umbanda and pentecostalism conducted in the preceding chapter is the first of its kind. It seems right that the full implications of a pneumatological theology of religions should be allowed to exert themselves before resorting to christological criteria. I suggested at the end of Chapter 8 some other areas of dialogue which require the employment of christological categories, and these will need to be brought into play in future dialogues.

The second reason for delaying the application of Christology to this dialogue is that the approach to other faiths proposed here is one of the first to explore the viability of a theology of religions within a systematically developed pneumatological framework. Relatively new models need to be severely tested on their own terms for their coherence, plausibility, and adaptability. It is best to proceed with such probation piecemeal so that categorical confusion is kept to a minimum. There comes a point in the application of the model that it is recognized to have exhausted its ability to provide further insights. I did not sense that to be the case in the above

---

4. Lederle and Clark, *What is Distinctive About Pentecostal Theology?*, 63; cf. McQueen, *Joel and the Spirit*, 15–16.

dialogue between pentecostalism and Umbanda. That said, however, at some point in any interreligious dialogue, Christians will need to correlate the findings provided by a pneumatological approach with christological categories and criteria in order to complete the dialogue and be faithful to the fully trinitarian structure of their faith.

This said, I need to reiterate my commitment to Christology as an essential feature of all things and events. There is no better way to do so than by acknowledging my own theological inclusivism, following the model developed by Clark Pinnock and John Sanders, among others. Ultimately, as Gerald Finnegan indicates, I suspect that perhaps my metaphysical intuitions have been so shaped by the Christian story that I have thus far been unable to read reality other than through a trinitarian lens. In discussing the question of Jesus Christ as the unique or only savior of the world, Finnegan comments that

> the uniqueness of all things historical and the ability to distinguish and evaluate such realities may be the underlying question here. We return here to intuition and the ancient question of the one and the many. For those who favor pluralism seem to be opting for multiplicity over unity, whereas those who accept the traditional understanding of Christian faith seem to presume the unity exists at a deeper level of reality, indeed at the deepest level, and multiplicity is a phenomenon which arises from it and returns to it in the end.[5]

Clearly, my adherence to the metaphysical hypothesis of God as creator of all things *ex nihilo* predisposes me ultimately toward a christological inclusivism within a trinitarian framework. For that reason, I can understand the meaningfulness of ultimate salvation expressed in the *Christ*-ian way and through the name of Jesus.[6]

Yet the metaphysical hypothesis undergirding this study also provides for a "pneumatological inclusivism" that enables me to defend pluralism in terms of the created order. As a pentecostal Christian, the pneumatological imagination does make the world a much more adventurous place to live in, even as it frees me to look for evidence of both hands of the Father in other religious traditions. In the long run, perhaps the pneumatological imagination will require a fundamental reorientation of Christology. Karl Rahner suggests as much in reflecting on the trinitarian and pneumatological framework of Eastern theology toward the end of his life:

---

5. Finnegan, "Jesus as Savior of the World," 149.
6. Cf. Surin, "Revelation, Salvation, the Uniqueness of Christ, and Other Religions."

Perhaps an Eastern theology will one day reverse this perspective [of Western christocentrism]. Because of the universal salvific will of God and in legitimate respect for all the major world religions outside of Christianity, it may perhaps make a pneumatology, a teaching of the inmost, divinizing gift of grace for all human beings (as an offer to their freedom), the fundamental point of departure for its entire theology, and then attempt from this point—and this is something that might be achieved only with considerable effort—to gain a real and radical understanding of Christology. For a theology of this kind John 7:39 ("There was no Spirit as yet because Jesus had not yet been glorified") will perhaps be less suitable and intelligible than scriptural passages which extol the universal salvific will of God and which let the Spirit speak through all the prophets and know that the Spirit has been poured out on all flesh.[7]

The third, and perhaps most important theological implication of this study is that the turn to pneumatology in the formation of a Christian theology of religions necessarily transforms the character of Christian theology for two related reasons. To begin with, if it is acknowledged that the Holy Spirit is at work perhaps even in the non-Christian religious traditions of humankind, it becomes incumbent on Christian theologians to cease ignoring other faiths in the doing of theology. The possible presence and activity of the Spirit in other traditions means the possible existence of theological insights in other traditions that may have a positive impact on Christian theology. To deny this latter possibility is to lapse to an extremely anemic pneumatology even on biblical grounds. Perhaps the pneumatological approach to other religions developed here can provide the impetus toward a theological appropriation of the insights of other traditions that has been suggested but rarely accomplished.[8]

---

7. Rahner, "Aspects of European Theology," 97–98. In this connection, see also Burgess, "Implications of Eastern Christian Pneumatology for Western Pentecostal Doctrine and Practice," suggestions about the value of bringing Eastern Orthodox pneumatology into dialogue with pentecostalism.

8. For a valiant beginning effort, see Smart and Konstantine, *Christian Systematic Theology in a World Context*. One of the more celebrated "failures" to follow through with the program of deriving theological insights from other faiths is Wolfhart Pannenberg's three-volume *Systematic Theology*. Whereas he clearly suggests in part one of the first volume that such is imperative for Christian theology at the present time, what we find throughout the second part and the remaining two volumes is a systematic and thoroughgoing engagement with the Christian tradition in a manner reminiscent of Barth! Pannenberg's *Systematic Theology* does not live up to the expectations generated in the theological community both by his methodological claims and by his previous work (e.g., Pannenberg, *Basic Questions in Theology*; cf. Bollinger, "Pannenberg's

Following from this, the universal presence and activity of the Holy Spirit speaks of the universality of truth. Christian theology that claims to be true and universally applicable cannot continue operating according to the parochial categories of a Western, institutionalized Christendom.[9] Theoretically, it is certainly possible and legitimate, from a Christian standpoint, to insist on divine revelation as being given in the form of the Hebrew Bible and the Christian Testament. Two caveats, however, should be registered. First, a pneumatological orientation cannot arbitrarily deny that other canonical traditions may also be divinely inspired in some way.[10] Such must be the conclusion of an extended investigation, not an assumption at the beginning. Second, even to insist that Christian Scripture is divinely inspired and normative does not do away with the requirement for careful exegesis and interpretation of both the Christian Bible and non-Christian canonical texts. Such processes inevitably involve the religio-cultural lenses of the interpreter and interpreting community in the hermeneutical spiral. To say that revelation is scriptural does not obviate the reality that the revelation that counts—i.e., that saves and transforms—emerges from the dialectical encounter between the text (or ritual, or symbol, etc.) and the person-in-community (more accurately, person with various levels of membership in multiple communities).[11] In the same way, Christian theology inevitably

---

Theology of the Religions and the Claim to Christian Superiority"; Braaten, "The Place of Christianity among the World Religions"; Grenz, "Commitment and Dialogue").

9. Cf. Stackhouse, *Apologia*.

10. Cf. Dupuis, *Jesus Christ and His Spirit*, 211–28.

11. This is Henry Knight's primary error. Knight clearly recognizes the contextuality of all interpretation. But he seems unaware that it is a purely semantic move to privilege the biblical narrative over the contemporary horizon. He is right to insist on guarding revelation against "cultural accommodation, ideological captivity, and reductionism" (*A Future for Truth*, 165). But such comes about by playing out the dialectic between text and context rather than simply asserting the priority of the former. It is unrealistic and self-deceiving to think oneself and one's community able to preserve the priority of biblical revelation since it is precisely such mechanisms which allow the ideological captivity Knight fears. The pneumatological dimension of revelation is precisely the open-endedness that temporally situated beings negotiate. It is therefore better, and more accurate, to say that the form of revelation is "influenced by the cultures and histories in which it occurs . . . It is a blend of human imagination and reflection and Divine . . . co-operative persuasion" (see also Ward, *Religion and Revelation*, 343; cf. D'Costa, "Revelation and Revelations"). The traditional Christian argument that general revelation leaves human beings without excuse (Rom 1:20; cf. Oden, "Without Excuse") is valid not because general revelation is only damning, but because general revelation imparts sufficient knowledge about the divine reality such that one neglects it to one's peril. To say that human beings are unable to appropriate general revelation salvifically due to total depravity is to go down the road to the kind of five-point Calvinism that finds no resonance with the pentecostal-charismatic experience.

results from the interface between Christian Scripture and the context of interpretation. In a multi-religio-cultural world, a Christian theology aware of the universal and prevenient presence and activity of the Spirit cannot but be open to the truths of the Spirit wherever they may be found. In that sense, a pneumatological theology of religions will therefore both require and enable a reconstruction of Christian systematic theology that engages the truths that are discovered in the global interreligious context.

In sum, a pentecostal-charismatic theology of religions embraces the tensions between pneumatology and Christology, between inclusivism and exclusivism, between divine presence and divine absence. The explosion of the pentecostal-charismatic movement attests to the vitality of its pneumatocentric spirituality and the promise of such spirituality for the wider ecumenism. I have therefore argued in this study that this imagination signifies a latent ability to engage religious "others" theologically. If it is in fact true that meaningful, engaging, and relevant theology has inevitably been founded upon authentic and vibrant spirituality, then pentecostal theology has plenty of pneumatological capital to draw from and is therefore under obligation to provide the kind of reflection that matches its life and practice. This theological potency has led some observers to comment that pentecostalism "will play a prominent role in the next millennium's Christian vision."[12] I suggest that this role includes the forging of a more holistic and trinitarian theology, one which gives proper place and emphasis to both Word and Spirit and that refuses to allow either to be dominated by the other. It is therefore correct to say that pentecostal-charismatic imagination is empowered by the Spirit to insist on both singularity and multiplicity, unity and plurality, the one and the many. In the words of Peter Hodgson, "I affirm a quest for a more radical pluralism, but let it be a pluralism of solidarity rather than of separation . . . Confidence in the possibility of mutual transformation through dialogue is properly grounded not in an optimistic humanism but in a realistic theology of spiritual presence: Spirit is the third, the Interpreter who interprets all in all."[13]

---

12. Cleary, "Introduction," 15.
13. Hodgson, *Winds of the Spirit*, 306.

1.2

Beyond the Impasse[1]

ASSESSING THE SITUATION

BEFORE MOVING AHEAD WITH the overarching question of discerning the religions, I think it is important to redress an important set of questions with its corollary concerns that may be lingering in our midst as a potential problem for pneumatological *theologia religionum*. This set of questions may be simply framed with regard to the *Filioque* since it basically concerns the relationship of pneumatology to christology in this project. This question, of course, is not new. It has been a perennial source of tension, going as far back as Irenaeus' view of the Word and the Spirit as the "two hands of God" and evidenced throughout the history of Christian dogmatics. Irenaeus' dictum has been generally assumed as summarizing the biblical distinction underlying the differentiation between the christological and pneumatological missions. Yet, at the same time, because the early Christian apologist understood the economies of the Son and the Spirit to be integrally related, he also insisted that "where the Church is, there is the Spirit of God; and where the Spirit of God is, there is the Church."[2] This question of the relationship of the Spirit to Christ and to his Church has been replayed down through the ages in the *Filioque* debate. In terms of the historical formulas, is the Spirit solely "from the Father," "from the Father and the Son," "from the Father of the Son," or even "from

1. Yong, *Beyond the Impasse*, 185–92.
2. Irenaeus, *Against Heresies* 3.24.

the Father through the Son"? The result of this debate may be pertinent to the question of whether or not a pneumatology of religions is possible. If indeed the *Filioque* is re-asserted, pneumatology may remain subordinated to christology thereby minimally securing the fulfillment theory—the notion that other faiths, including Judaism, are valid only as anticipations of the Christian revelation and therefore are fulfilled by Christ—and perhaps reinforcing the Catholic doctrine of *extra ecclesiam nulla salus*.

As previously discussed, however, there is growing agreement in the West regarding the dogmatic illegitimacy of the *Filioque* particularly in light of its intrusion into the creed outside the recognized conciliar processes. Rejection of the *Filioque* may free up some room for a development of a pneumatology of religions as a distinct or at least related stream in the history of salvation. Yet in a very real sense, removing the *Filioque* is but the beginning of the adjustment of a religious vision, leading to a complete reassessment of traditional formulations of christology, pneumatology, ecclesiology, and missiology.

There are many other aspects of this particular issue that have not been considered. I am certainly not arguing for a view of the economy of the Spirit as completely sovereign or unrelated to that of the Son. I am, however, affirming that the turn to pneumatology may allow for more neutral categories to emerge when attempting to discern the presence and activity of the Spirit in other traditions. Christological criteria will always remain and have their place. Yet they may perhaps be enhanced by other criteria thus retaining the integrity of the other tradition. How else should discernment proceed if not first paying serious attention to the "object"—I use this conceptually, realizing that often, discerning the religions includes discerning persons and personal activities—of discernment as radically other? Of course, discerning the demonic is itself not unambiguous. More often than not, as the Orthodox like to say, "we can only know with some assurance where the Spirit is, rather than where the Spirit is not" (the latter being divine absence).[3] In that case, certainly we can proceed only with confidence

---

3. For this saying, I am indebted to my friend, Father Andrew Jaye, formerly of St. Mary's Orthodox Church in Minneapolis, Minnesota. This finds confirmation in Bulgakov, *The Bride of the Lamb*, 313, which deserves to be quoted at length: "An even greater abstention from judgment is appropriate with regard to non-Christians. On the one hand, we know that Christ's Incarnation and Pentecost are universal. Their efficacy extends to all people without exception: all humankind is the body of Christ. On the other hand, it pleases the Lord to shroud in obscurity the ways of salvation and the eternal destinies of those to whom, in our age, the holy gospel has not been revealed and baptism has not been given, which perhaps is not even their fault but ours. The Church does not judge those on the outside but keeps silent about them, leaving them to God's mercy. Her practical attitude toward them consists of the duty of preaching..."

as we are enabled to discern the Spirit precisely as the Spirit of Jesus. The question is whether or not we can learn anything substantively new from engaging with religious otherness seriously, and if so, whether or not this will, ultimately, transform our own capacity to recognize the face of Jesus. Another way to pose this question is whether or not we as Christians ever encounter other faces which are only and generically human, rather than other faces which are also always-already religiously formed and expressive.

My own sense, as should be clear from this volume, is that the latter is always the case. Religiousness is not incidental to personal self-identity and not something that may be discarded at will. Even conversions, as radical as they may be, carry over former values, perspectives, and commitments, even if they proceed, at times, unnoticeably.[4] So, the interreligious dialogue turns out to include what Raimon Panikkar calls the "intra-religious" dialogue, the dialogue which occurs in the heart of every person who wrestles with two or more religious ways of being in the world and with the fact of religious plurality in general.[5] At this level, getting at the criteria for what is true, holy, beautiful, and good is a complex intersubjective process. Yet discern we must. Now it certainly may turn out to be the case that discernment in this model will reveal the other tradition to be destitute of the Spirit of God. However, in that instance, is it not within the province of the Spirit to avail himself to that tradition through the very process of dialogue itself as such occurs at many levels?

My argument is that this kind of discerning comparativism is absolutely central to the contemporary Christian engagement with other faiths. Yet we cannot judge the other without first understanding the other; all our judgments—which we inevitably must and do make from day to day—should be held tentatively, subject to the ongoing processes of engagement and discernment. I am optimistic, however, that the power of the pneumatological symbol lies precisely in its calling attention to and accentuating every and all particularities, and that precisely because of its universality. The doctrine of the Spirit thus requires that Christians take the empirical particularities of historical religious traditions seriously as data for theologizing. A pneumatological approach to the religions therefore demands reflection not only on Christian sources, but also on the sources provided by the religions themselves. Pneumatology therefore leads to global theology,

---

4. See, on conversion, Rambo, *Understanding Religious Conversion*; and Gelpi, *The Conversion Experience*.

5. Panikkar, *The Intra-Religious Dialogue*; cf. also Krieger, "Methodological Foundations for Interreligious Dialogue"; and Swidler, *After the Absolute*, esp. 52–53.

which methodologically includes the important tasks of comparative religion and comparative theology.⁶

LOOKING AHEAD

What, then, should a Christian theology that sustains an intensive dialogue with the religions of the world look like? Here, let me lay out in brief what I see as the task for Christian systematic theology in the twenty-first century global context. First, Christian theology is concerned with the truth. Truth, however, arises out of the dialectical relationship between divine revelation and human reception and interpretation. All Christians have responsibility for grappling with the truth. But, wrestling with the difficult question of truth is compounded when confronted by the question of the non-Christian faiths.⁷ Since Christians in Asia, Africa, and Latin America now far outnumber Christians in Europe and North America, Christian theology should work hard to include these non-Western readings of the gospel itself in order to understand the truth of divine revelation.⁸

This means, second, that to the extent the non-Western world is religiously infused with Hindu, Taoist, Confucian, Buddhist, etc., traditions of belief and practice, the gospel will itself be read and reread through those lenses.⁹ If we naïvely push ahead with our efforts to contextualize the gospel in the non-Western world as if these non-Western religious ways are not deeply embedded in the languages and socio-cultural practices of these peoples, should we be surprised if Christianity is rejected in the long run? This has certainly been the case in Japan, for instance, where after centuries of missionary activity, the Church remains practically non-existent. Of course, our ignoring other faiths could also result in an unconscious assimilation of tenets contradictory to the gospel. This is irresponsible religious syncretism

---

6. Here, I am in basic agreement with Fredericks, *Faith among Faiths*, that the way forward for Christian theology of religions is through the hard work of intercultural and interreligious comparisons and contrasts.

7. See, e.g., Adler, *Truth in Religion*; Pannenberg, "Religious Pluralism and Conflicting Truth Claims"; Ward, "Truth and the Diversity of Religions."

8. On this point, see also Cobb, "Global Theology in a Pluralistic Age"; Pittman et al., eds., *Ministry and Theology in Global Perspective*; and Barr, ed., *Constructive Christian Theology in the Worldwide Church*.

9. Cf. McDermott, "What If Paul Had Been from China?"; Lee and Hand, *A Taste of Water*; Griffiths, ed., *Christianity through Non-Christian Eyes*; England and Torrance, eds., *Doing Theology with the Spirit's Movement in Asia*; and Kim, *Christianity and the Encounter of Asian Religions*.

which we should rightly be cautious of and reject.[10] The problem, however, is that of distinguishing between valid forms of contextualization and invalid ones. This process involves, as I have argued in this book, extensive interreligious and intercultural engagement and comparative religion and theology at its depths rather than on its surfaces.

Alternatively, of course, we should take the Word-made-flesh (John 1:14) and the Spirit poured-out-on-all-flesh (Acts 2:17) seriously in developing what could be called either an incarnational or a "pentecostal" pneumatological model of contextualization (chapter one). To do so would be to ask what the gospel might look like if its primary dialogue partners are not Plato, Aristotle, Kant, Hegel, or Whitehead, but rather the Buddha, Confucius, Lao-tzu, Chuang-tzu, Nagarjuna, Shankara, Ramanuja, Chu Hsi, Dogen, Wang Yang Ming, and so on. Sure, these thinkers are not religiously neutral; but then, neither are any in the so-called philosophical tradition in the West. More important, where are we able to receive divine revelation in its purity apart from all cultural-linguistic "contamination"? The truth of the matter is that theological reflection has to continuously negotiate the dialectic between revelation and enculturation since divine revelation comes always-already inculturated, even as the Word-made-flesh was a first-century carpenter who was also male, Jewish, a Nazarene, and the Spirit is poured out, not on all people in the abstract, but on real people in particular places and times.

I have argued in this book that it is a pneumatological approach to the non-Christian faiths that provides the most rigorous theological, methodological, and epistemological rationale for engaging religious otherness in a serious, in depth, and discerning manner. Of course, the proof is in the pudding, and the value and promise of a pneumatological *theologia religionum* will need to be determined in the long run by the results this research project delivers. The long term result of the dialogical quest for truth driven by a pneumatological theology of religions will, I believe, be a thoroughly reconstructed Christian theology that will have passed over into the other faiths and returned home transformed in such a way as to be able to speak the gospel effectively and meaningfully in a world context generally and in the context of the diversity of religions in particular.[11]

The goal of reconstructed Christian systematic theology that takes the world religions and other non-Christian faiths seriously, however, cannot

---

10. I get the language of a "theologically responsible syncretism" from Hollenweger, *Pentecostalism*, chap. 11; cf. Gort et al., eds., *Dialogue and Syncretism*.

11. The model for this kind of theological work remains Cobb, *Beyond Dialogue*; cf. also Dunne, *The Way of All the Earth*.

be the product of one person's reflections.[12] I envision my own contribution to this project as one of testing the specifics of the pneumatological paradigm against the empirical reality of the world religions. In other words, I want to ask what the pneumatological categories of divine presence, divine activity, and divine absence, for example, would look like when brought into dialogue with the religious symbols of the non-Christian faiths. With regard to Buddhism, these categories lead to the comparison of metaphysical and ontological visions, of soteriological analyses, and of the role and function of the demonic.[13] Application of the pneumatological categories need to be tested against the world religious traditions—Hinduism, Taoism-Confucianism, Islam, Judaism—as well as against the phenomenon of new religious movements.

12. Tillich was moving in this direction at the end of his career (Tillich, *The Future of Religions*), even while Pannenberg has long called for Christian theology to be done in light of the history of religions even if he himself has not succeeded in heeding his own advice (see Pannenberg, *Basic Questions in Theology*, chap. 4; and idem, *Systematic Theology*). Yet still, progress has been made. See, e.g., Smith, *Towards a World Theology*; Martinson, *A Theology of World Religions*; Swidler, *Toward a Universal Theology of Religion*; Reat and Perry, *A World Theology*; Krieger, *The New Universalism*; Cornille and Neckebrouck, eds., *A Universal Faith?*; Smart and Konstantine, *Christian Systematic Theology in a World Context*; and Teasdale, *The Mystic Heart*; cf. also Meynell, "The Idea of a World Theology."

13. For preliminary comparative studies on the latter two categories, see my "Technologies of Liberation"; and idem, "The Demonic in Pentecostal-Charismatic Christianity and in the Religious Consciousness of Asia." I hope to incorporate, revise, and extend these inquiries in a book-length manuscript in progress, tentatively titled, "Does the Wind Blow through the Middle Way? Pneumatology and the Christian-Buddhist Dialogue." [Editor's Note: The published title is Yong, *Pneumatology and the Christian-Buddhist Dialogue*.]

1.3

The Spirit Bears Witness[1]

RELIGIOUS TRUTHS

WHEREAS THE ENLIGHTENMENT DEMANDED that religious truth be measured by the standards of objectivity established by the sciences, more recent discussions influenced by Wittgenstein have not only raised questions about the interconnectedness of facts and values even in scientific inquiry but also about the distinctiveness of meaning and truth in the domains of science and religion. Within a Wittgensteinian framework, words emit their significance in sentences, sentences in paragraphs, paragraphs in chapters, chapters in larger narratives, and so on. Truth in general therefore rests not on value-neutral (and in that sense, objectivist) archimedian vantage points, but is always set within certain social, cultural, and linguistic commitments, contexts, and forms of life (what Wittgenstein called "language games"). Put alternatively, religious truths derive more specifically from religious communities, and emerge from distinctively religious practices and commitments.[2]

Christian theologians have taken this Wittgensteinian insight as a reminder that religious truths cannot be abstract or self-evident propositions about things divine. Rather they are "grounded" in and emergent from specific socio-historical realities. But whereas scholars of religion may then be tempted to formulate (sometimes reductionistic) theories of

---

1. Yong, "The Spirit Bears Witness," 22–26, 32–35.
2. For an excellent overview, see Sherry, *Religion, Truth, and Language-Games*.

religious truth from various "secular" disciplinary perspectives—sociological, cultural-anthropological, psychological, economic—they have also challenged themselves to provide truly "thick descriptions" of the forms of life that sustain religious claims to truth.[3] Christian scholars, in turn, have taken this opportunity to explore the distinctively faith matrices which produce specifically Christian truths, even while availing themselves of insights from other scholarly disciplines. The result has been a veritable explosion of interconnected Christian self-understandings regarding the nature of religious and doctrinal truth. The Yale School spearheaded by George Lindbeck has suggested that religious doctrines do not so much refer to external truths about God and the world as function as a kind of grammar which structures and informs Christian conduct.[4] Closely connected are views which privilege narrative construals of Christian truth on the one side, or moral, communal, and liturgical forms of Christian praxis as undergirding Christian truth on the other.[5]

A few observations are pertinent at this juncture about the nature of religious truths. First, whereas objective truths are relatively trivial bits of knowledge about the way things are, religious truths being precisely about things transcendental and divine can never just be about the way things are—God not being another thing besides others in the world—but may rather suggest how things should (or, the ethical imperative, ought to) be. As such, religious truths are concerned with normative issues regarding ultimate reality and human origins on the one hand, and orienting human practices toward human destinies on the other. Second, whereas objective truths are dependent upon and relative to the way the world is, religious truths are similarly dependent upon and relative to the various traditions, narratives, and practices of religious communities. Whereas objective truths are publicly and empirically accessible to any and all who care about them, arguably the most momentous religious truths are disclosed only to those who inhabit and are committed to specific forms of life. Building on

---

3. The notion of "thick description" comes from Geertz, *The Interpretation of Cultures*.

4. See Lindbeck, *The Nature of Doctrine*. For further analysis and discussion, see Marshall, ed., *Theology and Dialogue*; Phillips and Okholm, eds., *The Nature of Confession*; and Goh, *Christian Tradition Today*.

5. The turn to narrative understandings of Christian doctrine are legion. I provide an overview in *Spirit-Word-Community*, 171–73. The argument for considering doctrine in terms of Christian praxis is also gaining momentum, most recently in Hütter, *Suffering Divine Things*; Buckley and Yeago, eds., *Knowing the Triune God*; and Volf and Bass, eds., *Practicing Theology*; but most extensively defended so far by James William McClendon, Jr.; for a more in-depth discussion, see my "The 'Baptist Vision' of James William McClendon, Jr."

this, whereas objective truths by nature assume (at least a minimalist understanding of) a dualism between knowers and knowns, religious truths seem to assume interpersonal and intersubjective relationships and commitments. Finally, whereas objective truths admit of theoretical certainty, religious truths admit (at best) of practical certainty.[6]

Of course, the question immediately arises that if religious truths are so dependent, are they no longer absolute but relative truths? Herein we arrive at the heart of the interreligious encounter. The multiplicity of world religious traditions and their many conflicting truth claims have been the cause of a great deal of existential anxiety to every one of us who has awoken from the dogmatic slumber of our own faith to the reality, plurality, and vigorousness of other faiths. Traditional apologetic strategies reliant upon empirical-rational methods designed to uncover objective truths seem powerless in this new context. The Christian who realizes at the end of the day that her only option may be to invite the religious other to "taste and see that the Lord is good" (Ps 34:8) also realizes the flip side of the coin: that the truth of the religious other is accessible to her only if she agrees to walk in the other's moccasins. Of course, this new situation brings us face to face with the complex questions regarding dual religious identities and the age-old concern regarding syncretism as human beings "try out" other faiths in their quest to discern the truths of the various religions.

But perhaps we are moving too fast to regain the absolute amidst the pluralism of religions. What if our experience of religious plurality signals the radical alterity or difference between the various traditions? In the Wittgensteinian framework, trees are trees and wooden tables are wooden tables. The family resemblance that connects the two is minimal, and trivial. Trees have their natural habitats and in those habitats serve natural functions. Wooden tables have their social habitats and in those habitats serve utilitarian human ends. Similarly, might it be the case that the family resemblances that lead us to label Christianity and Buddhism as religions—leaving aside the contemporary trend to pluralize all traditions, e.g. Christianities, Buddhisms—are trivial compared to the (momentously weighty) differences that exist between these two forms of life? If that is so, are they perhaps incommensurable to the point of prohibiting dual participation and thus requiring radical conversion in order for encounter, engagement, understanding, and assessment to occur?

Yet this incommensurability is itself threatening for a number of reasons. For one thing, it jeopardizes the traditional response which insisted

---

6. I defend a Peircean version of this understanding of religious truth in my "Tongues of Fire in the Pentecostal Imagination"; see also my *Spirit-Word-Community*, chap. 5.

that, ontologically, truth is one, but epistemically, truths are many.[7] This in turn raises questions regarding not only the relationship between religion and science—are these incommensurable activities or ways of engaging the world?—but also about the nature of scientific truths and the scientific enterprise as a whole. And finally, the implications for ethical relationships are potentially devastating if moral truths are associated with religious truths and hence also rendered incommensurable.

Responses at this point range across a wide spectrum. There are those who argue that the incommensurability thesis is either untrue (since if true we could never translate from one language to another) or unintelligible (since its intelligibility rests on the capacity to recognize the differences between two discourses, itself impossible per the incommensurability thesis),[8] and in this way salvage the possibility of interreligious encounter and assessment. The problem with this answer is that it assumes that (in)commensurability has to be either complete or non-existent, thus denying the general intuition of most persons that there are degrees of incommensurability stretching from the similar to the radically other. There are others who, in the interests of science, insist on the unity of the world to secure the unity of ontological truth, and then proceed to privilege the discourses and methods of science over the discourses and methods of the religions. This move undermines the integrity of all religious self-understandings, and not just those of other (non-Christian) religionists. Finally, there are those who distinguish between various types of incommensurability—(a) of languages, (b) of ways of thinking, and (c) of the capacity to judge competing theories to be inferior or superior, as more or less wrong or right[9]—and insist that outcomes of the debates over (a) and (b) do not impinge on (c). Most remain unconvinced about this latter claim.

So where does this leave us regarding the question of religious truth? In part with the familiar problem of faith versus reason. On the one side, religious truths are accessible only by, in, and through faith—faithful communities and faithful practices. In this case, religious truths are not only relativized to such communities and practices, but also perhaps parochialized. On the other side, religious truths are publicly accessible, in accordance with the epistemic convictions and practices agreed upon by reasonable human beings in the public square. In this case, religious truths are depleted of their content and integrity and rendered increasingly inconsequential

---

7. For a defense of the transcultural unity of truth from the philosophy of religion perspective, see Adler, *Truth in Religion*.

8. Davidson, *Inquiries into Truth and Interpretation*, chap. 13.

9. Wong, "Three Kinds of Incommensurability."

by the process of abstraction. Is the quest for religious truth caught on the horns of this dilemma? The question is, to use the words of Thomas Nagel, "how to combine the perspective of a particular person inside [a religious] world with an objective view of that same world, the person and his viewpoint included."[10]

A PNEUMATOLOGY OF ENCOUNTERING RELIGIOUS TRUTH: A BRIEF SKETCH

My primary thesis is that the Pentecost narrative provides for a pneumatology of encounter that preserves the integrity of religious truth beyond objectivism and subjectivism. Building on and locating the foregoing exposition of Acts 2 in the larger context of the scriptural, especially Johannine, witness, let me sketch several elements of what I call a "pneumatological account of encountering religious others truthfully" in expanding on this thesis.

First, the Spirit who is poured out on all flesh (Acts 2:17) is also the Spirit of truth (cf. John 14:17; 15:26; 1 John 5:6), including religious truths which are potentially of ultimate concern. As such, the Spirit testifies to the truth and leads those who seek after the truth into all truth (John 16:13). Moreover, the capacity to bear witness to the truth comes about through the Spirit's anointing and inspiration (cf. Acts 1:8). On the Day of Pentecost, the 120 spoke "about God's deeds of power" (Acts 2:11) as enabled by the powerful infilling of the Holy Spirit. In this way, it can be seen that the Spirit both is the truth and bears witness to the truth. This pneumatological insight confirms the previous discussion gleaned from the Pentecost narrative regarding the witness of the Spirit to truth which sublates the subject-object dualism—here, in the Hegelian sense of going beyond not by leaving behind but by including and preserving (mere) objectivity and subjectivity. Put alternatively, the religious other is not simply other, but the religious other is, in pneumatological respects, ourselves, thereby witnessing to the truth as in a mirror; yet, at the same time, the religious other retains her identity as radically other to us, and precisely as such is able to witness to and confront us with the truth.

Second, when confronted with truth in general and religious truth in particular, human beings are liberated. According to Jesus, who is also "the way, and the truth, and the life" (John 14:6), "you will know the truth, and the truth will make you free" (John 8:32). On the Day of Pentecost, Peter was miraculously (should we say?) delivered from the guilt and shame he

10. Nagel, *The View from Nowhere*, 3.

suffered in denying Christ three times. Empowered by the Spirit, it was he who proclaimed the liberating truth of Pentecost even to those who were amazed and perplexed on the one hand, and those who sneered on the other (Acts 2:12-13). Further, it was he who also witnessed to the truth now made known to all flesh that God is no respecter of persons (cf. 10:34), and that all—whether sons or daughters, young or old, slave or free (2:17-18)—have been caught up in the new work of God. Most importantly, it was Peter who, speaking by the Spirit, responded to the question "What should we do?" by making known to the crowd the saving and liberating gift of God available through the same Spirit (2:38-39 and 2:21). Thus is this outpouring of the Spirit in the world of cosmic significance (cf. 2:19-20). Truth is not merely an abstract property that we possess epistemically, but rather a relational and interpersonal property that orients us properly to one another and comports us and the world rightly toward the divine.

It is clear from this that we are liberated by the truth in order to live in the truth. In Johannine terms, not only shall we know and be set free by the truth, we are also called to abide in the truth (1 John 2:27). This is because the truth not only comes to us from without ourselves (by the Spirit), but is also mediated to and through us (again by the same Spirit). For this reason, Paul's calling the Galatians to a life of freedom is at the same time a call to life in the Spirit (Gal 5). And as the Spirit abides in us, so also does the truth (cf. 2 John 2), thus sanctifying (setting apart) and enabling our walking in the truth (cf. John 17:17-19; 3 John 3-4). This is both the existential and the practical dimension of truth as transformative. We realize we are grasped by the truth precisely because we exhibit the liberative power of truth in the concrete and even mundane aspects of our lives. In the Lukan narrative, to be filled with the Spirit is to be empowered to witness to Christ, both in terms of verbal proclamation and in terms of living testimony as a community of faith (Acts 2:42-47). As such, religious truth is neither (only) propositional nor abstract, but is participatory and pragmatic. Put another way, truth is for us a living, dynamic, and intersubjective relationship, not only with the Holy Spirit but also with one another.

This pneumatological theology of truth now ought to be, third, both Christological and thereby trinitarian. The Spirit is, after all, the Spirit of Jesus (Spirit of Christ) and the Spirit of God. More specifically, the Spirit bears witness to Jesus the Christ and to the testimony of Jesus (John 14:26; 16:13-15; cf. Acts 2:22-38). But if the Spirit bears witness to the truth by bearing witness to Christ, is not then all religious truth to be discerned according to the normative standard of Jesus the Christ? And if this is the case, then what about the witness to the truth of other faiths? How then can a pneumatological theology of truth account for the truth in other faiths and preserve the integrity of their radical alterity precisely as other to the Christian witness?

Two brief responses are in order. First, the Spirit bearing witness to the truth of Jesus the Christ means that religious truth is supremely personal—both personally embodied and interpersonally encountered and engaged.[11] While this does not deny the possibility of truth's propositional expression, it does point out the differences between merely objective truth, alleged absolute truth, and fully religious truth. A personal relationship with Jesus cannot be objectively measured because such is a qualitative rather than quantitative property. For this reason, even the category of absolute truth, especially as a propositional claim, is unhelpful. Christians bear witness to Jesus by faithful confession and praxis. Apart from the latter, any merely verbal confession remains null and void (Matt 7:21–23; 10:40–42; Jas 2:14–26; 1 John 4:20–21), in part because it remains epistemically inaccessible. But once this personalistic dimension of religious truth is recognized and affirmed, then a pneumatological theology of religious truth goes much further in explaining how this truth is encountered. The Logos and "true light, which enlightens everyone" (John 1:9) comes into the world precisely through the Spirit of God (Matt 1:18) in whom all persons live and have their being (Acts 17:28). In this case, then, the intuition that religious others are also caught up in some way by the truth of Jesus as light of the world is given a pneumatological grounding. Thus I suggest that Jesus' reference to "other sheep that do not belong to this fold" but who will yet listen to his voice (John 10:16) points to this pneumatological dimension of the Spirit bearing Jesus' witness, not only *to* those in the non-Christian faiths, but perhaps also *through* them.

Second, and just as important for preserving the integrity of other faiths in light of the Spirit's testifying of Jesus, is that such testimony is not only personal but also eschatological. The Spirit's outpouring upon all flesh is an eschatological event signaling the arrival of the last days (Acts 2:17). For this reason, the Spirit is elsewhere spoken of as the "seal of promise" and the "pledge of our inheritance toward redemption as God's own people" (Eph 1:13–14), even as she is said to lead us in prayers and groans for the redemption of all God's creation (Rom 8:18–27). But more precisely, the Spirit's work is eschatological because she bears witness to the eschatological Christ, the first fruits of those who are to be raised from the dead (1 Cor

---

11. By this, I don't assume an Aristotelian reading of person which requires additional metaphysical notions like an eternal or substantial soul. Rather, as will be clear in what follows, truth as a quality of interpersonal relationship simply recognizes the intersubjective and ethical dimensions of truthful living. As such, this is applicable, in principle, even to Buddhist notions of truth which deny the substantive self.

15:20–23). This is why the resurrection cannot be (merely) an objective truth. Neither can it be simply declared to be an absolute truth by Christians given its disputed epistemic status. Rather, it is properly a religious (and eschatological) truth which Christians confess by faith and in hope given the empty tomb.

This eschatological character of religious truth creates existential and dialogical space for the plurality of religious voices and their witnesses to the truth. The witness to the risen and living Christ cannot be fully captured in any one language, or even in the full chorus of tongues of all ethnic groups, tribes, peoples, and religious traditions combined. That is precisely what it means to say that religious truth is eschatological. If this is the case, then the Christian attestation to the truth is not threatened by other testimonies. Rather, since the eschatological truth will be borne by two or three (even a multitude of) witnesses (1 Tim 5:19), the non-Christian faiths need to be engaged dialogically, practically, and even existentially in anticipation of the full revelation of God.

1.4

Toward a Pneumatological Theology of Religions[1]

THE HOLY SPIRIT AS GOD PRESENT, ACTIVE, AND ABSENT IN THE RELIGIONS

TRAVELING IN THIS DIRECTION, we arrive at three hypotheses that provide a rudimentary framework for a pneumatological theology of religions:[2] (1) Granted that God is universally present by the Spirit, God in this sense sustains even the religions for divine purposes. (2) Granted that the Spirit's work is to usher in the kingdom of God, the Spirit is active in and through various aspects of the religions insofar as the signs of the kingdom are manifest. (3) Granted that the Spirit's universal presence and activity presume a resistant and retarding presence and activity that work against the kingdom of God, the Spirit is also absent from the religions to the extent either that the signs of the kingdom are absent or that they are being prohibited from being manifest.

First, to affirm the Spirit's presence in the religions is to make nothing more than a basic theological statement about the omnipresence of God. Where, after all, can we go away from the Spirit of the Lord? the Psalmist asks (Ps 139:7–12). Put alternatively, using Pauline language, what in all

---

1. Yong, *The Spirit Poured Out on All Flesh*, 250–57.

2. What follows brings together the three foundational pneumatological categories developed in Yong, *Discerning the Spirit(s)*, esp. 122–32, with the three axioms presented in Yong, *Beyond the Impasse*, 44–46.

creation can separate us from the love of God in Christ (Rom 8:39), which is no less than the Holy Spirit given to our hearts (Rom 5:5)? Following out the scriptural witness, why would the realm of the religions be exempt from the Spirit's presence? This is not to say that all religions are good, holy, and truthful, nor is it to say that the entirety of any particular religion (including Christianity as a historical religion)[3] is good, holy, and truthful. Further, this claims neither that any religion is fully salvific in the Christian sense nor that any religion is fully revelatory of God's mystery. To say that all governing authority is from God (Rom 13:1) requires saying neither that all governments are from God nor that the entirety of any particular government is from God. Whether any or all are from God is something that we will have to discern, and this goes also for the religions. Therefore, to affirm that the religions are not accidents of history that catch God by surprise is, at one level, a theological truism.

Second, to affirm the Spirit's activity in the religions is to confess much more, though all the qualifications of the first hypothesis apply here as well. One classic example is Cyrus the Medo-Persian king and patronizer of the Babylonian god Marduk, who was yet anointed with the Spirit of God to act on behalf of the people of God[4] (Isa 45:1; cf. Ezra 1). In this case, we have a pagan who was also a Christ figure (an anointed one) accomplishing the purposes of God. But it is not simply that God can use pagans (e.g., Balaam and his divination). Consider the nature of human religiosity (dependent, of course, on the world religious traditions) and its mediation through the material, social, cultural, political, economic, and other spheres of human existence. Human religiousness is not an accidental feature of human life that can be put on and taken off at will. Rather, it informs these spheres even as it is formed in and through them. Thus religion is resolutely intertwined with the human condition and with human hopes and aspirations and is only arbitrarily divorced from individual and communal identities. So the Christian claim that the kingdom of God is now coming (even if also not yet) cannot be limited only to any one sphere (e.g., the social, political, or economic) and detached from any other (e.g., the religious). This is no more than the claims previously made about the multidimensionality of salvation (§2.2.2), which locates God's saving deeds not only in the private space of the human heart but in the material, social, political, and other domains of life. For similar reasons, religious conversion, as previously discussed (§2.2.3), is precipitated by conversion in other realms even as it transvalues

---

3. This follows Barth, "The Revelation of God as the Abolition of Religion," §17.

4. On Cyrus the pagan, see Hauer and Young, *An Introduction to the Bible*, 132, 136, 198, 200.

conversion in these other realms. In short, given this interconnectedness, to say that the Spirit is active in the world at all is to say that the Spirit is active in the world of the religions in some way.

Third, although the Spirit is God present and active in the world, this presence and activity are still eschatological—not yet fully experienced but punctuated here and now by the Spirit. This points to our human experience of God's hiddenness or God's absence. Using religious parlance, I identify this with the demonic in order to preserve some means to retrieve and re-appropriate the traditional claim that the religions are bearers not only of the divine but also of the demonic.[5] But the demonic signifies not only the apparent absence of the divine but also the forces that actively resist the arrival of the divine kingdom. Because of this, the specifics of any demonology make sense only with an understanding of the perceived threats precipitating demonological reflection. Thus, insofar as the medievals were concerned with monastic purity, on the one side, and with the Turks, on the other, the demonic was identified with the seductions of the flesh and with the Islamic religion. Insofar as the fundamentalists were concerned with theological liberalism, on the one side, and with Darwinism, on the other, the demonic was identified with higher criticism and with the carriers of evolutionary theory—teachers, textbooks, school systems. Today, insofar as (evangelical) Christianity is concerned with terrorism and the Arab nations are concerned with secularization, the demonic is identified with Al-Qaeda, on the one hand, and with Western capitalism, on the other; and so on. Yet although religious persons and communities usually demonize religious traditions other than their own, the demonic is pervasive, from a Christian theological perspective, with traits of its presence and activity throughout the domains of human experience and even in Christian lives and institutions—anti-Semitism, the Crusades, the witch hunts, sexism, racism, and classism, to name a few of the demonic's most obvious manifestations in Christian history.

What about the demonic and the pentecostal imagination? Pentecostal demonologies respond to at least three kinds of threats. First is the threat of the former life from which we have been saved and that still may retain a certain degree of attractiveness to us (thus acting as a competitor

---

5. Since Tillich reintroduced the category of the demonic into Christian theological discourse, a number of proposals have been put forward to reconstruct a theology of the demonic for our time by, e.g., Walter Wink, Nigel Wright, Rene Girard, and Jeffrey Burton Russell. See my previous discussions in Yong, *Discerning the Spirit(s)*, 127–32, 235–45; idem, *Beyond the Impasse*, 137–39, 154–56, 164–66; idem, "The Demonic in Pentecostal-Charismatic Christianity and in the Religious Consciousness of Asia"; and idem, "Spirit Possession, the Living, and the Dead."

for our Christian commitment); at this level, the demonic is identified with everything that stands for that life—for example, sex, drugs, and rock 'n' roll. A second response is the personalizing and the psychologizing of the demonic; André Corten is right to say that "the Devil is a symbolic device used to designate social ills which oppress the poor: unemployment, hunger, prostitution, street children, drugs, and so on."[6] A third response is the socializing and the politicizing of the demonic, that the demonic is all that opposes the values of the kingdom and inhibits the fulfillment of the Great Commission, from the "spirit of blindness" to other kinds of territorial spirits. Insofar as the forces resisting the kingdom operate at every level and in every domain of human life, pentecostals are right to say, "The Devil is a ubiquitous presence."[7]

THE SPIRIT AND THE SPIRITS: DISCERNING THE SPIRIT(S) IN THE RELIGIONS

The challenge is to discern which spirit is which in the world of the religions. Where is the Holy Spirit? What is the Holy Spirit doing? What other spirits are present in the religions, and what are they doing? This task of discerning the religions can be an exceedingly complex affair.[8] I suggest three interrelated sets of questions that pertain to this challenge.

First, we need to discern the various background factors in our encounter with other faiths. There is not only a pluralism of religions but a plurality of contexts in and through which the religions subsist: geographical, historical, economic, political, and social. As important, there is also a pluralism of encounters between persons of faith: daily coexistence, domestic settings (interfaith marriages), social interactions, spiritual practices (meditation, worship, multifaith prayer), doctrinal understanding, the comparative science of religions (which brackets truth claims), formal intrareligious discourse (as in the Christian attempt at self-understanding in a religiously plural world), and formal interreligious dialogue. To discern the religions requires that we accurately discern the contexts within which our discernment proceeds.

Second, we need to pay close attention to what demands understanding—in this case, the multifarious phenomena of the religions. Insofar as discernment is always about concrete realities, discerning the religions will need to focus on the particularities of other faiths. How can we say anything

6. Corten, *Pentecostalism in Brazil*, 61–62.
7. Lehmann, *Struggle for the Spirit*, 139.
8. See Yong, *Beyond the Impasse*, chap. 6; and Yong, "Spiritual Discernment."

about the Spirit's presence, activity, or absence in the world of the religions without empirical investigation of this complex reality? We need to learn how to observe other faiths from an insider's perspective (so far as that is possible) so as to avoid our own biases, which pick out only what we have been trained to pick out. Still, discernment is about measuring a reality with previously established criteria (e.g., the marks of the kingdom) to determine congruence or divergence. So does not each side of the process undermine the other? Is it possible to fully adopt an insider's perspective so as to understand the religions and at the same time retain our Christian criteria in assessing them?[9]

I suggest that the pneumatological imagination derived from the outpouring of the Spirit enables this kind of impartial (so far as that is possible), sympathetic, and yet critical inquiry to proceed. This is because we realize that the pentecostal mission of the Spirit is never abstract but concretely and historically realized and manifest in actual persons, bodies, communities, experiences, languages, and so forth. The miracle of Pentecost is that the Spirit enables the difficult and even impossible task of understanding the other in all his or her otherness, strangeness, and difference (see §4.3.3). Only in the Spirit are we able to follow in the footsteps of Jesus, who fulfilled his mission by emptying himself and taking the form of another (Phil 2:5–8). Granted, the process of discernment is never easy. Discerning the Spirit in the world of the religions can never be the merely intellectual exercise of reading the doctrinal texts of other faiths (although this is a necessary task). Discernment further requires an incarnational mindset, made possible by the Spirit of Pentecost, that is willing to get one's hands dirty with and in the particularity of religious lives and practices of those in other faiths. And given that the religions are never static entities, discernment is always provisional—sufficient for the moment but requiring us to check again and again to see if our previous conclusions hold up. It is important to discern the various goals, purposes, and functions of the diversity of religions. But most important, with the Christian conviction that the Spirit is ever active in the world, even that of the religions, who knows whether a determination of the Spirit's absence today in a given religious phenomenon may not produce a determination of the Spirit's presence tomorrow in a phenomenon that is now both the same and yet different?

Finally, to discern the Spirit in the world of the religions is to pursue a multileveled inquiry that is best measured by its fruits. At one level, discerning the religions transforms (as does increased knowledge most of the

---

9. This is a complex matter, as brought out in Yong, Macchia, Del Colle, and Irvin, "Christ and Spirit." The following attempts to advance this conversation.

time) our understanding, attitudes, and approaches to those in other faiths. Here our neighborly, social, and missionary relationships are affected. We interact with those in other faiths who have a different demeanor and strategies because we see religious others first as complex human beings and only then as Buddhists, Hindus, Muslims, and so forth. To discern the Spirit in the world of the religions correlates with living in the Spirit with the world of the religions.

At another level, the interreligious encounter transforms us as Christians not only in relationship to religious others but also regarding our own self-understanding. To enter into relationships is to be transformed by them, as all genuine relationships are dialogical. This transformation affects our Christian identity.[10] To discern that other spirits are present and active there and then is to discern both the otherness of the religions and the presence and activity of the Spirit of Jesus and of his body here and now. In this sense, discernment is always twofold: of self and other simultaneously. On the one hand, to be a Christian is not to be a Buddhist, Hindu, or Muslim insofar as there are mutually contradictory elements of these identities. At the same time, there may be essential elements of Buddhism, Hinduism, or Islam that are not contradictory to the fruits of the Spirit and the marks of the kingdom. In these cases, that in itself enriches the Christian self-identity even while the challenging process of engaging religious others on their terms also deepens the Christian self-understanding.

Is it possible that our Christian identity might be transformed altogether? Theoretically, yes; since authentic relationships never decide in advance about how things will end up, we must be open to the idea that those who are doing the discernment may undergo various levels of conversion depending on what they find and on whether they are open to being transformed by their findings. This is how I understand the journey of faith, which requires that my confidence lie not in myself but in the Spirit of God, who is able to bring this work to completion.

At the third level of discerning the Spirit in the world of the religions is the question of criteria for discernment. According to the pneumatological soteriology and pneumatological ecclesiology developed in this volume, what are minimal clues to the Spirit's presence and activity? First, are the fruits of the Spirit being manifest in the religious phenomenon in question?

---

10. Harold Dollar points to the conversion of Peter and the Twelve in their encounters with Cornelius and the pagan converts to Christ (Acts 9–10, 15). Cornelius and the Gentile converts were not religious others in the contemporary sense of the term, but they were surely religious others, measured by the crisis of self-understanding these experiences precipitated in these early Jewish followers of Jesus. See Dollar, *A Biblical-Missiological Exploration of the Cross-Cultural Dimensions in Luke-Acts*, chaps. 6, 8.

Second, are the works of the kingdom manifest in the life and ministry of Jesus—after all, the Spirit witnesses to Jesus—seen in the religious phenomenon (§2.1.2)? Third, is salvation, understood in its various dimensions (§2.1.3; §2.2.1), discernible in the religious phenomenon? Fourth, is conversion in the various human domains (§2.2.3) occurring in the lives of those in other faiths? Fifth, is the ecclesial mark of holiness (§3.2.2), understood in its realized and eschatological senses, discernible, however dimly, in the religious phenomenon? Put alternatively, can the processes of purification according to a trajectory anticipating the coming kingdom be discerned in the religious tradition in question? These criteria are abstract in the extreme. Knowing how to apply them to the various contexts and religious phenomena will itself affect our understanding not only of the criteria—since the religions will have their own criteria—but also of how criteria function epistemologically and theologically. They are nevertheless heuristic devices representing our best, even if feeble, attempts to discern the Spirit in the world of the religions in our time.

For these reasons, then, at the level of theology proper, discernment will always leave as many questions as answers. And why should this not be the case in the theology of religions when it is the case in theology's relationships with the sciences and even in understanding the world of the Bible on its own terms? The point here is to forestall those who want to insist that unless discerning the religions can provide some hard and fast answers on whether the Spirit is present, revealing and saving through them, the interreligious encounter (and interreligious dialogue in particular) is a waste of time. Three brief responses are in order. First, not all are called to formal interreligious dialogue, even though all Christians are called to bear the witness of Jesus to their neighbors, including those in other faiths (§6.1.2). Second, if bearing Christian witness takes the form of establishing dialogical relationships with others, including those in other faiths, then the question to ask is whether having relationships is ever a waste of time. For those who measure valuable activities only by conversion to Christian faith, most things done in life are a waste of time. Finally, the Christian life is a journey toward the truth that is to be revealed fully in the day of the Lord. Life in the Spirit, directed toward that eschatological goal (cf. John 16:13; 1 John 2:27), will be impoverished and debilitated if the hard questions concerning the religions are subordinated to the pragmatic tasks of world mission and evangelization, traditionally understood.

1.5

Pneumatological Performance
Many Tongues, Many Practices[1]

I NOW WISH TO extend Dabney's first theology of the Spirit for a post-Christendom world in concert with Hütter's pneumatological theology of ecclesial practices toward a pneumatological theology of interreligious praxis. To do so, I need to identify how the church bears witness to the world through the Holy Spirit. There are three movements to my argument.

First, I suggest that the many tongues of Pentecost anticipate, herald, and even paradigmatically manifest the many gifts—*poiemata* (works)—of the Spirit in, to, and through the churches. In the congregational context, St. Paul identifies nine gifts "for the common good" (1 Cor 12:7). Yet the many gifts correlate with, are dispersed throughout, and are expressed through the many members of the body of Christ (1 Cor 12:12ff.). In fact, the distinctiveness of many members of the body is constituted by their having been given many different gifts. In asking the following questions—"Are all apostles? Are all prophets? Are all teachers? Do all work miracles? Do all possess gifts of healing? Do all speak in tongues? Do all interpret?" (1 Cor 12:29–30)—the answer is clearly "No!" Hence, the many gifts through many members are the *poiemata* of the Spirit for the edification of the body.

Yet, the gifts of the Spirit are designed not only for the believing congregation but also for those who may be on the margins, or even those without. In fact, St. Paul explicitly says that the gifts of tongues and prophecy

---

1. Yong, *Hospitality and the Other*, 62–64.

function differently in the congregational setting when unbelievers are present (1 Cor 14:22–24). Further, in another epistle, after identifying a number of "gifts that differ according to the grace given to us" (Rom 12:6–8), the apostle goes on to urge,

> Contribute to the needs of the saints; extend hospitality to strangers. Bless those who persecute you; bless and do not curse them. Rejoice with those who rejoice, weep with those who weep. Live in harmony with one another; do not be haughty, but associate with the lowly; do not claim to be wiser than you are. Do not repay anyone evil for evil, but take thought for what is noble in the sight of all. If it is possible, so far as it depends on you, live peaceably with all. Beloved, never avenge yourselves, but leave room for the wrath of God; for it is written, "Vengeance is mine, I will repay, says the Lord." No, "if your enemies are hungry, feed them; if they are thirsty, give them something to drink; for by doing this you will heap burning coals on their heads." Do not be overcome by evil, but overcome evil with good (Rom 12:13–21).

While most of these exhortations could apply also to those in the household of faith, they are clear expressions of the Christian virtues and of the grace of the Holy Spirit when manifest to unbelievers—for example, strangers, one's persecutors, the lowly, perpetrators of injustice, one's enemies—who are not only outside the body of Christ but also opposed to the saints.[2]

Second, I suggest that the many gifts of the Spirit at work through the church for the sake of the world are part of the divinely appointed means of grace through which the world is drawn into the saving work of God in Christ. But how is the salvation of God to be understood? Elsewhere I have argued that salvation is a multidimensional and dynamic work of God's Spirit.[3] The multidimensionality of salvation refers, in no necessary order, to the recognition and confession of sin, and to repentance from it; to the moral and spiritual transformation of human hearts by the Spirit; to the interpersonal healing and reconciling community that is the body

---

2. These exhortations complement others given to the diaspora Christians of Asia Minor: "Conduct yourselves honourably among the Gentiles, so that, though they malign you as evildoers, they may see your honourable deeds and glorify God when he comes to judge . . . For it is God's will that by doing right you should silence the ignorance of the foolish. As servants of God, live as free people, yet do not use your freedom as a pretext for evil. Honour everyone. Love the family of believers. Fear God. Honour the emperor" (1 Pet 2:12, 15–17).

3. In what follows, I summarize a pneumatological soteriology defended at length in *The Spirit Poured Out on All Flesh*, chap. 2.

of Christ; to the transformation of communities, societies, and even nations into realms of justice, peace, and righteousness; to the mending and redemption of the world, the cosmos, as a whole; to eschatological union with God—or *theosis*, as the Eastern Orthodox churches would say, etc. Relatedly, the dynamic process of salvation includes human conversion by the power of the Spirit throughout their lives. Thus, conversion through the Holy Spirit's means of grace involves, variously, taking responsibility for the different domains of life: the intellectual, the affective, the moral, and the sociopolitical.[4] Specifically, Christian conversion occurs when the encounter and union with Christ by the Spirit occurs, which in turn transforms all other conversions. At the same time, this does not diminish the importance of conversion in these various domains either before or after specifically Christian conversion. Rather, Christian conversion is itself facilitated by other forms of conversion—these are the constitutive works of the Spirit apart from which Christian conversion is impossible—even as it in turn provides a christomorphic shape to the converted and converting life.

Within this soteriological framework, then, I present the third step of my argument in the form of a hypothesis: insofar as Christian conversion is a complex and multifaceted process, and Christian salvation is a holistic and multidimensional work (*poiesis*) of the Holy Spirit, Christian praxis intended to bear witness to the God of Jesus Christ to a post-Christendom and postmodern world needs to take many forms, and this multiplicity of forms is manifest in the diversity of tongues and gifts of the Spirit. The many gifts of the Holy Spirit, which include many languages, discourses, and tongues, are the means through which Christian witness is borne and the salvation of the world is affected. So, on the one hand, insofar as Christians intend to bear witness to the gospel in a pluralistic world, they will adopt a variety of practices and speak a diversity of languages commensurate with their audiences in different times and places. On the other hand, inasmuch as people have received the gift of the Holy Spirit in their own times and places, they will testify to what God has done in their own tongues and in their own ways. Put succinctly, I suggest that the many tongues of Pentecost open up to many Christian practices in a pluralistic world, and vice versa. The remainder of this book consists of an extended explication and defense of this theological hypothesis specifically with regard to the world of many faiths.

In this chapter, we have explored the emergence of Christian doctrine from Christian practices, analyzed theological accounts of the interrelationship between beliefs and practices, and provided a pneumatological perspective on the performative aspects of Christian theology in a pluralistic

---

4. Here I draw specifically on Gelpi, *The Conversion Experience*, esp. chaps. 2–3.

world. I do insist we take seriously the interrelatedness of beliefs and experiences, doctrines and practices, theologies and performances. Neither one nor the other side is to be privileged or subordinated. The hermeneutical spiral requires that we move from beliefs informing practices, even as such are proceeded by practices shaping beliefs. I suggest that a pneumatological approach is better capable of sustaining this dialectical relationship without collapsing onto one or the other side.[5] We are now ready to see how a pneumatological theology of religions and interreligious praxis—in which "many tongues equals many practices"—plays out in a post-9/11 world of many faiths.

---

5. This point is highlighted in my *Spirit-Word-Community*, esp. 10–11, as central to the argument of that book.

1.6

Salvation

*Pneumatological and Buddhological
Comparisons and Contrasts*[1]

WE ARE ALREADY AWARE that the differences between Orthodox Christianity and Theravada Buddhism are most striking when theological and ultimate questions are posed. Here, the phenomenological, practical, psychological, and epistemic categories break down since the notion of divinity is itself foreign to Theravada Buddhism. Thus, the Orthodox goal of *theosis* and the Theravadin quest for *nibbana* summarize the radical divergence between these two spiritual paths. To be recreated in the image of God as seen in the incarnation of the Son is foreign to Buddhist sensibilities even while the final salvation understood as liberation from the cycle of rebirth is generally incomprehensible to Christians. At one level, the disjunction between religions in general and these two traditions particularly should not be downplayed. The differences, however, can be taken in at least two directions. One traditional approach would simply note the dissimilarities, and attribute the non-Christian religion to demonic sources.[2] Postmodern

---

1. Yong, *Pneumatology and the Christian-Buddhist Dialogue*, 171–77.

2. Thus the Bishop of Nafpaktos: "... so much the more does it [Eastern Orthodoxy] differ from the 'spirituality' of Eastern religions, which do not believe in the Theanthropic nature of Christ and the Holy Trinity. They are influenced by the philosophical dialectic, which in Orthodox theology has been surpassed by the Revelation of God ... There is no path leading their 'disciples' to *theosis*-divinization of the whole man. There are many elements of demonic 'spirituality' in Eastern religions" (Hierotheos

sensibilities, on the other hand, would be attracted to a Wittgensteinian or Lindbeckian cultural-linguistic approaches that understand theological and religious discourses to function as grammatical wholes that shape the practices of entire ways of life. Either way the dialogue between faiths breaks down. In the former case, the religious other is demonized, and in the latter case, the other's incommensurability prohibits engagement.

Yet at the same time, I suggest that there remain similarities even at this third moment of the two spiritual paths. Both the Orthodox saint and the Theravadin arahant experience perfection, albeit the former in terms of sanctification and divinization of the whole person and the latter in terms of purification of the virtues, of the mind, and of the understanding. As such, both experience liberation from lust, passion, ill-will, and hate, and both are freed to live in peace with others in the world. The cross is the foremost Christian symbol of the reconciliation that has been achieved, even while the Bodhi tree—under which the Buddha obtained awakening—has come to signify the equanimity that characterizes freedom from suffering.

But most significantly, both the Orthodox saint and the Theravadin arahant receive salvation or awakening by entering into a transcendental experience. For the Orthodox, reaching the inner stillness of the heart in the presence of God and attaining to the silence of the soul and spirit are signs of the experiential realization of union with God. At this moment, there is a renunciation of all discursivity in the saint's engagement with the divine, and the duality between God (in his energies) and humanity is overcome. The Theravadin parallel is the attainment of wisdom and insight that bypasses the usual perceptual and cognitive modalities of knowing. The arahant has overcome the delusions that drive him or her to lead a misguided life. In both traditions, then, there is the achievement of a non-discursive contemplation of the true nature of things. This feature of the third moment of Orthodox spirituality has caught the attention of other investigators as well. The Hesychast light mysticism, for example, supersedes ordinary intellectual conceptualism and is therefore beyond either empirical verification or falsification. Thus, Daniel Rogich has observed that on a comparative plane, "the teachings of Gregory Palamas can represent Christian spirituality quite well in a discussion with such Asian religious thought as the Advaita of Vedanta Hinduism, or the nondualist philosophy of Buddhism or Taoism—teachings which are attracting many in the West today for their holistic and nonrational approach to life and prayer in particular."[3]

[Vlachos], Bishop of Nafpaktos, *Orthodox Spirituality*, 30–31).

3. Rogich, "Introduction" to *Saint Gregory Palamas*, 19. Jean-Claude Barreau also suggests that the achievements of Eastern Christian mysticism are, for these reasons, comparable to that of Taoist or Zen mysticism; see Barreau's "Preface" to Clément, *The*

The question I want to raise at this point concerns that which motivates this entire comparative project: is there potential for a deepened understanding of Christianity and Buddhism when these similarities are understood within a pneumatological framework? I want to suggest two possible kinds of responses to this question. The first type of response might, once we get beyond the surface of things, also end the possibility of fruitful dialogue. I have in mind here the pluralistic hypothesis that the similarities of spiritual technologies suggests that the goals of these practices are not divergent but one and the same.[4] According to this line of thought, there is, finally, only one goal accessible through a global mysticism or universal interspirituality that is variously manifest in different traditions of spirituality over the centuries. In this theory, contemplative traditions are similar because the same divine or universal spirit mediates the one salvific experience through different cultural and religious contexts. We get a sense of this in Thomas Merton's suggestion that "the only source of the spiritual life is the Holy Spirit," and in Bede Griffiths's saying, "Clearly, all Christians meet with Hindus, Buddhists, and Muslims in the depth of the Spirit beyond reason, which is known in meditation as we open our hearts to what St. Paul calls the 'mystery of Christ' . . . The possibility of a Spirit beyond the rational mind can be a problem, since for some people the rational mind is the mind . . . So in meditation we are entering into that depth of the spirit where we encounter the Spirit of God."[5] But if this is the case, then there may be no need for interreligious encounter or dialogue, and perhaps no value in doing comparative theology, since the spiritual paths of all traditions, including that preserved in the *Philokalia* and the *Visuddhimagga*, simply use different languages to describe the same spiritual undertaking. Yet at the same time, both Merton's and Griffiths's observations should not be entirely discarded if we believe truth to be one.

The way forward, however, is not to conclude that it is only the Holy Spirit who is behind all forms of religiosity in general, or behind the *Philokalia* and *Visuddhimagga* more specifically, but to be open to the possibility of the Spirit's presence and activity in these cases. This leads to the

---

Roots of Christian Mysticism, 7.

4. See, e.g., Teasdale, *The Mystic Heart*. One form of the pluralistic hypothesis, albeit a quite sophisticated one that does not naively promulgate all of what critics of the hypothesis often decry, has been developed across the *oeuvre* of John Hick, argued most extensively in his Gifford Lectures: *An Interpretation of Religion*.

5. Merton, *Contemplation in a World of Action*, 271; and Griffiths, *The New Creation in Christ*, 67–68. Note that Nhat Hanh also uses pneumatological categories to talk about convergences between Buddhism and Christianity; see Hanh, *Living Buddha, Living Christ*, 13–24, 66–69, 130, 150–51, 177, 183, and, his engagement with St. Macarius (a fourth century Christian hermit) on 165–66.

second kind of response which should inform the Christian approach to and engagement with the non-Christian faiths: that given the possibility of the Holy Spirit's presence and activity in the world's religions, Christians should be respectful of other faiths and alert to what they may learn from non-Christian religious others on the one hand, even while they should be discerning about the presence and activity of the Spirit of God amidst the various forces—human, ideological, socio-cultural, natural, demonic, etc.— that are at work in the world, even in the world of the religions, on the other.

Within this framework, should Christians not consider the possibility that the Theravada Buddhist tradition has come to a deep awareness of the radical contingency of creation itself in a powerfully transformative experience which is pneumatologically mediated? Is it not the work of the Spirit to enable the overcoming of the lusts of the flesh, the pride of life, and the deceptive confusions of the mind? Does not the Holy Spirit bring about peace, tranquility, lovingkindness, joy, compassion, and equanimity? Should not the Theravadin experience of crossing over the floods and intoxicants of lust, ill-will, and delusion be attributed to the activity of divine Spirit? If all of this is the case, then is it possible that Buddhaghosa's *Visuddhimagga* captures in a general sense at least part of the truth of the gospel most explicitly displayed in the life, death, and resurrection of the Son, and does so through the Spirit's mediation?

At this moment, however, it is important to pause and be reminded of the claim made in the introductory chapter (1.2.1) that a pneumatological approach to the interreligious encounter provides theological sanction for multiple modes of engagement, including that of bearing verbal witness to the gospel. This juncture of the dialogue serves as a window into a more explicit confession of how Christians might understand Christ as the fulfillment of the aspirations of Theravada Buddhists, and would be conducive to Eastern Orthodox intuitions about the universality of the gospel as mediated through the Word and Spirit as the "two hands of the Father." Perhaps by now, the curiosity of even our most sophisticated Buddhist dialogue partners will have been sufficiently perked to allow for the conversation to go in such a direction.[6]

What needs to be made explicit is the theological criteria for discerning the Holy Spirit from other spirits, the divine presence and activity from

---

6. Not all Theravadin Buddhists are meditators in the tradition of Buddhaghosa, just as not all Eastern Orthodox are ascetics in the tradition of the Desert Fathers. For some evangelical and pentecostal Christians, this moment serves as a springboard for evangelizing not just lay Theravadins, but also the Orthodox faithful. And depending on the circumstances and the context, a pneumatological theology of interreligious engagement provides theological justification for these activities as well.

the divine absence, which sustains the preceding conclusions, even if hypothetically, provisionally, and tentatively stated. The biblical and theological criteria would begin with sanctification understood as walking in the Spirit and bearing the fruits of the Spirit rather than the works of the flesh (Gal 5:19–23). At this level, can we say that presence or absence of the Spirit in the religions in general and in Theravada Buddhism in particular is to be measured by whether or not either the virtues of love, joy, peace, patience, kindness, generosity, faithfulness, gentleness, and self-control are evidenced, or the works of the flesh such as fornication, impurity, licentiousness, idolatry, sorcery, enmities and strife, jealousy, anger, quarrels, dissensions, factions, envy, drunkenness, carousing, etc., persist? St. Paul links this criterion of presenting our bodies "as a living sacrifice, holy and acceptable to God," with "spiritual worship"; from here, a follow-up criterion would be sanctification understood as the transformation and renewal of the mind resulting in the capacity to discern the good, acceptable, and perfect will of God (Rom 12:1–2). Here again, the process involves the Spirit's presence and activity (1 Cor 2:9–16). At this level, can the good, acceptable, and perfect will of God be understood in moral and ethical terms reflected in the capacity to love one's neighbor (cf. Jas 2:8–17)? If this is the case, then can we discern the Spirit in other faiths if the commandment to love our neighbor is kept even if not explicitly connected with the name of Jesus (cf. 1 John 3:11–24)? But finally, the ultimate criterion of the Spirit's presence and activity is conformation to the image of the Son culminating in glorification (Rom 6–8, esp. 8:29–30). And here, does Theravada Buddhism appear finally bereft of the Spirit's presence and activity, especially for those who understand its religious end of *nibbana* as extinction (which would be impersonalistic at best and ontologically nihilistic at worst)? But given all this, might it still not be possible to discern and acknowledge the Spirit's provisional presence and activity along the Theravadin Buddhist path, if not in its ultimate destinations?

Yet I suggest that to grant even this is to have made important theological progress. The Holy Spirit's presence and activity in other faiths is what enables human beings to meet, dialogue, and understand each other. In the process, Christian theological self-understanding has been gained, and the significance of such has been expanded so as to be pertinent to a wider theological public, that of the world religions. The practical implications of this—for Christian mission, for those engaged in socio-political and environmental matters, for being good neighbors and co-workers, etc.—should not be underestimated.

Now the attempt to discern the religious other utilizing Christian criteria is valid from a Christian theological perspective. Yet at the same time, it is important to acknowledge that the value of the preceding set of hypotheses and claims would then be limited only to the Christian self-understanding. It cannot be passed off as an attempt to understand Buddhaghosa's *Visuddhimagga* for Buddhists without violating the integrity of the other tradition precisely because I cannot claim to be a Buddhist adept or to have participated as an insider in its practices.[7] The way forward, given the present pneumatological hypothesis, is to embrace the hermeneutical spiral: to attempt first to understand the other on its own terms, to proceed to ask about how the experience of the other challenges or deepens the Christian experience, and then to explore the possible lines of convergences, only to return to engaging the religious other again from this new vantage point, thus re-initiating the hermeneutical inquiry.[8] But having done as much of this as possible in the preceding, the question can no longer be avoided: what about the absence of the divine and presence of the demonic in the world of the religions in general and in Buddhism specifically? And we should not be surprised to discover that this is not only of Christian concern, but also that of Buddhists as well.

---

7. Recent discussions of the insider-outsider debate in religious studies include McCutcheon, ed., *The Insider/Outsider Problem in the Study of Religion*; and Arweck and Stringer, eds., *Theorizing Faith*.

8. In this regard, Shanta Ratnayaka's comparison of faith in Buddhaghosa and Wesley in his *Two Ways of Perfection*, is a model study, and a newer book by May, *Transcendence and Violence*, is an intriguing comparative reflection on how visions of transcendence facilitate (or not) the encounter of religion and culture.

1.7

Starting with the Spirit

*Pneumatology and the
Christian-Buddhist-Science Trialogue*[1]

MY METHODOLOGICAL THESIS IS that pneumatology opens us up to the possibility of a participatory epistemology which overcomes the dualistic and dichotomous thinking of subject and object—e.g., of theology and science, and of the world of Scripture and of nature—without collapsing the distinction between the two.[2] Similarly, a pneumatological approach to religious pluralism also opens up to a participatory epistemology of self and otherness—e.g., of religious beliefs and religious practices, of the worlds of Scripture and other sacred texts, and of Christianity and other faiths—again without collapsing the distinctions between them.[3] Allow me to elaborate on three basic elements of such a pneumatological epistemology and hermeneutic: its "grounding" in the Pentecost narrative of Acts 2; its furnishing dynamic categories for comprehending science and religion; and its provid-

---

1. Yong, *The Cosmic Breath*, 20–28.

2. My *Spirit-Word-Community*, esp. part II, provides the book-length argument; a briefer article is my "The Hermeneutical Trialectic."

3. To be chronologically precise, I come to the religion-science dialogue from much more extensive work in theology of religions, but my pneumatological epistemology and methodology developed contextually within the latter framework was also always intended to engage with matters related to the former; see my *Spirit-Word-Community*, esp. §6.2.

ing a dialogical and intersubjective means of adjudicating multi-disciplinary and multi-religious claims to truth.

PNEUMATOLOGY AND THE "GROUND" OF EPISTEMIC PLURALISM

First, a pneumatological theology proceeds at least in part from the Pentecost narrative of the Spirit of God being poured out "upon all flesh" (Acts 2:17).[4] This involves understanding "all flesh" to have universal application. This reading is supported by *both* the immediate context of this claim which includes sons and daughters, young and old, and slave and free, *and* the broader context of the Pentecostal outpouring of the Spirit upon the many who were gathered on the streets of Jerusalem from around the known (Mediterranean) world. While at one (exegetical) level it might be argued that "all flesh" is limited to the class of people drawn from the categories of sons, daughters, etc., at another (theological) level, the sons, daughters, etc., are who they are precisely because they are those upon whom the Spirit is poured out. In this latter reading, the "all flesh" would not be qualified by "Christians." Further, while some might argue that the "all flesh" is limited to Jews and proselytes to Judaism derived from the Jewish diaspora, this overlooks three more universalistic trajectories embedded in this text: a) that proselytes are not full converts: rather, being at different stages of their spiritual journeys, they embody in their lives multiple traditions and cultures in various degrees; b) that the summary list of regions and languages present in Jerusalem symbolize (weaker) or represent (stronger) the breadth of the known first century world; and c) that Luke's own narrative is guided by a universalistic vision whereby "all flesh" includes those from Jerusalem, Judea, Samaria, and "the ends of the earth" (Acts 1:8; cf. Acts 3:25).[5]

From this universalistic (epistemic, not soteriological) reading of the Pentecost narrative, it is but a short series of steps to understanding interdisciplinary and interreligious engagement in pneumatological perspective. First, it is undeniable that this Pentecost narrative should be read against the narrative of the Tower of Babel (Gen 11) when human beings were dispersed across the earth through the confusion of their languages. Against this background, the outpouring of the Spirit redeems the diversity of languages, enabling each tongue to become a vehicle to communicate the wondrousness of "God's deeds of power" (Acts 2:11). Building on this, the diversity of languages is also correlated with the diversity of cultures (or,

   4. The following is adapted from my *The Spirit Poured Out on All Flesh*, §4.3.3.
   5. I provide such a reading to the book of Acts in my *Who is the Holy Spirit?*.

nations, tribes, and peoples, to use first century Mediterranean categories; cf. Rev 7:9 and passim) and, by extension, to the diversity of symbol systems (including, I argue in a moment, that of the various sciences). In this reading, Pentecost becomes the theological basis for not only accepting but also valuing the plurality of cultures, and the missiological basis for methods that emphasize the inculturation, indigenization, and contextualization of the Christian gospel.

This connection between language and culture should then be extended to include, I suggest, other semiotic dimensions of human life, including both the world of the sciences and the world of the religions. With regard to the former, I propose that the world of the sciences is constituted by a plurality of semeiotic or symbolic systems (disciplines), each operating according to various grammars (rules), sustained by various practices, and directed to various functions, but all networked to one another by the common goal of inquiring into nature.[6] With regard to the latter, the world of the religions is intrinsically linked to the diversity of cultures and languages, and only a modernist compartmentalization would divide between them. Hence, I argue, the Pentecost principle of linguistic and cultural plurality necessarily includes that of scientific endeavor and of religious diversity, and divine redemption includes not only human languages and cultures, but also human scientific inquiry and human religiosity. However, just as this does not mean that all human words and all aspects of human culture are holy without qualification, so also it does not mean that all scientific inquiry and all forms of human religiousness are ultimately saved or sanctified. Language and culture, science and religion, must all be tested and discerned, even as each is potentially a vehicle for mediating the truth, beauty, goodness, wondrousness, and even grace of God. However, acceptance of this possibility establishes the Day of Pentecost as the narrative "ground" for engaging the world of the sciences and the world of religions in pneumatological perspective.

Now before proceeding, I need to be clear that I am not insisting that my elucidation of Acts 2 in the preceding (and following) pages captures the author's original meaning or the intended audience's understanding. Rather than being a strictly exegetical exercise, mine is a more theological interpretation wherein I am suggesting only one possible reading of Acts 2 for our twenty-first-century, pluralistic, scientific, and technological world. Now given that Luke's purpose was also to show how the Spirit of Pentecost was the Spirit of Jesus, we will need to return later to a discussion of what

---

6. See my "Academic Glossolalia?"

our pneumatological hermeneutic of the religion-science and interreligious dialogues has to say about christology.[7]

PNEUMATOLOGY AND THE DYNAMISM OF SCIENCE AND RELIGION

The second basic element of a pneumatological approach to science and religious pluralism is that pneumatology furnishes dynamic categories for comprehending both domains of human experience. Let me explicate this dynamism in terms of a two fundamental notions: tradition and praxis.

Tradition in pneumatological perspective is dynamic in light of the long-standing metaphor of the Spirit as the soul or life of the Church, especially when the latter is considered in its institutional form. Whereas the classical theological understanding of "tradition" (and the ecclesial tradition more specifically) emphasized its given once-and-for-all nature, a pneumatological view of church and tradition highlights the fluidity and dynamic movement of both. In this pneumatological framework, the Christian tradition and church not only *exist*, but are also *becoming*, because the tradition and church are concrete expressions of human responses to and participation in the Spirit's outpouring upon—presence and activity in—the world.

Similarly, this pneumatological perspective recognizes the dynamic character of scientific inquiry and of other religious traditions. In the same way as the Christian tradition can be discerned only through its continually changing empirical manifestations—to see if the Spirit's presence and activity can be detected or if the Spirit is absent in some respect—so also are the traditions of inquiry of the natural and human sciences, and of "Judaism," "Islam," "Buddhism," "Hinduism," etc., discernible through their permutations. A pneumatological perspective on science and a pneumatological theology of religions would be better equipped to recognize "science" and "religions" not as nouns, but as verbs: they are formed by the processes of human "traditioning" and are thereby shaped by the various human engagements with the world (the sciences) and various human responses to realities considered transcendent (the religions).[8]

---

7. Elsewhere, I respond more specifically and at length to this question of the Spirit of Pentecost as the Spirit of Jesus; see Yong, "A P(new)matological Paradigm for Christian Mission in a Religiously Plural World."

8. While the dynamic character of science is obvious, that of the religions is now much more widely accepted, especially since Smith's *The Meaning and End of Religion*; cf. also Irvin, *Christian Histories, Christian Traditioning*.

This leads to our consideration of *praxis*. From a pneumatological perspective, praxis becomes just as, if not more, important than beliefs (doctrines) and that precisely because pneumatology calls attention to divine activity rather than divine being (at one level), and to sanctification rather than to mere confession (at another). This contrasts with the classical understanding wherein "praxis" was secondary to "doctrine" in defining a religious tradition. The strength of a pneumatological theology is precisely its capacity to recognize the interrelatedness of praxis and doctrine without subordinating either to the other. Rather, praxis is understood to be guided by doctrine even as praxis shapes, clarifies, confirms (or not), and even transforms doctrinal formulations. A pneumatological viewpoint both acknowledges and is able to provide a theological account for the interrelatedness between praxis and doctrine.

For this reason, a pneumatological understanding of science emphasizes the process of inquiry rather than the content of scientific knowledge. This is especially important given the fallibility attached to all scientific discoveries, and the shifting nature of the scientific paradigms and frameworks. The advances of science are predicated on nothing less than the willingness to question previously accepted claims to truth and to start afresh. Scientific inquiry is therefore a set of practices oriented toward engagement with the world, and a pneumatological perspective on the religion-science dialogue would empower the practices of both religion and science in their common quest for truth.

Similarly, a pneumatologically informed theology of religions is better able to comprehend religious otherness not only in terms of the category of doctrine but also in terms of other dynamic praxis categories like ritual, piety, devotion, morality, and the like.[9] While many previous theologies of religions have had an almost exclusive focus on the beliefs of religious others,[10] a pneumatological *theologia religionum* is better able to account for the diversity of beliefs that are linked to and shaped by different social, moral, and religious practices.

Together, these brief discussions of tradition and praxis are suggestive of how a pneumatological approach inculcates a more dynamic

---

9. On the intrinsic relationship between Christian beliefs and practices, see McClendon, *Systematic Theology*; Hütter, *Suffering Divine Things*; and Volf and Bass, eds., *Practicing Theology*.

10. Some of the prominent exceptions, interestingly, have been those of pluralist theologians like John Hick (who has focused on the ethical-transformative processes of religious traditions) and Paul Knitter (whose emphases have been on orthopraxis); see Hick, *An Interpretation of Religion*; Knitter, *One Earth Many Religions*; and Knitter, *Jesus and the Other Names*.

understanding of theology and its work, especially in its engagement with the worlds of nature and the religions. In the same way as pneumatology points to eschatology (the doctrine of things related to the end), so also a pneumatological theology of science and a pneumatological theology of religions recognizes the open-endedness and unfinished character of scientific inquiry and of religious traditions. Certainly, scientists and scholars of religion have long been advocates of this more dynamic understanding of each domain. The contribution of a pneumatological perspective is a specifically theological (rather than philosophical or practical) rationale for this kind of dynamic interpretation of science and of religion.

PNEUMATOLOGY, TRUTH, AND THE RELIGIONS

This leads to the third basic element of a pneumatological approach to science and religious pluralism: its capacity to provide an intersubjective mode of engaging claims to truth.[11] Previous theological approaches to science and other religious doctrines have noticed and, often, emphasized their contradictory quality when explicated in terms of the correspondence theory of truth. So most scientists believe in evolution via random mutation and natural selection, while some Christians believe that God created each species distinctively; or most Buddhists believe that death leads either to reincarnation or nirvana, while Christians classically believe that death leads either to heaven or hell—in which cases, either scientists or Christians and either Buddhists or Christians are right (and the other wrong) since both sets of claims cannot be simultaneously true. With regard to the question of evolution, there is both the challenge of what counts as data and the deeper issue of how to interpret the data when the lines between science and metaphysics are blurred. With regard to the question of nirvana or reincarnation versus heaven or hell, the problem is that such claims are either transcendental or eschatological, resulting in Buddhist and Christian claims and counterclaims without any means of adjudicating conclusively in the present life the apparent contradictions assuming the correspondence theory of truth.

More recent developments have thus focused on the epistemological questions of how any particular truth claim is nested semiotically within a larger web of interlocking beliefs and practices. This is explicated in terms of the coherence theory regarding how truth is known. Considered in this way, the religion and science domains are disparate, with theological claims dealing with ultimate meaning, morality, sentiment, and piety that are

11. The following is a revision and adaptation of my "The Spirit Bears Witness."

embedded in religious practices, and scientific claims dealing with matters of fact regarding the world that are embedded in traditions of empirical enquiry.[12] Similarly, Buddhist or Christians claims only make sense within Buddhist or Christian frameworks since doctrines function with regard to religious traditions and practices in ways similar to how grammars function with regard to languages. In both the religion-science and interreligious dialogues, truth is to be assessed according to whether or not any statement coheres with other statements within the religious system (of beliefs *and* practices).

Yet the turn to epistemic coherentism does not resolve the alethic issues. The problem here is twofold: *either* scientific and the different religious frameworks are all incommensurable—based as they are on different semiotic and praxis systems—and hence apparently contrary claims are essentially non-adjudicable; *or* any attempt to adjudicate scientific-religious or multiple religious claims requires that one not only learns about or observes from a distance another tradition but also that one enters into and participates in its semiotic system and practices. With regard to the religion-science conversation, to adopt the former position—that religion and science are incompatible languages—ignores the fact that religion makes claims regarding matters of fact and that science provides explanations on matters related to morality and even metaphysics. To adopt the latter position—that engaging religion with science and vice-versa requires cross-over and return—risks either mixing the two domains inappropriately or privileging one and subordinating the other. How then do religion and theology engage with science given this dilemma connected with the coherence theory of truth?

With regard to the interreligious encounter, to assume that religious traditions are inapposite leads to relativism: what is true for the Buddhist is not true for the Christian and vice-versa. But to assume that adjudicating religious truth claims requires cross-over and return into another religious tradition and its practices threatens to compromise the kind of scholarly objectivity aspired to by scholars of religion,[13] and raises the question of how to retain one's Christian identity in the process of entering into the beliefs and practices of another faith. Is it not advisable to follow anthropologists and their participant-observatory methods that do not require them to embrace fully the ways of life (both beliefs and practices) of those who they

---

12. Expressed most straightforwardly in terms of the principle of religion and science providing "non-overlapping magisteria" by Gould, *Rocks of Ages*.

13. See McCutcheon, ed., *The Insider/Outsider Problem in the Study of Religion*; and Arweck and Stringer, eds., *Theorizing Faith*.

are studying? However, is it then possible in this way to adjudge between contrary claims to truth among the religions?

The pneumatological approach to this dilemma provides a specifically theological rationale for holding both correspondence and coherentist theories of truth and methods for their resolution in tension. Let me explicate this claim in two steps. First, going back to the theological reading of the Pentecost narrative proposed above, the outpouring of the Spirit enables each one to give witness to the wondrous works of God (Acts 2:11) in and through the diversity of languages. Now insofar as language can only be arbitrarily divorced from culture and from religion, to the same extent, then, cultures and religions are potentially vehicles for mediating the grace and truth of God. Therefore the Spirit who gives the capacity to speak in a foreign language also enables, by extension, participation in a foreign culture, a different semeiotic system of beliefs and practices, and even an alien religion, so that one can experience and testify to those realities to some degree "from within." If in more exegetical terms the Spirit's outpouring on the Day of Pentecost redeemed the various languages for the purposes of God, my more theological interpretation and application to the religion-science and interreligious dialogues would be to embrace the redemption of both domains of human knowledge and experience, but attempt to present and discuss them in ways that respect their distinctive languages and perspectives. Hence I say that our dialogue with science and other faiths allows and even invites our engagement with them on their own terms and, to that degree, emically "from within" rather than merely etically "from without."[14] I therefore suggest also that the same Spirit whose outpouring on the Day of Pentecost enabled the speaking in foreign tongues might today enable genuine engagement with the sciences and with other faiths.

This means, second, a pneumatological epistemology empowers a robustly dialogical and intersubjective approach to truth. On the one hand (from the Christian perspective), the Spirit graciously enables our entrance into, inhabitation of, and testimony to faith in Jesus Christ. On the other hand (from the religion-science or the theology of religions perspective), this same Spirit also graciously grants understanding of, guides participation in, and empowers engagement with other languages, cultures, semiotic systems, and even at least in some respects religious traditions. This dialogical relationship thus means that we engage our own and the other tradition both as "insiders" and as "outsiders," albeit in different respects. While it is

---

14. My colleague, Tony Richie, also discusses, in dialogue with other evangelical theologians, the importance of entering into the viewpoint of religious others to whatever degree possible, without compromising Christian faith; see Richie, *Speaking by the Spirit*, 92–94.

obvious how we are "insiders" to our own tradition, it is also important to note that we are theological "outsiders" even to the Christian tradition insofar as we are still not yet fully converted to the image of Christ (on this side of the eschaton).[15] On the other hand, while it is clear we are "outsiders" to other traditions, it is also important to note that we are potential "insiders" even to other traditions insofar as the Spirit enables us to speak in other languages and to cross over into other traditions. Hence we engage our own and other traditions neither merely "objectively" (as "outsiders") nor merely "subjectively" (as "insiders"), but intersubjectively—e.g., both within and outside each tradition, as individuals and as members of (both) communities, in terms of both beliefs (doctrines) and practices (participation and inhabitation), in historical reality (in dialogue with others), and yet anticipating eschatological consummation. This dialogical and intersubjective engagement with truth therefore neglects neither the criteria of coherence nor that of correspondence, but highlights the processes of adjudication as involving the mutual transformation of traditions in dialogue by the power of the eschatological Spirit.

---

15. I elaborate on the eschatological aspects of pneumatological theology in my "Performing Global Pentecostal Theology."

PART TWO

Religion and Science

2.1

The Spirit and the Orders of Creation[1]

IN OUR ENVIRONMENTALLY CONSCIOUS age, an increasing number of biblical interpreters are calling attention to the "Creator Spirit," the Spirit as being intimately involved with the orders of creation.[2] The Christian Testament's association of the groanings of creation with the eschatological work of the Spirit (Rom 8:22–23) can only be understood against the Hebrew Bible's depictions of creation as the theater of the Spirit's presence and activity. Not only does the Spirit transform deserts into fertile fields and forests (Isa 32:15), all creatures—donkeys, birds, goats, lions, fish, and so on—are nourished by the breath of Yahweh, apart from which "they die and return to their dust. When you send forth your spirit, they are created; and you renew the face of the ground" (Ps 104:29–30; cf. Job 34:14–15). And when the psalmist also says, "By the word of the LORD the heavens were made, and all their host by the breath of his mouth" (Ps 33:6), he is clearly echoing the Priestly author's account of the creation of the world by the *ruah* ("wind" or "breath") of God sweeping over the waters and the word of God speaking things into existence (Gen 1:2–3).

Yet the *ruah* of God does not make a solitary appearance at the beginning of the creation narrative; *ruah* is also present at its culmination, with the formation of *ha adam*. Only when the Lord God breathed into *ha adam* did *ha adam* become a living being (Gen 2:7). The Spirit's appearance

---

1. Yong, *The Spirit Poured Out on All Flesh*, 280–83.
2. Pannenberg, "The Doctrine of the Spirit"; Faricy, *Wind and Sea Obey Him*, chap. 2; Cantalamessa, *Come, Creator Spirit*; and Edwards, *Breath of Life*.

on both ends of the creation narrative justifies rereading the creation story within an explicitly pneumatological framework.[3] In this perspective, a few observations can be made toward a pneumatological theology of creation that bridges the Genesis narrative with the science-religion dialogue of the late modern world.

First, the *ruah* of God blowing across the primordial world and the breath of life given to *ha adam* provide insight into the interrelationality of the Spirit and the orders of creation. The Spirit is not contradictory to nature, as modernity would have it; rather, the Spirit infuses the world. The vivifying breath of God provides the ontological conditions not only for the relationality of the spiritual and the material dimensions of reality but also for the relationality of human beings as male and female (1:27) and of human beings with the natural world, with each other in community, and with the divine. Is this not suggestive for the more recent attempts to overcome the dualism between spirit and nature, long assumed in scientific circles?[4]

Second, even as the life breath given to *ha adam* empowers *ha adam* to be a responsive creature, capable of being addressed by the divine and of taking responsibility for the orders of creation (1:26), so also the wind of God blowing across the primordial waters enables creation to respond to the divine command. In fact, the breath of God vivifies the orders of creation and empowers them as creative agents in their own right. In some cases, the divine commands given in a passive voice are followed by specific divine actions of making (1:7, 16, 21, 25). But in other cases, God creates by saying (emphases mine): "Let the earth *put forth* vegetation: plants *yielding* seed, and fruit trees . . . that *bear* fruit" (1:11); "Let the waters *bring forth* swarms of living creatures" (1:20); and "Let the earth *bring forth* living creatures of every kind" (1:24). In the first and third case (but not the second), God's command is followed by "And it was so," before indicating God's response and activity. Further, on the third day, the dry land is allowed to appear, and God then proceeds only to call it earth (1:9–10), and the earth itself is said explicitly to bring forth vegetation (plants, fruits, and trees). A case can be made that these hints from the Priestly author are fully consistent with the nuanced accounts of contemporary science.[5]

Third, not only does creation respond to the divine; God also responds in turn and interacts with the orders of creation. God sees, evaluates, and pronounces: at the end of each day—long before the appearance of human

---

3. See Yong, "Ruach, the Primordial Waters, and the Breath of Life."

4. Thus the work of the John Templeton Foundation. See also Sharpe, *Sleuthing the Divine*.

5. E.g., Peters and Hewlett, *Evolution from Creation to New Creation*.

beings—what appears is good. In this sense, as Miroslav Volf puts it, creation is "an end in itself," having a value independent of human beings.[6] This demands a nonanthropocentric view of the orders of creation, including an environmental and ecological ethic of care for the earth on its own terms and not just for the benefit of human habitation.

Finally and perhaps most significantly for the contemporary science-religion dialogue, the *ruah* of God sweeping across the primordial waters infuses the orders of creation with a teleological dynamic, so that creation is best understood in terms of processes directed toward the eschatological intentions of God. Here we must be careful, given the many wrong turns and dead ends coughed up by the evolutionary process (e.g., the extinction of so many species of animals, not to mention the incalculably long periods of time before the appearance of life forms in the universe). Yet is not the evolutionary struggle also implicit in the "formless void and darkness" that covered the face of the deep (1:2)? Is it not precisely in and through this formlessness that the wind of God separates out, divides, and particularizes the orders of creation so as to bring forth complexity out of chaos? The cosmological, geological, and biological orders of creation emerge as increasingly complex systems of organization, each intrinsically connected to the others. Might the presence and activity of the *ruah* of God illuminate some of the topics much debated in the present science-religion dialogue: the teleological processes of emergence and the anthropic principle; the holistic interactivity and causal relations between systems and their constituent parts; and the interrelationality and interactivity of the mental and material domains of the world?

The challenge for Christian theology, however, is to translate these convictions into public discourse accessible to those without the community of faith and to provide for some means to clarify the validity of these interconnections besides just saying, "The Bible says so." Here we return to the task of doing theology in the public square, in this case, in dialogue with the sciences. Although mathematical proof can never be the goal of theological argument, neither is fideism an acceptable option. All this talk about the Spirit and the orders of creation—do they come together only in the figments of the exegetical imagination? My claim, however, is that all truth is God's truth and therefore communicable universally and verifiable in other tongues. How, then, can a pneumatological theology of creation proceed, especially when (at least historically) other voices, in particular the voices of the sciences, have made counterclaims? Do we not need a mediating discourse that allows for translation between the language of science

---

6. See Volf, *Work in the Spirit*, esp. 144-45.

and that of theology? For these particular needs, what we are calling for is a mutual context, a context as wide as the creation itself and amenable to the languages of the natural world, of the sciences, and of theology. Such would be a metaphysics, along with an interpretive account that justifies its articulation. Among various alternatives, the metaphysics of experience developed by Donald Gelpi in dialogue with the North American philosophical tradition provides one sure way forward. Its justification is the semiotic of C. S. Peirce.

2.2

The Emergence of Interdisciplinarity[1]

IN THIS FINAL PART of this chapter, I will suggest that an emergentist anthropology opens up an interdisciplinary framework for the theology and science dialogue, but that it does so for both scientific and theological reasons. Scientifically, the various levels of complexity that constitute the web of human life invite a pluralism of methods of inquiry and analysis. Theologically, the diversity of disciplinary and methodological perspectives functions analogously to the many tongues of the Pentecost narrative. In what follows, I develop this two-pronged rationale by looking at the pentecostal phenomenon of glossolalia.[2] My claim is not only that our understanding of glossolalia can be fruitfully illuminated by the various scientific perspectives, but also that our understanding of God's action in the world need not be threatened by the diversity of scientific explanations.

From the standpoint of the sciences, the first two parts of this chapter have already shown that tongues speaking can be analyzed at many different levels. Let us summarize the preceding discussion, moving up the ladder of the sciences, so to speak. Technological advances in the cognitive sciences now allow us to observe neural and synaptic functions of those engaged in glossolalic prayer. Unsurprisingly, we note distinctive cerebral patterns as well as the activation of certain brain sites that can be compared and

1. Yong, *The Spirit of Creation*, 65–71.
2. It might be countered that I picked the "easy case" of glossolalia, which involves a high degree of human participation anyway. I think, however, that my supervenience account can also illuminate claims about miraculous healings, among other charismatic phenomena, as I hope to show in chapter 4.

contrasted with what happens with people engaged in nonglossolalic but otherwise prayerful activity.[3] A reductionistic interpretation of such data might be tempted to eliminate the role of human mentality and thus "explain away" what happens in glossolalia as being no more than the epiphenomenal manifestation of various brain states. The argument might be that whatever else people might believe they are doing, the cognitive sciences tell us otherwise.

Yet while neuroscientists may be able to observe, from an outsider's point of view, the correlation between a person's brain functions and his or her conscious activity, this does not explain the insider's "first person" account of the same set of events. This argument of Murphy, Clayton, and others is not meant to demean the gains made in the cognitive sciences.[4] It only distinguishes much that can be illuminated by such studies, while also recognizing that outsider perspectives remain limited within the bigger scheme of things. This does not mean that the cognitive sciences are now in turn negligible since, as we have already noted, our embodiment constrains what can emerge and what happens after that. It means only that the neurophysiological, psychological, and psychosocial sciences are incomplete; put more strongly, apart from first-person accounts, we will not even be able to make the correlation between brain activities and mental states.

At these higher levels, we have already noted research suggesting that tongues speaking may be learned behavior or that glossolalists may fit certain psychological profiles. But gains certainly have been made, especially in overturning the earlier bias that identified glossolalia as pathological. More recent rigorous studies clearly indicate that tongues speakers are no more or less abnormal than non-tongues speakers. Instead, the former are less likely to experience depression, and they exhibit a less hostile personality type. On the whole, there may even be therapeutic benefits to consistent glossolalic practice.[5]

Still, pentecostal theologians, especially the more apologetically motivated, may be concerned about these psychological "findings." What if glossolalic profiling determines that only a small percentage of the human population is predisposed to speaking in tongues? Further, even if there is increasing evidence of the nonpathological nature of tongues speech, what about counterexamples, cases of genuinely pathological glossolalists,

---

3. E.g., Newberg et al., "Cerebral Blood Flow during Meditative Prayer."

4. This is not only a theistic issue; Buddhist scholars also resist any reductionism that eliminates the first-person account of what is happening; see my essay "Mind and Life, Religion and Science."

5. See, e.g., Castelein, "Glossolalia and the Psychology of the Self and Narcissism"; and Gritzmacher, Bolton, and Dana, "Psychological Characteristics of Pentecostals."

especially those snake handlers?[6] Last but certainly not least, if the psychological sciences are able to identify how the neurochemistry of tongues speaking functions therapeutically, does that not undermine the role and activity of the Holy Spirit as divine healing agent? To respond at least initially to the last question: If the Holy Spirit can heal through doctors and medicines, then why not through neurophysiological brain reactions? If embodiment is central to pentecostal spirituality,[7] then why wouldn't the work of the Spirit be mediated through human bodies and brains?

Similarly, we have seen that sociological analyses can also be illuminating. To be sure, such illumination can call attention to how glossolalia functions as a means of religious socialization (a relatively benign conclusion in some pentecostal circles, or one that is more amenable to those who view it as a sign or evidence of the Spirit's infilling), just as it can draw attention to the prevalence of glossolalia among more socially marginalized people groups (which may be less appealing for those in the upper classes). Parallel to this, as the research of Goodman and others has shown, cultural-anthropological perspectives have also documented how glossolalia serves as a semiotic marker among communities experiencing social upheaval in the transition from a premodern to a modern world. On the other hand, we also saw recent collaborative and multidisciplinary approaches that revealed glossolalia flourishing among well-adjusted and upwardly mobile people groups too.

Predictably, polemicists have attempted to draw from selected scientific data to attack pentecostals personally or undermine pentecostal spirituality and piety as a whole.[8] Such polemics are, however, inevitably reductionistic inasmuch as explanation provided at any one level—for example, neurobiology, psychology, or sociology—is thought to completely account for the phenomenon in question. But this is an extrascientific conclusion that is smuggled in rather than derived from any individual data set. It also assumes either that a lower-level explanation exhaustively captures all there is to be known about what is under discussion or that the world itself is a closed system of causes and effects that excludes a religious or theological

---

6. Snake handling is a very limited phenomenon among global pentecostalism, reflecting, as much as anything else, the historical and cultural peculiarities of the Appalachian region. For a sympathetic yet illuminating discussion that does not pathologize serpent handlers, see Hood and Williamson, *Them That Believe*. See also Burton, *Serpent-Handling Believers*; and Covington, *Salvation on Sand Mountain*.

7. The centrality of the body to pentecostal and charismatic piety is documented by Csordas, *The Sacred Self*; and idem, *Body/Meaning/Healing*.

8. E.g., Preus, "Tongues."

dimension. The latter, of course, is a metaphysical assumption that is contested especially among those working at the theology and science interface.

My claim is that each level of scientific inquiry is important and helpful for shedding light on the whole even as any adequate explanation of a religious phenomenon, including glossolalia, should also pay attention to the religious and theological explications of its practitioners. When this latter element is factored in, a genuine encounter between science and religion would proceed in two directions. On the one hand, scientific viewpoints would complement and even enrich our religious and theological descriptions, rather than threaten them; on the other hand, religious and theological perspectives would also add depth to scientific accounts by providing "thick descriptions" of the phenomenon under investigation.[9] So whereas a neurobiological, psychological, or sociological theory might be tempted to reduce tongues speaking to a single or lower-level variable, Malony and Lovekin's "transcendency deprivation" perspective would recognize each level of explanation as valid in its own way, yet seek a holistic viewpoint that includes the religious and theological dimensions involved in practitioner self-understandings.

In other words, to return momentarily to Murphy's supervenience hypothesis,[10] the lines of causal explanation can be understood to flow in multiple directions, including a "top-down" role for human, and even divine, agency. So any particular glossolalic manifestation may be viewed from any number of disciplinary perspectives, each illuminating the phenomenon in its own way (neurobiologically according to certain brain functions, psychologically according to certain personality propensities, sociologically according to certain social deprivations, etc.). But this need not—indeed should not—displace the first-person account, one that may be testified to as having the character of a spiritual yearning, or, to put it in pentecostal terms, a "tarrying before the Lord."[11] In this case, the mental exertion put forth in tarrying for this or that blessing from God is constrained by and supervenes upon the existing or underlying neurobiological and psychological realities, but is not reducible to these lower levels without loss of the higher-level account. (Later in this book, I will reflect further on how such a supervenience account is applicable also to an understanding of other pentecostal phenomena like miracles and healings.)

---

9. I provide such a "thick" account in my "Tongues, Theology, and the Social Sciences"; see also Yong, "Tongues of Fire in the Pentecostal Imagination."
10. See Murphy, *Anglo-Saxon Postmodernity*, chap. 10.
11. Castelo, "Tarrying on the Lord."

Note, however, that we are here not arbitrarily making room for pentecostal interpretations. Rather, there is an increasing recognition that phenomena at each level up the hierarchy of sciences—for example, physics, chemistry, biology, neuropsychology, sociology—are in some way causally constituted by the lower level, but yet, once having emerged, add something to the explanation of the whole without which our understanding would be significantly impoverished.[12] So while lower-level explanations can illuminate observations at the next level to some degree, only a blatant reductionism would claim to provide an exhaustive account. At the same time, the emergentist hypothesis also recognizes the validity of the various scientific discourses each at its own level—since the science at each level should be determined by the nature of the objects or things studied at that level—without negating the need for higher-level perspectives.[13]

The call for interdisciplinarity does not just seek to make room for theological perspectives. What is at stake is not just theology's "voice" but the integrity of each of the disciplines within and across the spectrum of the sciences. Anticipating here the defense in chapter 5 of a theology of evolutionary emergence, reductionism threatens not just theology but each science's investigation at higher or emergent levels. I insist on interdisciplinarity in order to preserve the relative autonomy of each of the scientific fields of inquiry.

The result is a scientific justification for methodological pluralism and interdisciplinarity that has a theological correlation. I am referring to an analogical interpretation of the many tongues of Pentecost. In my reading, the tongues of fire in the Acts narrative symbolize the many cultures, languages, and perspectives that constitute the human community, all of which combine, at least potentially if not actually, to declare the glory of God (Acts 2:11). Hence the many tongues of Pentecost serve metaphorically to suggest how many different linguistic and cultural perspectives can also be vehicles for declaring all truth as God's truth. By extension, in our contemporary world, I am suggesting that the many scientific disciplines and the diversity of viewpoints represented in the scientific enterprise constitute a multiplicity of modes of inquiry and discourses that also reveal how nature declares

---

12. E.g., Clayton and Davies, eds., *The Re-Emergence of Emergence*; and Murphy and Stoeger, eds., *Evolution and Emergence*.

13. For an argument for multilevel or stratigraphic disciplinary analysis, see McGrath, *The Science of God*, chapter 5, and also McGrath, *A Scientific Theology*, chapter 10 (who draws, in both cases, on the work of British philosopher Roy Bhasker). For an alternative argument against scientific reductionism, see Kauffman, *Reinventing the Sacred*, although I'm less enthused about Kauffman's naturalistic theism that hearkens of Spinoza's pantheism.

the glory of God (Ps 19:1). Each speaks distinctively from its vantage point, illuminating the world in its own way, while complementing our knowledge of the whole. None can be eliminated without substantial loss, but simultaneously, none can presume to subsume all other explanations under its own rubric. Theology can therefore allow the various sciences to do their work, and need not fear (at least not in general) about the deliverances of the sciences. The two books—of nature and of Scripture—should not contradict one another, assuming they are both being interpreted correctly.[14] Theology can learn from the sciences even while theology can also perhaps inform scientific inquiry.[15]

But we are missing one more element that has been percolating under our discussion throughout this chapter: the activity of God the Holy Spirit. Now for the record, I do *not* hold that God as spirit is also an emergent reality like human spirits. So since the preceding emergentist anthropology and interdisciplinary method open up space for human intentionality, made possible in terms of a supervening relationship between the mind and its environment (including the brain and the body), the question arises: What about divine intentionality? More precisely, how should we think about the person and workings of the Holy Spirit? How is science supposed to account for that?

This is not a moot question. In the glossolalic experience, many pentecostals will turn immediately to the biblical account, which states, "All of them were filled with the Holy Spirit and began to speak in other languages, as the Spirit gave them ability" (Acts 2:4). Quite apart from citing scriptural texts as explanations, pentecostal testimonies are pervasively infused with recognition of the Spirit's constant presence and activity in their lives. How can a pentecostal engagement with modern science register fairly this conviction about divine action? As we shall see from the argument of the next two chapters, I believe that pentecostal perspectives and emphases on the eschatological dimension of the Spirit's presence and activity can be understood as complementary to—even supervenient upon—the causal descriptions identified at the various levels of scientific inquiry.

---

14. See Yong, "Reading Scripture and Nature."

15. Russell, *Cosmology from Alpha to Omega*, 9–24, suggests that theology can influence scientific work in at least the following ways: informing assumptions behind empirical research; providing models and analogies for imaginative interpretation of data; and suggesting criteria for choosing among rival interpretive theories.

2.3

The Books of Scripture and of Nature
The Hermeneutics of Science[1]

THE PRECEDING PREPARES THE way for seeing how a pneumatological perspective can contribute to the ancient tradition that came to distinguish between the books of Scripture and of nature as two complementary sides of the same coin.[2] By this, I mean that Scripture, read in faith, provides us with the theological significance of nature, understood on its own terms. Thus there are two levels of importance, although each level has its own integrity. If concordism insists that Scripture and science are, or should be, about the same thing, then the Scripture-nature complementarity that I am suggesting says that the Scriptures provide a higher-level set of meanings for scientific findings without undermining the integrity of science or its methods. In order to see this, we will give a brief overview on the history of the two books metaphor before turning to more contemporary applications.

---

1. Yong, "Reading Scripture and Nature," 9–11.

2. This complementarity between the two books is associated, in my mind, to that which goes under the same label as applied to explaining the relationship between theology and science. Complementarity in the theology and science arena refers to the idea that each provides valid insights into the one world which we inhabit, and which should at least be noncontradictory, if not also convergent in some respects. My use of the term is informed by, among other sources, Loder and Neidhardt, *The Knight's Move*, especially section 1; Mackinnnon, "Complementarity"; and McGrath, *Science and Religion*, 165–74.

While Augustine was one of the first of the early church fathers to call nature a book,³ the basic idea goes back even further and certainly has seen major developments since the fifth century.⁴ The Christian tradition has perennially appealed to the Scriptures with regard to thinking about the revelatory power of the creation: "The heavens are telling the glory of God; and the firmament proclaims his handiwork" (Ps 19:1), and, in the New Testament, "since the creation of the world his eternal power and divine nature, invisible though they are, have been understood and seen through the things he has made" (Rom 1:20). There are other scriptural allusions, for example, to the sky being like a scroll (Isa 34:4 and Rev 6:14), which have lent themselves to the emergence of the metaphor of the book of nature.

During the patristic and especially medieval periods, then, Scripture and nature were interpreted in the light of each other. Following the dominance of Augustine and the neo-Platonic worldview, however, the visibility of the natural world was thought to point clearly toward the invisible things of the spiritual world. Hence, the interpretation of nature's symbolism was multileveled, parallel to that of Scripture, although both were considered revelatory instruments of the character and works of God. Hugh of St. Victor (1078–1141) understood that nature revealed God's power, wisdom, and goodness, and that attendance to the message of nature enabled participation in the sanctification and redemption of nature itself, so that in Christ, the world would be completed, reconciled with, and returned to God.⁵

The Renaissance, Reformation, and early modern periods, however, saw major shifts in the Christian understanding of the book of nature.⁶ First, the medieval conviction about nature's revelatory powers was expanded so that nature illuminated not just theological truths (like Scripture) but also could be expected, if properly mined (or interpreted), to disclose the secrets of the creation itself.⁷ Second, the medieval four-fold sense of interpretation—literal, moral, allegorical, and spiritual—was increasingly abandoned, especially among the magisterial Reformers, in favor of the literal sense.⁸

---

3. Augustine, *Contra Faustum Manichaeum*, 32.20; see Augustine, *Answer to Faustus, a Manichean*, 422.

4. The most complete discussion, and certainly now the standard account, is the four-volume work by van der Meer and Mandelbrote, eds., *Nature and Scripture in the Abrahamic Religions: Up to 1700*; and idem, *Nature and Scripture in the Abrahamic Religions: 1700–Present*.

5. On Hugh's theology of nature, see Mews, "The World as Text."

6. A book-length discussion is found in Harrison, *The Bible, Protestantism, and the Rise of Natural Science*.

7. Howell, *God's Two Books*.

8. This despite the strategic protestations of Galileo, in his letter to the grand duchess

Correspondingly, the clarity of nature was understood, not in terms of its universal accessibility (as was held during the first millennium), but as enabled by the emergence and use of the empirical methods of early modern science that brought the causal mechanisms of nature into plain view.[9] Third, the Reformers' insistence on interpreting Scripture directly, rather than relying on authorities favored the growing class of elite scientists, who also urged the importance of engaging nature directly (experientially and experimentally) rather than relying on the discoveries of their ancestors. Last but not least, if Jesus' mention of the Scriptures and the power of God (Matt 22:29) was an oblique reference to the two books, as Francis Bacon (1561–1626) took it to be,[10] then not only did the book of nature require its own distinctive methods of interpretation, but the identification of the powers of nature also suggested that nature was less a set of facts to be uncovered than a web of processes and potentials to be mastered and deployed.[11]

The result during early modernity, at least in part, was the emergence of the scientific method as the key to unlocking the book of nature. Whereas the medieval schoolmen distinguished ontological and divine causality from cosmological or creaturely causality—for instance, that God is the first or primary cause of all there is, while creatures are valid secondary causes—the early modern scientists began to focus their expertise on tracing the efficient and material causes operating in nature. As the scientific enterprise has continued to unfold over the last few hundred years, various disciplines have attempted to secure primacy of place, but each has defended itself against the encroachments of others. Contemporary science is thus characterized by a vigorous interdisciplinarity (in which the lines between disciplines are blurred) and multidisciplinarity (featuring collaborative inquiry between two or more disciplines), both of which combine to illuminate the natural world.

Non- or antireligious scientists might conclude that the revelatory power of the book of Scripture has been entirely eliminated by that of the book of nature and its scientific methods. Concordists who insist on the harmonization of the Bible and science have sought to restore the authority of the book of Scripture but go about it erroneously: by legitimating its

---

Christina, that Scripture remained ambiguous, subject to various interpretations (when compared with nature); see Galileo, *Discoveries and Opinions of Galileo*, 173–216.

9. With regard to the transformation of the two books metaphor in the early modern period, I have been helped by the overview of Tanzella-Nitti, "The Two Books Prior to the Scientific Revolution"; but the interpretation is mine and Tanzella-Nitti should not be held responsible for it.

10. Matthews, "Reading the Two Books with Francis Bacon," 67.

11. See Harrison, "Reinterpreting Nature in Early Modern Europe," esp. 33–38.

credentials on the basis of modernist assumptions about science. On the one hand, this is understandable, given the explanatory power of modern science—who would not want to affirm truths consistent with the most powerful fount of knowledge produced by the modern world? But on the other hand, concordists overlook the fact that the scientific method's focus on the book of nature means that its purview is by definition limited to the natural world. This means that science is not equipped to make metaphysical or religious claims, and it is only by transgressing these boundaries that science (or book of nature experts) can render or adjudicate such claims. In short, concordists have to stretch science beyond its boundaries in order to harmonize Scripture with it.

I suggest that pentecostals can contribute to a contemporary theology of the two books by developing its pneumatological imagination in ways that adapt both premodern and modern understandings.[12] In the following, I sketch two basic trajectories for a pentecostal reconsideration of the relationship between the books of Scripture and of nature. First, recognizing that the *ruah of God* both hovered *over* the primeval chaos and yet was dynamically at work as the breath *within* the creatures of the world, we can posit a pneumatological theology of creation that understands the Spirit to be present and active *over* and *within* history and creation, even while illuminating both worlds to human minds. Such illumination, however, is by nature theological, soteriological, and eschatological (related to God's final salvation of the world), providing a perspective on history's and nature's ends as intended by God. Second, what the history of Christian thought has called the interpretation of nature, pentecostals call discernment. But whereas theologians or scripturalists will discern (exegete) the books of Scripture and nature theologically and soteriologically, others will discern (interpret) the nature and history of the world from their respective disciplinary perspectives. The theological discernments (readings) inevitably will go beyond the nontheological interpretations, but that neither delegitimizes the latter nor undermines the possibility for complementary perspectives to emerge.[13]

---

12. I present the details of such a pneumatological imagination in my book, *Spirit-Word-Community*, part II. Many of my claims in this article are grounded in my views about epistemology and interdisciplinarity argued at (some would say, exhausting) length in this earlier volume.

13. I see my theological approach to the two books as consistent with what is suggested by others who have contributed to this journal—e.g., Menuge, "Interpreting the Book of Nature"; Thorson, "Hermeneutics for Reading the Book of Nature"; and Murphy, "Reading God's Two Books." Menuge and Thorson agree that nature is also interpreted, but they differ over whether intelligent design is to be read scientifically (Menuge) or theologically (Murphy). I tend to agree that contemporary intelligent

The preceding discussion invites us to think analogically about the relationship between theology, concerned with the book of Scripture, and contemporary science, concerned with the book of nature. The multi- and interdisciplinary character of the sciences require discursive practices that depend on peculiar methodological presuppositions, cultural practices, and institutional arrangements.[14] If the work of the Spirit was to harmonize the many tongues on the Day of Pentecost so as not to eliminate their differences but to declare the wonders of God (Acts 2:11), then might it not be possible for the same Spirit today to harmonize the many discursive practices of the various theological, natural, and human sciences so as not to eliminate their differences but to exalt the glory, power, and goodness of God?[15]

This means, then, that Christians can proceed in faith to suggest overarching theological interpretations of both books, while recognizing that the many disciplines also have their integrity, methods, and contributions. Therefore, historians might interpret the events of history (i.e., early Christianity of the book of Acts) in ways that complement pentecostal and Christian understandings, even as scientists might interpret the events of nature (i.e., the events of natural history behind the Genesis account) in ways that complement theological and soteriological perspectives. Concordism would insist that theological, historical, and scientific interpretations all proceed at the same level, and I believe this is a mistake. Instead, I suggest that the view of the two books as complementary is distinctively theological and does not need to claim either historical or scientific expertise in these respective domains. Thus historical-critical approaches and natural scientific methods can proceed to do their work. From a theological point of view, the truth will ultimately be complementary, even if, "For now we see in a mirror, dimly" (1 Cor 13:12). This is based on the nature of historical and scientific inquiry, which revises itself over time as each engages in the honest search after the truth and deploys the methods at its disposal.

Of course, biblical and theological interpretations should be consistent with the various historical and scientific consensuses[16]—that is what we

---

design is by and large a theologically funded project (here standing with Murphy, who sees ID as a natural theology) while also seeing that in some cases, discussion of some of the corollary issues such as function are more strictly scientific (so here, open to Menuge's claims about the scientific engagement of nature).

14. See Grinnell, *Everyday Practice of Science*, esp. part I.

15. See Yong, "Academic Glossolalia?"

16. Clayton, *Adventures in the Spirit*, esp. chap. 3 argues convincingly, about how theology's engagement with the sciences needs to recognize what can be said within scientific constraints. Thus, for example, the spherical nature of the earth confirmed by science dictates that intimations of a flat earth in the scriptural accounts need to be reinterpreted. I take this as meaning that science is not supremely authoritative, but

would expect if all truth were ultimately theologically funded. But given the fallibility and finitude of all human knowing—in things theological as well as in things historical and scientific—it may be that the desired complementarity does not arrive, either because of lack of consensus in one or more fields of inquiry, or because of contradictory perspectives within or across disciplines. In the case of the former, when no consensus has been achieved, biblical and theological accounts should be tendered provisionally, perhaps sufficiently vaguely so as to be consistent with alternative historical or scientific theories under adjudication (regardless of what happens),[17] or with the recognition that later findings may warrant revisitation of the issues. In the case of the latter, if contradictions persist, this simply means that those working on contrary sides of the issue need to be open to further researching the matter and to revising their position as appropriate (while being cognizant that the complexity of some disagreements may not yield complementary resolution even in their lifetime). Yet in all of these cases, those interested in the theology and science dialogue or those working in the sciences can rely on the Spirit's illumination in their endeavors, which is negotiated variously in their immediate confessional community, in wider communities of faith, amidst their disciplines, and within the backdrop of the broader scientific community.[18]

---

that when engaging specifically with the sciences, theologians need to understand that specific context and thus have to accommodate themselves, at least in part, to that field of discourse.

17. Thus, for example, theological interpretations should be potentially compatible with both intelligent design and theistic evolution, perhaps even with progressive and young-earth creationisms, all of which are currently being negotiated within evangelical Christianity. To affirm this of *theological* interpretation is not to say that each of these are equal options in the science classroom—in that arena, other experts with more than just theological interests need to adjudicate the issues. This is, in part, what it means to retain the integrity of disciplines rather than either to reduce any to others or to subsume all under theology, as it was during the medieval period. For further discussion of these matters, see my *The Spirit of Creation*, esp. chaps. 2 and 5.

18. For instances of such interconfessional and interdisciplinary inquiry, see Yong, ed., "Pentecostalism, Science, and Creation"; idem, *The Spirit Renews the Face of the Earth*; and Yong and Smith, eds., *Science and the Spirit*.

2.4

Faith and Science
Friend or Foe?[1]

MANY PENTECOSTALS HAVE ASSUMED or heard that the Bible conflicts with modern science. This is especially true when discussing scientific theories about the age of the earth and the origins and development of life. Often pastors broadcast this assumption from their pulpits in ways that move our college- and university-educated members to reconsider whether they can, with good conscience, remain in our churches. It is not necessarily that these members think they know better. But they do know there are a variety of views about scientific theories. A pastor's insistence that there is only one way to see things says to these members: "Leave your mind at the door before you come into church." This may not be the intended message, but it is implicit in the way pastors sometimes talk about the seven days of creation when our audience has come to understand the ancient Hebrews did not interpret these as literally as we do.

We should be aware, however, that over the last two generations more and more pentecostals have gone on for higher education, with an increasing number in the sciences. And as they have studied the theological and scientific disciplines, they also have come to entertain a spectrum of positions. While too many have, as a result, left our churches, a good number have remained faithful to the pentecostal message. For those who have

---

1. Yong, "Faith and Science," 46–51.

stayed, what binds them together is the conviction that their faith and their scientific knowledge are not necessarily antagonistic.

This article summarizes four basis positions of how theology and science have interacted and makes some recommendations.

FOUR POSITIONS CONCERNING THEOLOGY AND SCIENCE

Conflict

The first position is the historic position of *conflict*. Some pentecostals remain convinced that whenever science appears to contradict the plain sense of the Bible, science must be wrong. Therefore, if the Bible says that God created the world in seven days, then any theories that the earth is older than that must be false. This view assumes that the Book of Genesis provides an ancient scientific account that is in concordance with later scientific developments. However, the basis for such an assumption is not obvious. Genesis 1–3 could well reflect God's accommodation to the understanding of the ancient world instead. If so, then it tells us about God the Creator as opposed not to modern science, but to the creation myths of the ancient world.

The conflict position remains important if contemporary science oversteps its boundaries. Some scientists go beyond what science says to make metaphysical and theological claims. These claims also come with a set of presuppositions, such as matter or nature is all there is. This is not genuine science but scientism. Pentecostals need to resist such assertions.

Independent

The second position views theology and science as *independent*. In broad terms, those who hold this view say that science concerns nature and the material world, while theology concerns morality, the spiritual world, and the afterlife. Different norms and methods guide these two views, and they should not conflict with each other.

For many, the independence model works because there are differences in assumptions and approaches between theology and science. There is also a practical aspect to this position. It is probably most prevalent among pentecostals who end up working in the theological or scientific disciplines. Because it takes years of graduate-level education to master a discipline, most pentecostals have neither the time nor resources to gain sufficient expertise in both arenas to form a well-reasoned opinion.

However, while such a truce between theology and science might make it easy to do our work and retain our faith, it does not provide resources for integrating our faith and our work in the modern world. The result is that many pentecostal scientists go to church on Sundays and lift up holy hands but then go back to their scientific laboratories during the week and do not think much about the theological aspects of their work.

On the other side, pentecostal theologians and all Christians use scientific technology continuously—from electronics to communications to transportation to medicine and beyond. Yet theologians do not think much about how to reconcile their theology with the science that makes such technology possible. If this continues in our churches, our students who go off to secular colleges and universities will not be able to make theological sense of what they are learning. In reality, we do not live in compartmentalized silos. While we wear different hats—as theologians, scientists, spouses, parents, etc.—we still share a common world given to us by God.

Cooperating

The third position sees theology and science as *cooperating* with each other. There are certainly different forms of such cooperation. Two of the most popular currently among evangelical and pentecostal scientists and theologians are intelligent design (ID) and old-earth creationism (OEC). The ID movement has a formally organized platform but also includes many others who are not a part of the formal ID organizations yet believe we can detect design in nature. Most of the latter insist that whatever else science might tell us about *how* things came about, theology tells us *why* they have come about. Theology reveals what science currently struggles to recognize—that nature reveals features that suggest a designer, who believers worship as God.

The challenge for ID at this point is that most mainstream scientists say this belief does not employ the scientific method and has not produced any testable hypotheses. In short, ID might belong in a theology classroom but not in a science classroom. Things may change going forward, however, as many scientists are working diligently to develop the scientific aspects of this idea.

OEC also comes in many forms. What binds these forms together is a commitment to God's creative and providential activity in the world, and acceptance of the evidence for a very ancient earth and cosmos of at least millions if not billions of years. Some OEC advocates believe that the "days" of Genesis 1 refer to incalculable eons of time. Others believe in a primordial fall that inserts a lengthy period between the first and second verses of Genesis 1. A third group accepts the standard accounts of the sciences regarding an old earth and some kind of theory of progressive creation. Within this camp, many believe only in microevolution (within species), but a few also accept macroevolution (across species). Yet all OEC supporters accept that however things came about or developed, they did so directed by God's creative handiwork.

The challenge for those who believe in cooperation between theology and science is that there are so many variables to consider and so many possible positions to adhere to about how such cooperation ought to proceed. Some are willing to cooperate, but they are not as trusting of science since its hypotheses and theories are continuously subject to change. They would be concerned that others urging cooperation are too willing to assume science is right and risk undermining biblical faith.

Partnership

This leads to the fourth option: that of theology and science in *dialogue* or *partnership*. If the third model assumes a kind of cooperative enterprise, the fourth model simply says that we ought not to presume such cooperation is always possible. However, neither should we assume conflict or independence either. Instead, theologians and scientists need to be open to consulting and learning from each other. After all, as Paul wrote, "For now we see in a mirror, dimly, but then we will see face to face" (1 Cor 13:12). In some cases, we might find that we need to oppose what science suggests because of *scientism*. In other cases, there could be cooperation at various levels. Nevertheless, we must discern these on a case-by-case basis. This requires that both sides be willing to collaborate in a search for truth.

The challenge here, of course, is that the scientific establishment is not usually in the habit of consulting with pentecostals on matters related to their research. On the other side, neither have pentecostals prepared themselves to engage these matters through an informed Christian faith. We pentecostals appear content to use the results of modern science when it suits our purposes. Yet we fail to see that the underlying science that makes possible the comforts of modern life invite deeper theological reflection on biblical teachings as well.

If pentecostals inform themselves about both theology and the sciences, they might find that this partnership model provides a fruitful way forward. On the one hand, we will be more likely to encourage our scientists in their work and create opportunities for our scientists and theologians to work together. On the other hand, we will provide a model for our children to emulate so they can be better prepared for a world that will be even more complex than it currently is. Theologically, we might also come to see that our presuppositions about life in the Spirit do not oppose the life of the mind or the scientific vocation. In fact, the Scriptures teach the creation of all things not only through Jesus as the Word of God (Col 1:16–17 and Heb 1:2), but also through God's Spirit or breath, which "swept over the face of the waters" (Gen 1:2). Further, the work of the Spirit in the world is clear:

- "If he should take back his spirit to himself, and gather to himself his breath, all flesh would perish together, and all mortals return to dust" (Job 34:14–15);
- "When you hide your face, they are dismayed; when you take away their breath, they die and return to their dust. When you send forth your spirit, they are created; and you renew the face of the ground" (Ps 104:29–30);
- The prophet Isaiah also foretells that "until a spirit from on high is poured out on us, and the wilderness becomes a fruitful field, and the fruitful field is deemed a forest" (Isa 32:15).

In other words, whereas previous generations might have thought that the work of the Spirit was only in our hearts, the Bible tells us otherwise. The Spirit's work is intimately present and active in our bodies (which we experience daily), in the church, and in God's creation as a whole.

Perhaps we could also see that if God can speak to us through the many tongues and languages of Pentecost, then science, correctly understood, might also be a means to declare and witness "about God's deeds of power" (Acts 2:11). We need to support pioneering researchers and thinkers to venture into both fields. They might provide an interpretation and translations of the difficult languages that constitute both theology and science.

The church has long believed that God has revealed His glory in His two books: Scripture and nature. If the Holy Spirit leads the people of God into all truth, will not the Spirit lead theologians and scientists together also in unveiling the truth of God and the world? Of course, whatever our pronouncements, we need to always follow the apostle Paul's guidelines. When people give prophecies in the congregation, he warned, "Let two or three prophets speak, and let the others weigh what is said" (1 Cor 14:29). Why should this be any different for our theologians and scientists?

CONCLUSION

Here are a few recommendations. First, we need to realize that for much of the 2,000-year history of the Church, Christians were at the forefront of scientific discovery. As the Assemblies of God's position paper on "The Doctrine of Creation" (passed by the General Presbytery on July 30, 2011), says: "Believing scientists and biblical scholars consider no fundamental conflict to exist between God's Word and His works" (available at http://www.ag.org/top/beliefs/position_papers/). Let us not allow a strident set of atheistic voices from the science community or an equally anxious set of fundamentalist Christian perspectives perpetuate a warfare mentality between theology and science. Let us instead distinguish what is nonnegotiable, like the existence of God as Creator, from issues of second-tier import, and then allow our believing scientists and our faithful theologians to keep doing their work at this level.

Perhaps one way we can foster sound biblical and theological reflection on scientific matters is by inviting any scientists or science teachers in our congregations to share their testimonies. Another way is to incorporate the testimonies of believing scientists into our sermons and teaching.

Second, we need to support Assemblies of God higher education. The Alliance for AG Higher Education has been proactive in promoting the work of our schools and our faculties. Inquire about having faculty from one of our Assemblies of God universities visit your church. Many faculty, even those who work in the sciences, have a call to preach and carry ministerial credentials. Others can share how their pentecostal faith informs their work. Most of our schools have church ministries offices that can coordinate such visits from faculty. Such exposure to our church members will encourage our young people to aspire to all that God might call them to through a college education.

Jesus urged us to love God not only with all of our heart, soul, and strength, but also with all of our mind (Luke 10:27). Our colleges and universities can help us do better in this regard.

My final set of recommendations is that we need to continue to work to overcome the history and culture of anti-intellectualism that persists in some segments of the pentecostal church. When pentecostals first emerged in the early twentieth century, the educational establishment marginalized them and in turn pentecostals demonized the educational establishment. But times have changed. So how do we transform the climate from one that has been hostile to academia and science?

Pastors need to get to know the scientists, medical personnel, and science teachers attending their congregations. The latter listen to their pastors each week. Pastors need to find out about their work and their views, and perhaps read books they recommend on topics of mutual interest. Then, involve them more intentionally in the life of the church. Have them lead adult education classes or make presentations to the senior high group about how they integrate their faith and their work. Have open forums involving these resident experts that provide space to discuss questions our students are encountering in public schools. These events will go a long way to quelling the fears that are otherwise hyped by the volatile rhetoric of the media.

Do not make Christians in the scientific community feel like they do not belong. God has called them to their vocation, and they can help us do better in loving God with our minds. By fostering such discussions within our churches, and by furthering relationships between our colleges and our churches, we will create environments of research, scholarship, and dialogue. This will in turn motivate pastors and scientists to compare notes, listen to, and learn from one another. Along the way, this will inspire them to bring their pentecostal perspectives to the wider theology and science academies.

Why continue to allow the secular or non-pentecostal voices in the theology and science fields to set the research agendas? How might we also develop methods and approaches to explore and better understand pentecostal experiences and phenomena like healing and the miraculous? Our pentecostal faith should not be threatened by theological and scientific study; it should instead be enriched by it.

Continue to be vigilant in prayer for the pentecostal movement. The Father of Jesus Christ who has led us by the Spirit to the ends of the earth will not abandon us as we step into the halls of academia and scientific inquiry. Instead, the Spirit who leads the church of Christ into all truth will continue to guard our hearts and minds. The same Spirit will empower us to bear witness to the truth in ways that will turn others to Christ.

2.5

Speaking in Scientific Tongues[1]

AT THE BEGINNING OF his response, LeRon Shults suggests that my *The Spirit of Creation: Modern Science and Divine Action in the Pentecostal-Charismatic Imagination*, Pentecostal Manifestos 4 (Grand Rapids and Cambridge, UK: William B. Eerdmans Publishing Company, 2011), traverses domains where "even angels... might 'fear to tread.'" This is certainly not from any sense of my being extraordinarily courageous—after all, I don't even like to watch scary movies with my teenage daughters! Shults is also right to observe, however, that I am trying to make sense of my pentecostal tradition in a scientific world, and others on this panel, especially Thomas Oord, recognize that this will be important not only for pentecostals but also for those working at the theology and science interface. In what follows, I will begin by engaging with Shults's questions and suggestions, as doing so will also provide me with opportunity to interact with Joshua Moritz's and Craig Boyd's responses.

I have two sets of clarifying remarks to make in response to Shults before asking him a counter-question. First, Shults wants to know what I mean by matter, material, and materialism because he is unclear about what disembodied agency looks like in my proposal. I take responsibility for this obfuscation—it's not easy to describe what I am seeing as a pentecostal theologian doing pioneering work at the theology and science interface, not to mention that even as a pentecostal I am less full of the Spirit than I

1. Yong, "Speaking in Scientific Tongues," 130–39. See also the reviewers to which Yong responds, in *Canadian Journal of Pentecostal-Charismatic Christianity* 3, no. 1 (2012).

should be so that I have difficulty getting the "correct interpretation" of the pentecostal tongues that I sometimes speak. He especially wonders if my references to out of body experiences are meant to support a view of disembodied agency that undercuts the emergence theoretical framework I have adopted. This also is Moritz's primary concern: that there is a breakdown between the emergence of mind from body/brain and what I am positing as the emergence of disembodied spirits from embodied minds. Let me try to explain further what I am thinking about through two examples to see if it appeases both Shults and Moritz.

First, at the individual level, upon death, it is not uncommon that relatives or close friends have dreams, visions, or other perceptions of their deceased loved one. I do not think we need to merely subjectivize such experiences, as if they were merely projections of mourning minds (even if that may be true in some instances). Instead, I view this as remnants of the fields of force generated by living creatures that have emerged from out of but are now irreducible to their embodied parts and have the capacity to be sustained, to some degree, even after the demise of their bodily functions. In due course, however, these interactions fade away—which suggests that irreducibility does not mean the infinite capacity to be self-sustaining, a point to which I will return momentarily.

Second, at a corporate level, nations declare wars and then also agree to truces. However, the realities of war persist long after peace treaties are signed, both in memories (which are present realities, even if of past events) and in the very real effects and consequences of wars. The fields of force (the spiritual aspects of nations) generated by nations, in other words, are much stronger than those generated merely at the individual level. My way of putting it is to say that the national "spirits" oftentimes persist long after even the nations themselves have dissolved and ceased to exist in any definable manner. Hence we can still talk about the "spirit" of Nazi Germany, although strong counter-forces have arisen in the last sixty years to resist and ameliorate its demonic effect.

My point, however, is this: because spiritual beings are emergent from their underlying material substrates, they can exist in a disembodied sense only for as long as their force generating powers persist. The principalities and powers of Nazi Germany remained engaged much longer than that of my grandmother. The difference is that Christian faith confesses in the eschatological long run that my grandmother's body will be resurrected. That doctrinal commitment complements the emergence thesis that apart from embodiment in some respect, emergent levels of complexity cannot be infinitely self-perpetuating.

The second set of clarifications I want to address is Shults's related question about disembodied intentional agency. Now, however, I work in reverse order, beginning with corporate spiritual realities. In what sense can we say that national declaration of war reflects the intentional spiritual agencies? Only to the degree that we understand how groups of minds effect corporate intentions. My point is that if we do not wish to reduce personal human mentality to brain activities, then there is no reason to reduce the "decisions" or "actions" of nations (or any other corporate entity) to the decisions or actions of their parts.

What about the intentional agency of my grandmother's "disembodied" spirit as it interacted with my mother? Here, is where I think we can see continuity and discontinuity between living and dead human persons. Living persons exercise top down causality through their embodied presences in the world. Dead persons, however, exist only in a "spiritual" manner as sets of fields of force that have emerged from a complex life but will limp along with decreasing intensity unless or until the resurrection of the body. As such, dead persons may be able to exercise a degree of intentional agency, but only through ongoing interaction with living persons. So, for instance, my mother perceived, not too long after my grandmother passed away, that my grandmother had some unfinished business that needed attention, and that it was up to my mother to take it upon herself to attend to these matters. A reductionist model would simply say that my mother was imagining things. I see no reason within an emergentist frame of reference to deny that the emergent spirit of my grandmother was able, during this brief period of time after her death, to remain interactive with the world, in particular engaging with other kindred "spirits" who were sensitive to the legacy and influence of her field of force.

So now I would like to ask about Shults's theory of spiritual beings explicated in light of what he calls "theogonic (god-bearing) mechanisms of anthropomorphic promiscuity and sociographic prudery," about which I may have little qualms at their levels of explanation. But in the bigger scheme of things and at the personal level within which we both exist, what does Shults mean by exorcising spirits "(so to speak) both methodologically and materially"? His parenthetical remarks—"so to speak"—suggest that he is not being reductionistic about such exorcisms, but in that case, what is left after his exorcisms? Alternatively, he is simply using "exorcism" metaphorically, in which case, his is a thorough program of demythologization and reductionism.

My main point about a spirit-filled cosmology is this: if we do not wish to reduce human mental and spiritual capacity to brain and body activity, then why do so either with corporate realities or insist that such emergent personal realities cease to function upon death? Shults rightly notes that I do not seek a causal joint (that can be measured in terms of efficient causality) for divine action, and so he wonders how I think I can scientifically (i.e., quantitatively) measure other kinds of spirits in my pluralistic cosmos. Here is the difference between the activity of the divine Spirit (which causality I postulate in teleological and eschatological terms) and creaturely spirits, whether of human persons or their institutions. The latter are not self-sustaining and can and do exert efficient causal forces, and if so, such are, potentially, open to empirical detection. (As a side note, I believe that in staking out my position in this way, I am also parting ways with Oord, although for different reasons since he thinks, against Shults and me, that divine action also can be empirically measured scientifically; those interested can see our respective chapters in a new book edited by Matthew T. Lee and me, titled, *The Science and Theology of Godly Love*.)

Moritz believes that information theory can come to the rescue where emergence leaves us foundering with regard to a spirit-filled cosmos. I am very sympathetic to this suggestion, and it may be that in future work I will return to take up his assist in a more sustained manner. I do think that at some level, the role of information is key and it just needs to be unpacked. However, I don't think that the way forward is to replace emergence theory with information theory—although I'm not sure this is what Moritz is suggesting. Rather, they can be complementary. Information on its own is merely abstract—raising the perennial philosophical conundrum about the reality of mathematical truths. I think mathematical truths are abstractions, although I have not spent years on the philosophical disputes about this matter to be assured about my intuitions in this case. But if I am right, then such abstractions can nevertheless be realized in the world's many things, and we'll still need some kind of emergence theory to account for how the many things have emerged from pure possibility. (Here my Peircean triadic ontology shows its features: mathematical Thirdness is instantiated in brute Secondness that derive from Firstness.)

I should pause here to register two caveats. First, the recent work of others, including E. Janet Warren,[2] suggests that chaos theoretical models and linguistic rhetorical and metaphorical approaches may helpfully shed additional light particularly on the demonic aspects of human experience. If so, then the combination of information and chaos theories may also work in complementary fashion to illuminate what are otherwise scientifically obscure, even non-existent. Second, thesis 5 of my speculative cosmology (pp. 213–17 of my book) gives the misleading impression that personal

---

2. Warren, *Cleansing the Cosmos*.

manifestations of angelic beings appear first in the evolutionary scheme of things. I should have ordered the typology to begin with celestial, then proceed to terrestrial, personal, social, and ecclesial expressions. I also ought to have clarified that this is not meant to be an exhaustive classification. There appear to be at least partially animal-like "heavenly creatures" in Ezekiel 1 for instance, and there is no reason why other created things do not have inner spiritual aspects or dimensions as well. My speculative point is that different types of angelic realities have preceded and also continue to emerge subsequent to the personal ones that relate to human creatures, but that in each instance these spiritual entities are constituted by, but yet irreducible to, their material elements.

This leads us to Boyd's observations. His response reminds me of a paper written by Sally Shelton in one of my doctoral seminars in 2008 titled, "What Hath Amos to Do with Thomas?: Divergences and Convergences between the Theological Methodologies of Renewal Scholar Amos Yong and Renowned Scholastic Thomas Aquinas" (heretofore unpublished, to my knowledge). It is ironic to be mentioned in the same breath as the angelic doctor if Shults is right that my work treads where angels fear to tread, but I am flattered nonetheless. I do think that the "consonances" (Boyd's word) are more than coincidental since others have also observed such between my teleological account of divine action and Thomas's neo-Aristotelian argument from design. My heart is strangely warmed when I read from Boyd, who knows more about Thomas today than I ever will, even in eternity, that for Thomas, "that the most important of the [theistic] arguments is the argument from final causality," and that "teleology plays the central metaphysical role as creatures 'return' to God from whence they came." Peircean scholars like Menno Hulswit[3] are also beginning to explore other links between Thomas and Peirce, including matters related to that all-important notion of final causes that plays such an important role in my work. In conversation with Norris Clarke, the contemporary Jesuit and one of the most respected Thomist philosophers, Boyd calls attention to the "potencies" embedded within the created order that God "collaborates" with in order to bring about God's ultimate purposes. I am grateful to Boyd for interpreting Thomistic tongues for pentecostals like me and I hope that there is enough of the Spirit of truth in the spaces wherein we meet so that further light can be shed as renewal theologians continue the dialogue with the legacy of Thomas. If I might be so bold as to venture this comparative assessment as a prelude to the invitation for our contemporary common task: what Thomas did for his time in updating medieval theology in light

3. Hulswit, *From Cause to Causation*.

of Aristotelian philosophical and scientific knowledge invites us—from the ecumenical and theology-science communities—to re-theologize in light of the relational, holistic, and scientific cosmology of our twenty-first century.

In closing, then, I am hopeful that the theoretical sketch I have provided in my books and in this response can motivate others to also take up the research questions now opened up with the pentecostal entry to the theology and science discussion. This exchange, as well as others—e.g., other responses especially to *Science and the Spirit: A Pentecostal Engagement with the Sciences* edited by James K. A. Smith and me (Bloomington: Indiana University Press, 2010), with my rejoinder published in the *Cyberjournal for Pentecostal-Charismatic Research* 20 (2011), other responses to my *The Spirit of Creation*, plus my rejoinder, forthcoming in *Australasian Pentecostal Studies*,[4] and a book I am co-editing with Veli-Matti Kärkkäinen and Kirsteen Kim, *Interdisciplinary and Religio-Cultural Discourses on a Spirit-Filled World: Loosing the Spirits* (forthcoming with Palgrave Macmillan)[5]—are no more than the beginnings of what I anticipate will be a long conversation. The issues heretofore discussed in no way exhaust what needs to be engaged in the pentecostal encounter with science. As Oord indicated in his response, there is much work to be done. In particular, he is concerned about pentecostals attaining a sufficient level of both theological and scientific literacy in order to make a contribution to these discussions. I also am praying that more answer the Spirit's call to till in this particular section of the Lord's vineyard. We are also especially in need of biblical scholars, as Oord notes, who can address the hermeneutical and biblical interpretive issues as well. We are at the very beginning of a long-term discussion and there is much work to be done all the way around.

---

4. *Australasian Pentecostal Studies* 15, no. 1 (2013).

5. Yong, Kärkkäinen, and Kim, eds., *Interdisciplinary and Religio-Cultural Discourses on a Spirit-Filled World*.

2.6

Toward a Pneumato-Ecological Ethic
Christian-Buddhist Convergences[1]

YET EVEN WITH THE preceding response, it is important to note that this question is problematic not only within the Madhyamaka system (as developed specifically in the Huayen teaching) or within systems theory. In fact, it reflects, from the perspective of Christian theological discourse, the combined and related conundrums of both the problem of evil and the freedom of creatures. The former is the question of how evil arises in a world created and recognized by God to be good. The latter is the question not only of how free creatures can actualize evil states of affairs, but how such states of affairs can be rectified. The ethical, moral, and existential question is if and how free creatures such as human beings can go about doing the good which is necessary—in the case delineated above—to abolish nuclear weapons and save endangered plant species.

In the Christian theological tradition, of course, the combined problem of evil and creaturely freedom leads to the challenge of theodicy. In its starkest form: from whence comes evil if God as creator of the world is both omnipotent and omnibenevolent? If for Buddhists evil—with its desire and suffering—is simply part of the conventional world of samsara as we know it, for Christians, evil is simply part of the fallen human condition as we experience it. If Buddhists say that evil is ultimately related to the grasping and desiring of sentient beings, then Christians might say that evil is ultimately

---

1. Yong, *The Cosmic Breath*, 234–41.

due to the disobedient propensities and proclivities that affectively motivate creaturely—whether human or angelic or demonic—choices and behaviors. If the Buddhist argument is that evil is ultimately illusory, to be unveiled as such through human awakening to enlightenment and the true Buddha nature, the Christian version might say that what is thought to be evil from a finite perspective will ultimately—eschatologically—be shown, if not to be good, at least to have served the good purposes of God. Neither of these lines of responses, however, resolve the problem; they only push the question back even further: for Christians, is God justified for permitting creaturely freedom and the horrendous evils that has brought, and for Buddhists, even if illusion itself is the key evil, from whence comes illusion if the Buddha nature is true human nature?[2]

Neither religious tradition—nor their theological and philosophical counterparts—has satisfactorily resolved the intellectual aspects of the problem of evil. Yet the problem of evil as an intellectual puzzle is only one side of the question; more importantly on the other side is the ethical issue of how evil should be responded to.[3] This is also the more crucial issue if our task concerns the possibility of developing a Christian environmental ethic "after" (having crossed over and returned from) the dialogue with Buddhism given the Buddha's focus on the practicalities of liberation. On this front, then, the question concerns the possibility of such an ethical response given the implications of *pratityasamutpada* on the one side and the interpenetration of all things on the other.

As it is articulated within the Augustinian tradition, the problem simply put is this: in a fallen and sinful world, how can free creatures accomplish the required good in order to be saved? Translated into our present concerns, the question is: in a fallen and sinful world which includes both nuclear waste and endangered plant species, how can free creatures bring about a better world without these evils? The Augustinian response, of course, is that the problem is the result of free creatures left to their own fallen and sinful devises. In this state of affairs, such creatures are free only to perpetuate their fallen and sinful practices, and are throughout incapable in themselves of remedying their plight. As such, salvation has to come from outside the human condition. And it has, of course, been given to us purely gratuitously by God in Jesus Christ.

---

2. Some of these issues related to the problem of evil are discussed in Boyd, *Satan and Mara*; and Gregory, "The Problem of Theodicy in the Awakening of Faith." See also part III of my *Pneumatology and the Christian-Buddhist Dialogue*.

3. This is the argument of Tilley, *The Evils of Theodicy*. Another praxis- and ethically oriented response is provided by Pinnock, *Beyond Theodicy*.

Observe, however, the intriguing parallels precisely here with the soteriological claims of Buddhism. First, there is the emphasis on nirvana not as something to be gained or earned through effort but to be awakened to and realized here and now; more specifically, this is seen in the affirmation of enlightenment as a sudden awakening (in the Soto Zen traditions) rather than being the result of a long and gradual process of self-effort.[4] Further, there is the claim (in Huayen) that salvation derives from the vow of the bodhisattva to save all sentient beings. Finally, there is the insistence (in the Amida and Pure Land traditions) that entry into nirvana is purely a gift given (or accessed) in response to uttering the Buddha's name since, in the current age, sentient beings are thoroughly incapable of saving themselves. This would be to recall Tanabe's insistent emphasis on the vow of Amida Buddha as opposed to Nishida's deliberations about self-power (§7.3)

Now while the full force of these soteriological visions, both Christian and Buddhist, should not be blunted to avoid reducing the marvelous good news they proclaim, it is nevertheless clear that they implicitly sanction a kind of quietism that would undermine the necessity of ethical reflection at the theoretical level and of moral activity at the practical level. So how do we negotiate a middle way between understanding salvation or enlightenment as nothing but a gift even while affirming the centrality of response and activity? From the Christian point of view, how do we work out our salvation with fear and trembling even while affirming that it is God who is at work in us enabling our willing and working for his good pleasure (cf. Phil 2:12–13)? From a Buddhist perspective, what is the role of "self" power as opposed to the gratuitous and necessary gift of "other" power represented in taking refuge in the Dharma of the Buddha?

It should come as no surprise that the *via media* attempted here is also pneumatologically formulated.[5] Going back to the creation as emergent from the Spirit's hovering over the waters, three points should be recalled. First, creation itself was gifted with the capacity to participate in the creative work of God: the earth brought forth, co-created, as enabled by the empowering of the Spirit. Second, there was a genuine emergence of complexity, a movement from chaos to order, in varying "steps" and differentiated levels: the six days culminating with the final en-spiriting of specific forms of dust

---

4. See Park, *Buddhist Faith and Sudden Enlightenment*.

5. While the doctrine of the Holy Spirit has long been connected with the doctrine of sanctification, explicit articulation of a pneumatological ethics has been lacking. The starting point for such a task must be, Barth, *The Holy Spirit and the Christian Life*, which has since been expanded by Chung, *Spirituality and Social Ethics in John Calvin*. The following represents my minuscule contribution, focused on an environmental ethics.

resulting in living creatures. Finally, there is a genuine and systemic interrelationality—between male and female; between human and other sentient beings; between sentient beings and the natural world; between the natural and spiritual domains, etc.—brought about by the Spirit. Creation is herein realized as a web of living interconnectedness, but yet comprised of particularities, separatedness, and differentiatedness: each is in its own place amidst the whole, with its own functions and contributions to the whole, and having its own density and value among the whole.

So, from the Genesis account, I suggest that a pneumatological understanding of the creation is poised to negotiate the tensions between the created order as systematically interrelated and interconnected on the one hand, and the created order as en-spirited, emergent, and dynamic on the other. This allows emphasis on and valuation of the individuality and particularity of systemic levels and parts within the whole, while it permits and even encourages the ongoing transformation of the status quo in anticipation of the eschatological reign of God. Both are gifts from God. The former provides the relational matrices within which we live, move, and have our being, while the latter empowers the dynamism of creaturely activities and participation in actualizing the divine mandate to be, to bring forth, to reproduce. Understood pneumatically, freedom can be given a sufficiently robust account so as to illuminate how horrific evils such as nuclear waste and endangered plant species have actualized (not to mention the Holocaust) even while hope for the elimination of such evils can also be anticipated.

The creational breath of life enables and the pentecostal wind and fire of the Spirit empowers creaturely compliance with the common good, symbolized (for Christians) in the metanarrative as the coming reign of God and (for Buddhists) in the Mahayana vision as the Pure Land of compassionate bliss. While such hopes are ultimately eschatological confessions, they can begin to be actualized in the here and now as creatures align their directives with the divine will (for Christians) and the teachings of the Buddha (for those committed to Buddhist practice). For Christians, there is newness and novelty to the eschatological work of Spirit, and such comes about at least in part through their responses to the Spirit's enabling and prompting.

The connections between pneumatology and eschatology are most clearly pronounced in the Day of Pentecost narrative in Acts 2. In his account of the events on that day, the author of Acts recorded St. Peter's appeal to the Hebrew prophet Joel as prophesying that the outpouring of the Spirit upon all flesh would occur "In the last days" (Acts 2:17). My argument, however, is that such a thoroughly pneumatological approach to eschatology is more this-worldly than it is other-worldly: the outpouring of the Spirit announces the coming of the reign of God with ethical implications for human action, behavior, and responsibility in the here and now.[6]

So might a Christian pneumato-ecological theology of nature in global context "after" Buddhism see the convergence of the following themes and their attendant ethical implications? First, could the Spirit as the supremely mediational and relational symbol parallel the self-emptying nature of all things understood in terms of interdependence and interrelationality? If so, would this signify a possible convergence of theological and philosophical rationales for privileging a metaphysics of interconnectedness rather than one of substance? Second, might the Spirit as enabling the intersubjectivity of human persons and the interrelationality of humans and the environment parallel the self-emptying and interpenetrating character of all things? If so, would this signify a potential convergence of personalist and impersonalist rationales motivating environmental responsibility and ecological activity?[7] Third, if the Spirit is not only the source of life but also of gifts and charisms appropriate to creaturely functions in inviting their participation in the creative process, would this parallel *shunyata* as the locus or field of action and activity which invites—even nurtures—creaturely participation in the creative process? And if so, is this significant of a plausible convergence of the *ruah Elohim* with the Buddha's Dharma insofar as each is concerned with spirituality, community, ethics, values, and the quality of human life and flourishing?[8] Fourth, a pneumatological perspective would emphasize that the Spirit groans with human beings and with creation itself for its redemption and renewal (Rom 8:18–27) even as Buddhists earnestly await the illuminating power of the bodhisattva's vow, the Buddha's Dharma, and the coming of Matreiya Buddha to save all sentient beings.[9]

But perhaps most importantly, a pneumatological approach to a Christian environmental ethic after Buddhism can capitalize on the Buddhist resistance to any reductionistic or materialistic view of nature as well. This is because a pneumatological theology of nature, while not involving

---

6. I argue this pneumatological-eschatological-ethical connection in my *In the Days of Caesar*, esp. chap. 8; idem, *Spirit of Love*, esp. part II; and idem, *Who is the Holy Spirit?*.

7. Here, might I go even further and recognize with Michael Lodahl that the Spirit has a different sort of *persona* than that of Father or Son? After all, the Spirit is their common "breath" in communication and communion. Yet as Richard of St. Victor shows, the Spirit is "person" and personal precisely in and through the interpersonal bond of love between the Father and Son. See Lodahl, "*Una Natura Divina, Tres Nescio Quid*"; and on Richard, see my discussion in *Spirit-Word-Community*, 66–67.

8. This last question is motivated by Kosuke Koyama's discussion of "The Buddhist *Dharma* and the Christian *Ruah*"; see Koyama, "Observation and Revelation," 245–52.

9. See Wayman, "Eschatology in Buddhism."

a dualistic construal of spirit versus nature (as the preceding arguments should have made clear), nevertheless views nature as en-spirited with the divine breath of life. Nature does not consist ultimately only of inert matter, and Buddhist emphases on the fundamental nature of mind or consciousness also suggest a potential rapprochement regarding an enchanted world. This is not to suggest that there are "spirit beings" behind every tree, but that human beings have a responsibility to care for a world of which they are part, rather than being entirely distinct.

Granted the foregoing connections, the gift of the Spirit is supremely relevant for the contemporary environmental crisis. According to the words of the prophet Isaiah (32:15–17):

> . . . until a spirit from on high is poured out on us,
>   and the wilderness becomes a fruitful field,
>   and the fruitful field is deemed a forest.
> Then justice will dwell in the wilderness,
>   and righteousness abide in the fruitful field.
> The effect of righteousness will be peace,
>   and the result of righteousness, quietness and trust forever.

Here, the interdependence of the environment, living creatures, human flourishing, and the Spirit's presence and activity is clear. A pneumatological approach would sustain an ethic of embodiment, participation, and relationality vis-à-vis the environment.[10] Therefore, the call should thus be for a deeper and more conscious realization of the Spirit's presence and activity in our midst. In this case, might we be able to agree with Ruben Habito who writes:

> Zen practice brings all this from an abstract and conceptual theological plane down to a very concrete and experiential level in one's awareness, as one deepens in familiarity and intimacy with the Breath in day-to-day life. As I live my life in full attunement with the Breath and let it become the guiding power in my life, I experience the gift of being healed of my own woundedness and am empowered in my own little way to become an instrument of this breath in its work of healing a wounded Earth.[11]

A pneumatological ethics of the environment, then, would emphasize a threefold task in our contemporary multireligious context. First, humanity has the responsibility of restoring and renewing the environmental

---

10. E.g., Betcher, "Grounding the Spirit."
11. Habito, *Healing Breath*, 57; cf. Habito, *Total Liberation*, 104–06.

resources that are being used for human purposes; life in the Spirit involves participation in such renewing activity. Second, human beings ought to be mindful of the waste that is generated by modern ways of life and formulate appropriate responses to handling and disposing of such waste; life in the Spirit includes articulating and embodying a doctrine of sanctification which has implications for environmental care. Finally, humankind is obligated to develop a sustainable plan of environmental and ecological care that looks out for the wellbeing of our children and our children's children into the far off future; life in the Spirit is eschatological, which intertwines those who are coming with our lives in the present. These are interrelated and fundamental ethical tasks which details can be fleshed out in myriads of directions. A pneumatological theology of nature and environmental ethic will engage all voices—scientific, interdisciplinary, and interreligious—that can shed practical light on these tasks.

Notice then here that what is being proposed is not an un-thoughtful syncretism of Buddhist and Christian ideas, but a resolutely Christian ecological theology and environmental ethic, albeit one that is now more deeply Christian in part because it has also been informed by a dialogue with Buddhist traditions. It is more deeply Christian, I suggest, because it is now able to return to, retrieve, and reappropriate the scriptural resources of Christian theology albeit within a global, intercultural, interdisciplinary, and interreligious discursive context. Christians should not be hesitant about testing their beliefs in a pluralistic world and this testing happens in authentic dialogue with those in other faiths. If true for more than just Christians, such claims will survive dialogical testing, even if they might be reformulated in surprising ways. It is precisely because I believe in the truth of Christian theological claims that I have endeavored to comprehend these claims in a pluralistic world in dialogue with Buddhist traditions.[12]

Provisionally, then, I suggest that a pneumatological approach to the Christian-Buddhist-science trialogue opens up fruitful lines of mutual inquiry. It provides various perspectives on important contemporary issues ranging from the cosmological sciences through the cognitive sciences to the environmental sciences. It also has the potential to empower ethically compassionate feelings, thoughts, and actions on behalf of a suffering world. These are gains that we can now claim having accomplished, in the preceding, at least some of the hard work of conducting such a trialogue. Yet the last word has hardly been said. But enough has been said, I hope, to further

---

12. This is the constructive dimension to theology that has to be vulnerable to the widest possible public that might have an interest in its claims; for Christian theology, this would be the global context as a whole. See Yong, *Spirit-Word-Community*, part II.

the conversation and to demonstrate the potentiality of the pneumatological approach to the Christian-Buddhist-science trialogue.

2.7

A Trinitarian Theology of Creation[1]

A TRINITARIAN THEOLOGY OF creation therefore makes three interrelated affirmations. First, the world is neither self-originating nor self-sustaining. Rather, its ultimate origins, even its fallen character, are anticipated by the God of Jesus Christ, even from the foundations of the world. That is the theological significance of the creation narratives, not what can be rendered concordant with scientific perspectives. Second, the Christian doctrines of creation and providence are also intertwined. Christian theodicy is most successful explicating not the whence of evil but the whither of evil,[2] especially its eschatological redemption in Christ by the Spirit.[3] In fact, nature's constancy itself, within which human life evolves and flourishes, cannot be understood except as central to the Christian doctrine of providence. And the same constancy also undergirds the scientific enterprise. From a pneumatological perspective, the many scientific disciplines can all illuminate various (important) facets of human life and the (even tragic) processes of the world, even as the evolutionary sciences themselves provide a range of perspectives on the multifaceted nature of human tragedy. But it is theology that provides understanding of significance and meaning—both proximate and ultimate—amid the human condition. Finally, the goal of creation is redemption and community with the fellowship of

---

1. Yong, with Anderson, *Renewing Christian Theology*, 288–91.
2. Fretheim, *Creation Untamed*.
3. Wright, *Providence Made Flesh*.

the triune God.[4] The answer to the questions of suffering, evil, and death depends ultimately on human inquirers finding their lives mapped on to the divine story of the Father sending the Son to be reconciled with the world through the Spirit. Hence it is human response and action inspired by the manifest Spirit-empowered Son of God that is most central for generating and sustaining hope in the face of pain, suffering, and tragedy.[5] These are the basic elements of the whence, why, and whither of a trinitarian theology of creation.

We must now turn, even if briefly, to the performative aspects of a renewal theology of creation. Prior to this we discussed how the creation of the world can be comprehended as a dramatic exposé of sin and righteousness. The former is symbolized most vividly but paradoxically in the singularity of sin and selfishness of Adam anticipated in the natural history of the world before the arrival of *Homo sapiens* but actualized out of the sinfulness of all humans since. The latter is what is made possible in the light of God's creative, providential, and redemptive works in Christ and the Spirit. So whatever the historical Adam turns out to be, "the Adam in whom all men die lives on, the creation and the creator of history, a moral being whose every intellectual triumph is at once a temptation to evil and a power for good."[6] The meaning of the doctrines of creation and theological anthropology has little to do with understanding *how* God created the world or human beings—that is a question that science is best equipped to tell in the long run. Instead, these doctrines are invitations to free creatures like we to exercise choices that will ultimately be revealed, and judged, as either God-glorifying or self-obsessed. Human freedom is not absolute, constrained as it is by our finitude, creatureliness, sinfulness, and original victimhood, as previously asserted. We are all caught in Judas' predicament, himself a negative anti-type of Adam, somehow wishing to accomplish God's will but yet finding ourselves hopelessly, tragically, and destructively entangled in the cosmic forces of original sin and circumstances that strangle our lives. At the same time, we are now also open to the intervention of the other Adamic anti-type, that of Christ, whose yes to our befuddled and transgressive nos opens up the destructive singularities of our self-absorbed lives to the redemptive possibilities of the Spirit of God. As evolutionary predation and death produce ever-increasingly complex forms of life, so also do the saving and sanctifying works of the Spirit renew and recreate sinners in the image of Christ, as a new people of God.

4. Buxton, *The Trinity, Creation, and Pastoral Ministry*.
5. Tilley, *The Evils of Theodicy*; Swinton, *Raging with Compassion*.
6. Greene, *The Death of Adam*, 339.

Three avenues for living out the preceding trinitarian theology of creation thus recommend themselves. First, both testaments enjoin: "you shall love your neighbour as yourself" (Lev 19:18; cf. Matt 19:19; Mark 12:31; Luke 10:27; Rom 13:9; Gal 5:14; Jas 2:8). Ironically, it is precisely the evolutionary instincts of self-preservation that open up the self to the neighbor. Self-love includes, besides the potential of self-regard, self-concern, and selfishness, also cooperativeness, altruism, and benevolence.[7] What is exemplary of the latter is particularly the cruciform life of Christ, which itself was fully subjected to the world with all its contingencies and evils, but precisely in order to redeem nature's processes of death and violence. The stakes are all the higher in an evolutionary world that includes earthquakes, tsunamis, and hurricanes, among other natural but yet destructive phenomena. On this stage, human responses and choices are all the more ethically charged, capable of unveiling the depths of human self-centeredness but also making possible the revelation of a crucified but also resurrecting power. Hence there is something to those soul-making theodicies[8] that urge the capacity of God to bring something good out of what is otherwise wanton and gratuitous. When bad things happen, then the moral law written into human hearts judges each response (Rom 2:12–16). Creation and history are thereby the combined stage on which the ethical trajectories of human lives are sorted out. History itself will judge the consequences of our actions, whether they love only the self or also the other as well, and eternity will separate out the other-oriented sheep and the self-consumed goats in the light of God's loving and purifying judgment (Matt 25:31–46; 1 Cor 3:12–15). Simultaneously, we are not alone: the crucified and risen one who is in solidarity with the human condition has sent his Spirit to enable emergence of such self-sacrificial and self-giving lives for others out of an evolutionary cosmos.

Besides responding to our neighbors, with whose lives ours are irrevocably intertwined, there is a level of ethical response also to our environment, to the dust of the ground, which ultimately derives from the cosmic dust itself, with and through which we are symbiotically constituted. Human groaning that is inspired by the Holy Spirit echoes that of the creation itself across the inanimate-animate spectrum (see Gen 4:11).[9] The Scripture that says "the elements will be dissolved with fire, and the earth and everything that is done on it will be disclosed" (2 Pet 3:10b) refers not to the ultimate destruction of this world, as some dispensationalist accounts

---

7. Yong, *Spirit of Love*, chap. 2.
8. Corey, *Evolution and the Problem of Natural Evil*.
9. Cf. Park, *Triune Atonement*, 94–108.

suggest, but to the disclosure of God's judgmental fire. Hence the world and our human environment are not to be neglected as if they were to be finally discarded, but are rather to be cared for, appropriate to the divine stewardship with which humans have been entrusted and mandated (Gen 1:26).[10] What is redemptive is human participation in the creational work of God in Christ by the power of the Spirit.[11] Herein, then, is social justice inextricably linked to environmental and ecological justice, not because we have an overly realized eschatological imagination, but precisely because the cruciform cosmology and pneumatology of the cross developed in this chapter open up to what might also be called an eschatology of the cross[12] that works patiently in the present in anticipation of the cosmic reign to come.

Most importantly, the goal of human lives, along with the entire creation, is to become the temple of the living God.[13] As such, the eschatological point is for God to be enthroned not only in human hearts and minds or even "on the praises of Israel" (Ps 22:3) but "above" the creation itself. Hence any theology of creation, besides inspiring human ethics and motivating care for the earth, ought to inculcate the reverence that precedes authentic worship,[14] precisely what the first chapters of Romans tells us that human sin has incapacitated. The psalmist observed, "The heavens declare his righteousness, for God himself is judge" (Ps 50:6). The world is the stage upon which its various creatures are designed to reveal, adore, and worship God, each in its own way. So also with human creatures; as multidimensional and multifaceted as we are, our end is to give glory to God in a multitude of ways.[15]

---

10. Cf. Swoboda, *Tongues and Trees*.

11. Fulljames, *God and Creation in Intercultural Perspective*, chap. 7; Hefner, *The Human Factor*, esp. chap. 15.

12. Chester, *Mission and the Coming of God*, chap. 15.

13. Walton, *The Lost World of Genesis One*.

14. Dawn, *In the Beginning God*.

15. Harrison, *God's Many-Splendored Image*.

— PART THREE —

Theology and Disability

3.1

Theology and Down Syndrome[1]

THEOLOGICAL METHOD AND THE PNEUMATOLOGICAL IMAGINATION

BUT CAN THEOLOGIANS REALLY be advocates of the kind Blumenthal suggests, especially with regard to people with intellectual and physical disabilities? While in a real sense it will take me the rest of this book even to begin to respond adequately, let me comment in a preliminary sense by addressing the concerns behind this question related to theological methodology. In brief, I suggest that an approach to theological reflection informed and shaped by the Christian experience of the Holy Spirit provides what I call a "pneumatological imagination" that not only opens up space for the possibility of a dialogue with experiences of disability but also, arguably, requires such a conversation for Christian theology to maintain its credibility and plausibility in the twenty-first century.

The Pneumatological Imagination

Elsewhere, I have discussed the pneumatological imagination at length.[2] In brief, the pneumatological imagination can be said to be an epistemic posture shaped in part by the biblical narratives of the Holy Spirit and in

---

1. Yong, *Theology and Down Syndrome*, 10–14.
2. Yong, *Spirit-Word-Community*, pt. 2.

part by the Christian experience of the Spirit. From the biblical text, I draw especially from the account of Pentecost in the second chapter of Acts:

> All of them were filled with the Holy Spirit and began to speak in other languages, as the Spirit gave them ability. Now there were devout Jews from every nation under heaven living in Jerusalem. And at this sound the crowd gathered and was bewildered, because each one heard them speaking in the native language of each. Amazed and astonished, they asked, "Are not all these who are speaking Galileans? And how is it that we hear, each of us, in our own native language? Parthians, Medes, Elamites, and residents of Mesopotamia, Judea and Cappadocia, Pontus and Asia, Phrygia and Pamphylia, Egypt and the parts of Libya belonging to Cyrene, and visitors from Rome, both Jews and proselytes, Cretans and Arab—in our own languages we hear them speaking about God's deeds of power" (Acts 2:4–11).

From this narrative, I have argued that the many tongues of Pentecost signify both the universality of the gospel message and its capacity to be witnessed to by those who derive from the many nations, cultures, ethnicities, and languages of the world.[3] The significance of this pneumatological imagination, I suggest, is at least threefold. First, it provides an explicitly theological framework for thinking about the perennial metaphysical and philosophical question concerning the one and its relationship to the many. Second, and building on the first more explicitly for the purposes of this volume, it provides a theological rationale for preserving the integrity of difference and otherness, but not at the expense of engagement and understanding. Finally, it alerts and invites us to listen to the plurality of discourses and languages in the hope that even through "strange tongues," the voice of the Holy Spirit may still speak and communicate.

How this pneumatological imagination "works" might be more clearly seen in the concrete case of theology's engagement with the sciences, as will unfold in the pages to follow. Now some might say that the language of spirit is obsolete in the modern world dominated by science. Even if there are voices in late modernity that suggest the "end of science,"[4] the presence of modernity remains palpable in our midst, especially in our experience of being dependent on and often dominated by scientific technology. In this environment, science is chastened, but nevertheless ubiquitous. Theology in the late modern world therefore cannot avoid science but needs a specifically theological rationale for engaging with science. I suggest that

---

3. Yong, *The Spirit Poured Out on All Flesh*, chap. 4.
4. E.g., Horgan, *The End of Science*.

the pneumatological imagination provides such a rationale for the dialogue with science since, in a late modern context, the many languages of the Pentecost narrative can be understood to include the diversity of academic discourses and scientific disciplines.[5] The credibility of any contemporary theology of disability rests in large part on its capacity to engage both the broad spectrum of the humanities—and the various social, cultural, economic, political, and philosophical discourses of disability—and the wide range of medical, biogenetic, and evolutionary sciences, all of which continue to shape our understandings of disability. A pneumatological imagination alerts us to seek out, listen to, and discern the presence and activity of the Holy Spirit even in the "tongues" of the sciences, of modern technology, and of humanistic scholarship.

But beyond the sciences, as we have already discussed, the voices of people with intellectual and physical disabilities, and of all those who care for them, also need to be heard. This is the narrative dimension of Down Syndrome and disability so important for our understanding. I suggest that the tongues of Pentecost can be understood to include not only the diversity of academic discourses and scientific disciplines but also the emergent cultural traditions formed by new configurations of human interactions in our late modern world. This includes the postcolonial voices of women and persons of color from outside the Euro-American West, as well as those of people with disabilities (e.g., Deaf culture or disability culture). Again, the pneumatological imagination provides a theological rationale for engaging the (auto)biographies of people with Down Syndrome and other disabilities and invites us to pay attention to these experiences so as to discern how the Holy Spirit is present and active beyond our assumptions. In this case, the pneumatological imagination validates the conviction growing in theological circles that theology is rooted fundamentally in biography and narrative as much as it is in Scripture and tradition.[6]

Pneumatological Theology and Emancipation

So far, however, we have been concerned only with how the pneumatological imagination functions as an epistemology in terms of its securing input for theological reflection from the sciences and from personal narratives. Yet, the fact that the pneumatological imagination is grounded in the Pentecost narrative means that its epistemology is but part of a "larger" soteriological vision. There are both performative and redemptive aspects of this

5. Yong, "Academic Glossolalia?"
6. McClendon, *Biography as Theology*.

pneumatological soteriology that need to be mentioned in connection with issues of theological method under discussion.

First, because the Scriptures attest to the Holy Spirit as the Spirit of Jesus the Christ, the pneumatological imagination also inspires and shapes the body of Christ, the church. In this sense, the pneumatological imagination is never only of epistemic import but is always connected to the life of the church. An ecclesial theology of disability cannot be concerned with mere description but is always motivated by how the church's understanding, beliefs, and confessions can and must shape her practices. To be sure, the discussion in the following pages will include both metaphysical and theological speculation, but these are for the purposes of (re)shaping the Christian imagination and for (re)ordering ecclesial practices. At this level, we might say that the pneumatological imagination serves to empower the church's performative engagement with the world."[7] In this case, the theology of disability to be developed in this book is also a *performative theology* that informs, shapes, and guides the practices of the church."[8]

But to what ends are the church's performative engagement with the world directed? With regard to the topic of this book, we might say that the pneumatological imagination empowers Christian witness to establish a more peaceful and just society for all people, especially those with disabilities. Because the Holy Spirit empowers human witness, I claim that the pneumatological imagination not only enables human knowing but also directs liberative human activity. Again, our knowing by the Spirit is never only for knowing's sake but always correlates with the larger purposes of God's redemptive work in the world. The pneumatological imagination therefore serves not only the task of theological description, but also that of performative prescription. In other words, the empowering of the Spirit enables human witness both in word (testifying to the truth) and in deed (living the truth), so that we might work to establish righteousness, peace, and justice, and in that way participate in the redemptive work of God in the world. At this level, we might say that the pneumatological imagination serves to inform and transform the church so that her members can bear emancipatory witness to the gospel in our late modern world.

---

7. Another theologian who has made the connection between the Holy Spirit, Christian doctrine, and the practices of the church is Hütter, *Suffering Divine Things*, esp. pt. 3. We meet at this juncture, although my own approach is from a pentecostal perspective in contrast to Hütter's formerly Lutheran, now Roman Catholic background.

8. Others who are making the argument that theological doctrines are emergent from and normative measures of church practices include Lindbeck, *The Nature of Doctrine*; Cunningham, *These Three Are One*; Buckley and Yeago, eds., *Knowing the Triune God*; and Volf and Bass, eds., *Practicing Theology*.

3.2

Honoring the "Weaker" Member
A Disability Ecclesiology and Charismology[1]

IN ORDER TO SEE the full scope of Paul as a theologian of disability, we turn from the Second to the First Letter to the Corinthians.[2] Here we focus on a crucial passage that illuminates the wider ramifications of Paul's theology of weakness, particularly as that regards his ecclesiology and his understanding of ministry. In the previous chapter we employed a pneumatological imagination informed by the Day of Pentecost narrative to re-read Luke and Acts from a disability perspective. Here I invite us to develop a charismatic imagination derived from St. Paul's discussion of the Spirit-graced members of the body of Christ in order to understand what I will suggest are disability-inclusive and disability-friendly ecclesiological recommendations to the church at Corinth. I will quote a middle section of 1 Corinthians 12 as a springboard for our considerations:

> The eye cannot say to the hand, "I have no need of you," nor again the head to the feet, "I have no need of you." On the contrary, the members of the body that seem to be weaker [*asthenestera*] are indispensable, and those members of the body that we think less honorable we clothe with greater honor, and our less respectable members are treated with greater respect; whereas our more

---

1. Yong, *The Bible, Disability, and the Church*, 90–96.

2. In the remainder of this chapter, all parenthetical references to Scripture in the main text will be to 1 Corinthians unless otherwise noted.

respectable members do not need this. But God has so arranged the body, giving the greater honor to the inferior member, that there may be no dissension within the body, but the members may have the same care for one another. If one member suffers, all suffer together with it; if one member is honored, all rejoice together with it (12:21–26).

In what follows I will argue that a disability hermeneutic can help us re-read St. Paul toward a more disability-inclusive theology of the church (ecclesiology). There are three facets of this argument, particularly when this text is understood as situated within the broader contexts both of Paul's discussion of the spiritual or charismatic gifts operative within the church, and of this first Corinthian letter.

First, we have already seen that the reference to weakness in this passage, one of various cognates of *astheneia*, invites a disability perspective. To be sure, there is no historical-grammatical reason to limit weakness to those with bodily impairments or disabilities; but there is also no a priori reason to exclude such references. Rather, there are other textual and contextual grounds for such a more inclusive reading. More specifically, the self-understanding of the Corinthian believers highlighted from the second epistle—their pride, self-confidence, assertiveness, eloquence, and overall status as measured according to the world's standards (see the previous section)—can also be assumed as the social reality behind this first letter.[3] In fact, it is clear throughout this long correspondence that Paul's overarching worry was about those attitudes of elitism and superiority among the Corinthians that excluded others who were considered less spiritual and thus threatened to fragment the unity of the body (see 1 Corinthians 8 on food offered to idols and 1 Corinthians 14 on prophecy and tongues). Thus Paul repeatedly confronts and counters the sectarian divisiveness of those who thought themselves more knowledgeable, more eloquent, and wiser than others whom they treated as less articulate and more foolish (see 1 Cor 1:10–3:23). He also has to quell conflicts within the Corinthian congregation based on apostolic lineage (1 Cor 1:12 and 3:4) and social status (see 1 Corinthians 6 on congregational lawsuits, 1 Corinthians 11 on the "haves" and "have-nots" vis-a-vis the Lord's Supper, and the various references to slaves throughout the letter). We will elaborate on a few of these points shortly; here, this suffices to explain why a wider rather than a narrower semantic range for weakness is preferable: the former includes the socially devalued realities that contrast more starkly with the privileged Corinthian

---

3. The social divisions in the Corinthian context are highlighted by Theissen, "The Strong and the Weak in Corinth."

worldview. Read from this perspective, Paul's insistence that "the members of the body that seem to be weaker are indispensable" (12:22) is a stinging rebuke to the non-disabled Corinthian elite, a reprimand that is inclusive of marginalized people with infirmities and disabilities even if not limited to them. I insist on the importance of this point regardless of whether or not Paul himself was impaired or disabled.

Second, note the specifically ecclesiological applications of this Pauline claim regarding the weaker members as being essential to the body of Christ. In this context, the point is that the most disregarded, despised, and denigrated individuals associated with the Corinthian congregation are as important if not more important than the power brokers. By extension, a disability hermeneutic actually insists that the weaker, "less honorable," and "less respectable" (12:23) parishioners fit people with disabilities according to conventional stereotypes. And it is stereotypes that Paul is addressing, which is why he uses language like "that *seem to be* weaker" or "that *we think* less honorable" (12:22–23, emphasis added). In fact, the word for "less respectable" (*aschemona*) could very well mean "misshapen" or "ugly." While some scholars dismiss the idea that Paul might have been "referring to members of the congregation who were perhaps disabled or deformed or who otherwise lacked the physical beauty associated with nobility,"[4] my claim is that inclusion of people with disabilities in this context not only does no violence to Paul's rhetoric but fits well with the overall intent of what Paul is attempting to do in this passage—which is to break down the elitist, triumphalistic, and exclusionary attitudes that certain Corinthians had developed vis-a-vis others in the congregation.

But there is more to be said from a disability perspective regarding Paul's assertion that the weaker or less respectable parts of the body are necessary and indispensable. While scholars have debated what the weaker and the necessary body parts are, an important clue lies in the wider Greco-Roman context. Thus for Plutarch, the "necessary parts of the body ... are double, like the hands and feet, eyes and ears."[5] That each of these body parts appears in Paul's discussion (12:15–17, 21) suggests that these would have been associated with strength by the original readers of the epistle. However, a disability perspective would highlight that in the ancient Mediterranean context, these body parts are the nexuses through which human bodies interface and interact with the world. They are considered necessary because eyes see, ears hear, hands feel, and feet cross the external world.

---

4. Timothy Carter's response to this suggestion is that "there is nothing in the context of 1 Corinthians to suggest this meaning for the metaphor"; see Carter, "Looking at the Metaphor of Christ's Body in 1 Corinthians 12," 112.

5. See Collins, *First Corinthians*, 460.

They are strong (not weak) because they are the means by which people discern the world, do things, get around, even protect themselves. Thus the weaker body parts are those members that are "passive" by contrast—perhaps internal organs of the body in need of protection—not only incapable of acting out bodily desires and needs but also unable to fend for themselves and hence reliant on those members of the body who were "stronger." But if the necessary parts of the body—the hands, feet, and so on—are impaired, then they are no longer strong but weak.

By extension, people with disabilities are implicit in this metaphorical discourse. Their physical or sensory impairments define their weakness, both in the sense that they are less able than others without disabilities, and in the sense that they are reliant in some respects on the assistance of others. At the same time, Paul's insistence that even the weakest members of the body of Christ shouldn't be despised challenges the stereotypical thinking of non-disabled people. Accordingly, an ecclesiology of weakness would resist conventional ableist marginalization of people with disabilities as weaker, less respectable, or less-than-necessary members of the church with little to contribute.

This Pauline discussion leads, third, to an understanding of the weaker members of the body as equal recipients of, and conduits for, the Spirit's charisms. Paul's point leading up to his specifically ecclesiological reflections was focused on the charismatic gifts:

> Now there are varieties of gifts, but the same Spirit; and there are varieties of services, but the same Lord; and there are varieties of activities, but it is the same God who activates all of them in everyone. To each is given the manifestation of the Spirit for the common good . . . All these are activated by one and the same Spirit, who allots to each one individually just as the Spirit chooses. For just as the body is one and has many members, and all the members of the body, though many, are one body, so it is with Christ. For in the one Spirit we were all baptized into one body—Jews or Greeks, slaves or free—and we were all made to drink of one Spirit (12:4–7, 11–13).

The interconnections between this earlier passage and the later passage focused on the one-body-with-many-members need to be made explicit: the weaker members of the body who are of central import cannot be excluded from being channels of the Spirit's manifestations. More to the point, God freely distributes the Spirit's charisms to *all* members of the body so that each one can contribute to the common good of the body. This is also what allows Paul to say, "If one member suffers, all suffer together with it; if one member is honored, all rejoice together with it" (12:26). In this reading, people with disabilities are central to, rather than marginal to, the charismatically gifted body of Christ.

We need to be clear at this point. We are not saying that the many gifts of the Spirit are given to the stronger members of the body so that they may minister to the weaker members, and thus that people with disabilities are needed only as recipients of the ministry of such gifts. To be sure, that's part of what happens. But I'm making a stronger claim: that the many gifts of the Spirit are manifest through all members of the body, regardless of their ability or disability. In fact, it is more in keeping with Paul's theology of weakness that the more powerful manifestations are mediated through those whose abilities are less noticeable or who are thought to be lesser candidates for God's work from a worldly or "normal" point of view. The members of the body neither earn nor merit the Spirit's gifts, nor do they somehow have greater capacities or abilities that attract and dispose such gifts. In fact, here Paul emphasizes the opposite: that it is God the Spirit who chooses the recipients of the charismata, and that there is a variety of recipients precisely because of the diversity of the body's members. In short, the Spirit distributes gifts liberally and graciously so that people with disabilities are just as capable—if not more capable—of contributing to the edification of the community of faith, and hence are necessary in that sense.

These considerations suggest that the Pauline metaphor of one body with many (both strong and weak) members should lead us to say more than just that the unity of the body is constituted by its diversity.[6] The latter only parrots Paul's saying, "the body does not consist of one member but of many" (12:14). But our disability reading instead proclaims that the one body of Christ is centrally constituted by people across the spectrum of dis/abilities. The one Spirit distributes many gifts to many different members, and it is through such a diversity of members and gifts that the body is built up and edified. The health of the body requires the working of its many parts: the stronger and the weaker, those with more honor or respect and those with less, with each member recognized and honored as appropriate.

Thus, Paul says not only that the apparently weaker bodily members are equally necessary for the health of the whole group, but also that it is such marginalized members who are (to be) given greater honor and granted greater respect (12:23). Thus no gift—and no individual believer—is to be suppressed, dismissed, or minimized, and there is no hierarchy of gifts. Rather, all gifts are similarly indispensable, and each person is equally

---

6. This theme of the diversity of the body's many members is emphasized by Fee, *God's Empowering Presence*, 159.

important for the health of the whole. Indeed, each with his or her own distinctive gift has been made part of the same body of Christ by the Spirit.[7]

From a disability perspective, then, people with disabilities are by definition embraced as central and essential to a fully healthy and functioning congregation in particular, and to the ecclesial body in general. Beyond such a descriptive statement, however, is the implicit prescription of St. Paul: that "those members of the body that we think less honorable we clothe with greater honor" (12:22). Thus it is the responsibility of the whole body to end the stigmatization and marginalization of people with disabilities.

This translates into the following outline of an inclusive ecclesiology. First, the church is constituted first and foremost of the weak, not the strong: people with disabilities are thus at the center rather than at the margins of what it means to be the people of God.[8] Second, each person with disability, no matter how serious, severe, or even profound, contributes something essential to and for the body, through the presence and activity of the Spirit; people with disabilities are therefore ministers empowered by the Spirit of God, each in his or her own specific way, rather than merely recipients of the ministries of non-disabled people. Finally, people with disabilities become the paradigm for embodying the power of God and manifesting the divine glory.

Having said all this, it is important to register the following caveat before proceeding: that those in the disability rights movement today resist defining their personhood in terms of weakness because that perpetuates discriminatory perspectives that have been handed down for generations. We must be vigilant against either sentimentalizing or valorizing weakness or disability, or putting people with disabilities on a pedestal or expecting them to teach the rest of the ecclesial body because of their disabilities. There is also a fine line between honoring the diversity of the body's members, with and without disability, and overemphasizing either abilities or disabilities. Yet, while recognizing the potential of Paul's theology of weakness to continue to burden people with disabilities with negative stereotypes, I hope enough has been said here to show that the marvel of St. Paul's discussion is precisely to subvert such usually unquestioned presuppositions. In other words, if we take Paul seriously, our understandings of strong and weak—and ability and disability—will themselves be transformed.[9]

---

7. Carson, *Showing the Spirit*, 47–48.

8. This is understood by L'Arche, an international organization that exists to serve people with severe and profound disabilities. See Hauerwas and Vanier, *Living Gently in a Violent World*.

9. The first part of this chapter is consistent with much of Monteith, *Epistles of Inclusion*, a book which came to my attention too late for me to interact with it. Next, however, I shift in a direction that is heretofore uncharted, to my knowledge.

3.3

The Spirit Meets the Ethiopian Eunuch
Redeeming Disability[1]

IF THE INCLUSION OF the despised Samaritans in the coming kingdom was a stretch for many Jews of the first century, so also was the inclusion of the Ethiopian eunuch, although for other reasons. This man, known to us as the Ethiopian eunuch, had three strikes against him: (1) he was from the outskirts of the empire, thought then to be situated at the southern edge of human civilization; (2) he was probably of darker skin, as were those from Cush, Nubia, and Ethiopia (south of Egypt), and thus viewed by some as racially suspect or marginal; and (3) he was a eunuch, therefore probably castrated, and as such considered effeminate and not a fully able-bodied male. In some ways, strikes one and two were not as damaging, especially given some of the prophecies regarding the inclusion of Cushites and Ethiopians eventually in the redemption and restoration of Israel (Ps 68:31; Isa 45:14; Zeph 3:9–10), and the inclusive outpouring of the Spirit on all flesh on the Day of Pentecost.

Being a eunuch may have been more problematic for first-century Jews, especially since the law excluded eunuchs and those with crushed testicles from participating in the liturgical cult and worship of ancient Israel (Deut 23:1). Of course, castrated males were not being singled out; rather, they were categorized among those with physical, sensorial, and functional disabilities: the blind, lame, mutilated, hunchbacked, dwarfed, and so on

---

1. Yong, *Who is the Holy Spirit?*, 95–99. See Acts 8:26–40; cf. Luke 14:1–24.

(Lev 21:17–23). The Torah then later also clearly connected these "disabilities" with divine punishment for sin and disobedience (Deut 28:15–68). The result was so that even though in one case Jesus denied the link between the man born blind and the sins of himself or his parents (John 9:2–3), his response in another case to the paralytic—"Do not sin any more, so that nothing worse happens to you" (John 5:14)—as well as his linking sickness, blindness, deafness, and dumbness with evil spirits and healing these through exorcisms fit first-century Jewish assumptions about disability.

Yet Luke's inclusive vision of the redemption of Israel and the kingdom of God is revealed even in this case of people long marginalized because of their various disabilities. Just as Jesus had accepted the socially despised and short-statured Zacchaeus, so also here Philip accepts the racially questionable and physically impaired eunuch. Yes, in many other cases, Jesus and the apostles healed the sick and "disabled" by the power of the Spirit. However, in these two cases, Jesus pronounced the arrival of salvation to Zacchaeus' household (Luke 19:9) and Philip baptized the eunuch (Acts 8:38) without any reversal of their physical conditions.

The acceptance of the eunuch began to fulfill the promise of Yahweh to include eunuchs in the final redemption of Israel (Isa 56:3–5). Perhaps not coincidentally, the eunuch was reading about this final restoration when Philip came alongside his chariot. As one without the prospect of having children, the eunuch perhaps wondered about the fate and legacy of this figure he was reading about who also died without any descendants (Acts 8:32–33). Ethiopian tradition traces the origins of the church in that region to this eunuch's testimony. With his conversion, then, Luke not only anticipates the taking of the gospel to the ends of the known world but also clearly affirms that the diversity of tongues, cultures, and races in the coming kingdom includes the differences represented by human bodies.

Jesus' own teachings foreshadowed the inclusion of people like the eunuch. In Luke 14, Jesus dines in the home of a Pharisee. This is one of the many meal scenes in Luke's Gospel, with meals being socially defining occasions regarding who was considered "in" or "out" of one's community. On the one hand, Jesus heals the man with dropsy, a disability involving excess bodily fluids and inflammation (edema) caused by insatiable thirst. On the other hand, Jesus' intention was to challenge the Pharisees' understanding of the purpose of the Sabbath (14:3–5) and then to contrast their social conventions and values with that of the coming kingdom. The protocol for first-century client-patron relations clearly defined the rules of who invites whom, where each sits, what is then expected in return from such invitations, and so on. Jesus' two parables, of the wedding feast and the eschatological banquet, were intended to teach humility rather than to promote social status, to overturn the rules of you-invite-me-and-I-invite-you reciprocity, and to warn his hearers that the kingdom would include those at the bottom rather than at the top of the social, political, and religious hierarchy.

The main points of Jesus' teachings are brought home powerfully by his including the poor, the crippled, the lame, and the blind around the great banquet table (14:13, 21). These were the outcasts who had no status and were incapable of reciprocating the "generosity" of the host. For that very reason, social conventions would have dictated that they politely decline the invitation to begin with, so that Jesus insists that they need to be compelled to attend the banquet and carried in if necessary (14:23). What is truly astounding about this parable is the presence of people with clearly recognized disabilities at the eschatological banquet of the kingdom. So while Jesus' healing of people with disabilities would have confirmed some prophetic pronouncements that the blind, lame, and deaf would be cured on the coming Day of the Lord, in this case Jesus' inclusion of such people just as they are in the great banquet picks up on other prophetic themes about the coming kingdom involving the flourishing of all people not because we are physically cured but precisely because the social stigma of our disabilities no longer divides us (cf. Jer 31:8-9; Mic 4:6-7; Zeph 3:19). In short, the restoration and redemption of Israel would include people like the eunuch and Zacchaeus, not "fixed" so that they can conform to our social standards of beauty and desirability, but precisely as a testimony to the power of God to save all of us "normal" folk from our own discriminatory attitudes, inhospitable actions, and exclusionary social and political forms of life.

Does not the Holy Spirit still wish to do today what was accomplished two thousand years ago with this Ethiopian eunuch? Here is the redemption and restoration of one excluded geographically, racially, and physically. There is a massive revival occurring today on the African continent, and in many respects, the growing numbers of African Christians today can count themselves among the posterity of this Ethiopian official! But in a very real sense, we are still awaiting the day when the hospitality of the Spirit will be fully manifest in the church so that people with disabilities—those with physical, sensory, and intellectual differences—will be able to count themselves as descendants of this impaired eunuch. There are some indications that this is happening, for example in L'Arche communities where core members (who are people with disabilities) and assistants minister to each other in mutually transformative ways. Our prayer should be that more of us will be inspired by the Spirit of God to intentionally form fully inclusive communities that will be redemptive with good news for all people, both with and without disabilities.

3.4

Zaccheus
Short and Unseen[1]

CONTEMPORARY UNDERSTANDINGS OF DISABILITY are not identical to those of the biblical authors. Nevertheless, some interpretations of the Bible, often based on the normate and ableist assumptions, experiences, and perspectives of non-disabled people, have shaped popular views of disability throughout history.[2] On the one hand, many think that disabilities are ordained by God for God's purposes. But on the other hand, this is often accompanied by the feeling that people with disabilities are or ought to be pitiable and charitable objects of the care of others, and with the judgment that their condition is a sign of divine punishment for sin, or of the presence and activity of an evil spirit. By and large, then, disability has been viewed negatively, as a blot on an originally good creation.

Yet these views of disability can have negative effects. Images of Jesus and the apostles healing the sick, raising the lame, opening the eyes of the blind, and so on, fueled the historic quest for cures for disabling conditions, but they may lead people with disabilities to internalize the normate view and thereby wonder what is wrong with them that prevents their reception

---

1. Yong, "Zacchaeus," 11–17.

2. "Normate" in the field of disability studies refers to the assumptions about disabilities held by those without disabilities; "ableism," parallel to *sexism* or *ageism*, thus represents the discriminatory perspectives and practices imposed, sometimes unconsciously so, by non-disabled people, structures, and policies, on those with disabilities. For further discussion, see my *The Bible, Disability, and the Church*, 10–12.

of God's healing power. The further assumption that disabilities will be erased in the end—rooted in a belief that the resurrection body will be free from earthly disabilities, which overlooks the fact that the New Testament describes the raised body of Jesus as including the marks of the crucifixion—provides added impetus both to prevent the onset of disability and to cure or alleviate it if possible in the present life. It is no wonder that people with disabilities are often stigmatized and feel unwanted in public spaces. They remain in back rooms of homes around most of the world as even their families are ashamed by their existence. In technologically advanced societies, there have been initiatives to prevent people with disabilities from reproducing (motivated by the supposition that their children will perpetuate the parents' disability); in the worst case scenarios, eugenic projects have both attempted to select against disability and committed genocide against people with disabilities.[3] Is it any wonder that many people with disabilities do not feel welcome in the Church? Church leaders may claim that there are few people with disabilities in their congregations because there aren't many in the wider community. But up to twenty percent of Americans have disabilities of some sort and most believe that Christians think negatively about them rather than desire to include them in the Church.

In this essay I would like to highlight how our societal fears regarding disability can be seen in the way we read the Bible. Normate assumptions, which lead to the notion that disability is a problem needing to be fixed or eliminated, generate a hermeneutical approach that minimizes what the Bible features about disability.

In a recent book Jeremy Schipper has shown how the normate perspective ignores or even goes so far as to eliminate disability in the biblical message through his treatment of Isa 52:13–53:12's reception history (the passage widely known as describing the "suffering servant").[4] Schipper shows not only that the biblical text and context clearly denote that the servant suffered and perhaps even died from a skin anomaly, but also that it was precisely because of this skin condition that the servant was socially ostracized, marginalized, and, in this most fundamental sense, experienced suffering. Yet the interpretation of this passage over the centuries has by and large failed to recognize this, suggesting instead that the servant was injured, in some cases perhaps to the point of death. More intriguingly, what

---

3. The latter was enacted in Nazi Germany, but the Anglo-American world has also been tainted by eugenic assumptions, policies, and practices, especially now that we have the technology to identify disabilities *in utero* and up to 90 percent of parents (by some estimates) are opting for abortion in these cases. See also Russell, *Beyond Ramps*, chapter 2.

4. Schipper, *Disability and Isaiah's Suffering Servant*.

has consistently emerged is a view of the servant as able-bodied, rather than afflicted or plagued. The disability imagery present in the Isaianic text has been lost either in translation or in interpretation. Instead, what has been invented is an able-bodied suffering servant. The irony here is that people with disabilities have long felt the pressure to pass as able-bodied persons, and in this case, the impaired servant has been recreated in the able-bodied image of normate interpreters.

Schipper's study invites reconsideration of other scriptural narratives to see if similar interpretive bias can be identified. Although not a biblical scholar myself, I have spent a significant amount of time on the study of Luke-Acts. A Lukan story that many Christian readers are familiar with is that of Zacchaeus (Luke 19:1–10), a rich chief tax collector who is described as being "short in stature" (19:3). The Sunday school version has been told with a song:

> Zacchaeus was a wee little man,
> and a wee little man was he.
> He climbed up in a sycamore tree
> for the Lord he wanted to see . . .

A canonical reading of the Zacchaeus story could begin by connecting his short-staturedness to the dwarfism that is identified among a list of disabilities disqualifying priests from offering the sacrificial food or approaching the altar of the Holy of Holies in ancient Israel (Lev 21:16–24). Yet interpreters rarely attend to Zacchaeus' shortness, to the point of thinking that "short in stature" refers to no more than his youthfulness. Even when acknowledged, its import is subordinated to the assertion that in the story Zacchaeus seems "exceedingly large in spirit"; in this way his littleness of stature is spiritualized, understood for instance with reference to his humility.[5] Some commentators—even major ones like John Calvin and John Wesley—simply say nothing about Zacchaeus' lack of height. Instead, a great deal of attention is put on debating whether what he says about giving half his possession to the poor or repaying fourfold those he has defrauded (Luke 19:8) amounts to a set of resolutions following his conversion to Jesus or are statements vindicating his practices to local Judeans who would have despised a person in his official governmental position.

Beyond this, the major messages highlighted by scholars, commentators, and preachers appear to be communicable quite independently of Zacchaeus' shortness. His generosity has been understood as enacting the

---

5. Peter Chrysologus, "Sermon 54, On Zacchaeus the Tax Collector," 207. See also Cyril of Alexandria, "Sermon 127," 587–90, for another spiritualized view of Zacchaeus's short-staturedness.

Year of Jubilee economic vision running throughout the Lukan corpus. Jesus' pronouncement of his salvation as a son of Abraham (Luke 19:9) has been viewed both as contributing to the major theme of Israel's renewal and as an indictment of the crowd's beliefs that certain people, such as stigmatized tax collectors, were excluded from this restoration. Most generally, the conclusion of the pericope has been that "the Son of Man came to seek out and to save the lost" (19:10). Yet, none of these readings are dependent on or even remotely connected to Zacchaeus being a person of little stature, and thus it is warranted to conclude that interpreters think Luke's physical description is a minor, even negligible, part of the story. In effect, then, Zacchaeus' shortness has been overlooked, if not rendered invisible, by normate readers.

But does this dismissal of Zacchaeus' shortness inhabit the spirit of what Luke is attempting to communicate or reflect instead an ableist bias that literally handicaps readers from engaging the full meaning of the text? I suggest that while it is quite normal for normate interpreters to make little of Zacchaeus' littleness, this dismissal fails to recognize an essential aspect of his humanity and impoverishes our understanding of what is going on in this story and in Luke's overall message. Mikeal Parsons's analysis of ancient physiognomic assumptions regarding outward bodily traits expressing inward characteristics suggests that physical descriptions are not throw-away lines in the biblical account.[6] Rather, similar to how contemporary readings have been inspired by the reference to Zacchaeus' littleness to observe the largeness of his heart, so also did Luke deploy the physiognomic conventions of his day only to subvert them in light of the gospel of Christ.

Of the four Lukan characters explored in depth by Parsons—the bent over woman (Luke 13:10–17), Zacchaeus (Luke 19:1–10), the man lame from birth at the Beautiful Gate (Acts 3–4), and the Ethiopian eunuch (Acts 8:26–40)—our focus will be on the smallest one. Though grammatically the *hēlikiamicros* (being short of stature) in Luke 19:3 does not necessarily refer to dwarfism, and the Greeks had other more technical terms for this condition (*pygmē* and *nanos* or *nanosues*), Parsons documents that *mikros* was "also used for pathological dwarfism in texts from the fourth century BCE to the ninth century CE."[7] He also shows that the contemporary "science" of physiognomy would have read Luke's physical description of Zacchaeus not only as a window into the smallness of his character or of his lowly self-esteem, but also in a derogatory sense as indicative of small-mindedness and greed.

---

6. Parsons, *Body and Character in Luke and Acts*.

7. Parsons, *Body and Character in Luke and Acts*, 102.

Yet this is only what is most obvious. The assumption of Zacchaeus' pathological dwarfism more provocatively enables Luke to undermine the accepted physiognomic beliefs. The fact that Zacchaeus is later designated a sinner (19:7) would have provided further confirmation for his pathological dwarfism since congenital physical diminutiveness would have been assumed to be the result of sin. The image of Zacchaeus running ahead of the crowd and climbing a sycamore tree (19:4) would have provoked the derision of the crowd. Both those watching Zacchaeus and Luke's readers would have been fascinated by the awkward movements of a pathological dwarf with his less symmetrically proportioned body. My point is this: even if the technical grammatical construct in this passage suggests only that Zacchaeus is relatively short rather than that he is a dwarf (someone under 4'10" by today's measurements), there is nothing to prohibit viewing Zacchaeus as a dwarf and the Lukan strategy of subverting contemporary physiognomic conventions is much more effective precisely if that were the case.

I am not aware of any published readings of the Zacchaeus story by little people, but what if we were to deploy a *littlist* or *shortist* perspective in reapproaching this text?[8] Let me hazard three possible lines of reflection. First, although little people do not agree about whether or not they are part of the wider disability community, there is no doubt that pathological dwarfism across a very broad spectrum brings with it a wide range of physical disabilities and intellectual deficiencies. Beyond this, of course, is the social stigma and public ridicule elicited by their very visible condition resulting in unfair caricatures, discriminatory attitudes, and economic employability (and its concomitant poverty). Little people despair in this hostile climate, to the point that many live in self-denial or even avoid interacting with other little people since they do not want to be reminded of their condition.[9] What transpires, regardless of how physically capable little people might be, is the reality of a "social disability": they must deal daily with stereotypes of little people as bitter, disagreeable, and vengeful, and with accounts that rarely portray them "as thinking, feeling individuals who were at the center of their own lives, but rather . . . as adjuncts to the lives of others."[10] Against this background, however, Zacchaeus emerges

---

8. While "dwarf" remains the correct medical term, the nomenclature of "little people" or "LP" is the prevalent self-description today; see, e.g., Adelson, *The Lives of Dwarfs*, xvii. The following is inspired by what Orton, "We Felt Like Grasshoppers," calls a *shortist*—which is parallel, for instance, to *feminist*—reading or hermeneutic of Scripture, focused particularly on the *mikroi* or little ones who are repeatedly mentioned in the Gospel of Matthew.

9. Ablon, *Little People in America*, 91–94.

10. Adelson, *The Lives of Dwarfs*, 372; for the reference to dwarfism as a "social

not as a passive recipient of pity but as an agent in his own right. It is not so much that he was fully employed—after all, collecting taxes for the Romans was a despicable task that allowed few in the position to live at peace within their community—but that he was capable of and actively sought out Jesus, despite having to contend with the crowds. Further, his desire to see Jesus led him to expose himself to ridicule because "it was considered undignified for a grown man to run, and a man of his importance would certainly not climb a tree."[11] Yet he persisted and even got the opportunity to host the Son of Man in his own home. In these ways, Zacchaeus becomes a model for what little people can hope to accomplish.

Beyond this, however, little people would resonate with Parsons's reading of Luke as intending to subvert the physiognomic assumptions of his day. With Jesus' pronouncement, "Today salvation has come to this house, because he too is a son of Abraham" (Luke 19:9), the (Levitical) prohibition against dwarfs from full participation in the liturgical cult of ancient Israel was lifted. Little people are not only agents in their own right, but also in God's eyes, regardless of the limitations imposed on them by society or of the lowered expectations that they have to contend with.[12]

Thirdly, little people would also help us to notice that the structure of this passage results in the salvation or healing of both Zacchaeus and the people in ironic and counter-intuitive senses. On the one hand, normate assumptions would have expected Jesus to heal the sick, impaired, and disabled. Jesus does no such thing in this case, although he definitively acknowledges the presence of full health in the sense of salvation for Zacchaeus. On the other hand, the prejudices of the people are confronted, and Jesus' acceptance of Zacchaeus just as he is undermines their expectations that those who are impaired and disabled need to be "fixed" or cured in order to participate fully in the renewal and restoration of Israel. Zacchaeus becomes a disciple of the Messiah without having to go through the process of literally being stretched from his diminutive condition. Similarly, little people today need not undergo the various surgical procedures touted to increase the length of their limbs or their overall height in order to fit in with the aesthetic sensibilities of normate culture.

---

disability," see Ablon, *Living with Difference*, 7.

11. Keck, ed., *The New Interpreter's Bible*, 357. To be sure, besides the ambivalence toward dwarfs in the ancient Greco-Roman world, there was also some degree of acceptance, at least in Egypt and Greece, as documented by Dasen, *Dwarfs in Ancient Egypt and Greece*.

12. On having to live according to the lowered expectations of others, see the moving autobiographical account of Matt Roloff and Tracy Sumner, *Against Tall Odds*, especially chap. 12.

I do not present the preceding as representative of little people's understanding of the Zacchaeus story. Instead, I provide it as a counter to normate readings of Luke 19 that all too often minimize, eradicate, or even render invisible—as impossible as that seems!—Zacchaeus' littleness. It is not that disability and its various features are absent from the Bible; it is rather that normate interpretations are insensitive to their presence and thus overlook them as supplementary to the message that is, for them, obviously meant for normal people (like they). Of course most normate readers are not conscious of the marginalization of disability in their interactions with Scripture. The ableist bias is insensitive to the world of disability, and its normative assumption is that the world as it ought to be will not feature any signs or marks of impairment, even those related to littleness. It thus never occurs to them that what they are rendering invisible is actually essential to the message of the gospel that comes to specific human beings. The result is not only an overlooking of important features of a text expressive of the salvific message of the gospel, but the perpetuation of an oppressive social imagination that has negative repercussions for people with disabilities.

My claim, however, is that the Bible really is good news for all people, including those with disabilities and those who are temporarily able-bodied.[13] It is just that normate prejudices have created a chasm between people of varying abilities—separating "normals" like "us" from "them"—so that we are not able to stand in solidarity as human beings created in the image of God. Without such solidarity, normate folk are incapable of understanding the world from the perspective of their friends and therefore think that they need to do what they can to save, heal, or otherwise fix those who have disabilities. Perhaps what the Zacchaeus story teaches us is that human beings are equals both in their sinfulness and need for repentance, and in their being accepted as children of Abraham regardless of their physical characteristics or capabilities.

---

13. See my *Theology and Down Syndrome*.

3.5

Disability Theology of the Resurrection[1]

RYAN MULLINS APPEARS TO be reluctant to revise more traditional views regarding the resurrected body in favor of proposals informed by disability perspectives.[2] He thinks my claim "that persons with disabilities will be resurrected with their disabilities intact" is fundamentally misguided by Stanley Hauerwas's dictum—which states that to "eliminate the disability means to eliminate the subject"—and therefore argues my disability theology of the resurrection body confronts conceptual and other difficulties which require further elucidation and defense. This response recalls a number of important theological rationales previously provided in my work which Mullins has overlooked.[3] These clarifications are intended to not only answer Mullins's critical questions but also to invite him to further consider the tenability of classical theologies of the resurrected body in the face of our contemporary understanding of disability.

---

1. Yong, "Disability Theology of the Resurrection," 4–10.

2. See Mullins, "Some Difficulties for Amos Yong's Disability Theology of the Resurrection"; all further references to or quotations of this article in what follows will be made parenthetically by page number.

3. The perceptive reader will notice from Mullins's acknowledgments that he solicited my feedback, and that of others, on a previous draft of his article. I am happy to say that the published version is much improved from what I originally read although it remains misleading in a number of areas as he failed to follow through on my insistence that he locate his account of the resurrection body within the wider framework of my theological argument in *Theology and Down Syndrome*. This response intends to fill in the gaps of his portrayal of my views, so that readers can better judge the merits of my proposal vis-à-vis his reassertion of the more traditional view.

While it is arguable whether or not Hauerwas's dictum functions as a necessary truth claim, my use of it neither presumes nor requires such. As Mullins rightly notes, I do not claim that all disabilities are identity conferring. More important, this is only a minor strand of my argument for the persistence of the marks of disability in the resurrected body. Much more central is both the fact of the marks of impairment appearing on Jesus' resurrected body and—contra Mullins's reference to Augustine's articulation of the traditional view (30)—Gregory of Nyssa's reflections regarding his sister bearing the scars of a healed tumor in her resurrected body.[4] Even if the counter-proposals of Augustine and Gregory cancel each other, Mullins is curiously silent about the theological and eschatological implications of the scars on Jesus' resurrected body.

Perhaps I was not as clear as I could have been about two matters: the nature of the manifestation of disability in the resurrection body and the issue of pain. With regard to the former, Mullins characterizes my position as being that "persons with disabilities will retain their disabilities at the resurrection" (25), quoting in a footnote the following from my book: "To say that people with disabilities . . . will no longer be disabled in heaven threatens the continuity between their present identities and that of their resurrected bodies" (26n5). Yet within the broader context of my Christological argument, my claim is that what persists is at minimal the marks of our present disabilities and impairments. Such marks would include, but not be limited to, phenotypical appearances, mental capacities, behavioral expressions, and verbal, emotional, and interpersonal traits, among other perceivable—whether visually or audibly—features that emerge from and express human identities across the lifespan. In various ways, however, I would also maintain that these marks bear witness to the redemptive power of God. In other words, their presence signifies the continuities between the limitations that condition human creatureliness both in our present and future identities,[5] while simultaneously their transformed nature points to the discontinuities that pertain to the resurrection body (the heart murmur of many children with Down's that has not been closed, for example, would not be fatal!).

In the end, Mullins may be most exercised by the implications that the presence of disabilities in the eschaton involves the experience of pain. While he frames this objection as an entailment of Hauerwas's dictum, my

---

4. See Yong, *Theology and Down Syndrome*, 174–78, 274–75.

5. That human creatureliness is defined theologically by limits is argued convincingly by Creamer, *Disability and Christian Theology*, chap. 5.

account nowhere requires it.[6] In fact, here is where my discussion about the redemptive and transformative dimensions of the resurrection indicates discontinuity between our present experiences of disability in contrast with the persistence of the marks of impairment in the eschatological body. Further, I take great pains (pun intended!) to clarify, using Gregory of Nyssa's theory of epectasis—the eternal journey of the soul into the infinite mystery and presence of God—the dynamic character of everlasting life, not only with regard to each existential and embodied soul, but also in terms of each person's intersubjective and interpersonal relationships with others (and with God) and of the nature of each person's embodied experiences. In my account, our disabilities are not erased. Yet what endures is not their pain, or other negative elements of our experiences of disabilities; rather, even the stigma of disability and its discriminative social expressions, which are oftentimes more "painful" (and this especially in the case of people with intellectual disabilities!) than the physical aspect of impairment, is redeemed as ableist assumptions and conventions are overturned and the oppressed are vindicated. Hence, the marks of our disabilities continue precisely in order to bear witness to the gloriously redemptive work of God, but now without either the physical pain or the social stigma associated with the "normal" conventions of this world's wisdom.[7]

Thus Mullins's concerns about the particular experience of those who become disabled later in life is not an issue since my claim is that the resurrection body registers the peculiarity of each life's trajectory up to the point of death, so that what is raised from the dead will bear the unique marks of impairment to the degree that these have shaped (or not) the identity of that person over the course of a lifetime. Infants are thus raised as infants and octogenarians as octogenarians, etc., with each body marked variously according to the person's earthly journey—with its unique configurations of capacities and limitations—up to the point of death. What persists, and

---

6. I will leave it to Hauerwas to provide the definitive response to this matter, if he wishes to do so, but the context of his argument, as it was then framed, included his many years of working with people with intellectual disabilities. Perhaps this is a "necessary dictum" with respect to some of these people—I certainly think it applies to my brother with Down syndrome, although I nowhere claim that all impairments are equally identity formative.

7. In *Theology and Down Syndrome* I by and large characterize the nature of the discontinuities in terms of our being embraced and accepted by God and the community of saints regardless of who we are; other than that, I have a rather apophatic view of the nature of the discontinuity of the resurrected body: we know not what it will be—that is the nature of saying that our future bodies will be different from our present ones—except that it will not feature the physical pain and social ostracism that characterizes human life in this world.

what is eternally transformed within the community of faith in the presence of God, then, are the marks of our impairments relative to the formation of each identity. As I indicated, though, a dynamic eschatology does not need to insist that infants remain infants eternally, or that the redeemed bodies of octogenarians are incapable of reflecting even further maturation and growth, relative to the infinite glory of God as redeemer.[8]

Mullins's protests against my disability theology of the resurrection body thus seem to presume an either-or that overlooks the nuances of my more dynamic account. For him, it seems to be either the more traditional view in which our disabilities will be erased or "Yong's view" in which disabilities along with their pain will persist into eternity. But why would the nature of the resurrection body be mired in such a static condition? Does Mullins think with Augustine that all resurrection bodies—of the infant and the octogenarian included—will be that of the ideal age of thirty? If not, then does he not need a more flexible account of the resurrection body—even of physically or intellectually disabled ones—akin to the more dynamic view that I have proposed with the help of Gregory of Nyssa and others?

Further, Mullins suggests that Jesus' healings anticipate a resurrection life without disabilities. It is expected that this is what a "normal" or nondisabled perspective presumes—after all, we "normals" measure the world, including the world-to-come, according to our ableist standards! Let me reiterate three lines of response. First, Jesus' healings involve the making whole and saving of human beings as part of the inauguration of the coming reign of God. Oftentimes God's salvation involved curing of sick and impaired bodies, but not always. Zacchaeus' salvation, for instance, did not involve a curing of his short-staturedness, so wholeness, health, and salvation does not necessarily involve cures of disability.[9] Second, Jesus himself did not cure everyone, and even Paul left Trophimus sick at Miletus (2 Tim 4:20). But even if my distinction between curing and healing is ultimately difficult to sustain (although I think it is sufficiently useful to clarify why we ought to pray for a person with Down syndrome to be cured of pneumonia but not for God to cure such a person from the syndrome itself), and even if we grant that it is always God's will to cure (or heal), I don't think either

---

8. I should clarify that the everlasting lives we enjoy in our resurrection bodies are charted not according to counterfactual conditions pertaining to our earthly lives assuming we would live longer. Instead they unfold according to the unfathomable opportunities granted by divine eternal life. What is not lost, but is redeemed, are the various human experiences that have characterized individual lives to the point that they cross over into eternity.

9. See my *Theology and Down Syndrome*, chap. 8; and idem, *The Bible, Disability, and the Church*, chap. 3.

concession touches upon the disputed claim: that regarding the persistence of the marks of impairments on resurrected bodies. Remember, my suggestion is not that disabilities per se persist in the resurrected body, but that the marks of such impairments do. So people with disabilities can be cured of their sicknesses, but that may or may not involve the erasure of the marks of their impairments, as I have defined it above, in the resurrected body.[10]

My counter question to Mullins is this: how do we know for sure that God's redemptive work in the resurrection body will also be according to ableist sensibilities? More importantly, while Mullins is careful to highlight the discontinuities between our present and future bodies, what about the continuities? Will Kelli Mullins's identity be recognizable for her brother quite apart from the marks of her impairments (related to trisomy-21)? Mullins writes: "She [Kelli] has various character traits that are shaped by her Down Syndrome, but they are not causally determined by her Down Syndrome" (27). But aren't personal character traits that are "shaped by" trisomy-21 also identity conferring in some respects? The claim in my book is that personal identity is a complex interface of biological, physical, environmental, and even spiritual relations. Would it make sense to say that Mark, my brother with Down syndrome, has had "various character traits that are shaped by [his] Down Syndrome" but then insist that all of such traits will be completely removed in his resurrection body? What would be the point of such erasures of his character traits on the other side? What exactly does Mark need to be cured from that has not been addressed with open heart surgery, among other interventions? Is it not the rest of us who need healing from our oppressive presuppositions about Mark?

In the end, I think Mullins more traditional theology of the resurrection presumes a kind of Platonism (at best) or Gnosticism (at worst) that separates human embodiment from human identity. He wants me to articulate a more expansive theological anthropology in defense of my claim.[11] I for one do not think that the differences between the various emergentist or physicalist accounts are as important as he suggests—yes they might

---

10. So, for instance, if the bent over woman lived for many years after she was straightened by Jesus, she probably will not appear "in heaven" with any visible marks of her impairment. But what about Jacob's limp? Perhaps it might be barely noticeable, but is it not also conceivable that there will be marks of such a limp, even if they do not hinder the mobility of Jacob's resurrected body? I could be convinced either way in Jacob's case. Zacchaeus' short-staturedness, however, seems to me identity constitutive in an undeniable way, unless someone wants to argue that all resurrected bodies will be the same height, whatever that may be.

11. I do not intend to write a book on theological anthropology, so I may never meet Mullins's expectations on this issue. But I have further developed my emergentist anthropology in chapter 2 of my recent book, *The Spirit of Creation*.

prompt different speculative questions, but my speculative interests in the end are quite this-worldly and pragmatic (to which I return in a moment). Further, he cites with sympathetic agreement Pannenberg's insistence of a radical transformation of the earthly body. However Pannenberg's account, which says "nothing will remain unchanged," does not require that anything will be completely expunged. And to say that our hopes for the resurrection do not depend wholly on bodily continuity does not require that all continuities be eradicated and begs precisely the question of which character traits or "marks" will persist and which will not. Mullins seems to want to appeal to Pannenberg to defend an essentialist notion of human identity, one characterized by necessary and conditional or accidental features. But this ignores the fact that many of the "accidents" that mark our lives—from chromosomal ones to speech impediments to living in a wheelchair for an extended length of time, etc.—shape our identities in indelible ways. So even if Mullins is right to think with Pannenberg that personal identity is in no way dependent on the bodily resurrection (a conclusion which I doubt is derivable from a fair reading of the Pannenbergian corpus), that doesn't necessarily resolve the problem of how identities are registered on resurrected bodies. For instance, I doubt we will be resurrected without our racial features. And if racial and ethnic phenotypes continue to inform our personal identity in some respect (albeit no longer with the stigma attached to such identities in the present life), then why not the marks of impairment? So my claim is that as long as we are somehow the same people in our resurrected bodies as we are in this life, then I ask Mullins about the nature of the continuity between the now and the then.

Does Mullins want to disassociate our bodily characteristics and experiences, especially prolonged over our lives, from our identities? If not, then why resist the suggestion that our resurrected bodies will also bear the marks of our present impairments, and that these in turn inform and shape our eschatological identities, albeit in a continuously dynamic manner? To reject this possibility, or to not clarify the nature of the continuities between our present and future embodiment, seems to me to lapse into a Gnostic view of eschatological identities cleaved from our resurrection bodies.[12] In

12. Mullins's view seems to be like that of medieval Christians. Thomas Aquinas, for example, held to a unified view of soul and body in the present life, but this did not translate for the resurrection body. Thus Mullins seems to me to be subject to the criticism registered by Irina Metzler against the medieval theologians—that they appeared to have "had some kind of 'schizophrenic' perception of their body: an impaired body in life, a perfect body after the resurrection, so that in some ways they would not have the same body after life, even though they were taught that a person was only what they were because of their body and soul"; see Metzler, *Disability in Medieval Europe*, 61, italics orig.

the case of Nancy Eiesland's degenerative bone disease and Susan Wendell's myalgic encephalomyelitis, for example, I am simply following their cues about how these disabilities have shaped their lives, formed their identities, and even informed their hopes. My account allows for the possibility that their resurrection bodies will retain the marks of their impairments (without the pain, either physical or social, the latter even more important as I already noted), but which does not relegate them to spiritualized forms of their earthly experiences for all eternity; instead, a more dynamic eschatology will recognize the possibility of divine redemption of these disabling experiences and conditions not through their obliteration but through their everlasting transformation within the communion of saints and presence of the triune God.[13] Without the marks of impairment, what is the point of the resurrection of the body then? Spiritual "bodies" would suffice.

But in the end, let me re-assert, I base my speculations about the presence of the marks of impairment on resurrected bodies not on Hauerwas's dictum, as Mullins thinks, but on the scriptural witness to the persistence of those marks on the risen body of Jesus, a point that, as I have already mentioned, Mullins appears to have overlooked. The supporting argument has to do with the emergence of theologies of the body that do not dismiss embodiment as constitutive somehow of personal identity. I agree with Mullins that hard questions remain about how to conceive of personal identity in relationship to resurrected bodies. But the answer, I have tried to explain, involves the possibility of the marks of impairment (not disability per se) contributing to the resurrected identity rather than the erasure of such marks altogether.

In the bigger scheme of things, though, my eschatological speculations are designed to reimagine redemptive possibilities for our present lives together. My claims throughout are that the abolition of the marks of impairment in the resurrection minimizes their historical roles. The "normal" logic is that if heaven will be a certain way—i.e., one in which there are no disabilities, or their marks thereof—then so should we work in this life to eliminate them. This is precisely the kind of logic that leads at best to churches devoid of people with disabilities; at worst it leads to social, economic, biomedical, and other policies designed to eliminate such people, even to the point of preventing their births! I know that Mullins is not advocating any such approach. However, I also think he needs to reconsider

---

13. In Yong, "Disability, the Human Condition, and the Spirit of the Eschatological Long Run," I provide much more extensive consideration of Eiesland's theological reflections vis-à-vis the resurrection body. We need to consider continuities and discontinuities not just at the embodied level but also with regard to how these impact identity personally and socially.

that Kelli is in the image of God as a person with Down syndrome, and not apart from that. This has implications for thinking about the nature of her resurrection body in relationship to others, and that in turn has the potential to redeem and transform axiological systems of the present world so that they are more hospitable to and inclusive of all people, regardless of dis/abilities. This is not to say that we should not continue to fund research designed to cure diseases, etc. It is to say that for those who have lived with such disabling conditions—either because there are no cures or because they were born during periods of time before such cures were found—their resurrection bodies will give glory to God not because the marks of their impairments are no longer evident but because the discontinuities of the life to come only stand out in contrast to the evident continuities. In the eschatological long run, though, Kelli, as Mark and other people with disabilities, will experience the dynamic and transformative presence of the triune God within the community of faith. Identities are not stable, and neither will be the marks of their significance in our eternal journeys.

In conclusion, at least at this point of our "conversation," I invite Mullins to think more about the nature of the continuities that may persist between the Kelli he now knows and the Kelli whose body will be resurrected in the age to come. I appreciate his probing concerns, but suggest that our contemporary understandings of disability press questions that pertain not only to the outward manifestations of resurrected bodies but also to the more inward, behavioral, and socio-relational aspects of human identity. If the preceding provides helpful clarification, then perhaps they may also prompt further consideration of the important theological matters at stake for living with disability in the present.

3.6

Disability in the Christian Tradition[1]

INTRODUCTION

BRIAN BROCK AND JOHN Swinton's *Disability in the Christian Tradition: A Reader*[2] is a landmark volume in many ways. The two parts of this article summarize its contents and overview its main themes, and then provide a brief historiographic assessment. I suggest that the volume invites new historiographic approaches to the history of the Christian tradition. In particular, the *Reader* suggests fresh perspectives on narrating Christian history, recounting the history of Christian thought, and reconsidering the theological legacies of major thinkers. In this way, our contemporary experience and understanding of disability opens up innovative pathways not only for Christian historiography but also for theological education in the twenty-first century.

CONTENT SUMMARY AND OVERVIEW OF MAIN THEMES

Disability in the Christian Tradition: A Reader consists of a preliminary essay by Brock (who is on the Divinity faculty, in practical theology, at the University of Aberdeen, as is the coeditor Swinton) and fourteen chapters by other scholars. Each of these chapters, except two, focuses on a major historic figure or theologian, overviews that individual's ideas as a whole

---

1. Yong, "*Disability in the Christian Tradition*," 236–43.
2. Brock and Swinton, eds., *Disability in the Christian Tradition*.

and thinking about disability more specifically, and includes extracts of that person's writings related to the theme of disability. The two exceptions, however, also follow a similar format. Almut Caspary's discussion of the patristic period and Jana Bennett's handling of women and disability both zero in on select theologians (the Cappadocian Fathers in the case of the former and a triad of feminist theologians—Rosemary Radford Reuther, Nancy Eiesland, and Sarah Coakley—in the case of the latter). As such, each chapter both provides substantial summary remarks that situate ideas related to disability within a wider personal or broader framework and reproduces selections of original material. The downside to any anthological presentation is that portions of primary texts are lifted up from out of their original contexts, but the plus side is that these are judiciously chosen and adequately introduced. The result is that the outcome serves the overall purposes of the volume, which is to familiarize readers to a new way of reading the historic Christian tradition, i.e., through a disability lens, and to stimulate further research. For such goals, the editors and twelve other authors helpfully clarify why and how contemporary notions of disability do not always map easily onto past understandings, expertly situate each thinker's ideas about disability within broader contexts, and skillfully introduce primary sources.

The volume is structured historically, beginning with Caspary's discussion of early Christian attitudes toward disfigured outcasts and concluding with Swinton's discussion of theological ethicist Stanley Hauerwas. In between are five chapters on what might be called "pre-modern"—here used merely descriptively and not pejoratively—Christian theologians (Augustine, Aquinas, Julian of Norwich, Luther, and Calvin), three on modern thinkers (Hegel, Kierkegaard, and Willem van den Bergh, a Romanticist and Calvinist who founded Holland's first institution for the intellectually disabled), and three more, besides Bennett's chapter, on twentieth-century theologians (Dietrich Bonhoeffer, Karl Barth, and Jean Vanier). Those relatively familiar with the ideas of these figures will be initiated into new ways of reading them, while those even modestly familiar with the history of disability will come to a deepened appreciation for how these Christians were part of but yet also distinct from their times in thinking about disability.

Caspary highlights, for example, how patristic theologies departed from classical Greco-Roman attitudes and initiated the long history of pastoral care and philanthropy toward those socially excluded because of impairments. Brock's chapter on Augustine then situates this dominating Christian theologian's ideas about "normalcy" and disability within the overall contours of his hierarchical but yet christocentric theological anthropology, even as Miguel Romero's discussion of Aquinas observes how the Angelic Doctor includes the *amentes* ("imbecile" or "mindless") within his neo-Aristotelian and Augustinian theological anthropology. The chapter on Julian of Norwich by Amy Laura Hall nicely anticipates Bennett's more feminist-oriented approach, especially in the ways that this medieval woman understood the bodily character of her own debilitating suffering in christological and theological light.

Reformers Luther (by Stefan Heuser) and Calvin (by Deborah Creamer) also are presented as avoiding later binary notions, the former's theological anthropology as bypassing the normality-abnormality polarity and the latter's theology of divine sovereignty and pastoral care—note Calvin's commitment to developing institutions to care for people with disabilities at Geneva—as circumventing insider-outsider dualisms.

The chapters on modern thinkers provide three contrasting depictions. Martin Wendte shows that, in one regard, Hegel is one of the first to provide a more relational account of being human, but, in another regard, his views about rationality have also fed contemporary biases about mental illness and the lives of those plagued by such conditions. Known in some ways as reacting to Hegel's legacy, Christopher Craig Brittain's discussion of Kierkegaard here may perpetuate this reputation, if for no other reason than that the Danish philosopher both developed Hegel's relational account toward a more social anthropology and yet also subordinated his predecessor's rationalism toward a more theologically oriented existentialism so that disabling conditions are less the result of diminished cognitive capacities than they are related to human alienation and estrangement from God. The short life of van den Bergh (1850–1890), here recounted by Marjolein de Mooij, not only registers one of the few extended theological considerations of the origins of mental illness but also foregrounds van den Bergh's insistence on an ecclesiological rather than socio-political or governmental response to the challenge of care for those so afflicted. These anthropological, theological, and ecclesiological lines of thinking reflect how modern thinkers intersected and engaged variously with their increased awareness of the phenomenon of mental illness.

If Bonhoeffer's thinking about disability was forged directly through the political fires of the Nazi regime's program to euthanize people with disabilities, Barth's is more indirectly traceable only within his theocentric, trinitarian, and christologically oriented anthropology. Yet Bernd Wannenseetsch shows that the former's views were not bereft of christological moorings even as Donald Wood unveils how the latter's also led to a valuation of human life in all of its particularity, and that each person, no matter how impaired, has divine imprint and worth in the present life. These comparisons and contrasts between Bonhoeffer and Barth in the first half of the twentieth century also anticipate other associations and distinctions with the juxtaposing of the work of Vanier and Hauerwas in the latter half of the twentieth century and into the twenty-first century. Both are philosophically and theologically astute, although the insights of the former were honed through living communally with people with profound disabilities (in L'Arche, co-founded by Vanier) and those of the latter were shaped earlier in his scholarly life by his work as a hospital ethicist and chaplain. Vanier's communal theology, described by Hans Reinders, is both complemented and extended by Hauerwas's ecclesial approach, presented by John Swinton, while the former illuminates how people with disabilities can be appropriately considered as "teachers" and the latter shifts the questions related to the "problem of suffering" posed by non-disabled people.

As the first book to triangulate around theologies of disability, the Christian tradition, and primary sources related to disability, this volume is a groundbreaking and invaluable achievement. Of course, any historical treatment will have lacuna, and one could have imagined that chapters on Hildegard of Bingen, Paracelsus, Ambroise Paré, John Locke, and Teresa of Avila, among many others, could easily have been added. Certainly such considerations also apply to Bennett's chapter: Sarah Coakley's work on embodiment, while with implications for theology of disability, is less directly relevant than, for example, that of either Nancy Mairs or Joni Eareckson Tada, and Rosemary Radford Ruether's more recent *Many Forms of Madness: A Family's Struggle With Mental Illness and the Mental Health System* was omitted when it should have been woven into the discussion. Further, among contemporary voices, John Swinton's work is sufficiently wide-ranging, theologically original, and pastorally in-depth to have merited a chapter of its own, and many extracts from his expansive *oeuvre* on disability would have deserved an airing in this volume. Still, editors of (and contributors to) such volumes have to make hard choices, and for a book that is already more than 550 pages, students who have to read it for their course will perhaps be more grateful than is this reviewer about what is and isn't included.

A (BRIEF) HISTORIOGRAPHIC ASSESSMENT

This book can be read in a number of ways. Certainly it can be used as a supplement to traditional histories of Christianity, including historical theologies and histories of the Christian tradition. Of course, it can also provide historical and thematic—i.e., theological anthropology, theologies of embodiment, intellectual disability—perspective for courses on theologies of disability or other religion-and-disability or ministry-and-disability type courses. Last but not least, scholars working on any of the major theologians treated in this volume can certainly also gain new perspectives on their work from the discussions herein.

I want to suggest, however, that the book also inspires new possibilities for Christian historiography. Given how disability outlooks have more recently motivated rethinking both in the areas of biblical studies[3] and Christian theology,[4] the question arises: What are the implications of disability vantage points for the discipline of Christian history? As I approach this topic trained more as a theologian than a historian, I am wary about trespassing across disciplinary boundaries. Yet my work in theology of disability and the insightful pages of *Disability in the Christian Tradition* move me to sketch, in a very rudimentary manner, three lines of suggestions for the retelling of Christian history in light of disability experiences and perspectives.

First, if in fact history in general has traditionally been told by the winners or victors, then the emergence of disability voices in the theological academy invites revisitation of the grand narratives of Christian history from the disability "underside." While there is every concern not to presume the equivalence of people with disabilities and the alleged "losers" of Christian history—a point that contemporary disability rights advocates are keen to remind us—there is also no minimizing of the fact that in general, those with impairments have been the poor, the socially excluded, and the ecclesially marginalized throughout much of the history of the church. The challenge is twofold. In one regard, there is a need to retrieve their narratives and stories without being paternalistic about the ways in which this retrieval is done. This approach will enrich the Christian historical account with the voices and lives of people with disabilities whose contributions are otherwise forgotten. In another regard, there is also the need to interrogate the ways in which Christian history has been framed which privileges the institutional centres and hierarchies of the church while overlooking or ignoring those which society has identified as "weaker." In this way, a disability-inflected historiography comes alongside and complements social approaches that focus on the lives of ordinary people in ways that fill out our understanding of the past. Medievalists especially have been at the forefront of retelling the history of the Middle Ages in relationship to disability;[5]

---

3. E.g., Avalos, Melcher, and Schipper, eds., *This Abled Body*; Moss and Schipper, eds., *Disability Studies and Biblical Literature*; Yong, *The Bible, Disability, and the Church*.

4. See Yong, *Theology and Down Syndrome*; Betcher, *Spirit and the Politics of Disablement*; Reynolds, *Vulnerable Communion*; Creamer, *Disability and Christian Theology*.

5. E.g., Metzler, *Disability in Medieval Europe*; Eyler, ed., *Disability in the Middle Ages*; Turner and Pearman, eds., *The Treatment of Disabled Persons in Medieval Europe*.

Christian historians of these and other periods undoubtedly will remain hard at work into the foreseeable future re-examining the life of the church across the last two millennia from a disability point of view.

Second, I shift from Christian history in general to the field of historical theology more specifically. Here I am stirred in part by my reading of *Disability in the Christian Tradition*. This sub-field explores the history of (theological) ideas, the history of the development of doctrine, and the history of Christian thought, among other subfields of inquiry. The bottom line is this: Disability has been seen as a problem to be resolved (usually medically or technologically, if not supernaturally through divine healing) rather than as an epistemic posture. While I am all in favor of addressing the many real life and existential issues related to life with impairment, disability studies has taught us over the last few decades that the field has the potential to shed new light on other domains of knowledge. Here I am drawing less from the Foucauldian notion of subjugated knowledges (featuring the local agency, perspective, and experience of socio-historically embodied people)—as helpful as this is[6]—than from St. Paul himself, especially his theology of the cross and of weakness.[7] I am interested in asking what happens to our understanding of the history of Christian thought when disability insights are factored into the mix. For example, how might feminist and other women's perspectives be enriched and even complicated by disability experiences, as gestured to in the contributions of Amy Laura Hall (on Julian of Norwich) and Jana Bennett (on contemporary feminist theologians)? How further might the history of theological anthropology be told differently when Augustine's neoplatonic hierarchicalism is subverted by the Pauline theology of weakness, or when Aquinas's theology of *amentes* is foregrounded rather than rendered as marginal to the conversation, or when the Hegelian rationality is recognized to be only one mode of human intelligence rather than supremely enthroned? Last but not least, how might the history of the doctrine of salvation take different turns when Kierkegaardian notions of subjectivity, Van den Berghian etiologies of mental illness, or Vanierian views of personal realism are the norms, or at least not neglected to the margins, of what it means to be created in the image of God and to be in relationship with God? These are not merely interesting speculative questions. As the chapter on Bonhoeffer and the Nazi experiment reminds us, there are life or death consequences for people with disabilities dependent on these theological sensibilities and intuitions. A history of Christian thought that

---

6. See Tremain, ed., *Foucault and the Government of Disability*.

7. See Yong, "Disability and the Gifts of the Spirit"; and idem, "Running the (Special) Race."

includes, even if it does not centralize, disability perspectives will display a very different account of the theological commitments of the Christian tradition, one that, potentially, wards off even the specter of the Nazi threat.

Besides impacting Christian history and the history of Christian thought, a disability historiography might also lead to a reconsideration of the legacies of major theologians. This volume under review is exemplary in this regard. Almost to the person, each of the chapter authors is clear that disability is not a major thread in the *oeuvre* of the theologian (or theologians, with the exceptions of Nancy Eiesland and Jean Vanier) under consideration. The result of reading their work through a disability lens, however, is at least twofold. In one regard, identification of disability themes illuminates the power of their work in ways that otherwise might not be observed. This is best seen, for instance, in the thought of Aquinas, Julian of Norwich, Luther, Bonhoeffer, and Hauerwas. In each case, the ideas for which they are renowned come into new light when read through a disability angle. In another regard, new questions emerge when the theological ideas of others are refracted through a disability perspective. Augustine, Calvin, and Hegel, in this collection, are shown to be either inconsistent or biased in their analyses (the latter is not necessarily a pejorative claim since all theologians are biased!). Hegel, for example, needs to be read critically against himself, since the same cognitivism with which he predefines people with intellectual disability in negative light is challenged by his dialectical philosophy and phenomenology of embodied spirit that remains open to development even within this group of persons. The point is both that there are resources within any major theologian to counter ideas that have negative repercussions for people with disability and also that there may be major theological strands (i.e., Calvin on sovereignty), if not entire conceptual frameworks (e.g., Augustine's hierarchical cosmology), that ought to be reviewed when disability realities are brought to bear. This is not to say that an alternative disability reading of each of the theologians in this volume will not uncover counter-trajectories, contrary understandings, and contesting interpretations about disability and its related motifs than have been noted in this volume That is, in part, the nature of historical inquiry, including the truism that different readers situated in different times, spaces, and experiences will find different insights in the legacies of the great theologians and Christian thinkers of the past.

Any retrieval can be challenged, even as the contributors to this volume individually and the book as a whole are also challenging past readings of these important voices in the Christian tradition. But all of this suggests that the richness of the theological tradition remains in need of excavation from a disability historiographic perspective.

My reading of Brock and Swinton has led me to ponder historiographic questions about the Christian tradition. Our co-editors have done those working at the interface of disability studies and theology a favor in producing this reader. Yet in the process, they have also instigated the kinds of historiographic questions that we have only barely begun to consider. When combined with the hermeneutical and methodological fertility already in display in the wider theological academy, the addition of historiographic adjustments portends the revitalization of theological studies across the curriculum. It also bodes well for Christian theological education in general that each area of biblical studies, theology, and Christian history admits of disability blind spots and evinces openness to corrective and complementary approaches.[8] *Disability in the Christian Tradition: A Reader* is a major contribution to those working on this front.

---

8. See Yong, "Disability and the Renewal of Theological Education."

3.7

Be Healed!
Saving the Church, Redeeming the World[1]

HEALING IS AN EXISTENTIALLY palpable and extremely personal matter, especially for those who have experienced miraculous cures and for the afflicted who long for a divine touch in circumstances that seem hopeless. Yet what follows develops three aspects of a Christian theology of healing—the personal, the ecclesial, and the eschatological—in light of the preceding reflections. My major thesis is that authentic healing that includes but ought not be reduced to cures is always part of the salvific work of the Spirit of God in Christ, and as a "sign of the kingdom,"[2] invites our inhabitation of the coming reign of God. We conclude by considering how such a theology of healing is nevertheless commensurate with what might be paradoxically called a renewal theology of disability.

We begin with the personal experience of divine healing manifest in miraculous cures to which many have testified. There is no question that God meets human beings in remarkable and inexplicable ways by touching and curing infirm bodies. Pastoral, evangelistic, and missionary agents also have been and will continue to be ministers of healing through which God provides medically unexplainable cures that bring about a saving knowledge of Christ.[3] An important caveat, however, bridges this personal element and the wider ecclesial and eschatological dimensions of healing. To insist

1. Yong, with Anderson, *Renewing Christian Theology*, 215–21.
2. Ervin, *Healing*.
3. McGee, *Miracles, Missions, and American Pentecostalism*.

that God's healing involves curing does not mean that modern medicine can be dispensed with or that we can ignore other domains of knowledge that affect human health and wholeness. Human beings are complex creatures constituted by spiritual, material, psychical, social, political, economic, and environmental aspects. Science, medicine, and the humanities provide windows into various aspects of the human condition, and we would be irresponsible to ignore these insights. As God enables the human advance of knowledge in these areas, we may be able to explain more and more of how the Spirit can inspire and bring about an even wider range of remedies for human ills. This should not undermine faith in a healing God. Medical doctors can be agents of divine healing just as well as healing evangelists. Yet because medical diagnoses and prescriptions always address local symptoms, holistic health and (for our purposes) final healing lie beyond even the most exhaustively delineated scientific accounts.

This leads us to the ecclesial aspect of healing. Any testimony to or affirmation of divine curing involves an explicitly theological layer of explanation above either incredulity ("I don't know how this happened!") or other lower-level assessments ("The expert surgeon and his team were successful in removing the cancer"). Yet the effectiveness of such theological accounts is ecclesiological and christological simultaneously: they derive from an overarching faith community that believes in Jesus as savior and healer. Without this broader theological framework, there will be either no need or desire to testify to divine healing ("Oh, it was just a coincidence"). Yet within a Christian interpretive framework, the God who sent Jesus Christ to declare good news to sick and oppressed sinners invites their reconciliation with God, which includes reconciliation with others. In other words, there is no such thing as a merely individualistic perspective on the healing that God accomplishes. Healing occurs only in relationship to the believing community and its exaltation of the living Christ.

More concretely, this ecclesial dimension of healing indicates that any physical cures are part of the larger redemptive work of the Spirit of Christ. Thus the World Assemblies of God Fellowship Statement of Faith affirms that "deliverance from sickness is provided in the atonement," but the atonement involves saving individuals in the community of the faithful, the church. So also, a text that suggests a link between the atonement and healing points to the relational character of health: "He himself bore our sins in his body on the cross, so that, free from sins, we might live for righteousness; by his wounds you have been healed" (1 Pet 2:24). Physical health and wholeness thus are supported and completed by, if not also requiring the repair of, interpersonal and social relations. The removal of sins in the cross of Christ allows human beings to forgive one another and to accept one another as forgiven in Christ. Cures, even miraculous ones, may not persist without such forgiveness and relational reconciliation. Interpersonal and social alienation will undermine the long-term efficacy of any physical cure. The witness to Christ thus nurtures new relationships within the body of Christ and the fellowship of the Spirit, and these enable the flourishing of bodily cures into the full salvation that individuals experience only with others.

Beyond the confines of local congregations, however, the ecclesial aspect of healing points also to the social dimension of health and wholeness. The church's message of healing interfaces with the role of the larger society in at least three ways. First, the church can and ought to come alongside other social, economic, and developmental initiatives focused on health and health care. Christian organizations like World Vision, among many others, have led the way in this regard. Second, this ministerial approach may also need to be accompanied by a more prophetic posture. There are often structural impediments that keep communities impoverished and perpetuate ill health, and the church ought to be at the forefront of calling attention to and engaging these matters, so structural changes can be effected for the common good.[4] Last but not least, physical infirmities in many cases are variously symptomatic of and correlative with underlying moral, psychical, and most importantly, spiritual ailments. The last lies within the prerogative of the church and requires the full panoply of spiritual weapons from prayer and fasting to exorcism. Yet full healing will require that the social dimensions of ill health also be addressed.

This leads to healing's eschatological aspect, which, as has been consistently argued in this volume, is both already and not yet. Miraculous cures are present signs of the full reign of God, which is yet to be unveiled. The "natural laws" that operate within the divine rule that is coming now appear extraordinary according to our present understandings and expectations.[5] Thus, those with gifts of healing—whether healing evangelists or medical doctors, just to name two types—are made participants through the Spirit of Christ in the eschatological work of heralding the coming domain of God. In the new heavens and new earth, we are told that the "leaves of the tree are for the healing of the nations" (Rev 22:2b). Herein is indication that the healing power of God in some sense resides within the divinely ordered creation. On the one hand, sin has both wracked God's creatures with brokenness and illness even as it has also retarded the curative and healing capacities of the created order (see chap. 10). Yet on the other hand, this

---

4. Freeman, ed., *Pentecostalism and Development*.
5. Cf. Bulgakov, *Relics and Miracles*, 51–53.

also explains the discovery of the medicinal powers of the earth, of medical advances, and of healing traditions not specifically informed by the Christian theological vision. But with Christian healing, the works of the Spirit-anointed Christ as of those also now empowered with the Spirit accomplish bodily cures and nurture holistic health in the present life as signs of the full redemption to come.

Miraculous curing mediated through prayer, discernment, confession of sins, intercession, exorcism, and medicinal or other applications[6] provide humanity with a glimpse of the impending full salvation offered by God (Rom 13:11). On the one hand, then, we ought not to minimize the power of these curative signs for transforming lives and communities. On the other hand, we may also be seduced into seeking after miraculous signs and miss out on the fact that they are merely icons or windows into the eschatologically redemptive work of God that involves others, the world, even the whole creation. Bodily cures, from those affected more miraculously to those less extravagantly manifest, remain potent marks of the in-breaking of the reign of God.

How then does the preceding renewal theology of healing inform a theology of disability? There are many types of disabilities, for instance those derived from war, which we ought to avoid, as well as those resulting from contingent or accidental events. We now also know more about how chromosomal mutations occur that result in congenitally impairing conditions. Regardless of their source, disabilities need not be blamed on God. However, Christian faith can be hopeful that nothing lies beyond the pale of God's eschatologically redeeming work (cf. Genesis). Jesus' response to the question about why the man was born blind does not answer the question, but it does point to how God can bring good out of any situation: "Neither this man nor his parents sinned; he was born blind so that God's works might be revealed in him" (John 9:3). An eschatologically oriented renewal theology of disability focuses less on trying to understand why there are disabling conditions than on how we might be open to experiencing God's saving work even in and through such impairing situations.[7]

Hence a renewal theology of disability will understand the temporal and even limited experience of physical cures in the present life within the larger perspective of salvific healing in the coming reign of God. Some renewalists who might emphasize the present "finished work" of Christ may be less comfortable with such an eschatological framework than others.[8] Yet

---

6. Thomas, *The Devil, Disease, and Deliverance*; Kydd, *Healing through the Centuries*.
7. Yong, *Theology and Down Syndrome*, chaps. 6 and 9.
8. Alexander, *Pentecostal Healing*.

reception of divine favor in the form of physical cures now is no guarantee that full salvation follows, even as the latter—wholeness, health, and shalom—can indeed be experienced in the present life despite the absence of the former.[9] Rather, the real miracle of healing is the receipt of the gift of the triune deity, incarnationally given in the Son and pentecostally poured out in the Spirit, for life abundant realized in the reconciliation of all creatures with God and each other. The following therefore need to be kept in mind.

First, faith-filled prayers for physical cures are never out of order in light of Jesus' eschatological works; however, such prayers also ought to invoke God's full salvific work (rather than merely focusing on the physical maladies) on behalf of others. Second, however, even when cures are delayed, those with disabilities or impairments ought not be presumed to be lacking faith, persisting in sin, or oppressed by the devil; people ought not to internalize a "second-class Christian citizenship" just because they have not experienced physical cures. Third, people with disabilities are, like Zacchaeus (see section 9.1) and the Ethiopian eunuch, among others, full members of the body of Christ *in* and *with* their impairments; ecclesial membership is a spiritual and sacramental condition (see chaps. 6 and 7) distinct from our physical, sensory, or intellectual abilities or lack thereof. Fourth, full salvation will eventually involve physical cures (this is the point of the resurrection body), but such bodies will retain the marks of their impairments (as did Jesus' resurrected body). The retention of such marks, however, excludes the pain—both physical and social—accompanying disability in the present life, while potently testifying to the full salvation of individual lives in all their particularity and in relationship to others and the triune God.

Last but not least, the church continues its present ministry, in this time anticipating the Parousia, of ministry *to* people with disabilities and their families but also *with* those who are variously impaired. People with disabilities are not merely passive objects of pity needing the care of able-bodied people. Rather, all people, including those who are temporarily able-bodied ("normal" people come into the world dependent and if they are blessed to live long enough, they will exit the world in a similarly dependent state), are indispensable members of the body of Christ through whom the gifts of the Spirit can be manifest for the common good (1 Corinthians 12).[10] Perhaps more importantly, believers in the Messiah from Galilee should not underestimate the degree to which Christ remains in solidarity with the weak, the sick, and even people with disabilities, so their reception

---

9. Dawn, *Being Well When We're Ill*.
10. Yong, *The Bible, Disability, and the Church*, chap. 4.

of the ministries of compassion redounds to the salvation of those to serve in Jesus' name (Matt 25:31–46).[11]

Any theology of healing and of disability ought to inspire faith and hope in a curing but more importantly a healing and saving God, be linked to the forging of new personal identities in the body of Christ and the fellowship of the Spirit, and emphasize pastoral sensitivity and care, so that people can be empowered to deal with and overcome the afflictions derived from various spiritual, physical, psychical, emotional, interpersonal, and environmental maladies. We have seen that these practical guidelines only make sense within a robust ecclesiology, a trinitarian Christology, and an overarching theology of creation and fall. The ecclesiological issues have already been discussed. The next two chapters further elaborate on the christological and creational aspects of a renewed Christian theology.

---

11. Yong, *The Bible, Disability, and the Church*, chap. 5.

PART FOUR

Political Theology

4.1

The Multidimensionality of Salvation[1]

THE EARLY-TWENTIETH-CENTURY PENTECOSTALS TALKED about a "four-fold" gospel of Jesus as Savior, baptizer, healer, and coming king (which became the basis of Aimee Semple McPherson's [1890–1944] International Church of the Foursquare Gospel in 1923) and a "five-fold" gospel adding Jesus as sanctifier (prominent among the Holiness wing of the tradition).[2] The preceding analysis of Luke-Acts shows how the soteriological imagination of the early pentecostals was informed by their experiences of Jesus and the Spirit of God, experiences that were told about in the Bible. The fivefold gospel is expanded here in light of the foregoing Lukan Spirit soteriology by discussing the seven dimensions of salvation.

Personal salvation refers to the traditional understanding: individuals encountering and being transformed into the image of Jesus Christ by the Spirit. This includes, in part, deliverance from oppressive situations and conditions and, in part, release from spiritual captivity and the exorcism of demonic forces. It also includes, minimally, individual repentance, baptism, the forgiveness of sins, and the reception of the gift of the Holy Spirit (Acts 2:38; cf. also, in Paul's case, 9:17–18; 22:16). Already it is clear that personal salvation is never merely individualized, insofar as baptism involves the believing community. Yet the individual aspect of salvation cannot be neglected: there are (or should be) identifiable moments in human lives

---

1. Yong, *The Spirit Poured Out on All Flesh*, 91–98.
2. See Dayton, *Theological Roots of Pentecostalism*, esp. 21–23; and Land, *Pentecostal Spirituality*, 18–20.

when the awareness of the need for repentance comes to the fore and lives are turned in the opposite direction from which they were headed. Shortly we will unpack the meaning of personal salvation in terms of moral, intellectual, affective, sociopolitical, and religious conversion (§2.2.3).

Family salvation calls attention not only to the promise of the gift of the Spirit "for your children" (Acts 2:39) but also to the fact that individuals are who they are precisely as members of families. The salvation of the individual is thus intimately connected with the salvation of his or her family. This was declared to Cornelius (Acts 11:14), and proved to be the case for the households of Lydia (16:14–15), the Philippian jailer (16:31–33), and Crispus (18:8a). Some might argue that although family conversions were the norm for ancient societies, which followed the head of the household as a rule of thumb, individual conversion is the norm for modern societies. In light of the fact that "family" in the ancient world refers not to the nuclear family of modernity but to households, clans, and tribes,[3] I prefer to see the modern situation as an exception to the rule. Individuals still often come to repentance following after their family members, and many a fervent prayer has been offered up (and answered by God) on behalf of an unbelieving spouse by the believing spouse or on behalf of rebellious children by believing parents. This makes at least some sense of the otherwise enigmatic statement by Paul that families are made holy through believing spouses/parents (1 Cor 7:14).

Ecclesial salvation expands on the notion of family salvation and uses family metaphors (cf. Luke 8:19–21; Mark 3:31–35) to point to the communal dimension of what it means to be saved. Thus the connection between ecclesiology and soteriology that sees salvation effected through baptism: the death and burial of the unbelieving individual in and with Christ and his or her resurrection into a new life, existence, and community, the living body of Christ (cf. Rom 6:3–4; 1 Cor 12:13; Eph 4:15–16). Believing the good news of Jesus Christ leads to baptism (e.g., Acts 8:12, 36–38; 10:47–48). Salvation as ecclesial means being baptized into a new relationship with Jesus and his body by the power of the Spirit. Read another way, the outpouring of the Spirit (the book of Acts) not only made possible individual reception of the saving grace of God but also made real and actual the new people of God and a communal way of life.

Material salvation refers to the embodied nature of human beings (cf. §1.2.2). This includes the healing—of mind, soul, and body; mental, emotional, and physical—ministered by Jesus and made possible by the power of the Spirit. Material salvation is directed primarily to the poor, the

---

3. Barton, *Life Together*, chap. 3, esp. 41.

marginalized, and the oppressed, perhaps because they experience their diseased and deprived conditions in palpable ways.[4] The good news is specified as being for the poor, who are lifted up by the gospel; the hungry are fed while the rich are sent away (Luke 1:52-53). Unlike Matthew, who sees Jesus blessing the "poor *in spirit*" and those who "hunger and thirst *for righteousness*" (Matt 5:3, 6; italics added), Luke sees Jesus blessing the poor and the hungry *as such* and admonishing the rich and the full *as such* (Luke 6:20-21, 24-25). For these reasons, the early church ministered to the sick, the impoverished, the naked, the stranger, and those in prison (cf. Matt 25:31-46) and sought to care for widows and children, the most vulnerable members of society (Acts 6:1-6; cf. Jas 1:27).[5]

Social salvation is an extension of, and yet complementary to, ecclesial salvation.[6] It refers, on the one hand, to the healing and reconciliation of interpersonal relationships, most tangibly experienced in the church and to which the church is called to bear witness. It also refers, on the other hand, to the redemption of the socioeconomic and political structures—including fallen and destructive public structures, what Walter Wink calls the public and social manifestations of the demonic[7]—a redemption that, when accomplished in society at large, is also transformative for ecclesial relations (cf. §1.1.1; §1.1.3). These notions take some explication. This is most efficiently accomplished by following out the consequences of the outpouring of the Spirit on the day of Pentecost for what St. Paul refers to in terms of there being neither Jew nor Greek, neither slave nor free, neither male nor female (Gal 3:28),[8] and for what contemporary discourse refers to in terms of racial, class, and gender reconciliation.

Racial reconciliation: Seymour's reading of the Azusa Street outpouring of the Spirit as washing away the color line (§1.3.3) finds concrete justification in the Pentecost narrative. Included among the ethnicities and languages brought together at Pentecost were the Egyptians (this includes Africans, representative of the black race), Cretans (see the famous saying "Cretans are always liars, vicious brutes, lazy gluttons"; Titus 1:12), and the

---

4. Volf, "Materiality of Salvation."

5. For these reasons, Seccombe's thesis in *Possessions and the Poor in Luke-Acts*, esp. 24-43, is correct in what it affirms (that "the poor" refers to Israel under Roman oppression) but not in what it denies (that "the poor" therefore does not necessarily refer to the poor in a literal sense).

6. Pentecostal reflection on social salvation is emerging; see, e.g., Macchia, *Spirituality and Social Liberation*, esp. chap. 5; Villafañe, *The Liberating Spirit*; and Petersen, *Not by Might, nor by Power*.

7. See Wink's series: The Powers.

8. E.g., Thomas, "The Church at Antioch."

Arabs (Acts 2:9–11). From this group, three thousand were saved, the new work of God was inaugurated, and the new people of God was established. Imagine the reconciling power of the pentecostal gospel, which includes Semites alongside Africans (later specified in terms of the Ethiopian eunuch; Acts 8:26–40) and Arabs (all the more important given the more recent Arab-Israeli conflicts) and which breaks down and overcomes negative stereotypes of ethnic nationalities (such as that of Cretans). In retrospect, Acts 2 describes the worldwide church of the twenty-first century and anticipates the eschatological gathering of all peoples, tongues, tribes, and nations in the reign of God (Rev 5:9; 7:9; 13:7; cf. 21:22–26). Early modern pentecostalism captured this biblical vision through Seymour's leadership, but this did not last. An honest assessment of the current situation is that personal and sociostructural racism is still very much a present sin and manifestation of demonic power that needs to be confessed and dismantled by the church (see §4.2.3).

Class reconciliation: The outpouring of the Spirit upon all flesh not only reconciles ethnicities and races but also heals divisions erected by class. A new people of God emerged who had "all things in common" (cf. Acts 2:40–47; 4:32–37). The church brought together those otherwise socially segregated: the unschooled (4:13) and the well-educated (e.g., Paul and Apollos; cf. 18:24); the disenfranchised and those in religious or political power (e.g., Cornelius in Acts 10, Sergius Paulus in 13:7–12, Crispus in 18:8, Sosthenes in 18:17, and Publius of Malta in 28:7–10); and the socially marginalized and differently abled (e.g., the Ethiopian of Acts 8, who was a foreigner and a eunuch). No wonder modern pentecostalism, in providing space for and nurturing the poor, the sick, the social outcasts and misfits, the economically destitute, the spiritually impoverished, and the politically marginalized or invisible, has been called a "haven for the masses" and understood as representing the "vision of the disinherited."[9] Much work needs to be done to address inner-city slum conditions, violence on all scales, and economic structures of injustice that are demonically inspired to exploit mass labor for the gain of the rich, just to name three of the present challenges. But the church cannot ignore these matters if, as black pentecostal theologian Alonzo Johnson notes, "oppression is understood to include economic, political, cultural, as well as psychological and spiritual realities" (see §4.3.1).[10]

---

9. See Lalive d'Epinay, *Haven of the Masses*; and Anderson, *Vision of the Disinherited*, even if the sociological theories undergirding these arguments need to be scrutinized. See Miller, "Pentecostalism as a Social Movement."

10. Johnson, *Good News for the Disinherited*, chap. 4; quotation, 150. Also Bae, "Full Gospel Theology as a Distinctive Theological Practice for Korean Pentecostal

Gender reconciliation: The outpouring of the Spirit has been from the beginning also upon both male and female: sons *and* daughters would prophesy (Acts 2:17–18). The value and ministry of women are affirmed not only in Luke (e.g., 1:40; 2:36–38; 8:1–4; 11:27–28) but throughout Acts (e.g., Dorcas, Lydia, Damaris, Priscilla, Philip's evangelist-prophetess daughters, and other unnamed women). Modern pentecostalism has featured numerous women evangelists, pastors, church planters, missionaries, and leaders.[11] Nevertheless, sexism remains widespread not only in societies around the world but also in churches, including pentecostal churches. Full salvation includes the redemption of women and of the fallen social structures that have conspired to prohibit women's full realization of the image and calling of God in their lives (see §4.3.2).

Cosmic salvation refers not only to the interconnectedness of human beings and their environment (cf. Acts 2:19–20) but also to the redemption of all creation (perhaps not excluding the fallen principalities, spiritual authorities, and powers; cf. Eph 6:12).[12] In fact, Paul explicitly connects the cosmic salvation of all creation and the human redemption of the body with the work and groanings of the Spirit of God (Rom 8:19–23). Meanwhile the Spirit not only heralds the day of the Lord through the Messiah (Luke 4:19) but also works to bring it about. Indeed, the arrival of the day of the Lord is a thoroughly pneumatological event that transforms all creation (Isa 32:15–16) and effects even relationships between the wolf and the lamb, the leopard and the kid, the calf and the lion (cf. Isa 11:6–9; 65:25). For contemporary society, cosmic salvation is especially urgent given the pollution of the environment and bodies of water, the destruction of our ecosystems, the degradation of our rain forests, the erosion of our soils, and the greenhouse effect, among other concerns. Along with our tree-planting African Independent Churches in Zimbabwe (§1.3.1), recent "environmental spiritualities" are also drawing on pneumatological themes in their commitment to the greening of cities, the purifying of water and air systems, and the renewal of the natural environment (see §7.3.3).

Last but not least is *eschatological salvation*. Traditionally, this has been construed in individualistic terms related to one's final abode in either heaven or hell. These are the categories of the Apocalypse—the presence of God or the bottomless pit; the heavenly Jerusalem or the lake of fire; inside the city or outside the gates—and the full force of these powerful symbols should not be overlooked. Nevertheless, the foregoing analysis of Pentecost

---

Theology," esp. 175–77, 179–80.

11. See Griffith and Roebuck, "Women, Role of," 1203–09; cf. §1.1.2.
12. Wink, *Engaging the Powers*, 73–85.

as signifying the eschatological outpouring of the Spirit indicates that eschatological salvation is experienced now *and* awaited. Thus salvation is both historical and directed toward the future transformation of all creation into the new heavens and new earth.[13] Against the fundamentalist view, prevalent in many pentecostal circles, that sees all creation as apocalyptically destroyed, this transformational perspective suggests that (a) apocalyptic texts that on the surface imply the destruction of the world are better understood in terms of the eschatological purification of God; (b) the specific Christian hope for the resurrection of the body suggests both that there is a greater continuity than discontinuity between this and the next world and that God values the embodied nature of created things sufficiently to preserve them; and (c) God will finally save and vindicate the people of God, who yearn for divine intervention into their experiences of persecution, oppression, and alienation, and God will finally redeem the world, which was created good.[14] The apocalyptic elements of the New Testament anticipate the critique and judgment of the present sociopolitical and historical order. Jesus' exorcisms thereby overturn the reigning forces of this world and inaugurate the new order of the reign of God.[15]

The "not yet" aspect of eschatological salvation will include the saving work of the Spirit in the personal, familial, social, and cosmic dimensions as well. More specifically, as Miroslav Volf puts it, the final reconciliation is not only between God and human beings but also between humans themselves, including the reconciliation between victims and victimizers.[16] Hence it must necessarily accomplish the forgiveness of all sins, bring about justice, vindicate the oppressed, and yet reveal the mercy of God. Divine grace is manifest precisely in the eschatological redemption of sinners and those sinned against. In anticipation of this final redemption, the Spirit continues to issue an open-ended invitation to "anyone who wishes [to] take the water of life as a gift" (Rev 22:17), even as the Spirit blows forth the winds of refreshing preceding the return of the Messiah and the universal restoration of God (Acts 3:19–21). And although this cosmic salvation may not be

---

13. Kloppenburg, *Christian Salvation and Human Temporal Progress*. See also Althouse, *Spirit of the Last Days*; and Moltmann, *The Coming of God*, esp. 267–74.

14. The connections between (b) and (c) are argued explicitly in Green, "'Witnesses to His Resurrection.'"

15. Here I follow the argument of N. T. Wright regarding the apocalyptic eschatology of first-century Judaism as expecting a new world order rather than looking for the destruction of the present space-time cosmos. See Wright, *The New Testament and the People of God*, chap. 10; and idem, *Jesus and the Victory of God*, chap. 6.

16. See Volf, "The Final Reconciliation." For background discussion, see Volf, *Exclusion and Embrace*, chap. 5.

a literal universalism,[17] it certainly will entail the submission of all things under Jesus, the exaltation of his name (Phil 2:9–11), and the final subjection of both the Son and all things under God "so that God may be all in all" (1 Cor 15:28). Because of the continuity between the present historical work of the Spirit of God and the final redemptive act of the triune God, the eschatological motif runs as a thread woven throughout the entirety of this pentecostal theology instead of being set off as its own separate topic (or chapter) for discussion.

Salvation considered in these personal, familial, ecclesial, material, social, cosmic, and eschatological terms does not necessarily mean that individuals experience the saving work of God in this sequence or that these are updated categories for the older idea of the history of salvation. The point, rather, is that full salvation as concretely historical includes all of these dimensions and that to individualize salvation is to arbitrarily abstract one dimension from a much more complex and complicated process of relationships. This needs to be kept in mind as we work our way through what has traditionally been understood as the personal *ordo salutis* ("order of salvation") in the remainder of this chapter, before returning to the larger ecclesial and social pictures in the next two chapters.

17. See the most recent debate on this in Parry and Partridge, eds., *Universal Salvation?*

4.2

Poured Out on All Flesh

The Spirit, World Pentecostalism, and the Performance of Renewal Theology[1]

MANY WITNESSES: RENEWING SOCIETY

PENTECOSTALISM BEGAN AND CONTINUES first and foremost as a missionary movement. Its message has revolved around the four- (or five-) fold gospel of Jesus as savior, healer, baptizer, and coming king (or including Jesus as sanctifier). Pentecostal missionaries, evangelists, and pastors hence preached the gospel, laid hands on the sick and interceded for their healing, and prayed for the baptism of the Holy Spirit for all who were wishing for a deeper experience of God. And why not, if the same Spirit who anointed Jesus to preach the gospel and heal the sick is also the Spirit who now empowers the followers of Jesus to bear witness to his name and to do even greater things than he did (cf. John 14:12)?

Yet the works of Jesus involved not only healing the sick, but also, under the anointing of the Spirit, preaching to the poor, releasing the captives and oppressed, and announcing the liberative Day of the LORD (Luke 4:18–19). So Jesus delivers those oppressed by the devil through exorcisms, and heals lepers and other persons with severe disabilities, but does so in order that these individuals could be restored and reconciled to their communities. Further, Jesus is concerned not only about healing individuals but

---

1. Yong, "Poured Out on All Flesh," 31–34.

about doing so on the Sabbath in order that its original meaning and function might be restored, even as his interactions with widows and parables about them reveal both his compassion for an oppressed category of persons and his concern for justice. Most importantly, Jesus' proclamation of the impending kingdom of God resulted in his death at the hands of political rulers who were threatened by his message. Jesus' ministry, in other words, included a social and political dimension that went beyond his concern for individual lives and bodies. Hence, should not those empowered by the same Spirit also do these works of Jesus?

Pentecostals have increasingly begun to theorize (theologize) about how their religious convictions have informed their socio-political attitudes and activities. This is the case whether we are discussing classical-pentecostal pacifism during the first world war; Latino pentecostal civil rights activism and theology; Afropentecostal liberation theology; or contemporary pentecostal social ethics.[2] In each of these cases, and many others, pentecostals have argued that the gift of the Spirit empowers the Christian witness not only in terms of kerygmatic speech, but also in terms of prophetic action. The witness of the Spirit, in other words, both conjoins speech and action and includes the socio-political dimension.

A more holistic pentecostal missiological paradigm therefore includes at least the following interrelated elements. First, insofar as pentecostals have been touched by and continue to encounter God in Christ by the power of the Holy Spirit, they cannot but bear witness to this transformative reality; hence their witness will always include a narrative moment that testifies to the "this is that" of the biblical kerygma. Second, insofar as pentecostals have been touched by the Spirit, their witness will (or should) always be sensitive to the whole situation of their audience; hence their witness will (or should) always be borne by a sensitivity, empathy, and compassion for others.[3] Finally, insofar as pentecostals are moved to enact the works of Jesus by the power of the Spirit, their witness will include both prophetic and activist components that confront the injustices of the world and work with others who bear the same witness—both within and without pentecostalism and even the wider Christian community—to promote righteousness, reconciliation, and peace.

---

2. On pentecostal pacifism, see Shuman, "Pentecost and the End of Patriotism"; and Alexander, "Spirit Empowered Peacemaking." On Latino pentecostal activism and theology, see Busto, *King Tiger*; and Villafañe, *The Liberating Spirit*. On Afropentecostal theology, see Beckford, *Dread and Pentecostal*; and Cruz, *Masked Africanisms*. On pentecostal social ethics, see Macchia, *Spirituality and Social Liberation*; and Dempster, "Paradigm Shifts and Hermeneutics."

3. This is the point of Solivan, *The Spirit, Pathos, and Liberation*.

Whereas earlier I discussed similar themes under the rubric of a pentecostal theology of inclusion (§1.2), here I am specifically expanding the sphere of those deliberations with regard to the Christian mission to the ends of the earth. If human life cannot be neatly divided into social, political, and religious domains, then how can pentecostal prayer, preaching, and missionary endeavor not engage the socio-political realities of our time? But to do so, I suggest, is to participate in the work of the Spirit who has been poured out for the renewal of the world.

MANY VOICES:
TOWARD A RENEWAL THEOLOGY OF CULTURE

Focusing on the socio-political arena raises a further matter concerning pentecostal witness: the question of culture. Pentecostal missiologists have long been concerned about this issue, in large part because the largely evangelical approach to missions which has influenced them repeatedly frames the task of Christian mission as that of translating, contextualizing, or applying the gospel in and to different cultural realities. This begs a number of problematic assumptions: that the missionary is "in charge" of the translation, and that those being missionized are passive recipients of the gospel; that we can disentangle the eternal, unchanging, and essential core to the gospel from its first century Jewish Mediterranean context; and that the new vehicles of language and culture in which the gospel is presented are merely "accidents" which do not affect what is translated. More recent pentecostal thinking on culture, however, reveal shifts in several directions.

First, the Pentecost narrative is increasingly understood as anticipating the redemption not only of the diversity of languages but also the diversity of cultures.[4] Language and culture are distinct, but not unrelated, and the gift of many tongues can be understood as the gift of many cultures. This is not to uncritically baptize all that occurs in the many cultures of humankind (more on this momentarily), but it is to affirm that the image of God is both embodied, environmentally rooted, and socio-culturally situated. More important, it provides theological rather than politically correct rationale for embracing cultural diversity, and in so doing anticipates and even hastens the Day of the LORD which will include members from all tribes, languages, peoples, and nations. In this reading, the Day of Pentecost is but a prelude to and a foretaste of what is to come, when the glory and honor of all the nations (Rev 21:26) will participate in the light of the city of God.

---

4. Yong, "As the Spirit Gives Utterance."

From this starting point, then, emerges the realization that the relationship between gospel and culture is much more dialectical then previously understood. This is not to relativize the gospel, but to acknowledge the "hermeneutical spiral" whereby readers and reading communities receive the gospel in their own terms (languages) but are also simultaneously transformed by the gospel.[5] Hence there is a need for what might be called a "theologically responsible syncretism" which is able to be vigilant precisely because of the awareness that we might be able to receive from culture a witness to the gospel.[6] From a missiological perspective, however, such a posture flows forth from the "principle of indigeneity" long ago intuited and since operative in pentecostal discourse.[7] In this paradigm, indigenous perspectives, values, and leadership are to be embraced, albeit not uncritically. The many tongues of Pentecost thereby prefigures the capacity of many languages to receive the gospel on the one hand, and to bear its own distinctive witness to the gospel on the other hand.[8]

Last (for our purposes), but not least, this more pneumatological understanding of culture opens up theological space for pentecostal scholars to engage in the task of formulating a more comprehensive theology of culture. What about pentecostal perspectives on technology, not only with regard to the implications of medical technology for pentecostal healing practices (briefly mentioned above), but also with regard to modern telecommunications which pentecostals have adopted from its earliest moments? What about pentecostal and pneumatological perspectives on music and the arts, both with regard to the centrality of music to pentecostal worship, and with regard to the perennial question concerning the arts as expressing the deepest and most profound sensibilities of the human embodied spirit?[9] How do these realities manifest in the wide range of human cultures bear witness, if at all, to the work of the Spirit, and to the gospel of Christ?

These questions are not merely rhetorical. Rather, they are related both to the human quest for truth and to the human need to interact with the world in more truthful ways. With regard to culture, a pneumatological

---

5. See Osborne, *The Hermeneutical Spiral*; and Tate, *Biblical Interpretation*.

6. For more on "theologically responsible syncretism," see Hollenweger, *Pentecostalism*, chap. 11; cf. also Sepúlveda, "To Overcome the Fear of Syncretism."

7. The principle of indigeneity was developed by Hodges, *Build My Church*.

8. On the translatability of the gospel, see Sanneh, *Translating the Message*; and on the capacity of culture to bear distinctive witness to the gospel out of its own resources, see Tarr, *Double Image*.

9. On the former matter, see, e.g. McIntyre, *Black Pentecostal Music in Windsor*; and Becker, *Deep Listening*, esp. 97–100; on the latter, see Sherry, *Spirit and Beauty*; and Gorringe, *The Education of Desire*.

approach increases understanding, enables discernment, and empowers engagement. The renewal of the world includes the renewal of culture and its various domains, including but not limited to the linguistic, the technological, music, and the arts. Not everything in the realm of culture is to be naively received (hence discernment is so essential), but perhaps more will be redeemed and manifest in the kingdom than we realize (hence also the need for a theology of culture that empowers our performative engagement with the various cultural domains).

4.3

Many Tongues, Many Political Practices[1]

MY HYPOTHESIS IS THAT pentecostal reflections on political theology can be summarized with the motto, "many tongues, many political practices." There are three interlocking motifs that frame the thesis: the biblical, the pentecostal, and the political-theological.

Biblically, I posit that the dominant theme of the restoration of Israel and the renewal of the world in Luke-Acts opens up the people of God to a multiplicity of political stances, practices, and theologies.[2] The notion of the gospel going forth to the ends of the earth fulfills the Old Testament promise that through Abraham, all the nations of the earth would be blessed. At the same time, then, the multiplicity of political forms and structures in ancient Israel (2.1.1) anticipate the pluralism characteristic of "new Israel" in a predominantly Gentile world. In this case, the many tongues of the Spirit that represent the many cultures of diaspora Judaism (in Acts 2) not only foreshadow the many tribes, peoples, and nations (in the Apocalypse) but also the many political structures amidst which the church fulfills her vocation in the present age. I will attempt to make the case in Part II of this book that this biblical insight belongs not only to pentecostalism or to pentecostal theology but also to all Christians as well as those in search of a viable political theology for our time.

1. Yong, *In the Days of Caesar*, 109–11.
2. In a companion to this book, I provide an exegetical-political reading of Luke-Acts through a pentecostal and pneumatological lens; see Yong, *Who is the Holy Spirit?*. By contrast, my incursions into Luke and especially Acts throughout this volume will be primarily thematic.

From a pentecostal perspective, we have already seen that there is no one form of political, economic, or social engagement in global pentecostalism (chap. 1). Rather, there is a multiplicity of pentecostalisms in the global south, with distinct orientations toward the political, broadly construed. The preliminary biblical explorations provided in this chapter suggest that the many tongues of Pentecost, precisely because they represent a diversity of ethnic, linguistic, and cultural experiences, also imply the redemption of many political practices. If pentecostalism has been portable around the world because of its translatability—its capacity to be indigenized and vernacularized in local languages, customs, and experiences[3]—then any pentecostal approach to political theology will be similarly informed by the pluralism of the pentecostal body politic. In short, I suggest that pentecostals have intuitively correlated the "many tongues" motif central to their spirituality and piety with the complexity of their social, economic, and political lives. I will argue in the rest of this book that there are normative implications suggested in this pentecostal correlation for political theology.

Finally, then, from the standpoint of political theology itself, we have observed (chap. 2) that there is no one normative standard for how Christians should think about the political. Instead, there have always been a multiplicity of political structures in and through which the people of God have borne witness to the coming kingdom. Not without reason, we are beginning to see accounts that discuss political pluralism as if that itself were normative for Christian theology.[4] What I hope to provide in the remainder of this volume is a theological rationale for this pluralism in Christian political thinking. The task is to avoid either a relativism of political options or a politically correct legitimation that devolves into an ideology of the majority. Further, we must resist providing a merely pragmatic account that baptizes many theological beliefs derived from the diverse political contexts within which such beliefs are shaped.[5] Instead, if I am successful, my thesis will not only provide a theological justification for the diversity of Christian politics, but also empower the many different practices required to bear witness to the gospel in a politically pluralistic world.

In short, I am proposing that the many tongues of Pentecost and the many concomitant political practices may constitute a distinctive pentecostal contribution to the wider Christian discussion of political theology.

3. E.g., Dempster, Klaus, and Petersen, eds., *The Globalization of Pentecostalism*.

4. E.g., De Vries and Sullivan, eds., *Political Theologies*; and Budziszewski et al., *Evangelicals in the Public Square*.

5. Dumas, *Political Theology and the Life of the Church*, 20–22, almost suggests as much, that Christian thinking about the political is shaped by different political situations.

One might read the following as a "pentecostal political theology," and that would be appropriate at one level. I'm more interested, however, in how pentecostal perspectives can shape a Christian political theology that is viable for the church catholic.

4.4

The Spirit's New Economy of Salvation[1]

PETER'S QUOTATION FROM JOEL ends with the declaration that, on the glorious Day of the Lord when Yahweh would restore Israel, "everyone who calls on the name of the Lord shall be saved" (Acts 2:21). In that sense, the restoration of Israel involves the salvation both of the Jews and of all who call on the name of Yahweh. But there is more since, for Peter and Luke, who is retelling the history of Peter's sermon, salvation is bound up in "Jesus of Nazareth, a man attested to you by God with deeds of power, wonders, and signs that God did through him among you" (2:22). The heart of the Good News, then, was to "let the entire house of Israel know with certainty that God has made him both Lord and Messiah, this Jesus whom you crucified" (2:36).

We have already seen that the Jews were awaiting the Messiah, who would restore the house of Israel according to the promises made to Abraham, Moses, and David. Here in his first sermon, the Spirit-empowered Peter makes explicit Jesus' connections with the Davidic covenant. Not only does Peter mention David four times by name, but he also quotes or alludes to various royal psalms, songs that celebrate the restoration of the Davidic reign in the messianic age. One of these citations also confirms that Israel will be vindicated before her enemies (2:35; cf. Luke 1:71; Ps 110:1). The hope of the resurrection in ancient Israel was connected to the renewal of the Davidic covenant and the restoration of the nation (cf. Ezek 37:1–14).

---

1. Yong, *Who is the Holy Spirit?*, 19–23. See Acts 2:22–40.

Luke is thereby accentuating Jesus' credentials in the line of David. But more than that, since David remained in the grave, Jesus is the one who fulfills the covenant promises about resurrection life. For the Jews who believed in a general raising of the dead at the end of the age connected with the restoration of Israel, the resurrection of Jesus would have meant both that David's kingship now belongs to Jesus and that the redemption of Israel and the last days, the Day of the Lord, had indeed arrived in the person of the man from Nazareth.

Further, the resurrection of Jesus precipitates his exaltation to the right hand of God from where, "having received from the Father the promise of the Holy Spirit, he has poured out this that you both see and hear" (Acts 2:33). So while the Father has promised the Spirit (Luke 24:49), it is the resurrected Messiah who keeps the promise. Although salvation is based on the Spirit's work in and through the life, death, and resurrection of Lord Jesus (rather than Lord Caesar), it is realized and actualized through the ascended Messiah, who pours out that same Spirit on all flesh. If in the Gospel of Luke the Holy Spirit acts in the life of Jesus, in Acts, Jesus is present and active in the restored people of God in the power of the Spirit.

It is this exalted Messiah who has been crucified by a disbelieving and corrupt generation (2:40). Peter straightforwardly accuses his listeners, "You crucified and killed by the hands of those outside the law" (2:23; cf. 2:36). His audience is convicted by the fact that they have, however inadvertently, chosen to abide by the politics of Caesar and his lordship rather than that of the anointed Messiah. Wishing to avoid the judgment that befalls those who have executed an innocent man, they gasp, "What should we do?" (2:37). Peter responds: "Repent, and be baptized every one of you in the name of Jesus Christ so that your sins may be forgiven; and you will receive the gift of the Holy Spirit. For the promise is for you, for your children, and for all who are far away, everyone whom the Lord our God calls to him" (2:38-39).

Peter's response has drawn forth numerous interpretations during the two-thousand-year history of Christianity. I suggest that salvation consists not in emphasizing any one "thing," whether that be repentance, baptism, or the reception of the Spirit, but in repentance, baptism, the forgiveness of sins, and the receiving of the Holy Spirit *all together*. It must also be noted that forgiveness was originally a commercial notion that meant to be released from previous obligations and, in the first century, was also connected to the cleansing that had to occur in order for Israel to be renewed and restored.[2] So Peter's announcement offers his audience the forgiveness

---

2. Thus, does the Hebrew Bible frequently connect the restoration of Israel with the forgiveness of sins—e.g., Isa 40:1-2; 43:25-44:3; Lam 4:22; Jer 31:31-34; 33:4-11; Ezek 36:24-33.

of sins committed by them and their ancestors, against one another and against God and his appointed Messiah—that is good news indeed, indicating the time had come for the restoration of Israel!

By extension, for the rest of us, forgiveness frees us from our indebtedness to others and allows us to receive a new identity, the gift of the Spirit, that transforms us into servants and friends of the Messiah. Yet such forgiveness and salvation cannot be magically earned by "fulfilling" this short list of requirements; rather, salvation involves God's calling, which enables repentance, God's acting in Christ to make possible the gracious forgiving of sins, and God's free outpouring, through Christ, of the Holy Spirit.

This mode of God's salvation involving the full scope of repentance, and the gift of the Holy Spirit seems to establish God's way of salvation once for all. That these promises are "for your children, and all who are far away" (2:39) points to both the spatial/geographical and the temporal reach of God's salvation: to those in the farthermost reaches of the empire or even Gentiles who would be at the ends of the earth (1:8) and to the many generations of descendants who shall call on the name of the Lord. In other words, if the powers and wonders of God accomplished in Jesus inaugurated the day of the Lord promised by the prophets, then the salvific plan of God outlined here in Peter's sermon will continue that work until the Day of the Lord, when the kingdom is fully present. So while the kingdom may be in the world, it is not of the world; rather, the coming kingdom that is the promise of the Father, the way of the Son, and the gift of the Holy Spirit is in the process of turning the kingdoms of this world "upside down" (17:6).

Now, Peter said much more than what Luke records. Nevertheless, this text raises many important questions. For example, what exactly does it mean that salvation introduces a new economy of grace, and how exactly does this get worked out while we remain within the economies of this world?

Let me suggest that the salvation of God overturns the economy of this world. Whereas the world's economic system depends on each one of us paying our debts, the economy of God's Spirit involves the forgiveness of debts. Whereas the world's justice system involves our getting what we earn or deserve, the justice of God liberates us from the guilt and shame accompanying our actions. Whereas our humanly constructed economy depends on barter and exchange, the divine economy involves merely calling on God in repentance and receiving both the forgiveness of debts and the free gift of the Holy Spirit. God's way of doing business is contrary to the ways of the world. Rather than merely meeting the obligations imposed by the law, the coming of the trinitarian God establishes a new covenant of grace and a new economy of giving. The renewal of Israel, then, involves a kind of redemption that overthrows the rule (economy) of this world, albeit not precisely in the way that was expected.

4.5

Empowered Witness

The Reconciling Movement of Love[1]

ONE WAY IN WHICH the empowerment of the Spirit manifested itself concretely at the Azusa Street Mission is summarized, as one early observer puts it, in the saying, "the 'color line' was washed away in the blood."[2] To be sure, as we shall see, this line reasserted itself quite quickly upon its initial blurring.[3] But there is also no denying that for a limited period of time during the early years of the revival, the Mission was what we would today recognize as a multiracial and multiethnic congregation, led by William Seymour, a black man. I suggest that this was possible only because the baptism of the Holy Spirit was understood at the Mission also as involving the sanctifying and perfecting love of God. Such a baptism of holy love was thus received as forming a new spiritual unity in the body of Christ, reconciling people otherwise divided by class, culture, language, ethnicity, and race.

The first issue of the *Apostolic Faith*, for example, reports that "Jesus was too large for the synagogues. He preached outside because there was not room for him inside. This pentecostal movement is too large to

---

1. Yong, *Spirit of Love*, 64–68.
2. Bartleman, *Azusa Street*, 54.
3. See the insightful essay by Brathwaite, "The Azusa Street Revival and Racial Reconciliation." Brathwaite argues that an idealized view of the Mission overlooks how even within the very early days of the revival its racial harmony was contested and that this gradually unfolded into the segregated pentecostal movement that marked much of its development in the rest of the twentieth century.

be confined in any denomination or sect. It works outside, drawing all together in one bond of love, one church, one body of Christ."[4] This led one contemporary writer to note that "The voice of the Holy Spirit . . . early Pentecostals believed, was accompanied by a new eschatological baptism of love that would unite Christians beyond denominationalism founded on such creeds."[5] Yet this non- or even antidenominationalism overcame not only ecclesial boundaries and divisions but also other perennial human divides based on class, language, and ethnicity. "Since then multitudes have come. God makes no difference in nationality, Ethiopians, Chinese, Indians, Mexicans, and other nationalities worship together."[6] We should recall, as historian David Daniels points out, that "nationalities" was the preferred early twentieth century discursive concept, not our contemporary rhetoric of "race."[7] Thus was it noted of the Mission that "All classes and nationalities meet on a common level."[8]

In short, one of the unique features of the Azusa Street revival was its multiethnic and multiracial character, unusual in the Jim Crow era, even on the Pacific coast of the USA. It was precisely this mixing of ethnicities and races, not to mention the Africanisms manifest at the Mission, which repelled racists like Parham. But "William Seymour believed sanctification in the perfect love of God was necessary for Spirit baptism, essential to racial reconciliation and unity, and preparation for the return of Christ for a Bride without 'spot or wrinkle.'"[9] For him and the Azusa Street faithful, then, the baptism of the Spirit was an empowerment to love and a call to holiness, and this capacity enabled the crossing of human divides based on denomination, language, class, ethnicity, culture, and nationality. It was a baptism of holy love that enabled the inclusive acceptance of what was otherwise strange, and brought about, at least for a short while, the appearances of reconciliation among those who were otherwise far apart.

Seymour's vision of a church uniting black and white across the spectrum of cultures and nationalities was caught by one of his protégés, Charles Harrison Mason (1866–1961). Mason attended the Mission for five weeks in March and April of 1907, during which time he received the baptism of the Spirit, and then afterward returned to the South to spread the revival. For our purposes, what is important to emphasize is that Mason brought

4. Unnamed, "The Old Time Pentecost," 1.
5. Irvin, "Drawing All Together in One Bond of Love," 41.
6. Seymour, "The Same Old Way," 3.
7. See Daniels, "The Color of Charismatic Leadership," esp. 82.
8. Unnamed, "Beginning of a World Wide Revival," 1.
9. Land, "William J. Seymour," 225.

with him Seymour's mission for developing an interracial, ecumenical, and egalitarian fellowship.[10] Mason's organization, The Church of God in Christ (COGIC), facilitated an interracial pentecostal movement through the early 1930s by including whites within its congregations, by recognizing whites in high-ranking positions of leadership in the movement, and by ordaining whites as ministers both within the movement and to carry the pentecostal message beyond the formal confines of the reach of COGIC.[11] In so doing, Mason was doing nothing more than extending, even expanding, the mandate of the Azusa Street Mission to see the pentecostal baptism of powerful and reconciling love of God spread at least across the country, if not to the ends of the earth.

We should not underestimate Mason's resolve toward an interracial fellowship in the face of southern segregation during the first quarter of the twentieth century. Long after even Seymour had reacted defensively to white racism, paternalism, and antagonism—by revising in 1915 the Mission's *Doctrines and Discipline* to allow only "colored" leadership[12]—Mason continued to work with and include whites within the COGIC orbit. Throughout this early period, then, Mason's ministry wrestled in a very concrete manner with the potential of the pentecostal revival for reconciliation between classes, ethnicities, genders, and cultures. As noted more recently by COGIC historian and theologian Bishop Ithiel Clemmons, African American Holiness Pentecostals from Seymour to Mason and beyond did not view the pentecostal revival merely as a tongues movement as some whites would have it; rather, what they saw in the outpouring of the Spirit was the inauguration of a "prophetic social consciousness" such that "the Holy Spirit not only transforms persons but rearranges relationships and structures."[13] Thus within this pentecostal trajectory, "From the beginning, [the gift of reconciliation] was the very essence of the holiness pentecostal experience—not speaking in tongues."[14]

Yet as is well known, this interracial experiment was short lived, with cracks appearing within the movement already in the 1910s. While there is disagreement about whether the original formation of the Assemblies of God (AG), drawing at least some of its ministerial constituency from the ranks of those ordained by Mason, was intended to secure a nonblack (read: white) organizational option for southern pentecostals, there is no doubt

---

10. Ware, "The Church of God in Christ and the Azusa Street Revival," esp. 247–49.
11. For details, see Daniels, "Charles Harrison Mason."
12. Seymour, *Doctrines and Discipline*, 38–39.
13. Clemmons, *Bishop C. H. Mason and the Roots of the Church of God in Christ*, 57.
14. Clemmons, *Bishop C. H. Mason and the Roots of the Church of God in Christ*, 73.

that over the next half century,[15] the AG came not only to be representative of white American Pentecostalism as a whole, but also to adopt a face that was racist at least in its activities and structures, if not also theologically. Thus if from its founding until the late 1930s the AG viewed African Americans as simplistic or ignorant (as depicted in the fellowship's weeklies, for example) and clearly postured themselves in a paternalistic way toward blacks in the fellowship, in the next twenty plus years after that, there was a semiofficial policy of exclusion, including the refusal to credential or ordain blacks to the ministry.[16]

The climate began to change, of course, with the emergence of the civil rights movement in the late 1950s. Since then, white pentecostal groups such as the AG have become increasingly sensitized to the institutionally embedded dimensions of racism in their midst. What I find intriguing, however, is that it is predominantly white groups like the AG who, in following various aspects of Durham's Finished Work theology in distinguishing the doctrine of Spirit baptism from a more robust theology of sanctification, are the ones who have not retained the close connections between the baptism of power and of love.[17] Perhaps it should not be too surprising, then, if it is such groups who have not seen that the power of gospel involves the kind of reconciliatory vision long espoused by the African Americans in the holiness-pentecostal tradition. Equally noteworthy, then, is the fact that while other white Finished Work pentecostal groups have had similar track records to the AG in terms of their views regarding racial reconciliation, it has been the holiness-pentecostal organizations that did not sever the connections between sanctification, perfect love, and spiritual power who have been able to maintain interracial relations much longer, toward the end of the first and founding generation from the Mission.[18]

---

15. Newman, *Race and the Assemblies of God Church*, argues that the AG leaders were consciously motivated, even if only in part, by white-black issues, while Rodgers, "The Assemblies of God and the Long Journey toward Racial Reconciliation," 66, suggests that other reasons were more foundational and that race was largely beneath the surface of the denomination's founding. For our purposes, no resolution of this issue is required.

16. For details, see Newman, *Race and the Assemblies of God Church*, chap. 5. Cf. Olena, "I'm Sorry, My Brother," for a detailed examination of the case of Robert Harrison, who was originally refused credentials in 1951 but finally became a "poster child" African American in the AG when he was invited to join the Billy Graham evangelistic team in 1962 (he was also ordained by the AG that year).

17. For more on this observation, see Espinosa, "Ordinary Prophet," esp. 53–54.

18. See, e.g., Thompson, "On Account of Conditions that Seem Unbearable"; and Hunter, "A Journey toward Racial Reconciliation."

If it is the work of the Holy Spirit to always join together what human beings have put asunder, it also should not be surprising that the story of racial reconciliation within the pentecostal movement has not yet been concluded. To be sure, white pentecostals have recognized that they can rightly be indicted for responding to the issue of racism only long after the sociopolitical climate and cultural exigencies necessitated activity on their part.[19] Yet such wider developments have also prompted some first steps toward racial reconciliation among pentecostals. Most significant of these overtures was the disbanding of the all-white Pentecostal Fellowship of North America and its replacement by a racially integrated—at the leadership level as well—Pentecostal Charismatic Churches of North America at a historic meeting in Memphis, Tennessee, in October 1994. Observers recognized and have insisted since on the need for ongoing repentance that involves institutional restructuring, strategic expenditures of monies in a clearly interracial direction, revisitation of pentecostal statements of faith to reflect more inclusive commitments, involvement of other marginalized ethnic communities (in particular Latino/a Pentecostals), and full reconsideration of the role of women in classical-pentecostal churches and denominations. In other words, much remains to be achieved in the work of the Spirit initiated at the Mission and revitalized at the so-called "Memphis Miracle" event: whites need to continue to come to grips with the reality of racism and its institutional, structural, and ecclesial effects, while blacks need to walk a fine line between projecting a posture of prophetic justice and working in solidarity with those who are willing to implement the difficult processes of repentance and change.[20] The challenges along this front indicate that pentecostalism needs not just a historical pentecostal outpouring of the Spirit but ongoing baptisms of love in order that these "mountains" can indeed be moved.[21]

One way to foster an openness to the ongoing miracle of racial reconciliation is to retrieve the tradition launched, though not maintained, by Seymour, the leader of the Azusa Street Mission, who understood the baptism of the Spirit to be a baptism of holy love that had important implications for what it meant to be the church, the body of Christ. Chief among the accomplishments of the Spirit was a unity that transcended the divisions

---

19. The laments of Mostert, "Lessons from Our Struggle to Overcome Racial Segregation," are recognized as applicable also in the U.S.A. See also Robeck, "Historical Roots of Racial Unity and Disunity in American Pentecostalism."

20. See Macchia, "From Azusa to Memphis"; along with Macchia, "Roundtable."

21. In short, mere rhetoric needs to be translated into concrete action that dismantles racism; see Rosenior, "The Rhetoric of Pentecostal Racial Reconciliation," which is a distillation of Rosenior's dissertation, "Toward Racial Reconciliation."

of its time and, by extension, could continue to do so anytime if there were willing hearts and lives. Experience of and encounter with the love of God in Christ through the Holy Spirit thus had practical and performative ramifications; exclusionary forms of ordering the people of God had to give way to mutuality, cooperation, and solidarity. The Spirit-baptized fellowship could thereby potentially be a sign to the broader church ecumenical, as well as to the world, of the reconciling power of divine love in the midst of hostilities, out-group indifference and hatred, and historic divisions.

4.6

Toward a Pent-Evangelical Theology of Migration[1]

IN THE FINAL PAGES of this chapter, I want to sketch the rudiments of a migrant theology as informed by my Asian American perspective and my pentecostal rereading of the book of Acts. My goal is to build on Soerens and Hwang's theological insights toward an Asian American and pent-evangelical theology of migration. There are three dimensions to my summary reflections: missiological, political, and theological.

Missionally, any pent-evangelical theology of migration must begin with the missional character of the Spirit-filled life. On this matter, mission involves migration, and migration is undertaken for missional purposes.[2] Yet as our overview of the early messianic experience shows, at some point, roots are planted, and in those cases, migrants need to find homes. Note that the apostolic decision to receive leadership from migrants reflects the discernment that in that case, at that place and time, these migrants who were far from home (although having returned home in other respects) needed their own leaders. Here was a case of enabling local leaders on foreign soil, so to speak. Along the way, at least at the dawn of the modern world, including the beginnings of the modern missionary movement, we have forgotten such truths so that the missional task of Christianization has been co-opted by the colonial project of westernization instead. Hence we have had to relearn the hard way over the last century many lessons about the importance

1. Yong, *The Future of Evangelical Theology*, 180–85.
2. See Hanciles, "Migration and Mission."

of recognizing and empowering indigenous leaders.[3] Yet such should not be understood only in terms of what happens "out there," abroad, in the Global South; it may also be relevant here, "at home," in the Euro-American West, particularly in light of the reverse missionary movement from the rest to the West. Pentecostals have usually been alert to the need for establishing indigenous churches that are—following the famous missionary model of Roland Allen—self-supporting, self-governing, and self-propagating, at least in (missiological) theory if not in (evangelistic) practice.[4] Yet the current task for any theology of migration relative to the needs of the twenty-first century needs to be sensitive to the challenges experienced by migrant communities and their churches wherever they may be found.

From an Asian American missiological perspective, any pent-evangelical theology of migration ought to be mindful that the forces of globalization are not only causing upheavals in population movements but also open up new opportunities for mission and evangelization.[5] The Asian diaspora around the world, not to mention to North America, provides alternative pathways for carrying out the Great Commission, particularly with regard to people groups who are less accessible in their Asian homelands. More pertinent in the American context, many if not most Asian immigrants are open to learning about if not embracing the Christian religion since they are already primed to conform to the dominant American culture. There are missiological challenges involved here, but the opportunities are there nonetheless. The key is to be sensitive to Asian cultural dynamics so that ecclesial forms of life are nurtured that do not merely mimic Westernized church traditions. Empowering Asian American leaders to think through the contextual issues navigated by Asian American communities of faith will be central to the future of Asian American Evangelicalism in particular and to evangelical faith as a whole.

Politically: Our review of the Acts narrative also, however, highlights what we might not often hear much about in pentecostal circles—the political dimension of missional migration. Pentecostals have been, in general, so focused on the evangelistic dimension of missions that they have neglected to reflect more intentionally about the political relevance of their practices. In this respect, my initial efforts to construct a pentecostal theology of migration in this chapter involve also an element of deconstruction

---

3. Elsewhere, I sketch the broad contours of a postcolonial approach to the missionary task: Yong, "The Missiology of Jamestown."

4. See Yong, "Many Tongues, Many Practices," esp. 47–48.

5. See Im and Yong, eds., *Global Diasporas and Mission*.

of pentecostal assumptions about missional migration.⁶ What needs to be interrogated is the widely assumed notion in pentecostal mission and evangelism that the gospel is meant for human souls rather than for human lives in all of their political complexity. By political, of course, I am referring to the public constitutedness of human life, which includes not only the political narrowly conceived in relationship to the state but also the economic, social, cultural, and civic domains. Pentecostals are right to insist that neither Jesus nor Paul were directly concerned with such public structures in their migration. However, this does not mean that migrants have nothing to say about or contribute to the political formation of human lives. In fact, the subversive power of the gospel is precisely its capacity to interrogate the status quo of our political, social, and economic practices, even to the point of undermining the very nature of these presumed realities insofar as they do not measure up to the peace, justice, and righteousness of the coming reign of God.⁷ The power of migration is that it injects fresh perspectives into local situations, perspectives that can generate new insights into underlying causes of what needs to be fixed and that can identify what needs to be done. The key is that there need to be structures in place that welcome migrants and enable their settling into a new home yet that do not assimilate them to the point that they can no longer maintain a critical vantage point.⁸ The result should be a transformation of the margins so that new centers emerge in a globalized and post-Christendom world.⁹

From an Asian American perspective, the politics of migration are complicated not only ideologically but practically. In a real sense, this entire volume gestures toward a path forward for pent-evangelical Christians that includes but does not merely assimilate Asian Americans into the dominant (white) culture. If being yellow between black-and-white involves complex and challenging issues, perhaps we can take cues from how Jewish proselytes and Gentile Christ-followers in the early apostolic period navigated between traditional Jewish demands on the one hand and Greco-Roman obligations under the lordship of Caesar on the other. In this case, the

---

6. See further my "Global Pentecostalism and the Political." [Editor's Note: See Yong, "Global Pentecostalisms and the Public Sphere," forthcoming.]

7. As I try to suggest, with Samuel Zalanga, in "What Empire?"

8. Or, to facilitate what Andrew Sung Park calls "transmutation," which is not assimilation (wherein the emigrating identity is lost), amalgamation (wherein the emigrating and the new cultural identities are improperly syncretized), or mere coexistence (perpetuating ethnic enclaves and ghettoes), but where there is the possibility of the mutual enhancement, enrichment, and deepening of all groups by one another. See Park, "A Theology of Transmutation."

9. As argued by Hanciles, *Beyond Christendom*.

dilemmas confronted when the interests of Greek- and Hebrew-speaking widows collided in the early church becomes a window through which to think through an Asian American pent-evangelical political economy. The task involves the building up of vibrant ecclesial communities that can meet the needs of migrants in their many domains but neither devolve into a ghetto or ethnic enclave nor eventually get absorbed into the larger culture in ways that diminish or lose the gifts that each culture brings to enrich and beautify the body of Christ in anticipation of the reign of God to come. And when truly divine, the tribes and peoples of the church will also challenge the status quo from their sites of Spirit-inspired difference.

This leads, finally, to the theological axis: My pentecostal perspective that begins with the experience of Spirit infilling and empowerment for mission realizes that our migration is modeled on that of the Holy Spirit's.[10] The Spirit's migration, however, is also more precisely, from our perspective, an *im*migration, a movement of the Spirit that is incomplete until the Spirit takes up residence upon our heads, blows between our ears, enlivens our tongues, and gushes forth from within our hearts. Thus does Luke write,

> And suddenly from heaven there came a sound like the rush of a violent wind, and it filled the entire house where they were sitting. Divided tongues, as of fire, appeared among them, and a tongue rested on each of them. All of them were filled with the Holy Spirit and began to speak in other languages, as the Spirit gave them ability (Acts 2:2–4).

The movements of the Spirit are thus outward, from the Father on high (Luke 24:49) through the Son at his right hand (Acts 2:33), and then inward, into us (cf. Rom 5:5), so as to redeem us as the people of God. No wonder we are a migrant people, caught up in the migrations of the Spirit. Yet simultaneously, we are also an immigrant people, following the immigrations of the Spirit. But if the Spirit immigrates into human hearts, so do we, as living epistles, immigrate into the proximity of the lives of strangers, and there seek to take root, not in the sense of making their world our home, but in the sense of enabling the gospel to flourish deep in the hearts and lives of our hosts. Thus the call of the Spirit is the empowerment to take up and leave our homes and our comfort zones, to be guests of others in strange places, so that the triune God can become the home for us all. Herein is accomplished our own transformation, touched through the Spirit by the

---

10. Mine might be called an eschatological theology of migration, precisely due to its pneumatological dynamic, in which case it extends what Andrew Walls calls the Adamic (involuntary) and Abrahamic (redemptive) models of biblical migration; see Walls, "Toward a Theology of Migration."

differences represented in the hearts and lives of others. The Spirit immigrates betwixt, between, and through our own diasporic crossing (repeatedly: back and forth—sometimes literally but at least figuratively) over the borders and margins that had previously divided "us" from "them."

From an Asian American perspective, then, such a theologically funded hospitality works in multiple directions. On the one hand, Asian Americans, Christian or not, are guests and hosts in a multicultural United States; here Asian American Christians find ourselves playing multiple roles, depending on the context, with such roles often shifting. On the other hand, pent-evangelical Christians, Asian American or not, have the obligation, in following out the trinitarian life of God, to host others—nonevangelical Christians or even non-Christians—and to be guests of these neighbors as well; Evangelicals who may be more comfortable being hosts rather than guests in these contexts need to be more intentional about emulating Jesus, both the ultimate divine host yet also the ultimate human guest in his incarnational journey. Amid these trajectories of hospitality Asian American Pentecostals and Evangelicals find themselves relating to other (nonevangelical and non-Christian) Asian Americans, other non-Asian Americans, and other non-Asian American Evangelicals—being hosts in some circumstances and guests in others. Any pent-evangelical theology that is not capable of supporting or inspiring faithful Christian witness in these divergent and in some instances dissonant contexts will need to be reconstructed, since these are realities of the globalizing world of the twenty-first century that are not going to disappear anytime soon.

When all of this finally happens, the eschatological transmigration will occur, one that will involve the coming down of the new Jerusalem from out of heaven, and that will involve the renewal of the heavens and the earth so that they and all their inhabitants can become the final dwelling place of the living God.[11] This is the Christian and pent-evangelical hope, for sure; equally sure is that its realization, at least according to human standards, remains distant.

---

11. As beautifully argued, in the thesis that the cosmos is destined to become the dwelling place of the Spirit and the inhabitation of the triune God, by Frank D. Macchia, *Justified in the Spirit*.

4.7

Toward a Pentecostal-Political-Theology[1]

THE PRECEDING SUGGESTS THAT there is no one coherent formulation for pentecostal political theology; rather, at best there are many pentecostal political theologies related to the diversity of pentecostal political postures and practices. While some may despair then about the fortunes for pentecostal political theology, I here draw on prior work to suggest that there are resources within the pentecostal tradition for informing not just renewal theology in particular but the discussion of Christian political theology more generally.[2] The following extends the proposal by triangulating around the task politically, biblically, and theologically.

Politically, there can be no doubt that there is no one modality of pentecostal political response. Pentecostal churches, congregations, and communities in different political environments and eras have responded variously to their immediate contexts. In many cases, responses have shifted and been moderated over time: what may have been expedient and effective at one point for specific purposes has given way to other approaches more relevant to new conditions. Divergent strategies address the range of challenges and take advantage of different opportunities.

One way forward would be to draw from the five-fold gospel to also think pluralistically about pentecostal political theology. If the five-fold pentecostal christology announces that the person and saving work of Christ involves multiple aspects or dimensions, then there is no reason to

---

1. Yong, "Global Pentecostalisms and the Public Sphere," forthcoming.
2. See Yong, *In the Days of Caesar*.

think that this christological polyvalence is bereft of political implications. Jesus who meets embodied human beings in these various ways can thereby also be seen to inspire a range of political practices and commitments, ones that empower redemptive political engagement spiritually, materially, missionally, holistically, and transformatively.

It turns out that the scriptural heart of pentecostal spirituality, the Day of Pentecost narrative in the book of Acts, also supports such a multivalent approach to political theology. The many tongues enabled by the Holy Spirit announced the divine plan to redeem the many languages so they could declare God's wondrous works (Acts 2:4–11). Languages, however, exist not as abstractions, but are carried by material, social, and historical cultures. Hence, the salvaging of the many tongues potentially redeems also the many histories, the many cultures, and the many political economies through which such languages are constituted. This does not imply that all cultural, economic, and political arrangements are therefore equal and to be naively embraced; it does suggest that nothing can be presumed to be beyond the pale of God's redemptive purposes.[3] The New Testament vision itself suggests that in the end, the kings of the earth and the nations will bring their gifts into the New Jerusalem, to the glory and honor of God (Rev 21:24–26).

Theologically then, pentecostal political thought so construed is christological (according to the five-fold christology) and pneumatological (according to the Spirit's outpouring on all flesh on the Day of Pentecost), and hence thoroughly trinitarian. The Spirit of Christ enables discernment of the form of Christ in the many political environments wherein Christ-followers find themselves so as to empower a faithful type of political thinking and acting appropriate to that context. There is no one political theology for all times and places simply because there is no one time and place; but there is also always a proper and appropriate political praxis wherein followers of Christ are led by his Spirit to bear witness to the triune God in that public domain. Hence the many tongues of the Spirit empower Christ-like witness in word and deed relevant to the social, economic, and political demands made on historical human beings.[4]

Such an approach draws deeply from the wellsprings of pentecostal spirituality and theology rooted in the original pentecostal experience of the Azusa Street generation to open up multiple possibilities for thinking coherently about political theology beyond the other-worldly arc charted by dispensationalist eschatology. Just as the mission fostered racial reconciliation

---

3. I provide such a political-theological reading of Luke-Acts in my *Who is the Holy Spirit?*.

4. Yong, "What Spirit(s), Which Public(s)?"

(although its promise here has never been fulfilled), social ministry, and a holistic approach to Christian life that was capable of sustaining pentecostal mission toward the ends of the earth, so also are recent pentecostal and charismatic theologians attempting to retrieve and develop these more expansively as theologies of work, paradigms for liberative social ethics, and visions of personal and social transformation. Christian prosperity in this vein is understood to include the flourishing of whole communities, across vastly different historical and cultural contexts, and amidst divergent socio-economic and political domains, including not only other Christians but also all who find themselves in the public square.[5]

Many tongues and many practices, however, lead neither to the politically correct and bland tolerance of difference nor to political impotence. The pneumatological thrust of pentecostal political theology includes a prophetic dimension. The Spirit of Christ is also the Spirit of prophecy and hence empowers prophetic speech and activity even in the public sphere, not only as related to nation-states but especially in the civil, cultural, and social domains. In this case, the pentecostal prophethood of believers—an extension of the Reformation priesthood of believers[6]—ensures that for those called to bear witness in the public square, there may be occasions when a counter-cultural and counter-political voice will need to be registered. In some extreme cases, Spirit-inspired and empowered witness may involve martyrdom, consistent with the apostolic understanding that equated the two. Otherwise, a prophetic pentecostal political praxis takes as exemplary the Hebrew prophets who confronted the powers in the name of Yahweh; in contemporary parlance, this translates into confrontation with cultural, social, economic, and political evils in Christ's name.[7]

In the end, however, pentecostal political theology will simply need to reflect on pentecostal political praxis, however inconsistent and multifarious such may be. Continued pentecostal expansion predicted by almost all demographers suggests that renewal Christianity's influence in the public square will only continue to grow. Pentecostal media will extend further and further; pentecostal-charismatic economic power will create new markets, and their political numbers will demand appeasement; and renewal mission and evangelism will continue to grate at and even against other influences, agendas, interests, and ideologies.[8] Pentecostal pragmatism will continue to

5. E.g., Villafañe, *The Liberating Spirit*; Self, *Flourishing Churches and Communities*; Augustine, *Pentecost, Hospitality, and Transfiguration*.

6. See Stronstad, *The Prophethood of All Believers*.

7. As exemplified in Solivan, *The Spirit, Pathos, and Liberation*; and Beckford, *Dread and Pentecostal*.

8. See Kalu, *African Pentecostalism*.

drive renewal navigation in these public domains. If pentecostal theologians do not provide guidance that can inform pentecostal praxis in ever-shifting and complexifying contexts, then so much the worse for the renewal interface with the public square.

PART FIVE

Luke-Acts

5.1

Spirit Christology and Spirit Soteriology[1]

SPIRIT CHRISTOLOGY IN LUKE-ACTS

NOW FOR A THEOLOGICAL understanding of the good news for humankind: the person and work of Jesus Christ. Given the experiential dimension of pentecostal theology (chap. 1 above) and the exegetical privileging of Luke-Acts in pentecostal hermeneutics, I suggest a form of Spirit christology: Jesus is the revelation of God precisely as the man anointed by the Spirit of God to herald and usher in the reign of God.[2] This Spirit christology proposal is not meant, however, to replace the dominant Logos christology of the theological tradition. The two christologies are complementary (see further §2.3.1); Spirit christology is a fully biblical but marginalized theological perspective that can speak to, and needs to be reappropriated for, our time.

The conviction regarding Spirit christology derives from explicitly Lukan material. For starters, there is Jesus' own explicit self-understanding: "The Spirit of the Lord is upon me, because he has anointed me to bring good news to the poor. He has sent me to proclaim release to the captives and recovery of sight to the blind, to let the oppressed go free, to proclaim the year of the Lord's favor" (Luke 4:18–19, quoting Isa 61:1–2). Building on this, there are the early Christian kerygmatic claims regarding Jesus of Nazareth as "a man attested to you by God with deeds of power, wonders, and

1. Yong, *The Spirit Poured Out on All Flesh*, 86–91.

2. Here and in §2.1.3 are elaborated ideas about Spirit christology and Spirit soteriology previously sketched in Yong, *Spirit-Word-Community*, 28–34.

signs that God did through him among you, as you yourselves know—this man, handed over to you according to the definite plan and foreknowledge of God, you crucified and killed by the hands of those outside the law" (Acts 2:22b–23), and as the one "that God has made . . . both Lord and Messiah, this Jesus whom you crucified" (2:36).[3] Thus the earliest Christians prayed to God about "your holy servant Jesus, whom you anointed" (4:27), and spoke about "how God anointed Jesus of Nazareth with the Holy Spirit and with power, how he went about doing good and healing all who were oppressed by the devil, for God was with him" (Acts 10:38).

The emerging picture of Jesus as the Christ, the Spirit-anointed revelation of God, needs to be understood in terms of his person and work. Spirit christology sees Jesus not only as one anointed by the Spirit to do the mighty works of God but as a fully anointed one whose life from beginning to end was of the Spirit.[4] Luke records that Jesus was conceived by the Spirit in the womb of Mary (Luke 1:35; cf. Matt 1:18); that his dedication as a baby was presided over by the Spirit (2:25–32); that he grew strong in spirit and in wisdom (the latter associated with the Spirit; 1:80; 2:52; cf. Isa 11:2); that the Spirit descended upon him "in bodily form" at his baptism (3:21–22); that he was then led by the Spirit into the wilderness (4:1); that he overcame the temptations of the devil and returned to Galilee "filled with the power of the Spirit" (4:14); that his public ministry, inaugurated in the synagogue of Nazareth, was anointed by the Spirit from beginning to end (4:18–19); and that his death was a matter of his commending his spirit to the Father (23:46). The author of Hebrews makes explicit further details about the life and death of Christ, details consistent with Luke's portrait. Besides confirming the humanity of Jesus in no uncertain terms—that Jesus was "like his brothers and sisters in every respect" (Heb 2:17) and that he "offered up prayers and supplications, with loud cries and tears, to the one who was able to save him from death, and . . . he learned obedience through what he suffered" (5:7–8)—Hebrews also notes that Jesus offered himself up on the cross "through the eternal Spirit" (9:14). Finally, the life of Jesus ends not in death but in resurrection. Whereas Luke simply records Peter's proclamation that God raised Jesus from the dead (Acts 2:24, 32), Paul is much more specific about "the gospel concerning his Son, who was descended from David according to the flesh and was declared to be the Son of God with power according to the spirit of holiness by resurrection from the dead" (Rom 1:3–4; cf. 1 Tim 3:16; cf. 1 Pet 3:18).

3. Arguably, these references are at the heart of Luke's own original christology; see Zehnle, *Peter's Pentecost Discourse*, esp. 66–70.

4. See Hawthorne, *The Presence and the Power*; and Moltmann, *The Way of Jesus Christ*, esp. chap. 3.

This last Pauline claim is precisely Luke's thesis except that Luke applies it to the life and ministry of Jesus: if the Spirit of God who anointed Jesus dwells in you, the Spirit will empower you to do the same works (Acts) that Jesus did under the same anointing (Luke). Important here is the question concerning the works of Jesus. Luke's Gospel is about Jesus the messianic Christ, the anointed one, who fulfills the prophets (Luke 4:18–19; cf. Isa 61:1–2). His ministry throughout is to the poor, the downtrodden, the marginalized: witness his ministry to the lame, lepers, sinners, tax collectors, and so forth.[5] He releases the captives, literally freeing those oppressed by demons (4:32–34; 8:1–3, 26–40; 9:37–43; 11:13–15). He opens the eyes of the blind (e.g., 7:21–22; 18:35–43).[6] He sets the oppressed free, for example, the sinner woman (7:36–50), the family with the boy suffering from epileptic seizures (9:37–43), and women in general, especially in terms of their being valued as full human beings (e.g., 8:1–3; 10:38–42). Last, he proclaims the favorable year of the Lord, the liberative Day of Jubilee.[7] This refers not only to the cancellation of debts both literal (as in the Zacchaeus story; 19:1–10) and spiritual (as in the forgiveness of sins imparted by Jesus; e.g., 7:47–50) but also to the granting of a second chance at life, as was given to the widow of Nain, who, having lost her only son, would have been henceforth without voice, representation, or means in society (7:11–17).[8] Luke's Spirit christology is thus intimately tied in with the life and ministry of Jesus.

SPIRIT SOTERIOLOGY IN LUKE-ACTS

But also the Spirit's anointing of Jesus is promised to his followers (Luke 24:49). Hence the transition from Luke to Acts is the transition from Spirit christology to Spirit soteriology.[9] For Luke, the gift of the Spirit to the followers of Jesus empowers them to overcome sin, temptation, and the devil; authorizes them to cast out demons and heal the sick; and enables them to do the works of the ministry on behalf of the poor, the captives, and the oppressed—all as Jesus did. These themes need to be explicated briefly.

---

5. Pilgrim, *Good News to the Poor*; and Roth, *The Blind, the Lame, and the Poor*.

6. On these various aspects of Jesus' ministry, see Twelftree, *Jesus the Miracle Worker*.

7. Sloan, *The Favorable Year of the Lord*; and Graham, *There Shall Be No Poor among You*, chap. 1.

8. One of the few sources I have found that sees this miracle to be as much for the widow as for the son raised from the dead is Linskens, *Christ Liberator of the Poor*, 18.

9. See Shaull and Cesar, *Pentecostalism and the Future of the Christian Churches*, part II, chap. 6; and Del Colle, "Incarnation and the Holy Spirit," esp. 224–26.

First, the gospel (as good news) includes the forgiveness of sins. This was a feature of Jesus' ministry and repeatedly evidenced in early Christian proclamation (e.g., Acts 3:19; 5:31; 10:43; 13:38–39; 26:18; cf. Luke 24:47).[10] It is consistent with the Pauline claim that Christ enables the forgiveness of sins. Further, it heralds the day of the Lord's favor, when all sins and debts are canceled (cf. Matt 18:23–27). Most important, the forgiveness of sins is linked with the gift of the Holy Spirit (Acts 2:38; cf. John 20:22–23), a connection we will return to momentarily (§2.2.2).

Second, the gospel includes deliverance from the devil and his demons in realizing the eschatological reign of God. Jesus not only exorcised demons[11] but also declared that "if it is by the finger of God ['Spirit of God'; see Matt 12:28] that I cast out the demons, then the kingdom of God has come to you" (Luke 11:20).[12] The Twelve were given authority over demons and diseases even as they were commissioned to proclaim the kingdom of God (9:1–2), and the seventy returned rejoicing, "Lord, in your name even the demons submit to us" (10:17). The early church continued this ministry of deliverance as empowered by the Spirit (Acts 5:16; 8:6–7; 13:6–12; 16:16–18).[13]

Third, the gospel includes the healing of the sick. The Spirit who empowered Jesus to heal also empowered the early Christians to minister healing to the sick (Acts 5:16; 8:6–7; 9:32–35; 14:8–10; 28:8–9). But note that the ancients understood salvation as healing from disease followed by the restoration of the individual to the community.[14] This is subtly communicated in Jesus' giving back to his father the boy freed of the epileptic spirit (Luke 9:42) and in the return of the lame man at the Beautiful Gate to his community (Acts 3:1–10). But healing as a communal experience is most evident in the case of cured lepers (cf. Luke 5:12–14; 17:11–19) and demoniacs who were allowed to return to their homes and communities. In these instances, the Gospel healing accounts can be understood as processes of social transformation engaging the unbelieving community and breaking social taboos rather than merely in individualistic senses.[15] Salvation is now

---

10. I am helped here by Hurtado, *Lord Jesus Christ*, 185–88.

11. See the charismatic scholar Twelftree, *Jesus the Exorcist*.

12. Woods, *The Finger of God and Pneumatology in Luke-Acts*, argues that in this pericope (Luke 11:14–26) Luke's redactive preference for the "finger of God" rather than the "Holy Spirit" (Matt 12:28) signifies reference to God the Father as actor against Beelzebub. At the level of Lukan studies, Woods's argument has plenty going for it. But at the canonical level, the Matthean version justifies a pneumatological understanding of Luke's text.

13. Garrett, *The Demise of the Devil*.

14. See Witherington, *The Acts of the Apostles,* appendix 2, "Salvation and Health in Christian Antiquity."

15. Percy, *Power and the Church*, chap. 2.

understood in terms of "hospitality": being reconstituted into the divine community, the new people of God. The needy are best able to appreciate the divine hospitality given through Jesus and the Spirit (the affluent need a conversion of heart), and the saved then become instruments of divine hospitality heralding the eschatological kingdom.[16]

This leads, fourth, to the gospel as directed toward the needs of the poor, the freeing of captives, and the liberation of the oppressed, precisely through calling into reality a new community and social order wherein there is neither rich nor poor, slave nor free, oppressed nor oppressor (Gal 3:28; Col 3:11).[17] This is most clearly seen in the communalism of the early church, "All who believed were together and had all things in common" (Acts 2:44); in God's empowering and using uneducated and ordinary persons (Acts 4:13), including women (e.g., 21:8–9); and in the leaders of the early church as servants of all (Acts 6:1–6; cf. Luke 9:48), among other manifestations. These are essential features of the new community of God brought about by the outpouring of the Holy Spirit on the day of Pentecost (see §2.2.1).

Last but not least, the gospel also has an eschatological dimension that is both realized and future. Jesus himself notes that the reign of God is not merely coming: "For in fact, the kingdom of God is among you" (Luke 17:21). Further, the promised outpouring of the Spirit makes present the "last days" (Acts 2:17), which Jesus was anointed to proclaim and inaugurate (Luke 4:19). Certainly the church continues to anticipate the return of Jesus (Acts 1:11), and he "must remain in heaven until the time of universal restoration that God announced long ago through his holy prophets" (Acts 3:21). But in the meanwhile, the church lives betwixt and between; in the now and yet anticipating the not-yet; as saved, as being saved, and yet looking to full salvation. It looks to be saved from the wrath to come (Rom 5:9) even while believing that "salvation is nearer to us now than when we became believers" (Rom 13:11b).

These dimensions—the forgiveness of sins, the deliverance from evil powers, the healing of the body, the liberation of the poor and oppressed, the establishment of the new people of God, and the eschatological salvation of God—identify constitutive elements for a pentecostal understanding of salvation informed throughout by pneumatology. Here follows the sketch of a pneumatological soteriology that integrates these biblical themes and insights with the pentecostal experiences of the Spirit delineated in the preceding chapter.

16. Byrne, *The Hospitality of God*.
17. Cassidy, *Jesus, Politics, and Society*; and Wenk, *Community-Forming Power*.

5.2

Luke-Acts and the Trinitarian Shape of Hospitality[1]

JESUS AND HOSPITALITY

WE BEGIN WITH JESUS as the paradigm of hospitality because he represents and embodies the hospitality of God.[2] Indeed, as the authorized representative of God's salvific hospitality, Jesus is inhabited by and filled with the power of the Holy Spirit (Luke 4:1, 14; cf. Acts 10:38) in order "to bring good news to the poor . . . to proclaim release to the captives and recovery of sight to the blind, to let the oppressed go free, [and] to proclaim the year of the Lord's favor" (Luke 4:18b–19).[3] In the Lukan perspective, Jesus is the anointed one, the Christ, precisely as the one empowered in all aspects of his life and ministry by the Holy Spirit. It is in this sense that we can understand the entire life of Jesus, including his ministry of hospitality, as pneumatically or pneumatologically constituted. While much can be said about Jesus and his Spirit-inspired hospitality in Luke, we will focus on three motifs.

First, Jesus characterizes the hospitality of God in part as the exemplary recipient of hospitality. From his conception in Mary's womb by the

---

1. Yong, *Hospitality and the Other*, 101–05.
2. Byrne, *The Hospitality of God*.
3. That Jesus' ministry in Luke is focused on the traditionally marginalized of society is not insignificant; see Cardenal, *The Gospel in Solentiname*, passim; Hensman, *Agenda for the Poor*; and Prior, *Jesus the Liberator*.

power of the Holy Spirit to his birth in a manger through to his burial (in a tomb of Joseph of Arimathea), Jesus was dependent on the welcome of others. As "the Son of Man has nowhere to lay his head" (Luke 9:58), he relied on the goodwill of many, staying in their homes and receiving whatever they served (10:5-7). Thus during his public ministry, he is a guest of Simon Peter (4:38-39), Levi (5:29), Martha (10:38), Zacchaeus (19:5), and various Pharisees and unnamed homeowners (5:17; 7:36; 11:37; 14:1; 22:10-14).[4]

But it is precisely in his role as guest that Jesus also announces and enacts, through the Holy Spirit, the hospitality of God. As evidenced in one of the last scenes in the Gospel, for example, Jesus is invited by two disciples to stay with them because the night was at hand (24:29). Yet rather than they serving him, it is he who "took bread, blessed and broke it, and gave it to them" (24:30), at which moment they recognized that it was they who had been guests in the presence of the divine all along.[5] Similarly, throughout his public ministry, Jesus as the recipient of hospitality is at the same time the one who heralds and personifies the redemptive hospitality of God. He is the "journeying prophet" of the Spirit who eats at the tables of others but at the same time proclaims and brings to pass the eschatological banquet of God for all those who are willing to receive it.[6] Those who welcome Jesus into their homes become, in turn, guests of the redemptive hospitality of God.[7]

This leads, second, to the observation that it is in the various meal scenes in the Gospel wherein we see that the most eager recipients of the divine hospitality were not the religious leaders but the poor and the oppressed. In fact, the meal scenes can be understood as pneumatically constituted speech acts through which Jesus calls for the religious leaders to repent of their self-serving interests precisely in order to "share in the meal fellowship with repentant and forgiven sinners."[8] To do so, Jesus frequently breaks the rules of hospitality, upsets the social conventions of meal fellowship (e.g., Jesus does not wash before dinner), and even goes so far as to rebuke his hosts.[9] Luke thus shows that it is Jesus, not the religious lead-

---

4. This list can be supplemented by details in the other Gospels—e.g., Mark 3:20; 7:17, 24; 9:28; 10:10; 14:3; and Matt 9:10; 17:25; 26:6, 18.

5. Geitz, *Entertaining Angels*, 28-32.

6. Moessner, *Lord of the Banquet*; cf. Hultgren, "The Johannine Footwashing (13.1-11) as a Symbol of Eschatological Hospitality."

7. As in Zacchaeus, who though short in stature, has received salvation as a son of Abraham; cf. Luke 19:1-9, and Parsons, *Body and Character in Luke and Acts*, 107.

8. Heil, *The Meal Scenes in Luke-Acts*, 312.

9. Gowler, "Hospitality and Characterization in Luke 11:37-54."

ers, who is the broker of God's authority,[10] and it is on this basis that Jesus establishes, through the power of the Spirit, the inclusive hospitality of the kingdom. This involves not only women, children, and slaves,[11] but also the poor, the crippled, the blind, and the lame who are the oppressed and marginalized of the ancient world (Luke 14:21).[12]

Last for our purposes but not least, observe Jesus' teaching on hospitality in the parable of the Good Samaritan (10:25–37). In spite of the fact that the Samaritans had just rejected Jesus' visitation (9:51–56),[13] Jesus nevertheless presents the Samaritan as fulfilling the law, loving his neighbor, and embodying divine hospitality.[14] If the Samaritans were those of the other religion to the Jews of the first century, what implications does this parable hold regarding those in other faiths for Christians in the twenty-first century? Might people of other faiths not only be instruments through which God's revelation comes afresh to the people of God, but also perhaps be able to fulfill the requirements for inheriting eternal life (10:25) precisely through the hospitality that they show to their neighbors (which includes Christians)?[15]

Now the question for us is whether Luke intends his portrait of Jesus to be merely informative (locutionary) or commendable to and even normative for (illocutionary) his readers. Put alternatively, what does the hospitality of Jesus—that given as host and that received as guest—mean for those who confess him as Christ, the Spirit-anointed one, and Lord?[16] Part of Luke's answer comes in his follow-up volume, the book of Acts.

---

10. Thiselton, "Christology in Luke, Speech-Act Theory, and the Problem of Dualism in Christology after Kant," makes this argument about Jesus' performative speech acts representing the authority of God and thus functioning legally within this institutional framework.

11. On this point, see LaVerdiere, *Dining in the Kingdom of God*, 192–93; cf. Resseguie, *Spiritual Landscape*, chap. 4.

12. I argue at length elsewhere that this inclusion of people with disabilities is also not marginal to the message of the Gospel; see Yong, *Theology and Down Syndrome*.

13. For discussion of the acrimonious relations between Jews and Samaritans in the first century, see Ford, *My Enemy Is My Guest*, esp. 79–83. But note that in John's Gospel, the Samaritans actually do welcome Jesus through the witness of the woman at the well; see Fehribach, *The Women in the Life of the Bridegroom*, chap. 3.

14. Homrighausen, "Who Is My Neighbor?," esp. 405–07; and McFarland, "Who Is My Neighbor?"

15. I argue these points in detail in Yong, *The Spirit Poured Out on All Flesh*, 241–44.

16. These are the questions of Arens, "Jesus' Communicative Actions"; and Burrows, "The Hospitality of Christ and the Church's Resurrection."

HOSPITALITY AND THE EARLY CHURCH

Put succinctly, the hospitality of God manifest in Jesus the anointed one in Luke is now extended through the early church in Acts by the power of the same Holy Spirit.[17] On the one hand, the Spirit is the divine guest resident in the hearts and lives of all the people of God upon whom she has been poured out; on the other hand, the Spirit empowers from within the body of Christ (the anointed ones) to bear witness to the hospitable God to the ends of the earth (see Acts 1:8). We will focus our discussion on the missionary journeys of St. Paul.

As with Jesus and Peter before him,[18] Paul is also both a recipient and conduit of God's hospitality. He was first the beneficiary of divine hospitality through those who led him by the hand, and then through Judas on Straight Street, Ananias, other followers of Jesus who helped him escape from conspiring enemies, and Barnabas (Acts 9:8, 11, 17-19, 25, 27, 30; cf. 11:25-26). Then during his missionary journeys, he is "prevailed" upon by Lydia, a new convert, to stay in her home (16:15b),[19] and then has his wounds treated by the Philippian jailer (16:32-34). Paul is also a guest of Jason of Thessalonica (17:7), Prisca and Aquila at Corinth (18:3), Titius Justus also at Corinth (18:7), Philip the evangelist at Caesarea (21:8), Mnason in Jerusalem (21:16), and unnamed disciples at Troas, Tyre, Ptolemais, and Sidon (20:8; 21:4, 7; 27:3), staying with each varying lengths of time.

Along the way, Paul is escorted by Bereans (17:15), protected by two Roman centurions (23:23-24; 27:43), cared for by friends (24:23; 27:3), and entertained by Felix the governor (24:26). During the storm threatening the voyage to Rome, under custody, Paul hosts the breaking of bread, which itself becomes significant as a life-giving event that foreshadows the salvation of 276 people on the ship (27:33-37).[20] After the shipwreck, Paul is guest of

17. This motif of hospitality is evident throughout Acts; see Fernando, *The NIV Application Commentary*, esp. 127-28, 134-35, 314-15, 324-25, 330-31, 452-53, 510-11, and passim.

18. Due to space constraints, I pass over the ministry of Peter, who is both guest of and host to, albeit in different respects, Simon the tanner (Acts 10:6), Cornelius' servants (10:23)—note that Peter hosts Cornelius' servants while he himself is a guest of Simon the tanner!—Cornelius the centurion (10:48), and Mary the mother of John Mark (12:12-17).

19. John Gillman notes that for both Lydia and the jailer, ritual baptism was only part of their Christian initiation and "the acceptance of hospitality in their home was also an integral part of the full initiation experience ... From a theological perspective it is important that the authenticity of a believer's faith is acknowledged not only by the believer himself/herself but in interaction with the community of the faithful"; see Gillman, "Hospitality in Acts 16," esp. 194.

20. LaVerdiere, *The Breaking of the Bread*, chap. 6.

the Maltese islanders in general and of Publius the chief official in particular (28:2–10), and then later of some brothers on Puteoli (28:14). The book of Acts closes with Paul as host, welcoming all who were open to receiving the hospitality of God (28:23–30).

This giving and receiving of hospitality is also manifested throughout the first century church. For the early Christians, the house or home "becomes a new sort of sacred space, where the reign of God produces the community of grace, the house of God, *Beth-El*, where God dwells."[21] If the meal scenes in Luke's Gospel anticipated the eschatological banquet of God to come, in Acts they enact and realize the meal fellowship of God that marks the reconciliation of Jew, Samaritan, and Gentile, male and female, young and old, slave and free (cf. 2:17–18) in the present life of the church. Hence, the first Christians who had received the gift of God's Holy Spirit "had all things in common . . . broke bread at home and ate their food with glad and generous hearts" (2:44, 46; cf. 4:32–37 and 5:42). They cared for one another and ensured a "daily distribution of food" (6:1).[22] It is within this framework of mutuality and hospitality that "day by day the Lord added to their number those who were being saved" (2:47b).[23]

What is of central import for our purposes both in the life of Jesus and in the ministry of the early church is the themes of household relationships, table fellowship, and journeying and itinerancy.[24] In all of these cases, not only is Christian life and Christian mission mutually intertwined, but we have seen that the roles of guests and hosts are fluid, continuously reversing.[25] What implications does this Lukan portrayal have for a theology of hospitality?

---

21. Berryhill, "From Dreaded Guest to Welcoming Host," 85.

22. Capper, "Reciprocity and the Ethic of Acts," notes that after Acts chapter 6, this theme of mutual communion is replaced by almsgiving—e.g., 9:36; 10:2, 4, 31; 11:27–30; 20:35; 24:17—and suggests that "to restrict community of property to a past withdrawn from the present experience of the Church is also for Luke to postpone it to the eschatological future and not to demand its full realization in the present community" (511).

23. Riddle, "Early Christian Hospitality."

24. This theme of journeying has recently been studied in Luke-Acts by Baban, *On the Road Encounters in Luke-Acts*, although Baban's focus is specifically on the disciples on the road to Emmaus, Philip on the road to Gaza, and Saul on the road to Damascus. For more on hospitality understood within the framework of journey and pilgrimage, see George, *The Silent Roots*, chap. 3.

25. Koenig, *New Testament Hospitality*, 91–103.

5.3

"Times of Refreshing" from the Lord
A Lukan Glimpse of the Universal Restoration[1]

THE PETRINE (AND LUKAN) claim that the Spirit has been poured out on all flesh in the last days denotes that the time for the restoration of Israel is at hand, and that "everyone who calls on the name of the Lord shall be saved" (Acts 2:21). So far, I have presumed that such a Lukan eschatology is both Jewish and ecclesial, both present and future, and both now/already and not-yet—but I have not done much to defend this assumption. More comment is needed especially in light of Hans Conzelmann's effectively taking the study of Lukan theology to another whole level a generation ago precisely by arguing that the Lukan account was a salvation history narrative intended to address the disappointments regarding the delay of the Parousia.[2] If Conzelmann's resolution was to read Luke as redirecting belief in the imminent return of Christ to the hope for a future resurrection,[3] the alternative responses might either insist that Luke promulgated a realized eschatology of some sort or that there remains a future dimension of judgment and resurrection, with both proleptically anticipated in Jesus.[4]

---

1. Yong, *In the Days of Caesar*, 348–52.
2. Conzelmann, *The Theology of St. Luke*, esp. 131–32.
3. On this interpretation, fairly widespread among Lukan scholars at the time that Conzelmann wrote, Luke "is required by practical conditions to correct the over-expectant attitude by emphasizing the delay that was to be expected"; see Cadbury, "Acts and Eschatology," 320.
4. Bruce, "Eschatology in Acts."

I would think instead that a proper response would reject the available disjunctions—either realized or not, either eschatology or salvation history—and emphasize instead that with Jesus, in the Lukan view, "the end time, new age of salvation had broken into this world."⁵ This allows not merely for the maintenance of the already-but-not-yet tension, but also invites a living out of an eschatological faith in a way that links the gospel's "eschatological claims with one's present manner of life."⁶ Such a reading is more faithful to the Lukan vision, which rejects any speculation about Parousia and the final redemption (Acts 1:6–7) while simultaneously exhorting its hearers and readers to respond to the present moment when and where past history and the coming future are interrelated.⁷ It is in such a framework that I approach Peter's proclamation: "Repent therefore, and turn to God so that your sins may be wiped out, so that times of refreshing may come from the presence of the Lord, and that he may send the Messiah appointed for you, that is, Jesus, who must remain in heaven until the time of cosmic restoration that God announced long ago through his holy prophets" (3:19–21).

This declaration occurs in Peter's sermon following the healing of the lame man at the Beautiful Gate (7.3.1). In the following, I elucidate the eschatological elements of this text at four levels: that of the healing of the body, that of the restoration of Israel, that of the renewal of the jubilee economy, and that of the redemption of the world and of all things. First, the context of this assertion is Peter's sermon in response to the crowd that was "filled with wonder and amazement at what had happened" to the lame man (3:10). Peter said "the faith that is through Jesus has given him this perfect health in the presence of all of you" (3:16). As Jesus' healings of the sick by the power of the Spirit were signs of the coming kingdom (7.3.1), so also the Spirit's healing of the lame man through Peter and John's mediation of the name of Jesus was a sign of the "last days." It turned out that the (formerly) lame man stayed with Peter and John even through the night in prison,⁸ but this did not deter the apostles from insisting the next day that the man who remained in their midst provided an indubitable witness to the healing and saving power of Jesus' name (4:9–12). In short, the healing of the man crippled from birth was a sign that the power of the Spirit was present and that the beginning of the end of the age had dawned.

---

5. Chance, *Jerusalem, the Temple, and the New Age in Luke-Acts*, 3–4. I should note that Chance sees much more of a role for both Jerusalem and the temple in the future dimension of Luke's eschatology than might be suggested, for example, in Acts 7:44–50; cf. my *Who is the Holy Spirit?*, chap. 16.

6. Carroll, *Response to the End of History*, 167.

7. Nielsen, *Until It Is Fulfilled*, 280; see also Nielsen's discussion in chap. 6.

8. See Mundhenk, "The Invisible Man (Acts 4.9–10)."

Second, the healing of the lame man occurred at the temple and at a time of prayer (3:1),[9] and Peter's post-healing sermon was given in Solomon's Portico and address to his fellow Israelites (3:11–12). The sermon further includes references to the "God of Abraham, the God of Isaac, and the God of Jacob, the God of our ancestors" (3:13), links the miraculous healing and prophetic ministry of Jesus with that of Moses (3:22), warns that "everyone who does not listen to that prophet will be utterly rooted out from the people" (3:23), and specifically invites the repentance of the audience in order that they might experience the full restoration promised by the ancient prophets. There is no reason to bifurcate Israel from the church (as does dispensationalism) in this scenar0io, to think that the invitation extended to Israel's repentance has been withdrawn, or to read this only as applying to the specific historical circumstances surrounding the healing of the lame man. Instead, there is every reason in the pentecostal this-is-that hermeneutic (3.1.1) to view this call to repentance as an open-ended one extended to Israel in celebration of the healing of the crippled man and in anticipation of the nation's full restoration. As Dennis Hamm suggests, "Luke's paraenetic point is: repent and enter the times of refreshment already come upon us, for that is the view of the remainder of Acts regarding the opportunity of the Jews."[10]

Third, however, note that the promised "times of refreshing" are connected with the forgiveness of sins (3:19), which in the immediate context has to do not only with the individual sins of the audience but with the corporate sins of Israel for its role in putting Jesus to death (3:14–15).[11] But the forgiveness of sins had earlier been linked with baptism—now understandable as an eschatological sacrament—and the gift of the Holy Spirit (2:38), and we already know that the last-days outpouring of the Spirit had begun to usher in "the Lord's great and glorious day" (2:20), and that, in turn, was a sign of the arrival of the "year of the Lord's favor" (Luke 4:19) and of the age of Jubilee (7.3.1). Another clue that invites an equation of the times of jubilee with the healing of the crippled man is that while Peter and John have neither silver nor gold (Acts 3:6) they are conduits of the eschatological power of the Spirit to "proclaim release to the captives and . . . let the oppressed go free" (Luke 4:18). Finally, the reference to the healed

---

9. I should note that Chance, *Jerusalem, the Temple, and the New Age in Luke-Acts*, sees much more of a role for both Jerusalem and the temple in the future dimension of Luke's eschatology than might be suggested, for example, in Acts 7:44–50. My reading is that the eschatological rebuilding of the temple itself is not as significant for Luke's theology of Israel's final restoration. See Yong, *Who is the Holy Spirit?*, chap. 16.

10. Hamm, "Acts 3:12–26," 208.

11. Barrett, "Faith and Eschatology in Acts 3," esp. 10.

man "walking and leaping and praising God" (3:8) alludes to the messianic promises of the coming age when "the lame shall leap like a deer, and the tongue of the speechless sing for joy" (Isa 35:6).[12] I would thus agree with Goran Lennartsson that the promised restoration is the messianic era that can be "viewed both as an 'extended Sabbath,' and the release of Jubilee."[13] In other words, the pneumatological apocalyptic (unveiling) amidst these winds of refreshing bring about not the end-times economic upheaval and devastation anticipated in dispensationalism, but the eschatological shalom of the people of God.

Finally, then, I suggest that Peter's invitation to repentance is not limited to Israel. Rather, the promised "times of refreshing" are interconnected with the "time of universal restoration" that will envelop both the Gentiles and the creation as a whole. The latter cosmic restoration is what I am primarily interested in here. The Isaiah passage alluded to regarding the leaping man refers not only to the lame leaping like deer but also to the revitalization of creation itself:

> For waters shall break forth in the wilderness,
>   and streams in the desert;
> the burning sand shall become a pool,
>   and the thirsty ground springs of water;
> the haunt of jackals shall become a swamp,
>   the grass shall become reeds and rushes (Isa 35:6b–7).[14]

In other words, the "universal restoration" will involve the renewal of all creation, including (as I have already suggested—4.3.1) its principalities and powers. The Spirit who now groans in and through the creation for relief and redemption will then be given to bring about the refreshment and rest of the messianic age.[15]

Such a universal restoration does not, however, result in any simplistic doctrine of universalism. Rather, these eschatological contentions are best considered subjunctively, with their fulfillment hinging upon the response of free creatures. Thus, the Petrine call to repentance establishes one of the primary contingencies related to the universalistic hope. But if from the perspective of stubborn and hard-hearted humanity there is no hope for either the restoration of Israel or for the redemption of the world, then from

---

12. See further Hamm, "Acts 3,1–10."

13. Lennartsson, *Refreshing and Restoration*, 226.

14. The context is the messianic restoration of Israel from exile; see Grogan, "Isaiah," 221.

15. Shade, "The Restoration of Israel in Acts 3:12–26 and Lukan Eschatology," 153–57.

the view of the miraculous (even if subjunctively understood) outpouring of the Spirit upon all flesh, "What is impossible for mortals is possible for God" (Luke 18:27).

5.4

Promising to Restore the Kingdom of Israel, and the Spirit Came![1]

BUT WHAT EXACTLY WERE the disciples expecting with regard to Jesus and the kingdom of God? We've already seen that the Jewish hopes regarding the kingdom were connected to the Messiah, who would free them from foreign rule. More precisely, the coming of the kingdom would restore the land of Israel according to the covenants made with Abraham, Moses, and David. Now let's focus our attention on what the disciples as well as Luke's readers had been led to expect regarding what the Messiah would accomplish. To do so, we should look carefully at a number of passages from the infancy narrative of Luke's Gospel.

We can begin with Mary's song of praise, well known as the "Magnificat" (Luke 1:46–55). This lowly peasant girl was told by the angel Gabriel that the child she would conceive would receive "the throne of his ancestor David. He will reign over the house of Jacob forever, and of his kingdom there will be no end" (1:32–33). Clearly, then, this miracle involves God's remembering "the promise he made to our ancestors, to Abraham and to his descendants" (1:55). But what will happen as a result of the coming of the Messiah by the Holy Spirit? Mary anticipates that the powerful will be brought down and the lowly exalted, that the rich will be impoverished while the poor will be uplifted (1:52–53).

Zechariah, a faithful priest and husband of Elizabeth, Mary's relative, had already been told that his son, John (the Baptist), would "make ready

---

1. Yong, *Who is the Holy Spirit?*, 7–11. See Luke 1:46–55, 67–79; 2:22–38.

a people prepared for the Lord" (1:17). On the day of John's circumcision (dedication), Zechariah confirms Mary's song through a prophecy from the Holy Spirit (1:67):

> Blessed be the Lord God of Israel,
>   for he has looked favorably on his people and
>   redeemed them.
> He has raised up a mighty savior for us
>   in the house of his servant David,
> as he spoke through the mouth of his holy prophets from of old,
>   that we would be saved from our enemies and from the hand of all
> who hate us (1:68–71).

Zechariah also understood that the promised salvation of Israel would involve the peaceful forgiveness of their sins (1:78–79)—which necessarily had to precede the restoration of Israel—so he did not necessarily think that the messianic kingdom would involve a violent revolution. Nevertheless, God's redemption of Israel would shine a light on those who lived in the shadow of darkness and enable them once again to serve him in holiness and righteousness.

Last, when Jesus was presented in the temple, Simeon was said to be "looking forward to the consolation of Israel" (2:25) and Anna to be anticipating "the redemption of Jerusalem" (2:38). Under the inspiration of the Holy Spirit, Simeon comes to see that the consolation and restoration of Israel is necessarily intertwined with the fate of the rest of the world:

> My eyes have seen your salvation,
>   which you have prepared in the presence of all peoples,
> a light for revelation to the Gentiles
>   and for glory to your people Israel (2:30–32).

Undoubtedly the prosperity of Israel depends on her restoration and living in peace with her Gentile neighbors.

Many contemporary readers have come to understand these references to the redemption of Israel in spiritual terms. After all, Jesus neither overthrew the Roman rule over Palestine nor established Yahweh's political reign over Israel. In fact, not only was the temple itself razed to the ground a generation later (in 70 CE), but there are other passages (to be discussed later) in Luke-Acts that seem to transfer the promises of the covenant from the Jews to the Gentiles.

But Jesus' birth is presented by Luke in terms that clearly announce his kingdom as being at least superimposed on if not replacing Caesar's. By the first century, Caesar's birthday was celebrated as symbolizing the "good news" that the emperor brought to his subjects throughout the empire, and Caesar was exalted as divine "Son of God," "lord," "redeemer," and "savior" through the cult of the emperor. Jesus is announced in precisely these terms as the "Son of the Most High" (Luke 1:32) who would restore the Davidic kingdom. So if in those days even his parents were under the rule of king Herod of Judea and governor Quirinius of Syria, and even if they were subject to Augustus Caesar's decree of taxation, Jesus' birth brought forth the angelic proclamation regarding the arrival of "a Savior, who is the Messiah, the Lord" (2:11). Readers of the Gospel could hardly have missed Luke's understanding that Jesus' arrival challenged Caesar's assumed divinity, lordship, and salvific stature.

This background helps us to understand why the disciples, after following Jesus for three years and listening to him teach about the kingdom for forty days (Acts 1:3), still wondered if the times of restoration had finally arrived. If Jesus was the Messiah, then, according to the Old Testament—alluded to throughout Mary's Magnificat and Zechariah's prophecy—God was going to fulfill the covenant promises. Justice would be served on the enemies of Israel, on those powerful, proud, and rich Roman rulers and their aristocratic patrons (political, religious, and cultural leaders) who had conspired to keep the peasant farmworkers and landowners in poverty (through high taxation, sometimes of up to 50 percent of total crop) and thereby oppressed the lower classes. From the perspective of Mary, Joseph (a carpenter), and others at the bottom rung of Israelite society, the good news—the *euangelion*—of the Messiah's arrival brought with it tangible material expectations. If in fact Israel was to be saved from her enemies, God would have to raise up the Messiah to bring about a massive revolution.

Meanwhile, think for a moment about how the ruling classes of the first century might have reacted to news coming out of Palestine that the king long anticipated by the Jews had been born. What if they had heard that the kingdom of Jesus would be established over and against that of Caesar and his patrons and that part of the upheaval that would occur involved the leveling of the rich and powerful and the exaltation of the socially marginalized? Even if we grant for the moment that the kingdom proclaimed by Jesus was purely spiritual, the messianic expectations of the common people combined with the fears of the upper classes regarding the instability of their own social position would have been enough to cause a stir. Is it any wonder, then, that the Jewish religious leaders—groups like the chief priests, scribes, Pharisees, and Sadducees that, unlike most modern political parties, were both religious and political—were concerned enough about how Jesus might upset their own place in the sociopolitical hierarchy that they led the charge eventually to execute him?

What is clear is that the promise to restore the kingdom was connected to the promise of the Holy Spirit. We shall see later that, just as the Holy Spirit worked in the life of Jesus to bring about the kingdom, so also the Spirit empowered his followers to herald the kingdom. What does this then say about us today who are recipients of the same Holy Spirit? Perhaps there is a middle ground between thinking either that the kingdom proclaimed by Jesus is a spiritual reality located in the coming future or that we are called to be revolutionaries who would overthrow the ruling empires of our world today. Maybe this middle ground involves our being open to receiving the Spirit's empowerment so that we also might be agents who hasten the kingdom, which is in some respects already present, even if it is in other respects still to come. Maybe it might involve our engaging with and dismantling, by the power of the Spirit, the unjust structures that keep the poor impoverished, as sung about by Mary. More unimaginably, maybe the Spirit will enable the reconciliation of enemies so that salvation would come upon traditional enemies, as Zechariah prophesied, but through just peacemaking rather than by the overthrow or annihilation of the historical adversaries. Why would it be impossible to imagine today, for example, peace between Jews and Palestinians, or between Israelis and Arabs? Is it not possible that the coming of the Spirit was intended to complete the work of restoring Israel but to do so precisely by including and reconciling Jews and Gentiles rather than by perpetuating their divisions? If so, then the promise to restore the kingdom is still in the making, by the power of the Holy Spirit.

5.5

The Gift of Pentecost

Intimations of a Pneumatological Theology of Love[1]

IF THE PRECEDING CHAPTER was the pivot upon which the argument of the book turned theologically, then it has set us upon the constructive theological task that will occupy most of the remainder of our time. Central to this reconstruction will be a return to the scriptural narratives. This chapter is the first of three forays into the New Testament, each of which will wind as one strand of a threefold cord toward a pneumatological theology of love.[2] I locate this chapter here in part II because it continues the explicitly pentecostal reflections on love, albeit moving from the earlier more phenomenological, performative, and theological considerations to rereadings of Luke-Acts. Then, in the next two chapters we continue our

---

1. Yong, *Spirit of Love*, 94–99.

2. While we will stay close to the New Testament text for most of the remainder of this book, our focus is not on the grammatical level. Instead, we will be working theologically in general and from out of our pentecostal resources in particular. For this reason, while there are various words for love in the Greek New Testament—e.g., *philia, storge, epithymia, agape*—we will, unless otherwise indicated, not rely on these distinctions, staying with the general word love, since these meanings are more intertwined than not. For excellent discussions of how vast and overlapping the semantic range of these New Testament terms for love was in the first century, see Morris, *Testaments of Love*, esp. chap. 6; Furnish, *The Love Command in the New Testament*, the appendix; and Barr, "Words for Love in Biblical Greek." A more comprehensive discussion focused on agape but noting appearances and synonymous uses of the other terms is Spicq, *Agape in the New Testament*.

biblical retrieval by looking at the Pauline and Johannine materials, respectively. While our exegeses in part III will not be guided by specifically pentecostal concerns, they will be informed by the ideas developed in this part of the book. But we are getting ahead of ourselves.

Earlier (in chap. 3) we noted that the language of love has played a minimal role in more recent pentecostal theological reflection. Besides the historical reasons outlined above for this neglect, a further explanation is related to the centrality of Acts in the pentecostal scriptural imagination, and the fact that the word "love" does not appear at all in this New Testament writing.[3] Actually, Barnabas and Paul are identified as "beloved" (ἀγαπητοῖς) by the apostles in their recommendation letter to the churches in Acts 15:25. But other than this, there is no mention of love. We know, however, the book of Acts is about the Holy Spirit, and that the gift of the Holy Spirit has been associated with the gift of love in the Christian tradition. Might we be able to reframe the narrative of the Day of Pentecost outpouring of the Holy Spirit as an expression of what the Christian tradition calls the gift of love and what many early modern pentecostals called the baptism of love?

To be sure, the book of Acts is very clear that the Holy Spirit is nothing less than the gift of God.[4] Luke puts the "gift of the Holy Spirit" on the lips of Peter (Acts 2:38)[5] and associates the Spirit with gift elsewhere in his two-volume work (10:45; cf. 8:18–20 and 11:17 with Luke 11:13). And as the gift of God, the Spirit is thus also the gratuitous self-outpouring of God upon and into all of creation. Nothing requires, demands, or necessitates this self-giving—that is, in effect, the definition of the Gift, absolutely considered. In the Lukan case, such a gracious and unconditional gift of God is nothing less than the Holy Spirit of God herself.

But why is the Spirit given in the book of Acts? The most immediate explanation provided, in the Day of Pentecost narrative, can be extrapolated from Peter's reference to Joel (2:14–20; cf. Joel 2:28–32): that the gift of the Spirit is to enable prophesying by men and women, slave and free, to give dreams and visions to young and old, and, perhaps most importantly, to make it possible that *"everyone* who calls on the name of the Lord shall be saved" (2:21, emphasis added).[6] In a very real sense, these effects of the

---

3. See Hays, *The Moral Vision of the New Testament*, 201–02.

4. One of the more important books written by a pentecostal biblical scholar on this theme is Keener, *Gift and Giver*. See also Saarinen, *God and the Gift*, 36–45, for a discussion of the pervasiveness of the notion of giving and the gift in the New Testament.

5. Unless otherwise noted, all scriptural references in this section will be to the book of Acts.

6. Williams, "Upon All Flesh," deploys ideological criticism to alert us to how a

Spirit's outpouring provide insight into the purpose of the gift of the Spirit, which ultimately relate to God's desires to save all people, even the whole world, as we shall see played out in the rest of the book of Acts.

The universal scope of the redemptive work of God structuring the Acts narrative is highlighted in its first chapter, in a verse that also lies at the center of the pentecostal imagination: "you will receive power when the Holy Spirit has come upon you; and you will be my witnesses in Jerusalem, in all Judea and Samaria, and to the ends of the earth" (1:8). Whereas pentecostal interpretation has focused on the empowerment clause, I wish to emphasize the breadth of God's saving intentions instead. That the "ends of the earth" were always included in Luke's horizon is clear also in his first volume.[7] At the end of that book, it is recorded that Jesus instructed the disciples to wait in Jerusalem "until you have been clothed with power from on high" (Luke 24:49) so that they can be witnesses of the good news that "forgiveness of sins is to be proclaimed in his name to all nations, beginning from Jerusalem" (Luke 24:47). Even at the birth of Jesus, Simeon praised God that he had been privileged to have witnessed the divine salvation prepared "in the presence of all peoples, a light for revelation to the Gentiles" (Luke 2:31–32). The Acts narrative then unfolds God's redeeming work through the Spirit according to the geographical divisions laid out in 1:8. The apostolic testimony spreads from Jerusalem (2:1–5:11) through Judea (5:12–7:60) and Samaria (8:1–25), and all the way to Rome (chaps. 9–28), representative of the ends of the earth from the apostolic vantage point centered in Jerusalem.

Let us now return to the Day of Pentecost narrative in order to observe the effects of the gift of the Spirit in light of God's intended universal redemption. At the end of his explanatory sermon, Peter urges his audience, "Repent, and be baptized every one of you in the name of Jesus Christ so that your sins may be forgiven; and you will receive the gift of the Holy Spirit" (2:38). While salvation involves human repentance and baptism, it is nevertheless constituted by the person of Jesus, especially in the forgiveness

---

merely universalistic reading of Acts 2 without the appreciation of the many particular ways in which humans are constituted—ethnically, racially, socially, economically, in terms of class and gender, etc.—ends up being exclusive of such particularities. My own work has been sensitive to these readings of Acts specifically from an Asian American perspective—e.g., "The Future of Asian Pentecostal Theology," among a number of other articles and book chapters on pentecostal and evangelical readings of Acts. The following presumes the importance of particularity amidst the universalizing thrust of the Acts narrative.

7. For more on how the Third Gospel foreshadows the universal scope of the apostolic mission in Acts, see Lane, *Luke and the Gentile Mission*; and Wilson, *The Gentiles and the Gentile Mission in Luke-Acts*.

of sins. This is significant for a number of reasons, including the fact that the forgiveness of sins was precisely what this original audience needed as those who were responsible, even if only indirectly, for the crucifixion and murder of Jesus (2:36). If Jesus himself had forgiven his persecutors and tormentors (Luke 23:34), then so also was forgiveness of sins available through those who were commissioned to proclaim the good news in his name (3:19; 5:31; 8:22; 10:43; 13:38-39; 22:16; 26:18). In this case, then, the gift of God could be understood not so much in terms of the reception of something tangible but as the overlooking of the fault accruing to human sin. But the divine gift of grace is not to be understood merely in negative terms; rather, it is also to be seen as the positive capacity to receive forgiveness. Hence, God's gift results in a cleansed conscience and the removal of guilt.

In fact, this marvelous gift of forgiveness is not only made possible in Jesus' name but is interconnected with the gift of the Holy Spirit (2:38). One might say that the removal of sins (forgiveness) logically anticipates the outpouring (gift) of the Spirit. These are two sides to the one coin of God's redemptive work in human hearts and lives. Put alternatively, the Day of Pentecost outpouring of the Spirit upon all flesh is God's prevenient gift that makes possible the repentance of individuals hearts so that any who call upon the name of the Lord will experience for him- or herself the forgiveness of sins and receive the Holy Spirit. And make no mistake, "For the promise is for you, for your children, and for all who are far away, everyone whom the Lord our God calls to him" (2:39). In other words, the forgiveness of sins and the gift of the Spirit are not only available to the ends of the earth but also to the ends of time.[8] The universality of God's redemptive work has both synchronic and diachronic dimensions, covering geographic barriers while also overcoming temporal ones. This perhaps explains why Peter also says that both the forgiveness of sins and the "times of refreshing . . . from the presence of the Lord" (3:20)—arguably an oblique canonical reference to the reviving, reinvigorating work, and regenerating of the Spirit—anticipate "the time of universal restoration that God announced long ago through his holy prophets" (3:21).[9]

---

8. In fact, the "ends of the earth" (ἐσχάτου τῆς γῆς) of Acts 1:8 literally means the "ends of time"; see also Westhelle, "Liberation Theology," esp. 320-23.

9. Note that my references to God's "universal redemption" even in light of this Lukan "universal restoration" do not presume the heterodox doctrine of universalism—that all will actually be saved—since I am agnostic about what will happen in this regard. My claim is only that God "desires everyone to be saved and to come to the knowledge of the truth" (1 Tim 2:4), and in that sense the gospel has universal reach and range. Elsewhere (see *In the Days of Caesar*, 351-52) I have suggested that the possibility of the salvation of any, much less of all, is dependent in part on if, how, and to what extent those who have received the Holy Spirit bear witness to the gospel.

The immediate effects of the Day of Pentecost gift of the Spirit are described in a passage that deserves to be quoted at length:

> They devoted themselves to the apostles' teaching and fellowship, to the breaking of bread and the prayers. Awe came upon everyone, because many wonders and signs were being done by the apostles. All who believed were together and had all things in common; they would sell their possessions and goods and distribute the proceeds to all, as any had need. Day by day, as they spent much time together in the temple, they broke bread at home and ate their food with glad and generous hearts, praising God and having the goodwill of all the people. And day by day the Lord added to their number those who were being saved (2:42–47).

Two sets of comments should be made in this regard. First, the charismatic experience of the Spirit graciously empowers altruistic benevolence. Those of means were willing to part with what they had for the benefit of others who were needy. Later, Luke also notes that "There was not a needy person among them, for as many as owned lands or houses sold them and brought the proceeds of what was sold. They laid it at the apostles' feet, and it was distributed to each as any had need" (4:34–35). What Luke records here is consistent with the findings of the Godly Love project (see chap. 3). More important, it communicates an important theological truth: that the gift of the Spirit generates other gifts, in this case, economic gifts for the common good. Divine grace is in effect self-perpetuating, precisely because what is given is not just any things but the very gift of the Spirit of God herself. The result is love in action, even if it is not love as usually conceived.

Second, the pentecostal outpouring formed a community of the Spirit, a fellowship—the Greek word in 2:42 is κοινωνία—affectively united by joy, practically bound together by generosity, and spiritually oriented in worship. If we understand the Day of Pentecost gift as a baptism of love, according to the argument of the last few chapters, then we can also see the resulting fellowship of the Spirit (cf. 2 Cor 13:14) as a gracious community of love. In this case, the love of God ignites love for God, expressed in the prayers and praises of the people directed to God, and generates neighborly love, seen in the generosity and solidarity of the people with each other, as well as with those who were added to the community on a daily basis. While I want to return to elaborate more on this theme later, for now we can extend the theological truth formulated at the end of the preceding paragraph: that the gift of the Spirit generates all kinds of other gifts, some in response to God and others in the formation of a community of love around the name and person of Jesus. In other words, a gracious God forms a gracious—a grace-filled—community, and that because of the divine gift of the Spirit of love. Is this not also a manifestation of the love of God, even if not explicitly called such here?

And that is precisely the main point I want to argue about the Spirit of Pentecost: that it is nothing less than the gift of a loving God to the world. This has both salvation-historical and individual dimensions. With regard to the former, the gift of the Spirit is God's response to those who were yearning for the restoration of the kingdom of Israel (1:6) and for the redemption of Jerusalem (Luke 2:38; cf. Luke 1:55-56, 68). What most first-century Jews did not expect, however, was that God's response to this cry of their hearts would also involve the salvation of the Gentiles,[10] so that the covenantal promise made to Abraham, that "in your descendants all the families of the earth shall be blessed" (3:25; cf. Gen 12:1-3), might be fulfilled. When set within a theology of love framework, then, the Day of Pentecost outpouring is God's excessive and universal gift of love to the world, in and through the gift of the Spirit of God. God's love for Israel is thus manifest not only in her renewal and restoration but in God's keeping of the promises of the covenant so that the love of God can be poured out upon and given to all flesh.

Thus this salvation-historical rendition of the gift of the Spirit of divine love also finds concrete individual fulfillment. The gift of God's Spirit is, after all, described as a "baptism" (1:5; 11:16; cf. Luke 3:16), an inundation of the heart and the soul with the living breath of God. Thus the gift of the Holy Spirit is also talked about as an *infilling*—as a *being-filled-with* or a *being-made-full-of* the Spirit (2:4; 4:8, 31; 7:55; 9:17; 13:9, 52)—connoting an overflowing of God into human lives so that they are no longer full of themselves but full of God. The God who gives graciously of the Spirit thus spares nothing that will hinder the excessive flooding of human hearts and lives. Of course, what is suggested is that the human vessels are "space" for the divine life. Equally, it suggests that God also yearns to be yoked with human creatures, longs even to be reconciled with them, and through Christ pours out the Spirit into men and women, young and old, slave and free—in short, all flesh—as an expression of this desirous love.

On the human side, the infilling of the gift of God can only be *received* (8:15; 10:47; 19:2). This is Aquinas's passive potency, denoting the capacity of human hearts to become the dwelling or resting place (Luke 2:25) of God. Thus do human beings "suffer" the divine gift that is dispensed liberally but yet mysteriously through the presence and activity of the Spirit of love,

---

10. I have expanded on this thesis in my *Who is the Holy Spirit?*, which provides a pentecostal reading of the book of Acts as well as of the Third Gospel.

and in doing so are transformed into human receptacles of divine love. But divine love also waits patiently for human openness, thus also "suffering" human rebellion and resistance. And when hearts are finally turned to God, then, they are also ready to receive—to be impressed by and upon, to be impassioned with—the gift of God's love in the Spirit.

5.6

Pentecost and a New Theology of Diverse Dis/Abilities[1]

THE MIRACLE OF PENTECOST: A DISABILITY-INCLUSIVE READING

IT IS BY NOW commonplace to consider the inclusiveness of the Day of Pentecost narrative in linguistic and cultural terms.[2] These are, of course, connected. However, given the results of our physiognomic reading of Luke and Acts, I would resist limiting the inclusiveness of the Day of Pentecost to these two categories. More explicitly, I would argue that Jesus' acceptance of Zacchaeus and the apostle's acceptance of the eunuch invite us to think about how the early Christians were subversive of conventions that excluded those with defective and blemished bodies. To make this point, I begin first by noting in the Pentecost narrative not just the diversity of tongues but the plurality of modes of communication.[3]

---

1. Yong, *The Bible, Disability, and the Church*, 70–75.

2. See, for example, Solivan, *The Spirit, Pathos, and Liberation*, 112–18; and Macchia, "The Tongues of Pentecost."

3. I realize that my interpretation of Acts 2 in the following paragraphs is more inferential than some may be comfortable with. I'm simply proposing a possible rather than a necessary reading, as informed by a disability hermeneutic. While in the end readers will probably agree or not for different reasons, my claim is that Luke can be read from a contemporary perspective as being friendlier to rather than hostile to disability. Hence this particular disability interpretation of Acts 2 needs to be understood against my rereading of Luke-Acts as a whole. See also my *Who is the Holy Spirit?*.

The miracle of Pentecost has perennially been understood to consist, at least in part, of the miracle of inspired speech. But this miracle is only a means to an end, which is the manifestation of "God's deeds of power" (Acts 2:11). Read this way, the means can be seen as subordinate to the end, and God could just as well have chosen other means to accomplish this end. Following out this line of thinking, if God not only is capable of inspiring speech but has also created the bodily members through which speech is produced, then the incapacity to speak is no hindrance to what God can do, since God is just as capable of accomplishing his communicative intentions using other means. From a disability perspective, then, the God who creates the mute or enables the speech of the stutterer (Exod 4:10–12) is the one who empowers all communication about God's wondrous works.

But, second, there is also a minority reading of the Pentecost narrative which views its miracle as one of inspired hearing. Luke records the crowd's response that "each one *heard* them speaking in the native language of each" (Acts 2:6) and that "in our own languages we *hear* them speaking about God's deeds of power" (Acts 2:11).[4] So, the Spirit empowers not *xenolalia*, the speaking of unlearned languages, but *akolalia*, the hearing and understanding of unlearned languages.[5] But again, this miracle of hearing can be viewed as subordinate to the intended ends that manifest God's wondrous deeds. So in this case, if God not only is capable of enabling hearing but also has created the bodily members through which hearing is accomplished, I suggest that the incapacity to hear is in and of itself no hindrance to what God can do to reveal his glorious works, since God can adopt other means to accomplish his communicative intentions. In short, a disability perspective would simply insist that the God who creates the deaf or enables communication through signs (e.g., as seen in Zechariah, who is said to be only mute, not deaf; Luke 1:22, 62–63) is also the One whose speech-acts are capable of being manifest and received through the diversity of phenomenological and embodied interactions.

This leads, third, to my proposal that God's communicative speech-acts engage us through the multiplicity of our sensory capacities. On the Day of Pentecost, Peter himself recognized that the outpouring and gift of the Holy Spirit was both seen and heard (Acts 2:33). Pentecostals have generally focused on what has been most explicit in the Acts 2 narrative: the "sound like the rush of a violent wind" and the "divided tongues, as of fire" which alighted on each one (2:2–3). I suggest, however, that such

---

4. I have added the italics in both verses; thanks to Steven Fettke for reminding me to emphasize this point.

5. For some of the distinctions between xenolalia and akolalia, see Spittler, "Glossolalia," 670.

explicitly thematized sounds and images, along with the sensory capacities that mediate them (hearing and seeing), are not exclusive of the other sensory modalities that constitute our being-in-the-world. What if the miracle of Pentecost isn't limited to speaking, hearing, and seeing, but also includes touching, feeling, and perceiving? What if inspired speech is not the only means to bear witness to God's wondrous works but is one of a plurality of embodied sensory and kinesthetic capacities through which God is present and active in our midst? What if the pentecostal gift of the Spirit redeems all people—Zacchaeus and the Ethiopian eunuch included—not by transforming "them" into able-bodied standards of normalcy or by "fixing" their incapacities or impairments so that they can interact with us on our terms, but by transforming and fixing us all so that we can together be the people of God?

I see this set of proposals as an extension of the view that the list of ethnic and national provenance in Acts 2:7–11 is representative rather than exhaustive. My point is that Luke's inclusive vision of the coming Day of the Lord intersects not only with the coordinates of language, ethnicity, gender, class, and culture, but also with the coordinate of embodiment, including ability and disability. Accordingly, the miracle of Pentecost is irreducible to that of speech or of hearing; instead, the outpouring of the Spirit unleashes many tongues and many senses—many different communicative modalities—to bear witness to and receive the witness of the wondrous works of God. All forms and all types of dis/abilities, then, would be possible conduits for the Spirit's revelatory work, to those who would be receptive of the outpouring of the Spirit. If this is true, then regardless of whether or not Luke's credentials as a physician withstand critical scrutiny, he can be understood to have fulfilled the Hippocratic oath—except that rather than (merely) reporting about the healing of the sick and disabled, his narrative would be a performative speech-act, an invitation to each of us to inhabit the new world of the Spirit in which the stigmatization and marginalization of people with disabilities and sensory impairments will be no more.

THE EPISTEMOLOGY OF PENTECOST: MANY TONGUES, MANY SENSES, MANY ABILITIES

Let us now see if a more secure case can be made for the theological motif of "many tongues and many senses" capable of giving testimony to and receiving the witness of the wondrous works of God. There are two basic parts to the following argument: a general overview of the epistemology operative in Luke's narrative which shows how there are multiple modes of human knowing and interaction (this subsection), and a more focused discussion of Luke's holistic theology of embodiment, especially in its kinesiological dimensions as manifest in the touch that is inspired by the Spirit (next subsection). Throughout, I presume the Spirit's charismatic anointing of the entire life and ministry of Jesus in the Third Gospel and the extension of that anointing in the outpouring of the Spirit on all flesh in Acts, so that the entire Lukan narrative can be understood to be about the "acts of the Holy Spirit." My goal is to sketch a holistic pentecostal theology of embodiment that in turn opens up conceptual space for a pneumatological theology of disability beyond emphasizing only the healing of disabled bodies and minds.

Toward this end, I want to explore further the significance of both seeing and hearing as central to Luke's theology of bearing and receiving the witness of the Spirit. This coupling occurs throughout Luke's account. The shepherds praised God "for all they had heard and seen" (Luke 2:20); the disciples had seen and heard what prophets and kings had not (Luke 10:24), and later they could not but testify to what they had seen and heard (Acts 4:20); the Samaritan crowds heard and saw the signs that Philip did (Acts 8:6); and Paul himself was called to bear witness to the world of all he had seen and heard (Acts 22:15). This combination of seeing and hearing is a fairly standard characterization of the two dominant epistemic senses. As is evident from the preceding, neither is privileged over the other; there is no standard form whereby one always precedes and the other follows. But I want to suggest that from a disability perspective, their pairing is significant because it points to not one but two basic modalities of human knowing.

This observation already advances the discussion of pentecostal and pneumatological epistemology.[6] Within a pentecostal schema in which inspired speech is perhaps the central manifestation of the Spirit's empowerment for witness, the principal form of communication is speaking, and the primary mode of knowing is hearing. Yet our discussion shows that seeing is also important, and not only when paired with hearing. Thus there are also occasions within the Lukan narrative when the salvation of God is specifically noted as seen rather than heard (Luke 2:30; 3:6; Acts 3:17). Even at the heart of the Pentecost narrative itself, not only will sons and daughters prophesy, but "your young men shall see visions, and your old men shall dream dreams" (Acts 2:17b). Here, seeing occurs under the power

---

6. Proposals for a pentecostal epistemology are still in the initial stages; for starter discussions, see Cartledge, *Practical Theology*, chap. 3; and Smith, *Thinking in Tongues*, chap. 3. In my own work, I have sketched the contours of what I call a "pneumatological epistemology" as informed by pentecostal spirituality: see Yong, *Spirit-Word-Community*, part II.

and inspiration of the Spirit even when our eyes are closed, even when we are asleep! My point is that besides speaking and hearing, there is seeing, and that the Spirit's revelatory and saving work is accomplished not only through the oral medium of testimony but also through the "visual" media of seeing, envisioning, and dreaming.

From this perspective, let's re-read the Lukan narrative of the blind man (Luke 18:35–43) as a case in point of the multisensory modalities and the multidimensional activities in and through which he witnessed (to) the presence and activity of God. (1) While *sitting* on the roadside, he is nevertheless not entirely passive: he is *begging*. (2) He *hears* the crowd going by, and *asks* what's going on. (3) His persistence results in his *being brought* or *led to* Jesus (by others). (4) He *persists in shouting*, "Jesus, Son of David, have mercy on me!" and when asked by Jesus what he wants, *replies*, "Lord, let me see again." (5) Upon receiving his sight, he *follows* Jesus and *glorifies* God. Note that the blind man bears witness to the wondrous works of God not only in receiving his sight at the command of the Spirit-anointed Son of God, but also in exhibiting faith—as manifest in his alertness, aggressiveness, and response. Note also that his healing is mediated by those around him who took the time to witness to and interact with him (leading him to Jesus), and then rejoiced with him.

My claim is an extension of David Daniels's emphasis on the reception of sound and hearing rather than what pentecostals traditionally focus on (speech and words).[7] Since pentecostalism is constituted in an essential way by its music, worship, sound, "primal cries," and joyful noises, pentecostal orality requires pentecostal audio for its completion. Thus hearing is central to pentecostal spirituality and piety, perhaps as much as if not more than speech is central to pentecostal witness. Daniels also mentions in passing the sense of touch (in the gift of instrumentalization), sight (seeing visions), speaking (singing), and writing (poetry), and concludes, "Within the Pentecostal sensorium, the orality-literacy binary of the Enlightenment was recast in ways that challenged the coupling of reason and literacy and the hierarchy of the senses that privilege sight."[8]

Building on Daniels's proposals, I would observe from a disability perspective that rather than "normalizing" either seeing or hearing in ways that marginalize people who are blind and/or deaf, the Lukan text suggests that only one of these sensory capacities is needed for encountering and then bearing witness to the work of the Spirit. If so, then neither blindness nor deafness would exclude people from being recipients or vehicles of the

---

7. Daniels, "Gotta Moan Sometime."
8. Daniels, "Gotta Moan Sometime," 29.

Spirit's gracious and charismatic work. By extension, people who are deaf and mute would also be capable of receiving the gift of the Spirit and bearing the fruits of the Spirit.[9]

---

9. Recent research on a deaf theology bearing out this point has been done by Hitching, *The Church and Deaf People*; Lewis, *Deaf Liberation Theology*; and Morris, *Theology without Words*.

5.7

The Early Church in Jerusalem as a Migrant Community[1]

I WANT TO MAKE three broad observations about the migratory nature of the earliest messianic community that is described in the initial chapters of the book of Acts. First, it is clear that the initial followers of Jesus as the messiah were mostly Jews and God-fearers from around the Mediterranean who had come "home" to celebrate the Feast of Pentecost (Acts 2:5–11). Luke states that the original "congregation" of three thousand was constituted by these migrants "from every nation under heaven" (cf. Acts 2:5, 41).[2] Within a short time, the number of messianists had grown to over five thousand, not including women and children (Acts 4:4), although their numbers were being added to by those from the countryside around Jerusalem (Acts 5:16). It appears that as a result of what had happened many of those who had returned from the diaspora decided to stay in the area, leading to major organizational conundrums for housing and feeding so many families in the longer term.

Thus, second, the earliest Christian community was confronted with its most severe challenge—and opportunity—because of its migrant

1. Yong, *The Future of Evangelical Theology*, 168–71.

2. I assume the traditional and scholarly consensus about Luke being the author of Acts and thus will refer to him in shorthand vis-à-vis the one responsible for this early Christian historical narrative; however, the thrust of my exegetical and theological reflections do not depend on any naive one-to-one correlation between "Luke" and the authorship of Acts.

constitution. As Luke records it, "During those days, when the disciples were increasing in number, the Hellenists complained against the Hebrews because their widows were being neglected in the daily distribution of food" (Acts 6:1). On the surface, this "problem" can be understood as no more or less than an economic one: migration brings with it economic risks and hazards. However, we have already been told that somehow, there were sufficient resources that the growing community pooled together to meet the needs of all (Acts 2:45; 4:34). Something more is going on, reflecting perhaps the inequalities common to migration experiences from the beginning of time. In this case, the local Hebrew widows, at least some of whom were Aramaic speakers, appeared to have been able to control the distribution of food, resulting in the neglect of the "outsiders," the Greek-speaking or Hellenist widows. Note, though, that the problem was not so much that Hellenist widows were not getting food but that they were not participants in the distribution of food, resulting, perhaps, in the lack of food not only for Hellenist widows but also for Hellenist families as a whole.[3] Yet why should we be surprised that factions had developed in the early messianic community? No doubt there were miscommunications, misunderstandings, and even jealousies that characterized such a diverse community, drawn together by Jewish and messianic commitments to some extent, yet deeply diverse in terms of linguistic, customary, and cultural differences that inevitably emerged over time. Just as predictably, when such disagreements boiled over, those "in charge," the Aramaic-speaking messianists, acted exclusively and maybe even condescendingly vis-à-vis the migrants in their midst. After all, outsiders, or at least those whose ties to the local area had been stretched or even broken for a time in some instances, did not deserve the same level of treatment as insiders. That has been the undeniable experience of migrants since human beings have launched or been cast out (as the case may be) from their home regions in search of a better tomorrow.[4]

This leads to my third observation about the burgeoning messianic community: they worked hard to develop an egalitarian leadership by putting migrants in charge. The apostles appointed seven deacons, all apparently—if their names are any indication—leading members of the migrant Hellenist Jews, one of which, Nicholas, is said explicitly to have been from the diaspora, that is, from Antioch in what is today called Asia Minor (Acts 6:5). Herein I think we learn a further lesson about theological indigenization commensurate with the Day of Pentecost narrative. If the outpouring

---

3. See Finger, *Of Widows and Meals*, chap. 11, for details of this argument.
4. See Goette and Hong, "A Theological Reflection on the Cultural Tensions"; cf. also Hertig, "Cross-Cultural Mediation."

of the Spirit empowered the speaking of many tongues and languages to declare "God's deeds of power" (Acts 2:11), then part of the outworking of this dynamic gift of the Spirit should be the empowering of people from many cultures to incarnate the gospel on their own terms. The Pentecost event did not erase the diversity of tongues but redeemed it, in fact, loosing the plurality of human expressions while orchestrating such dissonance miraculously for the glory of God. Similarly, then, the experience of migration, which brings very different people together, should result not in a homogenization of the messianic community but in its diversification. And appreciation for such diversity and pluralism depends on our following the Spirit's lead in empowering leadership across the spectrum, even when that means putting migrants in charge![5]

Of course, this is not to say that the apostolic leaders had made all the right decisions in empowering the Hellenist Jews to take responsibility for their widows. In point of fact, initially there remained a distinction between the authority of the apostles themselves, as pray-ers and preachers/proclaimers, and that of the deacons, "to wait on tables" (Acts 6:2-4). Yet once released as deacons, the empowerment of the Spirit, which ultimately sought to take the gospel beyond the confines of Jerusalem and Judea, began to move upon these Hellenist Jewish leaders to undertake tasks beyond that of their initial assignment. It was Stephen the deacon who began to see, and to proclaim under the Spirit's inspiration, that the scope of the presence and activity of God's Spirit was not limited to Jerusalem or to the temple. Here was a Hellenist Jew who began to discern that this eschatological outpouring of the Spirit had diasporic implications. The entire history of Israel pointed to the universal character of God's redemptive activity (Acts 7). Stephen berated the Sanhedrin and other Jerusalem- and temple-centered Jews about their parochial perspectives, and the result was his stoning for blasphemy against Moses and the temple (Acts 7:44-53).[6] Is it too much to say that it was Stephen's migrant point of view, from the margins, that allowed him to realize the extent of the salvation in Christ that the more centrally located apostolic leaders might have discerned but failed to act out?[7]

---

5. This builds off my discussion of the early church's ministry in "Conclusion—From Demonization to Kin-domization," esp. 167-68.

6. See, e.g., Simon, *St. Stephen and the Hellenists in the Primitive Church*.

7. I came upon González, "Reading from My Bicultural Place: Acts 6:1-7," after I completed this section, but am happy to note that our observations are largely consistent, although I come at this from a different angle than González's Latin American point of view. I did, however, nuance my discussion in a few places in light of González's chapter.

PART SIX

Theological Method

6.1

Spirit-Word-Community[1]

WE HAVE TRAVELED A long way since the claim was submitted in the introductory chapter that the task of developing a theological hermeneutics cannot be separated from the question of a hermeneutical theology. For this reason, our journey begun in the Spirit has taken us through the technicalities of trinitarian theology—explored according to the two hands and the mutual love models—as correlated with a metaphysics and ontology—one that is triadic, relational, and social—and an epistemology—more specifically, the pneumatological imagination. The gains made during this pilgrimage were suggestive of a hermeneutical and methodological trialectic: all theological interpretation and reflection proceeds by way of Spirit and Word in Community. By way of concluding provisionally, one major and two minor points should be emphasized.

First, this trinitarian proposal undercuts once for all any hermeneutical claim based on a single principle. Such logocentrism needs to be exposed and prescriptively rejected not only because the complexity of the world and of human activity resists any totalizing metanarrative, but also because, at the descriptive level, interpretation cannot succeed if driven by a single engine. A brief look at each moment of the trialectic isolation will confirm this basic point.

What would *sola spiritus* look like? I propose that Paul Feyerabend's *Against Method* reflects *sola spiritus* applied to scientific method. Feyerabend's thesis is that:

1. Yong, *Spirit-Word-Community*, 311–16.

the events, procedures and results that constitute the sciences have no common structure; there are no elements that occur in every scientific investigation but are missing elsewhere. Concrete developments (such as the overthrow of steady state cosmologies and the discovery of the structure of DNA) have distinct features and we can often explain why and how these features led to success. But not every discovery can be accounted for in the same manner, and procedures that paid off in the past may create havoc when imposed on the future. Successful research does not obey general standards; it relies now on one trick, now on another; the moves that advance it and the standards that define what counts as an advance are not always known to the movers . . . A theory of science that devises standards and structural elements for all scientific activities and authorizes them by reference to "Reason" or "Rationality" may impress outsiders—but it is much too crude an instrument for the people on the spot, that is, for scientists facing some concrete research problem.[2]

Feyerabend's claims that scientific advances are not the product of a homogeneous method, that they do not reflect a single type of rationality, that they do not proceed from within a common structural framework, etc., may have parallels in the theological sciences as well. A pneumatic and charismatic bias in theological reflection, for example, might reject any and all attempts at defining either a hermeneutic or a method as constricting the free leading of the Spirit.[3] Certainly, such a bias would reject the authority of the author and the text over the reader, apply the hermeneutics of suspicion toward exposing the ideological elements of interpretive communities, and favor either the authority of the (usually charismatic) individual to discern truth by the power of the Spirit, or a rank plurality of interpretive authorities. Fundamentalists, some kinds of pentecostals, and contemporary reader-response theorists all espouse a kind of *sola spiritus* hermeneutic and methodology at least in practice if not in theory. The result is that *sola spiritus* inspires an "enthusiastic" or radically individualistic Christianity which has perennially fallen prey to a thoroughgoing subjectivism.

To be sure, our own argument began with the Spirit. However, the claim made in Part One is that the dynamic of the Spirit opens up and requires trinitarian theology since the divine Breath points not to herself but to the Son and the Father. The theologian's response to Feyerabend et al., is not to exempt either scientific or theological method from criticism, but

2. Feyerabend, *Against Method*, 1; emphasis original.
3. Cf. Maier, *Biblical Hermeneutics*, 320–26.

to examine closely the hermeneutical and methodological structures and movements themselves. Spirit, Word, and Community in that case can be understood as heuristic categories which actually better express the insights of *sola spiritus*. Certainly, the community of scientists and of researchers follow inspired hypotheses and abductions, often unpredictable in terms both of their formulation and their outcomes, and as such, perhaps conceivable as the leading of the Spirit. Equally certain, both communities of inquiry deal with givens that, while subjectively accessed and dynamic, nonetheless make claims on the researchers. Scientific and theological inquiry is focused not only on the self but on the world in all of its complexity. And, such inquiry is nourished by communities of researchers and scholars who are, in the long run, responsible to validate discoveries and advances in their respective disciplines. In short, *sola spiritus* does not work. A pneumatological method needs to be set within the triadic framework of Spirit, Word, and Community.

As much has already been said about *sola scriptura* [chapter eight]. Negatively put, the emerging consensus today is that *sola scriptura* never did function strictly according to its claims.[4] In fact, *sola scriptura* provides its own defeater since it cannot be biblically defended. Appeal cannot be made to the Church Fathers since they understood Scripture as one soteriological means of grace alongside other elements of the apostolic tradition. Clearly, it is a historically emergent hermeneutical principle that developed during the early modern period *after* the collapse of ecclesial authority in order to serve the epistemic function of providing a criterion of justification for theology. As such, *sola scriptura* advocates have never been able to develop an ecclesiology (theology of tradition) or pneumatology sufficient to the epistemic demands of the gospel.

Put positively, however, *sola scriptura* points to the radical alterity of the scriptural texts which confront us with the Word of God. And, when set within a triadic framework, it enables us to hear that Word in a meaningful way. In fact, I would go so far as to argue that biblical hermeneuticians are implicitly recognizing that all interpretation of Scripture needs to take place by the Spirit and within a community of faith. Consider, for example, the following hermeneutical principles suggested by Gerald O' Collins and Daniel Kendall:[5]

---

4. See, e.g., Lane, "Sola Scriptura?"; Williams, *Retrieving the Tradition and Renewing Evangelicalism*, esp. 229–34; and Abraham, *Canon and Criterion in Christian Theology*, chap. 6, esp. 148–55.

5. O'Collins and Kendall, *The Bible for Theology*.

1. The principle of faithful hearing: theologians need to be faithful and regular hearers of God's Word through the Scriptures.
2. The principle of active hearing: interpretation should be undertaken with prayer, study, and action.
3. The principle of the community and its creeds: theological interpretation and appropriation are done within a living community of faith and in light of its classic creeds.
4. The principle of biblical convergence: the entirety of the biblical testimony should be brought to bear on theological issues and questions.
5. The principle of exegetical consensus: centrist exegesis should guide the theological interpretation of Scripture.
6. The principle of metathemes and metanarratives: theological interpretation of the Bible should observe and take account of metathemes and metanarratives.
7. The principle of continuity and discontinuity: all interpretation results in discontinuities within continuities.
8. The principle of eschatological provisionality: all theological interpretation is tentative vis-à-vis the eschatological horizon of Christian experience.
9. The principle of philosophical assistance: theological interpretation of Scripture occurs in dialogue with philosophy.
10. The principle of inculturation: inculturating Scripture in diverse social and historical contexts shapes theological appropriation.

There is no explicit reference to the Spirit, although pneumatology is discussed in the Appendix of this book, specifically with regard to the inspiration of Scripture, but also with regard to the theological task. Yet clearly, principles two, seven, and eight are all suggestive of the pneumatic moment of biblical interpretation, whether that be the activity of the pneumatological imagination, or the novelty, dynamism, and provisionality of interpretation. Principles one, three, five, and ten require a faithful community and demand that attention be paid to contextual variables. In short, faithful and submissive reading and interpretation of the Bible—the intention of *sola scriptura*—cannot proceed apart from Spirit and Community.

Finally, claims for *sola traditus* or *sola communitas* (if there be any) inevitably struggle to make relevant the ancient stories, creeds, doctrines, and practices to vastly different places and times, and to those who are outside the community in question. This is the burden of Eastern Orthodoxy, regardless of its present attractiveness. But the reality is that all communities labor under constraints since the boundaries of communities, no matter how clearly defined, are constituted at least in part by those on the margins. Communitarian activities (and interpretations) are therefore checked by voices and actions that resist the hegemony of the center. Further, communities are not static entities. Rather, their dynamic and continuously shifting nature means that even communities are not immune to the movements of spirit. Finally, "majority rules" does not guarantee truth. False ideologies can capture the hearts and minds of communities, even communities of faith. Community needs to be transformed by the Spirit and checked by the Word.

But, if the *solas* which have laid claim to hermeneutical and methodological rule need to be rejected, so do the various dyadic combinations. Theological interpretation that functions either monologically or dialogically will always struggle to achieve clarity, coherence, and relevance. The absence of the Spirit from the hermeneutical spiral means a lifeless repetition of the Word by the tradition. The absence of the Word means the domination of either enthusiasm or anarchy (or both) in the tradition. The absence of tradition means a primitivistic, biblicistic, fundamentalistic, and enthusiastic orientation. Positively put, I am arguing here that Spirit in conjunction with Word and Community means that the Spirit is the dynamic of interpretation on the one hand, and that Spirit is delivered from its ideological captivity by those who would claim to be solely spiritual on the other. The Word in conjunction with Spirit and Community means that Scripture is a heuristic norm on the one hand, and that it is delivered from its ideological captivity by those who would claim to be solely biblical on the other. Community in conjunction with Spirit and Word means that tradition provides the context of interpretation on the one hand, and that tradition is delivered from its own ideological captivity by those who would claim control over interpretation on the other. In short, two moments without the third still runs the hermeneutical risk of insufficient checks and balances.

Put succinctly, and this is my second major concluding point, I have argued for a theological hermeneutic that is triadic, trialectical, and trialogical. It is *triadic* in that it includes three moments: that of Spirit (praxis, experience, actor interpretation), that of Word (thought, object, given of interpretation), and that of Community (context, tradition, public of interpretation). It should be clear by now that these concepts are heuristic and descriptive on the one hand, even while being normative in the sense of making claims on theological interpretation on the other. It is *trialectical* in that these three moments are inter-structurally given, interdependent, interconnected, interrelated, interpenetrating and inter-influential, and reciprocal (one hopes the point is made!). None operate apart from the other two; each informs and is shaped by the other two; each requires the other two in order for it to be itself. It is *trialogical* in that the methodological procedure of theological hermeneutics requires the ongoing demand by and submission of each moment to the other two. One can and does begin anywhere in the hermeneutical trialectic, but must at some point confront the implications for the question at hand raised by and for the other two moments of the triad. The corrections that follow can and do come from everywhere even as they are fallible and subject to correction from other perspectives of the triad as these are engaged in the hermeneutical process. The possibilities of theological knowledge are propelled by this trialectic of interpretation: Spirit and Word in Community means that object and subject, text and context, interpreter and community/communities of interpretation all coinhere and inform each other as pairs (dialectically) and across pairings (trialectically).

The primary rationale for the hermeneutical trialectic is the pneumatologically driven doctrine of trinitarian perichoresis. While pneumatology contributes the emphases on relationality, otherness, and dynamic, incessant activity, the triune subsistent relations are suggestive of mutuality, indwelling, and sociality. Applied hermeneutically and methodologically, the result is close to what Stephen Dunning calls "transactional interpretation,"[6] which endeavors to find reciprocal relations, and "transformational interpretation," which attempts to discern and resolve oppositional meanings through a paradoxical union that nevertheless retains the opposing poles. In terms of the primary categories employed in this study, theological interpretation is an activity that bridges Word and Community, that transforms Word and Community, and holds together in tension, Word and Community; theological interpretation is also emergent from the Spirit transforming Community, and holds in tension continuity and discontinuity; finally, theological interpretation is a communal enterprise to discern the Spirit, to understand the Word, and to be transformed by the Spirit and the Word.

My third and final (for the purposes of this book) remark can be put in the form of a question: is this hermeneutical trialectic a novel idea? Yes and no. It connects well with other models of theological hermeneutics including canonical hermeneutics (e.g., Brevard Childs, James Sanders, Charles Scalise); the Anglican Triad of Scripture, tradition, and reason;[7] the Wes-

---

6. Dunning, *Dialectical Readings*.

7. Cf. Bauckham and Drewery, eds., *Scripture, Tradition, and Reason*; Abraham, *Canon and Criterion in Christian Theology*, chap. 8.

leyan quadrilateral of the Triad plus experience;[8] and the hermeneutical circle or spiral.[9] It incorporates many, if not all, of the features of theological interpretation advocated by contemporary theological hermeneuticians. It has aesthetic, descriptive, and normative components reflecting the triune God Christians worship and serve. It recognizes the multi-dimensionality of truth, the limitations of epistemic conditionality, and the multifarious operations of canonical norms and measures. In these ways and more, the hermeneutical trialectic is simply re-stating old truths perhaps in a new way.

In what ways, then, Yes? Perhaps only in recognizing the thoroughgoing interplay of Spirit, Word, and Community in the processes of theological interpretation. This would not be only a pentecostal (with emphasis on Spirit), or Protestant (with emphasis on Word) or Roman Catholic/Orthodox (with emphasis on Community) hermeneutic. It strives to describe theological interpretation as it actually occurs, and prescribe a model of doing theology relevant to the Church catholic and directed toward the eschaton. As such, I present this as a consensual hermeneutic and methodology, perhaps already discernible to be operative in Christian theological interpretation and theological method wherever such may be occurring. And, in adhering to Peirce's fallibilism, I expect to be corrected on points of details and even of major scope by others inquiring into the persisting question of theological hermeneutics and theological method.

---

8. Cf. Thorsen, *The Wesleyan Quadrilateral*; Coppedge, "How Wesleyans Do Theology"; Gunter et al., *Wesley and the Quadrilateral*.

9. Cf. Osborne, *The Hermeneutical Spiral*.

6.2

The Hermeneutical Trialectic[1]

HERMENEUTICS, METAPHYSICS, EPISTEMOLOGY

MY VISION OF THE hermeneutical trialectic derives from the conviction that theological reflection is a process of inquiry that is always *in media via*, always betwixt and between. This is, perhaps, what might be cited as a pneumatological intuition, emergent from the dynamic nature of life in the Spirit. If true, then why does the theological quest seemingly always shut down prematurely, inevitably corralled by one or the other side of the dialectic of thought? My hypothesis is that a sufficiently robust "pneumatological engine" is lacking to drive the process of inquiry. In what follows, I hope to pursue this hypothesis by way of fleshing out various details of the trialectic, beginning specifically with matters hermeneutical, metaphysical, and epistemological.

To begin with, I suggest that the trialectic provides a third way between emphasizing the priority either of hermeneutics and method on the oneside or of theology on the other. The emergence of a hermeneutical consciousness over the last few hundred years has finally led postmodern deconstructionists to insist that it is interpretation "all the way down," and that language never gets outside itself. Throughout this same period of time, theologians have searched for ways to secure or ground interpretation, whether that be in history, in experience, in the stability of the text,

---

1. Yong, "The Hermeneutical Trialectic," 29–35.

or of the author's intention.² The debate, of course, turns on whether interpretation drives theology (thereby resulting in a potentially vicious hermeneutical circularity) or whether theology drives methodology (thereby producing sure foundational results). But are not both sides correct insofar as all theology is always interpretation even as explicit hermeneutical and methodological reflections are also always theologically informed (even if unacknowledged)? To admit this is not to advocate incoherence since the options are not limited to the endless maze of postmodernist deconstruction on the one side or to modernistic foundationalism on the other. Rather, the trialectic would endeavor to preserve insights from both camps without compromising their fundamental convictions by way of imaging theological inquiry as sustained by the Spirit and proceeding through a hermeneutical spiral toward an eschatological horizon. In this manner, the convictions that theology is interpretation all the way down (we now see through a glass dimly; cf. 1 Cor 13:8) and that theology is established securely (on the one foundation of Jesus the Christ; cf. 1 Cor 3:11) can be retained within an eschatological horizon and structure (we shall see him as he is; cf. 1 John 3:2).

Second, and following from this, the trialectic would affirm theological reflection as concerning or bridging the gap between subject and object, between subjectivity and objectivity, between knowledge and reality. As such, the trialectic entails or presumes epistemological and metaphysical or ontological commitments of sorts. In both cases, the same hermeneutical relationship as that established above holds: epistemology and metaphysics are informed by theology even as theology emerges epistemically from the way things are (metaphysics). To begin with the latter—metaphysics—I would suggest that a pneumatologically informed trinitarian theology provides clues for overcoming the disastrous dualisms of (among other metaphysical systems) Platonism, Thomism, Cartesianism, and Kantianism, even while preserving their valid insights toward a trinitarian ontology and metaphysics.³ Following the American logician, C. S. Peirce, reality as a whole and realities in particular are seen to be constituted triadically as essential qualities, concrete facts and actualities, and inner habits, dispositions, and laws.⁴ The speculative metaphysical hypothesis that emerges suggests this: things are present to other things through their qualities, are engaged phenomenologically through their concrete manifestations, and are sustained legally through their dispositions. I further suggest that such a

---

2. On these various efforts to ground theological interpretation, see Fiorenza, *Foundational Theology*, chaps. 9–10.

3. This argument has most recently been developed extensively by Gelpi, *Varieties of Transcendental Experience*; and idem, *The Gracing of Human Experience*.

4. For details, see my "The Demise of Foundationalism and the Retention of Truth."

metaphysical vision correlates well with the patristic theological claim that God works all things through God's two hands: the Word and the Spirit. Pneumatologically considered, the spiritual (*ruah* or *pneuma*) dimension of any thing may be imaged as the internal or inner legal, energetic, habitual, dispositional, and relational field of force that constitutes it as a concrete actuality.[5] (Of course, a thing's field of force is never solely singular but always a convergence of various fields of force which inform and influence the thing in question.)

Within this conceptual framework, the Spirit as the key to intra- and extra-trinitarian relations points in the direction of a relational or social metaphysics. Further, the Spirit as the dynamic power of life is suggestive of a radically temporal (and hence, eschatologically directed) ontology which does not privilege either the past or the present, but includes the future (without diminishing the importance of the other temporal modalities). Finally, the universal Spirit was and always is also the Spirit of particularity—especially of Jesus the Christ, the incarnate Logos—and hence requires recognition of the particularities, concreteness, and embodied character of otherness in all of its varied dimensions. Perhaps a pneumatologically informed metaphysic and ontology would then be a form of critical realism which affirms otherness as complex, dynamic, and legitimate "entities" (whether or not recognized by selves, and certainly not constituted by selves) that are in relationship (and hence, engaged or encountered perspectivally in relationship to selves). In short, such a metaphysic or ontology—what I suggest we call a foundational pneumatology[6]—would be dynamic, realistic, and social.

Some might object that the inclusion of a metaphysics and an ontology (not to mention the epistemology which follows shortly) in a proposal directed toward a consensual hermeneutic and theological method unnecessarily burdens the conversation with heavily debated and debatable philosophical notions. My rationale for this is both philosophical and theological. Philosophically, it should be clearly stated that the metaphysical and epistemological components of this project are presented as speculative hypotheses (rather than dogmatic theses) designed to ensure that claims to truth can be measured by the realities which such claims engage.[7] Failure

---

5. Theological exegesis in support of this hypothesis is drawn from Walter Wink's The Powers series, especially *Naming the Powers*.

6. Here, of course, I build on the work of Gelpi who builds also on the work of Peirce and the North American philosophical tradition; see Gelpi, *The Divine Mother*.

7. Hence, metaphysical thinking would not be aprioristic as in the onto-theological tradition, but rather fallibilistically preferred speculative hypotheses, open to revision and correction; on the notions of metaphysics as speculative hypotheses and of truth

to come clean with one's metaphysical presuppositions or arguments leaves one open to the charge of operating within some kind of self-enclosed narrative or cultural-linguistic world.[8] While those doing work in theological hermeneutics and theological method do not need to adopt the particular details of the metaphysical speculations proposed here, some account or other will need to be explored and developed in order to claim that the proposed hermeneutic gets at reality rather than being self-referentially enclosed within a linguistic or symbolic system.

Theologically, of course, the Christian claim is that the encounter with the Spirit of God is not just a figment of the psychological imagination (Feuerbach), but a real engagement with God who is both immanent to and yet transcendent from us. And, the precise pneumatological claim is that God is present to and active in our world by the Spirit, implying a real otherness amidst a real unity. A foundational pneumatology therefore has to assume such difference-in-unity, such radical alterity to the knowing self, and the task of reflecting on or explicating this notion involves metaphysical, ontological, and epistemological speculation. But is not such speculative endeavour emergent from theoretical criteria developed by communities of inquiry, and if so, does not such elevate the Community over both Spirit and Word? Yes to the former question—all criteriologies emerged from the ongoing inquiry and conversation—but no to the latter for two reasons. First, since communities of inquiry can ossify and settle on certain discoveries as final in a non-fallibilistic and dogmatic sense, such communities would in these cases effectively cease to journey on the path of inquiry. Getting off this path, I suggest, quenches the Spirit who always seeks to breathe new life into the community. Second, insofar as communities of inquiry are continuously impacted by their engagements with realities other than themselves, they are dynamically and thereby pneumatically constituted. The capacity of communities of inquiry to change their collective minds suggests an interactive process—what I call the trialectic—which informs its movements and possibilities. Community therefore remains essential to the hermeneutical trialectic without being elevated in an arbitrary manner over either Spirit or Word.

What then about a pneumatologically informed epistemology which would undergird the transformative processes of communities of inquiry? In a very general sense, all knowledge is pneumatological insofar as, from a Christian theological perspective, human beings are rational and knowing

---

claims being measured by reality, I follow the lead of my *Doktorvater*, Robert Cummings Neville, "Sketch of a System"; and idem, *Recovery of the Measure*.

8. So, for example, George Lindbeck has had to labor to defend his theory of doctrine against charges of insularity coming from a variety of fronts.

beings because of the life breath of the Spirit of God (cf. Gen 2:7). But more specifically, a pneumatological epistemology—what I call the pneumatological imagination—suggests that knowledge is, among other things, unpredictably dynamic, critically realistic, and semiotically triadic. A dynamic pneumatological epistemology would emphasize the finitude and fallibility of knowledge (always subject to the ongoing processes of deconstruction and reconstruction), as well as its perspectival character (knowledge as always emergent from particular locations, spaces, and times). Here, a pneumatologically informed metaphysics dovetails with a pneumatologically informed epistemology. After all, a continuously evolving, open, and dynamic reality requires a dynamic and creative epistemology alert to its fallibilistic character. At the same time, a critical realistic metaphysics assumes a realistic epistemology. Only if knowers and knowns were already distinct but also in relationship in some way (within some social context or other) would knowledge be possible. Finally, again building on and extending Peirce's idea, the Spirit who is relational leads toward both a relational metaphysic and a relational epistemology. The latter can be said to overcome the dyadic and dualistic framework of both the Cartesian *cogito* and the Saussurean sign precisely by recognizing the triadic character of the sign-relation: all signs (the semiotic fact) stand for something (the other) to someone (the interpreter). This means that knowing subjects never engage known objects directly, but always through signs, *ad infinitum* (hence: interpretation continues "all the way down").

The problems that arise for theological hermeneutics, of course, are familiar to those who are even vaguely familiar with the current ferment in the area of epistemology. How can finite minds ever hope to engage the (theologically alleged) infinite reality of God? What does epistemic fallibility entail for speculative and (especially) dogmatic theology, especially given the eschatological dimension of God's relationship with the world? Can perspectival, semiotic, and hermeneutical knowing wherein knowing subjects who and which participate in some social field or other with known objects be squared with absolute claims?

Here, the normative dimensions of the pneumatological imagination are important. The Spirit is, after all, not every spirit, but always the Spirit of Jesus the Christ in all his particularity who makes claims on us. Put simplistically, theological claims will be measured or normed finally by the concrete and particular historical-eschatological reality of this Jesus Christ. In the meantime, all theological claims are fallible at worst and partial at best, subject to the ongoing quest driven by the pneumatological imagination. Put metaphysically, theological claims will be measured or normed by the realities to which they aim: the divine Other, human others, and nature's otherness. Put hermeneutically, theological claims will be measured or normed variously by human experience, reasonable language or rational discourse, and communal traditions. Put alethically, theological claims will be measured or normed by its usage (truth as pragmatic) and its coherence with other known claims (truth as coherence). In this case, of course, truth is the property of the dyadic correspondence of any particular claim with the reality or realities it is directed toward even as the measurement of such correspondence is a triadic and interpretive relationship among the knowing subject, the claim itself in all of its semiotic complexity, and the known object. As such, theological hermeneutics and method is constituted subjectively (by the questing knower directed toward certain ends), objectively (by the known realities constituted over and against but also with the knower in various ways), and communally (by the various purposive, semiotic, and socio-historical contexts within and through which the knowing subject engages the known objects)—hence, the metaphor of "Spirit-Word-Community."

TOWARD A HERMENEUTICAL TRIALECTIC

My claim, in brief, is that theological hermeneutics and theological method is an interpretive enterprise, and as such, is always a pneumatologically (cf. also 1 Cor 2:10–16) and triadically structured semiotic relationship of knowers, knowns, and signs. As such, I suggest that theological hermeneutics and method should negotiate three moments in the hermeneutical spiral, albeit not in any necessary order: the hermeneutics of the knowing subject; the hermeneutics of the known object; and the hermeneutics of the contexts or communities of interpretation. And, following from the pneumatological impulse that feeds this hermeneutical trialogue, I will use synonymously the notions of discernment, reading, and interpretation, as appropriate. Succinctly put, the goal of theological hermeneutics and theological method is an ongoing task of discerning the Spirit, reading the Word, and critically interpreting both amidst various communities of inquiry—a trialogical or trialectical relationship because each moment is or should always be in dialogue with the other two. Let me briefly elaborate on each in turn.

In one sense, spiritual discernment lies at the centre of the doing of theology. We are called to discern the voice, presence, and activity of the Spirit in our experiences, in our reading of the Scriptures, and in the world around us. Herein lies what I call the explicit pneumatological moment of theological inquiry. More explicitly, this pneumatological moment calls attention to interpretation as a triadic activity involving interpreting subjects, interpreted objects, and interpretive goals. Human beings interpret as oriented teleologically toward certain transformative and liberative practices, as constrained by situational, environmental, and other factors, and as expressions of their potential to exercise creativity and freedom. Theological interpretation occurs insofar as each of these activities of interpretation are consciously opened to and intentionally designed to engage the divine. Herein lies the source of theological creativity and, dare we say, novelty, insofar as human beings engage reflectively in understanding God's relationship to the world in their unique spaces and times. As such, the hermeneutics of the knowing subject requires critical self-reflection in order to determine the personal and social motivations, intentions, and purposes that influence the activity of interpretation. The sources of these motivations can and should be traced to the unique psychological dispositions, the concrete physiological comportments, and the socio-historical and communal locations of interpreting subjects. For these reasons, I suggest that theological hermeneutics and theological method necessarily include this moment of self-discernment.

But of course, interpretation is explicitly concerned with engaging otherness, who or which is over-and-against-us, the moment captured by what I call "Word." So while interpretation cannot (should not) avoid self-discernment, it is directly interested in the discernment of others. Otherness, of course, can be the experiences of the self as objectified. Herein lies the clearest instance of the mutuality of the knowing subject and known object insofar as both lie within fields that are emergent from the interpreting self. But even in other cases, knowing subjects and known objects converge relationally, thus allowing for knowledge to emerge. This is the case, for example, when we hear or read Scripture, participate in the liturgy, recite the confessions of the Church, etc. But again, Scripture itself points to the living Word, Jesus the Christ, with whom, in a sense, all Christian theology finally has to do. And Scripture itself is emergent from the ecclesial tradition finally founded on the apostles and the prophets and handed down by a dynamic and ongoing process of traditioning. As such, the hermeneutics of the known object requires careful attention to the claims that these others—the living Word, the written word, the sacramental word, the traditioned (spoken, heard, recited) word, etc.[9]—make on us as interpreters. How does Jesus the Christ confront us through the Word and through the living tradition of the Church? Herein lies the over-and-againstness of the known

---

9. Rather than relativizing the importance of the written Word, I am simply emphasizing its functional location within the larger matrix of Christian life and practice. On this point, see, e.g., Abraham, *Canon and Criterion in Christian Theology*; and Work, *Living and Active*.

object to the knowing subject, even if there is a participatory character to their relational mutuality within a communal context.

What are the communal contexts of theological interpretation? There are a multiplicity of such communal contexts. David Tracy correlates such with the praxis of the Church, the identity of the Church, and the theological and wider academy.[10] Certainly the publics are intertwined not only insofar as any theological discourse can be translated appropriately for other publics, but also in that the articulation of any theology is shaped by the Church being in and for, if not of, the world. This said, however, the particularity of various theological discourses, adapted as they are toward ecclesial praxis, ecclesial self-understanding, and ecclesial engagement with the world, needs to be discerned in order for misunderstanding to be minimized. Political-liberation (and even feminist) theologies, pastoral-care theologies, theological ethics, etc., reflect theological discourses directed toward ecclesial praxis that are nevertheless informed by theologies intended for other audiences. Biblical theologies, historical theologies, dogmatics, etc., reflect theological discourses attempting ecclesial self-understanding (what Edward Farley calls "theological portraiture"[11]). Systematic theologies, philosophical (or fundamental) theologies, theologies of nature, theologies of culture, etc., reflect theological discourses emergent from Christian engagement with the wider academy, with culture, and with the world in all its complexity.

Are there overlaps in theological publics, in content, and in intentionality? Absolutely. The point surely is that practical theology—theology by the Church and for the ministry of the Church—is informed by, and has implications for, the Church's self-understanding and for academic theology; that ecclesial theology, likewise, is informed by and has implications for practical and academic theology; and that academic theology is also informed by, and has implications for, practical and ecclesial theology. The correlation with the theory of truth briefly articulated above—truth as pragmatic, as corresponding with reality, and as coherent, the first and third being means of measuring truth properly understood as the dyadic relationship between a claim and reality—is intentional. As such, dogmatic theology is true (corresponding to reality) insofar as its theological claims are both pragmatic (transformative or, in theological terms, soteriological) and coherent (in the widest, including eschatological, senses). Theological

---

10. Tracy, *The Analogical Imagination*. Other classifications are also possible, as in Rush's distinction of twelve sites of reception for theological proposals, *The Reception of Doctrine*, 206–07, and 331–58. Again, however, for simplicity's sake, I will use Tracy's categories.

11. Farley, *Ecclesial Reflection*, chap. 9.

discernment therefore attempts to measure the truthfulness of any claim according to its logic of consequences (its pragmatics) and its translatability into other discourses and contexts of engagement (its coherence). That being the case, practical theology (theology as ecclesial praxis) is checked by ecclesial and academic theology even as ecclesial theology is checked by practical and academic theology and as academic theology is checked by practical and ecclesial theology.

6.3

Theology and/as Performance[1]

CHRISTIAN DOCTRINE AS ECCLESIAL GRAMMAR

IT WAS THE LUTHERAN ecumenical theologian George Lindbeck who called attention to the similarity between how doctrines function with regard to religious traditions and how grammars serve languages.[2] Whereas a cognitivist approach to religion understood doctrines in propositional terms focused on the question of truth (the classical tradition), and whereas (what Lindbeck calls) an "experiential-expressivist" approach understood doctrines in symbolic terms focused on inner feelings, existential attitudes, and overall orientations (the tradition of modern liberalism), Lindbeck proposes instead a cultural-linguistic alternative that understands doctrines as illocutionary rules informed by and in turn formative for the religious community's practices. This postliberal option emphasizes religious traditions as entire ways of life embodied in texts (myths and narratives), rites, and other practices, which in turn combine to serve as comprehensive interpretive schemes (doctrines) that claim to be able to account for all of reality. Just as grammars dictate the use of language and language shapes the nature of experience, to that same degree, narratives and doctrines dictate the practice of religion and shape the nature of religious experience.

---

1. Yong, *Hospitality and the Other*, 50–56.
2. See Lindbeck, *The Nature of Doctrine*. Before Lindbeck, others had made similar points—e.g., Mananzan, *The "Language Game" of Confessing One's Belief*—but it was *The Nature of Doctrine* that effectively launched the "postliberal" movement.

While Lindbeck's proposal was designed to deal with intra-Christian ecumenical concerns, he based his theory primarily on breakthroughs in the philosophy of language (drawing from Austin and, especially, the linguistic philosopher Ludwig Wittgenstein) and cultural anthropology (Clifford Geertz).[3] Lindbeck argued that his proposed cultural-linguistic theory of doctrine had to be, at least in principle, also applicable to issues related to extra-Christian or interreligious ecumenism. At this level, Lindbeck made five points:[4] (1) that a cultural linguistic approach did not presume a common framework between religious traditions either for adjudicating conflicting truth claims or for assuming a common-core religious experience lying behind the diverse doctrinal assertions; (2) that because of this possibility regarding the incommensurability of religious traditions,[5] we should proceed cautiously in comparing religious traditions and not rush to make claims regarding the superiority of any one religious tradition over others; (3) but insofar as religious traditions make such claims, these have to be understood eschatologically (to use theological language) or performatively according to the logic of promise as awaiting actualization or realization rather than as accomplished matters of fact; (4) that rather than religious doctrines expressing the experiences of salvation, salvation is instead the process of being shaped, formed, and transformed by religious doctrines (by their illocutionary acts and their perlocutionary effects, to use Austinian language);[6] and (5) that there are hence many different modes of interreligious engagement, and the processes of interreligious dialogue arise ad hoc out of the encounter between representatives of the various traditions as they discover similarities and differences in beliefs and practices. In the postliberal scheme of things, the logic of any religion, as spelled out by its rules and doctrines, is shaped by its communal practices—its interpretive, ritual, institutional, and interpersonal performances—so that its adherents both interpret the world according to how they see the world fitting into

---

3. Wittgenstein and Geertz both helped Lindbeck view religion as a cultural and linguistic system; see Geertz's "Religion as a Cultural System," in *The Interpretation of Cultures*.

4. See Lindbeck, *The Nature of Doctrine*, chap. 3.

5. Elsewhere, Lindbeck discusses this incommensurability in terms of "untranslatability," by which he means that religions as comprehensive ways of life and thought are (a) not fully translatable into the language of another tradition, and (b) would resist such translation, preferring instead to itself translate every other conceivable reality, including the realities of other religions, into its own terms; see Lindbeck, "The Gospel's Uniqueness."

6. So Lindbeck said, citing Austin, that "a religious utterance ... acquires the propositional truth of ontological correspondence only insofar as it is a performance, an act or deed, which helps create that correspondence" (*The Nature of Doctrine*, 65).

their ways of thinking, on the one hand, even as they engage the world according to their rules of thought in order to change it, on the other hand.[7]

Lindbeck's work has generated a good deal of discussion, even an entire "postliberal" theological school or movement.[8] Because we cannot afford to get sidetracked with all of the controversy, I want to focus briefly on the implications of the cultural-linguistic theory for interreligious relations. Two points are especially noteworthy. First, if religious traditions as comprehensive ways of life and thought are in fact distinct as whole systems, then it would be inadequate for us to compare them as being equally (or not) salvific. Insofar as Islam, Buddhism, and Hinduism, for example, each provides a range of practices commensurate with their ideals and goals, to the same degree none of them can be said either to aspire to Christian salvation or to provide the requisite practices pertinent to obtaining or receiving such salvation.[9] In this case, Christian theologies of exclusivism, inclusivism, and pluralism all miss the mark because they do not engage other religious traditions on their own terms.[10] On the other hand, if Christianity is itself a comprehensive system of life and thought, these theologies of religions are various ways that Christians attempt to account for and engage

---

7. Here, Lindbeck's work intersects with those of a number of other theorists, both philosophers and theologians, such as C. S. Peirce's notion of the meaning of beliefs as unfolded in practices; Alasdair MacIntyre's notion of tradition as arguments that meanings are based on social practices; Stanley Hauerwas's claim that truthfulness lies in the practices of the community; Hans Frei's insistence that narratives shape both (nondiscursive) practices and (discursively articulated) beliefs; Ronald Thiemann's proposal regarding the gospel as narrative promise; James W. McClendon, Jr.'s suggestion that biography is intimately linked to theology and vice versa; Johann Baptist Metz's argument for the interrelatedness of fundamental theology and political theology; Helmut Peukert's theology of communicative action; Nicholas Lash's idea that theological languages shape the practices that provide access to God, etc. For discussion of many of these ideas in relationship to the postliberal school of thought, see Vidu, *Postliberal Theological Method*. I assess McClendon's project in my essay "The 'Baptist Vision' of James William McClendon, Jr."

8. See, e.g., Marshall, ed., *Theology and Dialogue*; Phillips and Okholm, eds., *The Nature of Confession*; and Goh, *Christian Tradition Today*.

9. From the Christian point of view, the one exception may be the Jewish tradition. But even here, we have to be careful to walk a fine line between continuity and discontinuity, between understanding the church as a new Israel in some sense and yet avoiding a supersessionistic interpretation of such relationship. Lindbeck himself attempts such a via media in his "The Church as Israel," 78–94, and does so by insisting on, among other points, the importance of the church being ready to share in the sufferings of Israel.

10. This is the point of Di Noia, "Varieties of Religious Aims." In a later work, Di Noia provides a book-length argument defending this hypothesis—*The Diversity of Religions*.

other faith traditions. We will return to discuss this issue in more detail in the next chapter.

But second, if the main lines of the cultural-linguistic theory of religion are correct—and for the record, I think that they are—then fully understanding the logic of any doctrinal or theological system requires participating in or embracing its practices.[11] This does not mean understanding cannot be achieved apart from such an endeavor, but it does mean the insider-outsider distinction is not an unimportant one when it comes to the meaning and truth of religious, doctrinal, and theological claims. Further, this does not mean interreligious engagement is impossible, but it does mean such can proceed only ad hoc, and that its shape, scope, degree of depth, and so forth, will depend on various factors such as who is involved, the context or background of the encounter, and the practices deployed. Finally, Lindbeck himself grants that the cultural-linguistic theory of religion does not eliminate a propositional understanding of doctrinal references, but it does mean that the significance of such assertions cannot be abstracted from ways of life as a whole. In this case, the adjudication of divergent doctrinal claims is as much a matter of the disputants engaging in religious (and interreligious) practices as it is a matter of them apologizing for or clarifying religious beliefs.

Having said this, there remains a nagging concern that any Christian community's "performance" of the Scriptures "makes it so" in a way that shields it from criticism. Is Lindbeck's cultural-linguistic theory of doctrine susceptible of being used to legitimize the dismissal of other points of view because they are neither congruent with one's beliefs nor informed by one's practices? While there are valid arguments for forms of Christian sectarianism that can serve as correctives to Christian expressions that are overly accommodating to cultural dynamics and fads, there are also unhealthy fundamentalisms shaped by religious (even "biblical") convictions and forms of life that are immune to external criticism. In the big picture, I will argue that the space for self-reflexivity and criticism is opened up precisely in the hospitable encounter with the stranger, the alien, and even the religious other. But if so, then the concern arises from the other side of the skeptical response to Lindbeck: that cultural-linguistic systems are never as homogeneous as one might think, and, in that case, insiders and outsiders are not so clearly demarcated and boundaries are blurred, especially in a global and postcolonial situation where migration and hybridity are so prevalent. In these cases, what keeps Christian communities from fragmentation? Is what is needed not a dynamic internal to the cultural-linguistic theory of

---

11. I have argued this point in my "The Spirit Bears Witness."

doctrine that can move, invite, and even sustain such engagement, but do so in ways that maintain continuity with the historic Christian tradition? I suggest that a "pneumatological assist" to Lindbeck's proposal is precisely what is required,[12] and for this, we turn to the work of evangelical-ecumenical theologian Kevin Vanhoozer.

THEOLOGY AS DRAMATIC PERFORMANCE

Building on Lindbeck's work, Vanhoozer has been concerned to recenter Scripture at the heart of the theological task. Hence, he calls his project "a canonical-linguistic approach to Christian theology."[13] Drawing also from continental philosophy, speech-act theory,[14] and dramatic theory, Vanhoozer provides not only a theory of doctrine but also an overarching vision of the theological enterprise understood according to the model of dramatic performance.

Vanhoozer's project is subtle and his argument sophisticated. For our purposes, however, it can be summarized thus: the gospel is itself a drama whose director is God, whose script is the canonical Scriptures, whose players or actors (dramaturges) are theologians in particular and the church in general, and whose stage is the church and whose theater is the world.[15] For Vanhoozer, as for Wolterstorff, Scripture is understood as a canon of God's illocutionary speech acts. Hence, Scripture is to be privileged so that the interpretive community—including the dramaturges—always attempts to perform the drama in accordance with the illocutions of the canonical authors, including God. Put alternatively, the players and actors as members of the church seek to be appropriately effected (the perlocutionary sense) by the canonical illocutions.

As with any dramatic play, the performance of the gospel must be enacted not woodenly but creatively, and not irresponsibly but faithfully. Hence, theologians as dramaturges have as their task "that of knowing how to transpose the drama of redemption into the present in a different cultural

---

12. Moulaison, *Lord, Giver of Life*, is suggestive along these lines, although not as helpful with regard to the question of Christianity's relationship to the world's religions.

13. Vanhoozer, *The Drama of Doctrine*.

14. See Vanhoozer's earlier books: *Biblical Narrative in the Philosophy of Paul Ricoeur*; *Is There a Meaning in This Text?*; and *First Theology*.

15. This is the argument of *The Drama of Doctrine*; a shorter version anticipating the book is Vanhoozer, "The Voice and the Actor." Other recent efforts to discuss theology in dramatic terms are Horton, *Covenant and Eschatology*; and Heyduck, *The Recovery of Doctrine in the Contemporary Church*.

key."[16] Faithfulness to the canonical script involves, then, what Vanhoozer calls "dramatic fittingness" (recall Austin's notion of the felicitousness or happiness of performatives) so that it "will require different performances in different situations. This is a kind of relativism, to be sure, but one that *establishes* rather than undermines biblical authority."[17] This is because dramatic fittingness ensures that the canonical illocutions are norms that guide Christian performances in different ways in different times and places.

Yet, it is important to note that dramatic and performative fittingness requires not only fidelity but also improvisation.[18] Nicholas Lash, Vanhoozer's *Doktorvater* (and to whom *The Drama of Doctrine* is dedicated), had already compared the task of performing the Scriptures to that of playing a score of one of Beethoven's quartets or enacting *King Lear*. In each case, "as the history of the meaning of the text [or score, or play] continues, we can and must tell the story differently. But we do so under constraint: what we may *not* do, if it is *this* text which we are to continue to perform, is to tell a different story."[19] Going one step beyond Lash, N. T. Wright proposed that biblical interpretation should be understood in terms of the church's performance of the scriptural narrative and how this might be parallel to a group of actors' performance of an unwritten fifth act of a Shakespearean play based on the script of the first four acts.[20] In line with Wright's hypothetical scenario, a Lukan perspective would ask how the church faithfully improvises the performance of the twenty-ninth chapter of Acts in times and places far removed from Theophilus' original situation. With Lash and Wright, this Lukan-inspired query raises the important issue for Vanhoozer: To what degree is performative creativity or novelty constrained by the canonical script when the stage has been shifted to and set up in a very different context?

It is here that Vanhoozer's understanding of the Holy Spirit comes into view.[21] He affirms that the church can be understood as a performance of the Holy Spirit insofar as the play is faithful to the canonical script. Hence, he agrees with Reinhard Hütter, who argues that the work of the Spirit is to

16. Vanhoozer, *The Drama of Doctrine*, 254.

17. Vanhoozer, *The Drama of Doctrine*, 261, italics in original.

18. See Young, *The Art of Performance*, chap. 8 ("Improvisation and Inspiration"), which suggests that the improvisation that goes with biblical interpretation always falls short of the originally inspired version, but at the same time anticipates "the great eschatological performance to come" (182). I am not as pessimistic as Young, as the following discussion shows.

19. See Lash's essay, "Performing the Scriptures," 44, italics in original.

20. Wright, *The New Testament and the People of God*, 140–43.

21. See *The Drama of Doctrine*, chaps. 6–7.

be found in the practices of the church (see below, 59–62). More precisely, for Vanhoozer the Holy Spirit is the "executor" of the Word in at least three senses: as prompting the canonical authors; as enlivening the canonical script; and as bringing about faithful improvisations through the dramaturgical performances. As such, the Spirit brings about the perlocutionary effects of the canonical illocutions.[22] Hence, Vanhoozer affirms both a unified understanding of the canonical text and a plurality of perlocutionary results: "*I affirm a 'Pentecostal plurality,' which maintains that the one true interpretation is best approximated by a diversity of particular methods and contexts of reading.* The Word remains the interpretive norm, but no one culture or interpretive scheme is sufficient to exhaust its meaning, much less its significance."[23] In this way, Vanhoozer insists on understanding how the "spirited practices" of the church are normed by the scriptural canon.[24]

Now as we have already noted, Vanhoozer's dramatic theory is not just a canonical supplementation to Lindbeck's cultural-linguistic theory; rather, Vanhoozer's is an expansion from a doctrinal theory toward a theory of theology. In other words, Vanhoozer is concerned not only with the nature of doctrine but also the nature of theology in general. At this level, Vanhoozer is led to ask the more general hermeneutical and epistemological questions. Whereas the hermeneutical tradition from Friedrich Schleiermacher to Hans-Georg Gadamer suggested that human understanding happens somewhat miraculously, Vanhoozer boldly suggests a Christian theological framework for explicating human understanding. More precisely, insofar as certain virtues such as openness, humility, and attention are needed in order for understanding to "happen," and to "the extent that these virtues are fruits of the Spirit, or at the very least evidences of common grace, a hermeneutics will be able to get beyond 'thin' descriptions of the event of understanding only by employing distinctly theological categories . . . [To] the extent that the interpretative virtues . . . are spiritual virtues, it may be that the Spirit performs a ministry of 'word' and [the matter of the text] as well."[25] In short, Vanhoozer's canonical-linguistic theory requires a robust pneumatological-theological framework.

---

22. Vanhoozer, *Is There a Meaning in This Text?*, 428–29.
23. Vanhoozer, *Is There a Meaning in This Text?*, 419, italics in original.
24. Vanhoozer, *The Drama of Doctrine*, esp. 226–31.
25. Vanhoozer, "Discourse on Matter," 25–26.

6.4

Method in Political Theology
A Pentecostal Perspective[1]

PENTECOSTALISM AND THEOLOGICAL METHOD: CHALLENGES AND OPPORTUNITIES

THEOLOGICAL METHOD HAS BEEN a modern academic preoccupation concerned with the question of the sources and authorities of, and procedures involved in, theological reflection.[2] Its problematic can be traced to the confluence of interrelated trajectories in early modernity including the post-Reformation dissolution of ecclesial authority (especially after the Wars of Religion), the emergence of the post-Cartesian and post-Kantian subject as a locus of epistemology, and the ascendancy of Enlightenment rationality as a technical model of inquiry. In the late-modern West, the task of theological method sought to adjudicate the questions raised by each of these issues, and this inevitably converged in the debates over foundationalism.

Although we have neither the time nor the space to enter fully into the disputes regarding foundationalism,[3] suffice it to say that at a very basic level, the theological issue has to do with the starting points or grounding

---

1. Yong, *In the Days of Caesar*, 88–95.

2. Arguably, the high point of the discussion was Lonergan's magisterial *Method in Theology*.

3. For those interested, I explore the terrain in *Spirit-Word-Community*, 96–101. For a fuller discussion, see Grenz and Franke, *Beyond Foundationalism*.

of any theological system. In order to highlight how difficult it is to locate pentecostalism in the existing theological landscape, I will simplify matters by distinguishing three major methodological responses developed in the modern period to the foundationalist question: the Reformation and post-Reformation *sola scriptura*, the liberal Protestant turn to experience, and the Orthodox and Catholic approach that sees Scripture as the book of the church and therefore in continuity with the church's teachings and traditions.

At one level, most pentecostals would unhesitatingly align themselves with the Reformation tradition of *sola scriptura*.[4] Pentecostals who are self-identifying Protestants would affirm the normativity of the Bible for the church and its teachings,[5] even as many lay pentecostals would go even further and insist that the Bible alone is all that is needed for Christian faith and practice. Yet even as the postmodern discussion is illuminating how there is no direct approach to the biblical (or any other historical) text that is not mediated by the contemporary horizon,[6] so also have pentecostals discerned their own approach to Scripture to have been informed by their encounters with the living Spirit of God.[7] Theirs is not, in other words, a reliance only on the Bible in any simplistic sense; instead, their contemporary experiences of the Holy Spirit lead them to resonate with the biblical narratives, so that they utilize what might be called a "this is that!" hermeneutic which sees the "this" of the present connecting with the "that" of (especially) the apostolic life (as recorded in the book of Acts) and vice versa.[8] It is this experientially informed hermeneutic that most radically distinguishes pentecostals from their fundamentalist cousins, many of whom are cessationists regarding the charismata of the Spirit, since any possibility of the ongoing revelation of the Spirit would threaten the rule of "Scripture alone."[9]

Is pentecostal hermeneutics then experientially driven? In light of the preceding, the answer will have to be a nuanced "yes" and "no." Yes, in the sense that experience plays an undeniable role in the pentecostal reading

---

4. I cannot here provide any extensive discussion of this complicated idea. For recent articulations with which some classical pentecostals, especially in North America, would be sympathetic, see Kistler, ed., *Sola Scriptura!*; and Sproul, *Scripture Alone*.

5. See Riggins, "God's Inspired Word."

6. As articulated most forcefully by Gadamer, *Truth and Method*.

7. See Menzies, "Synoptic Theology."

8. I discuss the "this is that" approach to Scripture further in my "The 'Baptist Vision' of James William McClendon, Jr.," esp. 33–34.

9. For a pentecostal response to the cessationism that drives many conservative Reformed theological traditions, see Ruthven, *On the Cessation of the Charismata*.

and interpretation of the Bible, and that astute observers have noted the parallels here with the experientialism characteristic of the more liberal or mainstream Protestant theological traditions.[10] Of course, the major problem with relying on experience is that this can sometimes develop into an ideological agenda that in turn reads Scripture selectively.[11] But pentecostals cannot be said to have adopted an experientialist hermeneutic in the sense that the Bible remains, in most cases,[12] authoritative and normative for pentecostal self-understanding and theological reflection. Philip Jenkins has recently provided a sketch of pentecostal Bible-reading habits in the global south and identified how, in a fundamental way, pentecostals remain a people of the Bible.[13] Yet, any consideration of the role of experience in pentecostal hermeneutics will be complicated by two additional factors: the unresolved question of what precisely is meant by experience and the pluralism of pentecostalism "on the ground." The former question has been registered most forcefully by Donald Gelpi,[14] a theologian of the Roman Catholic charismatic renewal, and his work cautions us about too naive an understanding of the notion of experience, particularly as that interfaces with issues of theological hermeneutics and methodology. The latter concerns the variety of pentecostal experience, especially in the global south.[15] My discussion in chapter 1 highlights pentecostal pluralism with regard to its interface with the public square; beyond these domains, pentecostalism is even more diverse and resistant to categorization. Hence any discussion of pentecostal experience has to be sensitive to the bewildering diversity of the movement, and this inevitably will defy efforts to homogenize the notion for hermeneutical or methodological purposes.

In light of the preceding, pentecostals have recently come to appreciate the important role of community and tradition in the theological task.

10. As suggested by Cox, *Fire from Heaven*, esp. chap. 15.

11. Thus Martin, "The Political Oeconomy of the Holy Ghost," esp. 60–61, discusses how pentecostalism's experience of the Spirit can be hijacked, especially by charismatic leaders, to legitimate sectarian and parochial goals.

12. An exception might be the Friday Masowe apostolics of Zimbabwe—as documented by Engelke, *A Problem of Presence*—who reject the printed Bible as representative of God's word, and operate instead with an understanding of the living word of God as mediated by the Holy Spirit's work in the congregation; however, a close reading of this book will reveal how the church is dependent on the scriptural witness even while publicly eschewing the materiality of the Bible in its own self-understanding.

13. See Jenkins, *The New Faces of Christianity*, esp. chap. 2 and passim.

14. See Gelpi, *The Turn to Experience in Contemporary Theology*, esp. the "Preface"; see also my discussion in "In Search of Foundations," esp. 13–18.

15. An overview is provided by Hollenweger, *The Pentecostals*; see also, more recently, Anderson, *An Introduction to Pentecostalism*.

Experience itself is not only pluriform, but is also open to a multiplicity of interpretations. A theological tradition, however, has to have some unifying features that hold the differences together. Orthodox and Roman Catholic traditions are unified in the early ecumenical councils and (for the latter) the church's teaching magisterium, and these provide a distinctive ecclesial identity even while staking out the hermeneutical and methodological parameters for theological reflection. The unavoidability of tradition has registered itself even among Protestant churches, so much so that many—e.g., Reformed, Anabaptist, Wesleyan, among others—have "founding fathers," authoritative confessions, and a range of canonical voices that shape and guide their ongoing self-understanding. Some pentecostals have therefore begun to identify a historical genealogy especially in the first generation of the movement for theological purposes,[16] and I am not unsympathetic with such a quest. However, one does not have to dig too much in order to discover that the pluralism of pentecostalism is not only a contemporary "problem," but one that is lodged even within the first generation itself.[17] Then there is the additional challenge of Oneness Pentecostalism—which numbers up to one-fourth of the movement worldwide and therefore cannot be ignored—since its rejection of Nicene orthodoxy is a brutal reminder both that the notion of tradition remains problematic theologically and that the historic pluralism of pentecostal traditions will not be unifying anytime soon.

In short, pentecostals appear to be a hodgepodge in terms of theological method. They are, in turn, traditional Protestants regarding the authority of Scripture even while simultaneously being strange bedfellows with liberalism in terms of how experience functions to shape theological understanding. And, with the emergence of pentecostalism in the theological academy, there is now a quest to identify the contours of the pentecostal theological tradition. Whither then pentecostal hermeneutics and theological method?

"STARTING WITH THE SPIRIT": TOWARD A PENTECOSTAL THEOLOGICAL METHOD

I propose that internal to pentecostal spirituality is a distinctive theological impulse that not only values and preserves the diversity of pentecostal experience but also opens up to an ecumenical methodology without

---

16. See especially Archer, *A Pentecostal Hermeneutic for the Twenty-First Century*.

17. Thus Hollenweger, *Pentecostalism*, identifies five roots of pentecostalism: black/African, Catholic, evangelical, critical/prophetic, and ecumenical.

undermining the centrality of Scripture in the theological task. My hypothesis is that starting with the Holy Spirit allows pentecostalism to enter into the debates in theological method on its own terms, even as it invites a specifically pentecostal contribution to the discussion. As I have elsewhere provided extended elaborations of this proposal,[18] let me very briefly summarize the key moves in what follows.

First, the pentecostal "this is that" presumes that the same Holy Spirit who was poured out upon the apostles remains present and active today, and that there is no Christian encounter with God that is not always and already a visitation from, with, and in the Spirit of God. From this, theology, as a second-order activity of reflecting on experience, is informed by life in the Spirit.[19] Having stated it thus, the claim that we begin with the Spirit, both experientially and methodologically, would seem uncontestable. Yet in the history of Christian thought, this insight has rarely been either articulated or its corollary theological project pursued. Part of the reason for this may be that the Spirit has, perennially, been neglected as the "shy" or "hidden" member of the Trinity.[20] I submit that the emergence of this insight came, not coincidentally, following the explosion of the pentecostal and charismatic movement in the twentieth century.[21]

From a pentecostal and charismatic perspective, however, I submit that starting with the Spirit provides a specifically theological rationale for doing theology pluralistically. Let me explicate this claim at three levels: that of experience, that of community, and that of the canonical Scripture. From an experiential perspective, the Lukan account of the Day of Pentecost provides a narrative template that preserves the many languages that separately and together bear witness to the mighty deeds of God (Acts 2:4, 6, 7, 11). Peter's explanation, drawing from the prophet Joel, was that this was the Spirit's eschatological outpouring upon all flesh, equally upon men and women, young and old, slave and free (Acts 2:17–18). In other words, the experiences and voices of those previously marginalized and excluded were now central to the church's witness. The crucial late-modern insight

---

18. The argument is laid out more abstractly in *Spirit-Word-Community*, while the method is clarified in *The Spirit Poured Out on All Flesh*, esp. 27–30, and then exemplified throughout that book.

19. See Yong, "On Divine Presence and Divine Agency," drawing especially from the work of D. Lyle Dabney, as developed in his following essays: "Otherwise Engaged in the Spirit"; "Starting with the Spirit"; and "Why Should the Last Be First?"

20. See Bruner and Hordern, *The Holy Spirit*.

21. For the correlation between pentecostalism and a pneumatological approach to theology, see Pinnock, *Flame of Love*, and Kärkkäinen, *Toward a Pneumatological Theology*.

applicable here is that there is a much more reciprocal and interconnected relationship between language, culture, and experience rather than any simplistic movement from the latter to the former.[22] The strong and perhaps unmistakable inference to be drawn is that the preservation of the many tongues of the Day of Pentecost is an indication that God values not only linguistic diversity but also cultural plurality.[23] In short, the Spirit was given on the Day of Pentecost without partiality to all (cf. Acts 10:34), and this in turn enabled each one to give testimony to the wondrous works of God in his or her own language and from out of his or her own cultural experience.

Yet the pentecostal outpouring not only warrants the diversity of experience at the individual level, but also at the corporate level. Here, we need to turn to St. Paul's reflections on the charismata to see that he observed how the one Spirit gave many gifts (1 Cor 12:4), and baptized all—Jews and Greeks, slave and free—into one body (12:13); yet, the one body is constituted without remainder by many members (12:14-26), and such constitution is accomplished by the Spirit who distributes many gifts. Hence, he concludes, "Now you are the body of Christ and individually members of it" (12:27). I am less interested in how the many gifts of the Spirit reside within the church and function congregationally than I am in the ecumenical implications of Paul's theology of the Spirit's charisms. If the many members constitute one local congregation, then the many local congregations constitute one body of Christ. In this case, the many congregations each contribute something distinctive—derived from the contextual particularities of experience, language, culture, etc.—to the church universal by way of the Spirit's special presence and activity in each locale, and it is only when the many members are recognized and their gifts received that the whole body of Christ is healthy. In short, the many tongues and many gifts of the Spirit are particular expressions of the church universal, each with its own role in the wider church and indispensable regardless of how small or insignificant such may appear.[24]

Last for our purposes (but not least), starting with the Spirit allows us to appreciate the diversity of voices and perspectives that constitute the canonical Scripture. There are two related pneumatological claims here: that involving the pluralism of the Scriptures themselves and that involving the plurality of interpretations of the Scriptures. With regard to the former, I

---

22. This was one of the main arguments in George Lindbeck's influential *The Nature of Doctrine*.

23. For a more extended argument, see also Macchia, "The Tongues of Pentecost"; and Solivan, *The Spirit, Pathos, and Liberation*, 112–18.

24. For elaboration, see Ryan, "Sharing Spiritual Gifts at the Dawn of the Third Millennium"; and Cantalamessa, *Come, Creator Spirit*, esp. chap. 10.

am referring here not only to the theological notion that all Scripture is God-breathed or Spirit-inspired (θεόπνευστος or *theopneustos*—2 Tim 3:16; cf. 2 Pet 1:21), but also to fact that the earliest followers of Jesus also encountered the risen Christ and read the sacred Scripture in the Holy Spirit. In other words, the Scriptures that record these pneumatic encounters and experiences themselves are products of the Spirit's inspiration, so that there are four Gospels, not one; there are multiple ecclesial/communal traditions within the pages of the New Testament—e.g., Matthean, Lukan, Johannine, Pauline, Petrine, and others—not one; and there are, even within one authorial corpus (like St. Paul's), a diversity of perspectives, not one. With regard to the latter, I only note how James's summary at the Jerusalem council (c. 49 CE)—that "For it has seemed good to the Holy Spirit and to us" (Acts 15:28)—points to how the Spirit brings forth new light from the sacred Scripture. In short, the Spirit both inspires the sacred text in all of its pluriformity and illuminates that same text to the many Christian readers and communities of faith across space and time.

I further suggest that given the centrality of the Pentecost narrative in the pentecostal theological imagination, there is a real sense in which pentecostalism is comfortable with the cacophony of the many tongues. What seems to others like drunkenness early in the morning (Acts 2:13–15) is but a sign of the multitudes that have been caught up in the work of the Spirit. In this case, the Pentecost account provides a theological rather than a merely politically correct rationale for methodological pluralism. Yet from a theological perspective, we cannot simply assert that mere pluralism makes sense without some indication of how there can be coherence amidst the many. More importantly, without further theological interpretation, mere pluralism is incapable of discerning the truth of the Holy Spirit from the falsity of many other spirits. So w(h)ither pentecostal pluralism and theological method?

6.5

Pneumatology and Interreligious Engagement[1]

I HAVE PREVIOUSLY ARGUED at length that a pneumatological approach to Christian theology of religions empowers Christian engagement in the interreligious dialogue.[2] I now wish to expand my argument by proposing that a pneumatological theology of religions actually sustains a much wider range of Christian practices vis-à-vis the interreligious encounter,[3] and that this invites, even requires, Christians to discern what the Holy Spirit is saying and doing in specific contexts rather than assume there is only one way to proceed in any interreligious arena. Thus, if we re-examine the witness of the early Christians upon their being empowered by the Holy Spirit on the Day of Pentecost, we find that Christian engagement with the world proceeded at least along three lines.

First, to be sure, the earliest Christians understood themselves as empowered by the Holy Spirit to bear witness to Jesus in Jerusalem, Judea, Samaria, and the ends of the earth (Acts 1:8). This witness bearing included declaring the name and works of Jesus, proclaiming his messiahship, and defending against whatever charges were brought by Jewish or Gentile authorities. No doubt the early Christians understood this pneumatic empowerment to fulfill the promise of Jesus that, "When they bring you before the

1. Yong, *Pneumatology and the Christian-Buddhist Dialogue*, 8–12.

2. See my *Beyond the Impasse*, and also, before that, *Discerning the Spirit(s)*.

3. The following summarizes what is argued at length in my *Hospitality and the Other*.

synagogues, the rulers, and the authorities, do not worry about how you are to defend yourselves or what you are to say; for the Holy Spirit will teach you at that very hour what you ought to say" (Luke 12:11–12).

To be sure, this mode of kerygmatic preaching and apologetic evangelism has been dominant in the traditional history of Christian missionary expansion. Even in a post-9/11 age, however, I suggest that Christian convictions regarding the empowering witness of the Spirit are not misplaced. While there is a greater need than ever to be sensitive to colonialistic, imperialistic, and triumphalistic approaches to the Christian mission and evangelism, this does not mean that the gospel witness to the poor, the sick, and the oppressed—one that "proclaim[s] the year of the Lord's favour," to follow in the footsteps of the Spirit-anointed ministry of Jesus (Luke 4:18)—should be curtailed. Within this context, there will always be opportunities for Christians to share their story, especially with people who are inquiring into the Christian faith. Further, in democratic countries, the freedom to practice religion applies not only to non-Christians but also to Christians. And last but not least (in this regard), the interreligious encounter will remain inauthentic if all people of faith, including Christians, betray their ultimate commitments. Genuine interreligious interaction can only proceed if people of faith engage one another in faith, rather than pretending to be something or someone else. In all of these cases and more, Christians are rightly encouraged to see a pneumatological approach to the interreligious encounter as empowering their bearing witness to the gospel in ways that continue to involve various aspects of the traditional understanding of missionary preaching, evangelism, and apologetics, especially as adapted to the new realities of the twenty-first century.[4]

At a second level, the Spirit's empowering witness also brought about a wide range of interpersonal relations and social practices besides the verbal confession of faith. The communalism described in the early chapters of the book of Acts (2:42–47; 4:34–37; 6:1–3) was no doubt a direct result of their having to learn to live in unity amidst the diversity of cultural, linguistic, and social characteristics that shaped the lives of the earliest Christians. Later on, the Jewish followers of Jesus had to learn that table fellowship and other interactions with Gentiles—beginning with Cornelius but extending to many others in the rest of the Acts narrative—were essential features of their commitments to the Messiah. There were also various kinds of relationships that the early Christians had with those in power, whether that be religious leaders like Simon the magician, political authorities like Felix

---

4. For an astute contemporary defense of interreligious apologetics, see Griffiths, *An Apology for Apologetics*.

and Festus of Caesarea, Agrippa and Bernice, or Publius of Malta, or civic servants like the Philippian jailer or Julius the centurion.

I suggest that a pneumatological theology of the interreligious encounter will identify in these varied interactions between Christians and non-Christians during the early church a diversity of approaches that can be empowered by the Holy Spirit. More specifically, I see that in certain contexts, the Spirit empowers and inspires Christian witness in the social and political domains that include people in other faiths. Oftentimes these social and political relations are most palpably felt at the meal table, with Christians sometimes serving as hosts and other times being treated as guests.[5] In all of this, I propose that a pneumatological theology of religions is better equipped to recognize the plurality of the approaches inspired by the Spirit in the Christian encounter with those in other faiths.

Yet, from the beginning Christian witness has not only included proclamation and service but also has been dialogical, at least in the broad sense of that notion. Paul reasoned and debated (*dialogos*) with philosophers at Athens, and with Jews and Greeks at Thessalonica (Acts 17:2), Corinth (18:4), and Ephesus (19:8–10), among other places. From this we can see that the question is not *whether* the interreligious dialogue but the *how* of dialogue in any particular situation. More pointedly, a pneumatological approach suggests that all effective interreligious engagement—from kerygmatic apologetics to social witness—involves a dialogical component, apart from which authentic interaction breaks down and ethical activity stalls. My claim is that interreligious dialogue is not just about verbal exchanges but about relational interconnection. Further, dialogue involves but is not limited to discursive interlocution. Even the latter can be non-dialogical, and when that happens, dialogue has degenerated into monologue (wherein either both sides are speaking and neither hearing or one side is speaking but the other is not understanding). Dialogical conversation, however, involves not only speech but also listening, reception, and comprehension. Thus dialogue as I understand it is a thoroughly pneumatic or "spiritual" activity involving human persons. What are exchanged are not just words but meaning and relationship, which in their very essence are pneumatologically mediated.[6]

Let me be clear here, however, about how I understand the limits and goals of interreligious dialogue. I have no delusions that interfaith dialogue either will solve all the problems of the world or that it will somehow lead us

---

5. For elaboration, see my articles, "The Spirit of Hospitality"; "The Inviting Spirit"; and "Guests, Hosts, and the Holy Ghost."

6. See also Dabney, "Otherwise Engaged in the Spirit."

to the ultimate truth of all things. Humans are finite creatures and hence all dialogical undertaking cannot escape our halting efforts to tell of the things about which we are convinced or to understand the depth dimensions of the religious life of others. As a Christian and pentecostal theologian, I believe in and am committed to the Lordship of Christ in the power of the Spirit, and our conversation partners from other faiths have their own commitments. My engaging in interfaith discussion is premised on my Christian convictions, not designed to dissolve them. Christian theologians usually do not embark on the dialogical enterprise anticipating to find truth that will be contrary to their deepest convictions. But dialogue will clear away our misunderstandings about religious others. Further, dialogue might also help us recover things we have forgotten about in our tradition. Last, but not least, dialogue may enable us to see things that our tradition either has been silent about or has not so far been pressed to give an account of.

The fact of the matter is that in the kind of pluralistic world that we inhabit today, interfaith dialogue is not a luxury but mandatory. We can no longer remain ignorant about our neighbors of other faiths. Similarly, Christian theology cannot understand itself as isolated from the pluralism of religions. My claim is that a pneumatological theology of the interfaith encounter will empower us to engage afresh this task of self-understanding in a pluralistic world. And while as a Christian I do not expect to discover truths that are contrary to the Spirit of Christ, I also think it possible that the Spirit can illuminate aspects of Christ more clearly in and through our encounter with others, including those in other faiths. This book is predicated on the assumption both that the Holy Spirit will lead Christians into truth, even through encounter with those in other faiths, and that such truth, if it is there to be found, will not contradict but will enhance the truth revealed in Christ. I also believe that only such a pneumatological approach to interreligious dialogue can sustain openness to those in other faiths while simultaneously preserving the nonnegotiable truths of Christian faith. How is this possible again?

I suggest that a pneumatological theology of religions enables both openness to others and Christian commitment through the forging of authenticity in the interreligious dialogue. Such authentic encounter includes at least three components: a) the ability to clearly articulate one's own position; b) the patience to listen carefully to another position and the courage to grapple with what is heard on its own terms first; and c) the capacity to fairly compare, contrast, and evaluate the two positions. The preceding has addressed the first component; the next two sub-sections will provide further justification for the next two aspects of interfaith dialogue.

6.6

Evangelical Theology in the Twenty-First Century

Hybrid Soundings from the Asian American Pent-Evangelical Diaspora[1]

AS A THEOLOGIAN SHAPED by this history, then, I find myself continuously navigating betwixt and between various identities, realities, and relationships. What has emerged can be considered a hybridized identity. By this, however, I mean not just a jumble of confused elements drawn from hither and thither, although sometimes it might feel that (for me) or even seem that (from the perspective of others). Rather, I mean that who I am is the result of a range of histories and particularities that are now interwoven into the fabric of who I am. I can still distinguish the Asian and the American features, although they hold together more in creative tension than they do as if their seams were obliterated. Jesus Christ, himself the "reflection of God's glory and the exact imprint of God's very being" (Heb 1:3), nevertheless took up in his person human nature as well, albeit without either confusing such with or separating such from the divine nature, as the early church taught. By the grace of God, then, according to the image of the incarnate Son into which I am being transformed through the purifying and sanctifying power of the Holy Spirit, these various elements of my identity are being eschatologically redeemed, not eliminated.

1. Yong, *The Future of Evangelical Theology*, 238–49.

Hence my Asian American hybrid identity cannot be understood apart from the other more specifically theological domains that also constitute my life (hi)story. Hybridity does not just cut across our lives variously in the globalizing world of the twenty-first century but is fundamentally theological. In order to see this, let me elucidate ten axes of creative and hybridic tensions that I find intertwined in my own life, each representing distinctive realities that yet precisely in their togetherness inform my testimony and witness to the saving work of God. I explicate these in no particular order.[2]

First, I find myself always between East and West, between Asian and American cultural traditions. In some respects, I am comfortable in either world, but in other respects, I find myself belonging in neither. This is in part because of my ethnic and racial identity, complicated certainly by the dominant black-white framework through which such issues are adjudicated in North America (to which I return in a moment). It is also in part because I now believe that various cultural aspects of my identity are constitutive of the primordial goodness of creation and, in that sense, also anticipate the redemptive work of God. This is not to say that all cultural realities are to be naively adopted into Christian faith. It is to say that there is much more to be considered about the cultural dimensions of Christian life than we have heretofore been open to. Beyond these factors, I ought to note that while I am grateful for the opportunities afforded to me and my immediate family in the United States, I know that part of my identity will always belong in Asia, with my extended family members and their children who remain there. As a person of Chinese descent, I will be on the margins of American life in some or other respect at least for the rest of my lifetime, even as my family members (and myself, if I were to ever return to Malaysia for more than a short-term visit) will remain at the margins of Malaysian life for the foreseeable future. In short, neither can be an ultimate resting place. And I cannot even return to China: any relatives going back a few generations would not know me, not to mention that my American Chinese would be largely incomprehensible to native speakers. Some people might find this situatedness between East and West debilitating; perhaps being *both* Asian *and* American—rather than *either* one or some unrecognizable or synthetic *tertium quid*—it can be a resource for theological reflection relevant to the contemporary global context instead.[3]

---

2. I apologize in advance for the brevity of these presentations, although I have cited mostly my other work wherein I engage with many of these issues more substantively. I urge readers who are interested in my own constructive thinking on these matters to consult these prior publications.

3. See, e.g., my two books, *Pneumatology and the Christian-Buddhist Dialogue*; and *The Cosmic Breath*.

Second, I live as yellow between white and black, but this is now also complicated by shades of browns, not to mention other spectra. As already indicated, my yellowness renders me both a perpetual foreigner and a model minority; yet the latter is also a threatening signifier for the darker hues of browns through blacks. More complexly, my interracial marriage (to a Mexican American woman) cuts against the unspoken prohibition, in the West, of yellow men marrying nonyellow women even as our children are racial hybrids—"Chexicans," as my son has publicly embraced—who may still be best characterized by what they are not: neither white nor black; neither yellow nor brown, "purely" speaking. Still, there are more and more of "them" even if in overall numbers, "they"—Chexicans, that is—are relatively few. Similarly, there are more and more black-white, black-yellow, black-brown, brown-white, brown-yellow, yellow-white and other "combinations," and these will only increase going forward. None of this means that the history of race and ethnicity, in fact and as socially constructed, will be any less important. Their significance, however, will need to be freshly construed by each generation.[4] Perhaps being yellow allows for mediating between other "colors" in ways that preserve their distinctive witnesses while yet also forging a new whole that anticipates the fullness of the coming reign of God. This book presents one effort to think theologically through the implications of Asian American racial and ethnic hybridity within the broader discussion.

Third, I live uneasily between a colonial and postcolonial world. We are about a generation or two removed from independence of most colonized nations. At one level, as a Christian, there is much to be grateful for about how missionaries brought the gospel to the Majority World, including, in my case, pentecostal missionaries who went to Malaysia. And while there were certainly missionaries who were supported and benefited from the colonial enterprise, many were also not politically motivated or directly implicated. On the postindependence side of things, it is also essential to note that the various countries of the world that have emerged from under colonial rule need to take responsibility for themselves and not blame the history of colonization for their woes. Many nations have made successful adjustments since independence, so others can as well. Still, the legacy of colonialism remains to this day, and its mechanisms, deeply embedded in countries and regions of the world across the Global South, continue to reverberate in our shrinking global village. In the United States, the long history of slavery and Native American racism remain palpable in certain parts of this country and continue to haunt our existence in a subterranean manner despite the gains

4. My work in this area is limited to some articles and one edited book—e.g., Yong, "Justice Deprived, Justice Demanded"; and Yong and Alexander, eds., *Afro-Pentecostalism*.

made during the civil rights revolution in the 1960s. In this context and as a member of the Chinese diaspora (twice removed, as I indicated above), I wrestle with the fact that the dominant theological tradition has been implicated in the colonial enterprise. New postcolonial voices and perspectives are emerging, some resisting and rejecting the historic tradition, others (among whom I count myself) seeking to revise, retrieve, or reappropriate the Christian faith for a postcolonial—not to mention postmodern, post-Western, and post-Enlightenment—world.[5] What does it mean to think Christianly and to reconceive Christian theology in light of the historical, social, and political realities after colonialism, not only for Malaysia but for the United States as well? Can we preserve the gains of the Enlightenment while being open also to what late modernity has to offer through subaltern perspectives? How in the end can a hybridic identity that is trinitarianly shaped—christomorphic and pneumatically empowered—redeem the colonial legacy on the one hand yet inspire postcolonial efforts on the other?[6]

Fourth, I live with some ambivalence on this course of upward socioeconomic mobility that I and my family have been traversing. As immigrants to the United States, we came "sponsored" (that is the technical term that includes the promise of financial support for as long as needed) by a missionary and a network of churches, and I looked forward every Christmas to receiving hand-me-downs from charitable Christians who would bless us missionary families who could not otherwise afford to purchase new clothes. My wife was born on the Mexican American migrant trail (her Texan parents were picking cucumbers in Wisconsin when she arrived) and remembers working in the fields every summer even through her college years. Now our combined income places us solidly in the upper-middle-class bracket, and we are awash in our consumerist and materialist cultural way of life. While our fortune in life makes it easier to talk about the providence of God, it also removes us somewhat from the solidarity with the poor that the Scriptures enjoin. In fact, sometimes I think that the individualistic, evangelical gospel of justification by grace through faith legitimates my way of life: it justifies my home ownership while being presumptive about others who lack such as simply not working hard enough. After all, my own Asian American upbringing instilled in me that if I worked hard enough, got straight A's, and completed medical school (I did a PhD instead!) that I could live the American dream. So when I read about

---

5. See my concluding reflections to a volume on the Christian mission to Native America: Yong, "The Missiology of Jamestown"; cf. Yong and Winn, "The Apocalypse of Colonialism, Colonialism as Apocalyptic Mission."

6. Two books of mine address different aspects of this issue: theologically in *In the Days of Caesar*, and scripturally in *Who is the Holy Spirit?*.

Jesus having nowhere to lay his head and Paul being a missionary tentmaker who was content in whatever situation he found himself, I ask myself if my contentment derives from Christ or from my relatively financially secure situation. John Wesley's maxim regarding generosity—that is, "Having, First, gained all you can, and, Secondly saved all you can, Then 'give all you can'"[7]—is haunting since I am sure we can give more, especially to those less well-off. I justify our condition saying that compared to others, we are only relatively comfortable, but it is undeniable that a much larger percentage of the world lives with much, much less than we do. In short, we sometimes are guilty about our prosperity, yet also often are thankful that our debt load is minimal and that we have enough to pay our bills at the end of the month. What is the fine line here between having enough and having too much, between living in a plentiful United States (or any other "promised land") and elsewhere in regions struck by famine, war, and other conditions inimical to economic stability, development, and growth? Perhaps it is possible to live faithfully and creatively either in simplicity or in plenty—or between them—as appropriate in accordance with various life stages, vocational calls, and circumstantial periods.[8]

Fifth, I struggle strenuously with how my Christian faith commitments are in some ways fundamentally opposed to yet also in other ways not exclusive of other faiths. This is my reality—I cannot deny that what I am as a person of Chinese descent is already a hybrid combination of the philosophical, cultural, and religious traditions of East and Southeast Asia. In the West, we might think these various strands are detachable from one another and therefore that it might be acceptable to embrace the cultures but not the religions of the East. But in reality, these are overlapping domains. Part of the challenge is that at least some traditions of Christianity consider any association with other religious traditions in negative terms as "syncretism." I desire neither an uncritical syncretism nor a bland, lowest-common-denominator theology that is inclusive of other faiths. Simultaneously, I also do not think that some versions of theological exclusivism can account for the complicated interreligious lives and identities that are being formed through the gospel. While being for Christ will entail being against some aspects of other faiths, perhaps this leads not to complete repudiation but anticipates their eschatological fulfillment.[9] If Paul's identity in Christ, for instance, did not eradicate his Jewishness even as it prompted substantial interrogation of what it meant to be a faithful Christ follower, might this

---

7. See Wesley's sermon (1760), "The Use of Money," 355.
8. See my chapter in Yong and Attanasi, eds., *Pentecostalism and Prosperity*.
9. As expertly argued by Satyavrata, *God Has Not Left Himself Without Witness*.

not also be the case for those in other faiths? Meanwhile, then, perhaps the tensions amid these domains can serve as a resource for creatively rethinking Christian commitments in a global multireligious context as outlined at the end of the previous chapter.[10]

The preceding Pauline example leads, sixthly, to discussion of identity in Christ that is between ancient Israel and contemporary Judaism. Is Christianity Jewish or not? Yes and no are probably both correct answers. The issues are particularly urgent in light of the long history of Christian anti-Semitism culminating in the Holocaust. Post-Shoah Christian self-understandings cannot afford to ignore how Christian views of the Jews have had tragic political and historical consequences. Complicating contemporary Christian and Jewish relationships are the emergence of messianic Jews and back-to-Jerusalem movements. The former are certainly well received in evangelical Christian circles but severely contested among Jews, while the latter are prominent in East Asian contexts and growing in global influence. On the one hand, many Christians insist on the ongoing evangelization of Jews; on the other hand, our theological self-understanding is not as deeply informed by the Hebrew Bible as it ought to be. In fact, there is a spectrum of response across the Christian community about how to understand the relevance of that portion of the biblical canon in relationship to the New Testament. Has the ancient covenant with Israel been subsumed into the church, or does it persist in some respects parallel to that of the new covenant in Christ? Therein lies part of the challenge about how Christians should relate to Jews in the contemporary world. No doubt, intermarriages between Jews and Christians have complicated this question of identity for both Christians and Jews. Rather than having to be either for or against Judaism today, the Christian way forward may be more adequately charted as one that embraces the Jewish roots of Christian faith in a post-Holocaust world. If so, then Christian faith is neither Jewish nor anti-Jewish but involves instead a hybridic posture between these options, one with the potential to transform the world in anticipation of the coming reign of God.[11]

Seventh, as a pentecostal I ride the tension that persists between more evangelical and more ecumenical forms of Christianity today. To be sure, such tensions are more relaxed today than at any time in the last century. Nevertheless, there are still debates between "conservatives" and "liberals," between "orthodoxy" and "progressivism," between confessional and mainline Protestantism (and Catholicism and Orthodoxy as well). In the

---

10. I have long wrestled with these matters, most recently in my *Hospitality and the Other*.

11. I struggle with this question in the final (eighth) chapter of my *In the Days of Caesar*; see also the literature cited there.

United States, and especially in the Asian American evangelical arena, the lines between "right" and "left" are more hard and fast than in other parts of the English-speaking world, even if the emergence of postconservative forms of Evangelicalism is erasing some of the rigidity. Certainly, as I have indicated above, in some parts of the Majority World, there is much more cooperation when confronted by the need to mobilize smaller numbers for common causes. This is not to say that pentecostals and Evangelicals need to give up on all their theological convictions. Neither is it to say that both sides are beyond critique in their respective commitments. It is to say that there may be better ways of holding to at least some of these convictions that more appropriately engage contemporary challenges. My point is that a hybridic response requires neither a negation of the good and true on either side nor some unwieldy and inauthentic both-and amalgamation but rather a redemptive way beyond either-or that seeks to be faithful to Scripture according to the image of Christ by the power of the Spirit.[12]

This leads, eighth, to a discussion of how pentecostal identity has existed in creative tension from its emergence at the beginning of the twentieth century with the self-understanding of the broader Christian tradition. On the one hand, the pentecostal belief in the baptism of the Holy Spirit that empowers Christian witness, as evidenced by speaking in tongues, suggests that those without such experiences are second-tier Christians (at best), if not members of nonvital churches from which they should depart (at worst). This view fosters a kind of pentecostal elitism that, not surprisingly, rubs other Christians the wrong way. On the other hand, the fact that pentecostals often attract nominal Christians from other churches has led also to concerns and accusations about pentecostal proselytism and "sheep stealing." These tensions are exacerbated in Asian and other ecumenical contexts internationally when pentecostal missionaries and evangelists approach other putatively Christian groups with an aggressive message of conversion. Against this backdrop, how can I maintain my pentecostal commitments without perpetuating the triumphalism characteristic of pentecostal attitudes from earlier eras? In addition, there is also the phenomenon of Oneness Pentecostalism—trinitarian pentecostals do not like to acknowledge this aspect of the modern renewal movement, but it is present nonetheless, especially in the ways that even trinitarian pentecostals count the demographics of global renewal. Is it possible to consider pentecostal Christianity as presenting certain gifts to the churches, even from the Oneness

---

12. I would argue that the issues are in part hermeneutical and in part methodological; see my *Spirit-Word-Community*.

perspective,[13] while yet inviting pentecostals to be open to receiving the gifts of other churches at the same time? Can such a mutual gift exchange preserve the distinctiveness and uniqueness of the pentecostal message—even across the trinitarian and Oneness divide—while not demeaning those of other Christian traditions? Is this what it might mean to receive the many gifts of the Holy Spirit that are given through the many and different members of the church?[14] Again, the hybridic response is that pentecostal Christianity remains distinctive yet is not set off completely from the broader Christian tradition; instead, there are opportunities for distinctive witness to resound, resulting in mutual edification and even transformation.

Ninth, I am a committed egalitarian when it comes to gender relations yet one who is continuously navigating the via media between evangelical complementarianism on the one side and evangelical feminism on the other. As already discussed, from a pent-evangelical perspective, the biblical case for the Spirit's empowering women across the full range of ministries is clearly arguable. However, many Asian American evangelical churches and congregations are hesitant about reading certain epistolary passages in light of the Day of Pentecost narrative in Acts, an attitude consistent with wider swaths of the evangelical world that affirm that male and female are equal in the sight of God yet assigned complementary (distinct) ministerial and other roles. On the other side, it is also undeniable that the renewalist fire that has swept across the world, even in the Asian context, has been lighted by women, both going back to nineteenth-century evangelical missionaries and certainly featuring consistently across the twentieth-century pentecostal and charismatic renewal movements. How to affirm this basic pentecostal principle while honoring culturally particular perspectives and alternative readings of the Scriptures in global context? How to empower women within biblical frames of reference while distancing from the more radically construed feminist political ideologies? How might the work and ministry of women be lifted up in ways that are edifying for others—for men, for the church, and for the world—and yet not imposed (imperialistically) on those who do not currently see such matters similarly (and may never come around to this egalitarian position)? In some circles, church unity is threatened precisely on this point. A hybridic response, however, would neither minimize nor exacerbate the differences but rather seek for mutual understanding within the broader quest for common witness in

---

13. As done so brilliantly by Reed, *"In Jesus' Name"*.

14. I confront the Oneness challenge plus explicate an expansive pentecostal theology in my *The Spirit Poured Out on All Flesh*, esp. chap. 5.

Christ. As in every one of these cases, perhaps what is needed is nothing less than a fresh and global outpouring of the Holy Spirit.[15]

Perhaps the nine tensions that have been described so far participate in this last one I will describe: that of living between now and eternity. The New Testament does, in various places, identify followers of Jesus Christ as "aliens and exiles" (1 Pet 2:11) who are seeking another, heavenly, city and country (Heb 11:17). Thus we are sojourners, continuously living a diasporic existence, thrust into a world that is in some ways not our home. At the same time, the goal is not merely to escape from the world, as we anticipate a transformation of the present world and its remaking as a new one fit for the presence of God and the new city of God. Thus the book of Revelation clearly indicates that "the kings of the earth will bring their glory into it [the new Jerusalem that descends to the earth]," and that "people will bring into it the glory and the honor of the nations" (Rev 21:24, 26). In that sense, then, we live between the now and the not-yet, between this world and the coming reign of God, between the Asian America of the present era and the whole world that will be redeemed by the triune God. There are certainly discontinuities between the present age and the one to come; but there are also continuities in how the redemption of this world will contribute to the glory of the one that is coming. This is hybridic Christian life: fully in but not of the coming world, while yet now anticipating, in Christ, the coming reign of God.[16]

I am motivated also by the scenario in Revelation that there will be around the throne of the Lamb "saints from every tribe and language and people and nation" (Rev 5:9; cf. Rev 7:9; 14:6). This tells me that God's final redemptive work will include not just souls in the abstract but real flesh-and-blood peoples in all of their linguistic, cultural, sociopolitical, and historical particularity. This is also consistent with the description of God's salvific work manifest through the Day of Pentecost narrative that lies at the center of my own pentecostal faith. The outpouring of the Spirit was also not on souls in the abstract but on men *and* women, older *and* younger, free *and* slave, from various regions of the known world, and embodying different histories, sufferings, experiences, and hopes. These pilgrims to Jerusalem, while all Jews at varying depths of commitment, were encountered by the living God. Their lives in all their complexity were there and then recruited to declare the wondrous works of God.[17]

15. See Yong and Alexander, eds., *Philip's Daughters*.

16. I develop such an eschatological theology in my book, with Anderson, *Renewing Christian Theology*; cf. Yong, *The Spirit of Creation*, chaps. 3–4.

17. As developed in my book *Spirit of Love*.

My claim would be that our status as aliens and strangers invites us to think about diaspora and hybridity not as marginal or incidental aspects of Christian faith but indeed as central to it. Hybridized identities hold together particularities in productive tension; as such, historical identities are also never pure, as if untinged by otherness. This does not mean that all languages, all cultures, all ethnic or racial aspects of human identity, and all religious traditions are equal. The gospel comes to judge as well as to purify. But my account here suggests also that the gospel comes to redeem, which means literally to "buy back." This means that in God's scheme of things, various aspects of our histories and life stories will find new meaning in light of our encounter with the God of the divine-human Jesus Christ, whose light has shone into every heart (John 1:9) and whose Spirit has been poured out upon all flesh (Acts 2:17) and potentially also into each human soul (Rom 5:5). This also means that we no longer have to be ashamed of our hybridized identities, neither as individuals nor as congregations, churches, and even as the church catholic. Instead, it is the nature of the church as the people of God, the body of Christ, and the fellowship of the Spirit to be constituted by manyness, difference, and plurality, albeit not in ways that perpetuate hostilities or antagonisms. To embrace our hybridized identities—whether yellow or "red," or even black or white—is to not have to assimilate to the dominant culture in ways that erase our differences but to be able to maintain solidarity in differentiated ways, with others nearer and further, and to be able to navigate these multiple spectrums, colors, and discourses in order to participate in and facilitate the pentecostal fellowship of the one Spirit with its many voices.[18] Hence for me as an Asian American and pent-evangelical yet ecumenical theologian, this is a redemptive word that I hope resounds also for others—all of us in some way or other—caught betwixt and between multiple worlds.

I present these soundings from the Asian American diaspora to my evangelical and Christian sisters and brothers in part because I think any centering of the church on any of these axes (rather than on Christ) portends its ossification. When the above tensions are resolved, voices from the margins, from the diasporas wherein the winds of the Spirit blows, will need to infuse new life into institutionalized forms of faith. The diaspora now no longer remains the frontier where Christianity is expanding, and the hybridic is now no longer, in Christ and the Spirit, the marginalized alien or mulattic other. Instead, diaspora captures the very heart of God's saving work, no matter when, where or among whom, and hybridity reflects the promise of trinitarian redemption of the many into the eschatological

---

18. See also Yong, *Who is the Holy Spirit?*.

harmony. No tribes are too "primitive"; no languages are too "barbaric"; no peoples are too uncultured; and no nations are too pagan. All are hybrids in some or other respect, and anyone, anywhere, anytime, may represent the surprising work of the Spirit in anticipation of the coming reign of God. Perhaps the preceding pages will help us to recognize the gospel notes within what otherwise might be no more than a cacophony of Asian American and pent-evangelical voices in the contemporary global situation.

6.7

The Dialogical Spirit[1]

THE *DIALOGICAL* SPIRIT

WE BEGIN WITH SOME remarks on the nature of dialogue going forward. This volume has suggested that Christian theological method is empowered by dialogical activity. The dialogical undertakings modeled here are those with other individuals: philosophers, theologians, theologian-scientists, scholars of other faiths, comparativists, anthropologists, missiologists—the list could be expanded if this were a longer book. To be sure, the question of why these twelve specific discussion partners and not another twelve (or however many) is a bit arbitrary. In some ways, we choose our friends (or interlocutors), but in other ways, our friends choose us. I have given some reasons (in the Introduction) for how my thinking with these "friends" emerged, but I will never be able to exhaustively rationalize how they arrived or why they remain (or not) within my conversation orbit. As a Christian theologian, I would thank God for these blessings, yes, even for my Buddhist conversation partners. What each one has taught me is that to appreciate and understand (to the extent that has happened at all) requires respectful and patient listening. To the degree that these have challenged and informed my own thinking, that is because they themselves have wrestled deeply with the difficult questions of theological (or philosophical or religious) methodology in our complex postfoundationalist, et al., domain. If I am going to disagree with them, I cannot do so apart from prolonged

---

1. Yong, *The Dialogical Spirit*, 282–90.

and sustained accompaniment with their ideas and even ways of life. More often than not, I feel less motivated to critically oppose their views; rather, I see many opportunities to expand my own thinking in conversation with them. This reflects my sense that Christian theologians like me aspire to make universal truth claims, but realize that in our contemporary public square, such proceeds best as an a posteriori achievement rather than an a priori assumption.

Of course, there will be some who will balk at the kinds of conversation partners I have chosen, or perhaps counter-suggest that there are limits to who ought to be around the discussion table. I agree: in some instances, when greeted by the devil, for example, the dialogical approach ought to be replaced expeditiously by an exorcistic strategy.[2] Part of the difficulty here, of course, is that the Satan, however "he" may be understood, comes as an angel of light (2 Cor 11:14) so as to be somewhat unrecognizable, even as, on the other side, we might believe we are encountering the Satan when we are not. Without minimizing the import for proper discernment, I would clarify that theological dialogue proceeds both contextually (within specific situations) and teleologically (for specific purposes), among other criteria.

The present discussion has been lifted up under four overarching contexts: an epistemological environment after the demise of early modern foundationalism; a cultural period after the passing of Christianity as a politically dominant reality; an information age beyond the sacred-secular divide that brings science and the religions together in the public square in new ways; and a late if not postmodern era within which the meeting of the religions portends either a clash of civilizations or a debilitating subjectivism and relativism. Together, these contexts emphatically announce that ours is an exceedingly pluralistic world, one in which a multitude of voices are both clamoring to be heard as well as attempting to resound over those of others. To be sure, who the appropriate dialogue partners are for any conversations will need to be discerned on a case-by-case basis. But it also may well be that any discussions will be attended by many others. Even any more narrowly circumscribed dialogue will be conducted in the presence of others, some more, others less interested. Hence the dialogical spirit is always already polyphonic and multivocal, both in fact and potentially.

None of this is to say that any case will not be contested; such disputes can derive from arguing variously about the appropriateness of potential discussants while others might result in disagreement either about the nature of the context(s) or the prioritization of the various issues. In any case, although Christian proclamation will always be carried out in the public

---

2. I discuss the challenges involved in my *Hospitality and the Other*, 118–25.

square and will proceed at least where there are democratic governments and religious freedom, Christian theological reflection only goes as far as making the case for such succeeds. So if in the twenty-first century Christian claims to universality cannot be presumed amidst the many voices, then arguments will have to be made on at least the four fronts that I have identified in this book, if not more. Some might want to argue that the universality of Christian truth can be asserted regardless of the contexts—that by nature is what Christian truth consists of, however scandalous such may sound to politically correct ears. Even if such scandal were presumed theologically, declaration without argumentation—the rhetorical scandal—will not convince, not to mention also will not be heard by, those who otherwise exist amidst at least these four contexts I have identified.

But even if we agreed on the horizons toward which global Christian theology traverses, what is the goal of such navigation? Why dialogue at all? What are the ends in view? There are at least three reasons for the Christian theological tasks in the present global context. First, Christian self-understanding is contextually situated; hence, mature Christian identities, for individual persons or groups of persons (congregations), or collections of faith communities (networks, denominations, church traditions, etc.) will need to be articulated at least in part vis-à-vis the identities of others, both within (ecumenically) and without (interreligiously) the Christian faith. Hence dialogue accomplishes the important purpose of getting to know others in order that we can understand ourselves better, how we are distinct from others, and what commonalities we may or may not share.

Second, dialogue that leads to the understanding of others enables more faithful, appropriate, and relevant Christian witness in relationship to and with the other, especially those of other or no faith, although also ecumenically. Such witness might be relational, ethical, social, activistic, or kerygmatic (involving Christian proclamation of the gospel). In any case, such witness unfolds more effectively—as measured not necessarily by conversions (although that may be one criterion) but by the full scope of the Scriptural witness concerning the Christian testimony—when informed by dialogical interchange. At the very least, we are better prevented from bearing false witness against our neighbor because authentic dialogue exposes our prejudices and replaces them with a more truthful portrait. At its best, the Christian witness brings about repentance and the expansion of the gospel message.

Last but not least, dialogue with others, Christians and religious or unreligious others, informs faithful Christian praxis. How then do we live faithfully in the complicated postfoundationalist, post-Christendom, post-secular, postmodern, and pluralist context of our present situation? Faithful living means, in part, being able to flourish with others, and such flourishing requires that we know our neighbors in order that we can develop common cause toward a more just and humane world. Dialogue enables such vital praxis to emerge. The Christian theological endeavor contributes to such an important objective when it proceeds dialogically in and with the company of others.[3]

THE DIALOGICAL *SPIRIT*

So far, my comments in this concluding chapter have unpacked the dialogical aspect of theological work in terms of its nature, context, and aims. In this section, however, we have to make an explicitly theological turn. More particularly, our pivot will be pneumatological, in light of this major thrust over the course of this book. The argument throughout is that only a pneumatologically inspired and empowered imagination is capable of both listening to the many voices but also critically discerning their contributions. Put alternatively, only a pneumatological imagination is able to sustain the dialogical task in a pluralistic world. However, although the pneumatological imagination proposed is informed specifically by pentecostal-charismatic spirituality and perspective, in theological terms, the Holy Spirit is still no less than the Spirit of Jesus and the Spirit of God. How then might we further understand the dialogical character of theological reflection and formulation in light of these pneumatological themes?

First and foremost, the dialogue enabled by the Holy Spirit will ultimately point to Jesus Christ. This means that Christians who are dialogically engaged will inevitably, even if also incessantly, revolve around Christ. Here the life of Christ, his teachings, and his selfless and atoning death are the normative shape of the Spirit's presence and activity. Voices, behaviors, and phenomena that are contrary to this Christic and cruciform character are those of the antichrist and hence opposed also to the spirit of Jesus. Those that manifest the fruits of the spirit of Christ (Gal 5:22-24) and are consistent with the values of the *shalom* Jesus, proclaimed and embodied, can be said to at least anticipate, if not also participate in, the coming reign of God.

At the same time, because Christ is the one who is also yet to come and we see through a glass dimly (1 Cor 13:12), it may well be that this testimony to Christ proceeds without the awareness of those who are witnessing, at least for the moment. Furthermore, our reception of the testimony of others may also lead us to deeper awareness and new appreciation of the

---

3. See Jensen, *In the Company of Others*; see also my review essay, "Globalizing Christology."

living Christ, even if we are initially unable to communicate why. We may find ourselves transformed into greater Christlike-ness only in hindsight, even as others come into more consciously thematized knowledge of Christ only eschatologically. On the other hand, if we gradually or otherwise cease to bear the fruits of the spirit of Christ in the course of our dialogical encounter, then the conversation will be animated by other spirits—at least our own, certainly—rather than the spirit of Jesus. Similarly, others who bear fruits opposed to those of the Holy Spirit are animated also by forces other than Christ. And when moved by the spirit of Jesus, there may come moments when dialogue ceases and other activities commence. Christians will often disagree about if and when such moments arrive. Arguably, the more christomorphic the pneumatological imagination, the more sensitivity exists about whether to press ahead dialogically versus shifting the *modus operandi*.

Christian trinitarianism also insists that however else the doctrine of the triune deity is understood, the spirit of Jesus is also the spirit of God and these aspects of the Spirit's identity are both related and distinct. Certainly, this distinction-in-relationship cannot involve internal contradictions so that to be the Spirit of one disallows being the Spirit of the other. Simultaneously, this relationship-in-distinction can open up to complementarity so that the light of the spirit of God can illuminate the person of Christ while the sending of the spirit of Jesus can unveil or reveal the image of God. Hence that the spirit of Jesus is the spirit of God accentuates the eschatological horizon of the dialogical journey. In the end, those who are of the spirit of Jesus will also be subordinate to the living God "so that God may be all in all" (1 Cor 15:28), even as those who are of the spirit of God will bend their knee at the name of Jesus and confess Christ's lordship "to the glory of God the Father" (Phil 2:12). In some cases in this time before the end, we may not recognize the one from the other; in other cases, there will be harmony and rejoicing when we come to see the other in the light of our commitments. If the disagreements obstruct the manifestation of the Spirit's fruits, then the spirit of God and of Christ has been grieved. On the other side, the appearance of the fruits of the Spirit is no guarantee. Somehow, "no one can say 'Jesus is Lord' except by the Holy Spirit" (1 Cor. 12:3), even as some will say "Lord, Lord" but Jesus will respond: "I never knew you; go away from me, you evildoers" (Matt 7:21, 23). The point for Christians is both not to be overly confident that their confession always reflects the spirit of Jesus and to realize that others who do not (yet) have the spirit of Christ, at least epistemologically, may nevertheless have the spirit of God, at least provisionally even if partially. But in the latter case the proper response should always be Christian witness, and this engages, again, the dialogical Spirit.

Last but not least, the spirit of Christ is also the Spirit of Pentecost, the Spirit of the church understood as the body of Christ, the people of God, and the fellowship of the Holy Spirit. This means that the church plays a distinctive role in bearing witness to Jesus by the power of his Holy Spirit. Simultaneously, the Spirit has been poured out eschatologically on all flesh (Acts 2:17) so as to make possible the witness to Jesus through the many tongues of the human condition. Hence the church boldly declares the name of Jesus even while it receives the testimony of others "about God's deeds of power" (Acts 2:11). This is the nature of the dialogical Spirit, to empower the witness of all to all, albeit in different respects. Those of the gathering of God—the *ekklesia* or congregation—are filled with the spirit of Jesus to lift up his name so that not only will Israel "know with certainty that God has made him both Lord and Messiah, this Jesus whom you crucified" (Acts 2:36), but that "all the families of the earth shall be blessed" (Acts 3:25). Simultaneously, those with the spirit of God will encounter dreams and visions, not to mention "portents in the heaven above and signs on the earth below" (Acts 2:19) so that "everyone who calls on the name of the Lord shall be saved" (Acts 2:21) according to his salvific power achieved through the spirit of Jesus. The scriptural reference to the eschatological outpouring of the Spirit "on all flesh" (Acts 2:17) would in this case involve also a perlocutionary invitation to those filled with the Spirit to bear witness to Christ to the ends of the earth (Acts 1:8).

The dialogical Spirit hence resolutely lifts up the person of Christ through his body; simultaneously, the dialogical Spirit builds up the body of Christ through the testimony of others, precisely so that the fellowship of the Spirit can bear more and more adequate witness to the God of Jesus Christ, as delineated above. Hence the spirit of Christ is present and at work in and through dialogue even as the spirit of God makes dialogue with others possible at all.

THE PNEUMATOLOGICAL IMAGINATION AND THEOLOGICAL METHOD FOR THE TWENTY-FIRST CENTURY

We are now on the final stretch, and I need to sketch some responses to one final set of questions before we conclude this discussion. Treatises on theological method classically deal both with the sources for theological reflection and their operational procedures.[4] This volume has argued that

---

4. The Anglican "triad" of Scripture, tradition, and reason, and the Wesleyan "quadrilateral" that added experience, focus on theological sources; the classical operational "manual," as it were, is Lonergan's *Method in Theology*.

a pneumatological imagination inspires and enables dialogical relationality that furthers the thinking and doing of theology. Yet we have said little about how to bring Scripture and tradition into the conversation. In this final section I briefly and quickly outline three models of such dialogical integration—one scripturally oriented, another communally shaped, and a third systematically construed—from my own work in order to illustrate the pneumatological imagination's capacity for bringing the past into the present and future.

First, one approach to Scripture and tradition attempts to foreground especially Scripture's own horizons of understanding. Classically, such a hermeneutical model emphasizes exegesis or a biblical-theological methodology that privileges Scripture's own categories and discursive rationality. My book, *Who is the Holy Spirit?: A Walk with the Apostles*,[5] is the closest I come to such a scripturally framed argument, beginning and working through the book of Acts and then, every other chapter, returning to the Gospel of Luke to reflect on the life and teachings of Jesus as may have been pertinent to whatever it was the apostolic community was encountering and having to resolve. Even in this sense, however, the Acts narrative provides the framework for reading the third Gospel and some exegetes might complain that this reversal does not honor Luke's own ordered sequence (in the sense that the Gospel was written before the Acts narrative). Beyond this important point, *Who is the Holy Spirit?* presents a reading of the Acts-Luke material framed by the quest to understand the public rather than only the ecclesial work of the Holy Spirit. Yet although I argue in the book that such an approach is consistent with Luke's own insistence that the outpouring of the Spirit is to the ends of the earth and upon all flesh, and thus has explicitly public scope, others might disagree that my justification is warranted.[6] In my own defense, I can only say that any reading of Scripture that tries only to stay with the scriptural horizon will be of little interest to third-millennium, much less twenty-fist-century, concerns. And once the latter is factored into the equation, then what often emerges is a conflict of interpretations (as Paul Ricoeur put it)[7] for many reasons, including how dialogical (or not) the intersection is between the scriptural and contemporary vistas.

Who is the Holy Spirit?, while not being a work of pentecostal hermeneutics per se, reflects my own quest as a pentecostal Christian to understand the Holy Spirit's wider work in the world. In that respect, I would insist that the Scriptures, including Luke-Acts, do not stand alone but are

---

5. Yong, *Who is the Holy Spirit?*.
6. Most vociferous here is Stronstad, "Review Essay on Amos Yong."
7. Ricoeur, *The Conflict of Interpretations*.

what they are as the authoritative word of God precisely as and through belonging to the church, the people of God. Hence, every faithful reading of Scripture is ecclesial or traditioned in some respect. My own is specifically pentecostal in overall hermeneutical sensibilities,[8] although as should be apparent from this book, such a pentecostal orientation is not set off from evangelical, ecumenical, and even broader cultural and interfaith concerns. The point is that Scripture is mediated in part by tradition and hence has a communal or ecclesial dimension. The dialogical imagination thus involves Scripture, tradition, and the church, along with contemporary voices.

My book *In the Days of Caesar: Pentecostalism and Political Theology*[9] reflects both how Scripture (again Luke-Acts, which predominates here) is carried ecclesially and how specific ecclesial perspective's (in this case pentecostal communities) reading and retrieving Scripture combine to enable engagement with important matters of the present time (in this case related to the political arena of Christian life). What emerges out of this book are five sustained interfaces with the Lukan material in the five constructive chapters of the book (Part II), informed by the pentecostal "five-fold gospel" (of Jesus as savior, sanctifier, Spirit-baptizer, healer, and coming king), and applied to matters of public and political importance. Scripture is here read as informing contemporary issues, although care is taken to ensure that the biblical authors' commitments are not taken in directions that they would have opposed. The point is that communal concerns and motivations (pentecostal ones here) shape, at least in part, how the scriptural message is reappropriated from age to age. The dialogical imagination is thus mediated by the opportunities and challenges confronted by ecclesial communities in attempting to remain faithful to the apostolic witness in the present global political context.

As first and foremost a systematic theologian,[10] however, the genre and its traditional manifestations could also shape my reading of Scripture and engagement with the tradition. How then might the dialogical and pneumatological imagination developed in this volume structure systematic theological reflection in the twenty-first century global context? I am glad you asked, as one of my newest books, *Renewing Christian Theology: Systematics for a Global Christianity*, presents precisely such a model.[11] Three interconnected aspects of *Renewing Christian Theology's* methodology concretely unfold the claims of the present volume. First, starting with the Spirit means

---

8. Which I summarize briefly in an article, "Reading Scripture and Nature."
9. Yong, *In the Days of Caesar*.
10. One of my earliest essays was "Whither Systematic Theology?."
11. See Yong, with Anderson, *Renewing Christian Theology*.

we begin with pneumatology and eschatology, the Spirit being the triune person of the present and coming age who reconciles creation back to the Father in and through the Son. Our systematic theology thus proceeds from eschatology (where we are going) to the doctrine of Scripture so that the foundations of Scripture are illuminated within an ecclesial and theological framework rather than the other way around. Second, the focus is on the renewal movement that is at the vanguard of contemporary global Christianity, so each doctrinal locus is discussed not only historically in light of the church's traditional teachings but also with regard to the dogmatic commitments of a specific renewal movement (the classical Pentecostal Assemblies of God church) and vis-à-vis the global theological ferment. Third, then, the third section of each chapter focuses on reading a specific book of the New Testament in light of the historical, ecclesial, and contextual issues and directed toward reconsidering how to understand the doctrinal theme that chapter addresses in the present time.

I have opted for such a methodological approach to the scriptural traditions in order to weave two kinds of dialogical commitments into the systematic theological task. First, rather than a proof-text approach, the various theological and doctrinal considerations will benefit from sustained interactions with whole scriptural texts (i.e., Gospels, letters). Thus we will be able to develop a deeper scriptural treatment when we unveil what the biblical author has to say about any particular topic in light of the whole of that writing. Second, of course, what is proposed within the scope of a limited volume, as long as it might be, is still only a model for reading Scripture, and readers are invited to continue their reflection by adding other scriptural books, eventually even consulting the entirety of the scriptural canon, for a more thorough set of authoritative perspectives. In other words, the dialogue with Scripture is fluid and dynamic, always ever unfolding, ebbing and flowing as those motivated to theological reflection continue to mine the wellsprings of the Christian tradition and revision new and faithful responses in ever-changing contemporary contexts. The result is, as the book's title aspires to achieve, the renewal of Christian theology.

Much more can be said about reading Scripture and tradition in dialogue with present circumstances and realities. I can only suggest that all of my monographs attempt such a dialogical approach and each is informed by the authority of Scripture, albeit in its own way (related to the topic, audience, purposes, etc.). Any dialogical theology will feature multiple modalities of not only thinking with Scripture but also of engaging the tradition with current opportunities and challenges. The pneumatological imagination that we have presented in this book thus can be seen to not only invite such an expansive dialogical vision but also in many ways to mandate that any theology desiring to speak boldly and faithfully will need to listen to and interact with the many voices and engage with, even enter practically into, the many ways of life present in the third millennium.

Bibliography

Ablon, Joan. *Little People in America: The Social Dimensions of Dwarfism.* New York: Praeger, 1984.

———. *Living with Difference: Families with Dwarf Children.* New York: Praeger, 1988.

Abraham, William J. *Canon and Criterion in Christian Theology: From the Fathers to Feminism.* Oxford: Clarendon, 1998.

Adelson, Betty M. *The Lives of Dwarfs: Their Journey from Public Curiosity toward Social Liberation.* New Brunswick, NJ: Rutgers University Press, 2005.

Adler, Mortimer J. *Truth in Religion: The Plurality of Religions and the Unity of Truth.* New York: Macmillan/Collier, 1990.

Alexander, Kimberly Ervin. *Pentecostal Healing: Models in Theology and Practice.* Blandford Forum: Deo, 2006.

Alexander, P. N. "Spirit Empowered Peacemaking: Toward a Pentecostal Peace Fellowship." *Journal of the European Pentecostal Theological Association* 22 (2002) 78–102.

Althouse, Peter. *Spirit of the Last Days: Pentecostal Eschatology in Conversation with Jürgen Moltmann.* London: T&T Clark, 2003.

Anderson, Allan. *An Introduction to Pentecostalism: Global Charismatic Christianity.* Cambridge: Cambridge University Press, 2004.

Anderson, Robert Mapes. *Vision of the Disinherited: The Making of American Pentecostalism.* New York: Oxford University Press, 1979.

Archer, Kenneth J. *A Pentecostal Hermeneutic for the Twenty-First Century: Spirit, Scripture, and Community.* London: T&T Clark, 2004.

Arens, Edmund. "Jesus' Communicative Actions: The Basis for Christian Faith Praxis, Witnessing, and Confessing." *The Conrad Grebel Review* 3, no. 1 (1985) 67–85.

Arweck, Elisabeth, and Martin D. Stringer, eds. *Theorizing Faith: The Insider/Outsider Problem in the Study of Ritual.* Birmingham: University of Birmingham Press, 2002.

Augustine. *Answer to Faustus, a Manichean.* The Works of Saint Augustine: A Translation for the 21st Century Part I, vol. 20. Translated by Roland Teske. Hyde Park, NY: New City, 2007.

Augustine, Daniela C. *Pentecost, Hospitality, and Transfiguration: Toward A Spirit-Inspired Vision of Social Transformation.* Cleveland, TN: CPT, 2012.

Avalos, H., S. Melcher, and J. Schipper, eds. *This Abled Body: Rethinking Disabilities in Biblical Studies.* Atlanta, GA: Society of Biblical Literature, 2007.

Baban, Octavian D. *On the Road Encounters in Luke-Acts: Hellenistic Mimesis and Luke's Theology of the Way*. Milton Keynes: Paternoster, 2006.

Bae, Hyeon Sung. "Full Gospel Theology as a Distinctive Theological Practice for Korean Pentecostal Theology." *Spirit and the Church* 2, no. 2 (2000) 169–81.

Barr, James. "Words for Love in Biblical Greek." In *The Glory of Christ in the New Testament: Studies in Christology in Memory of George Bradford Caird*, edited by L. D. Hurst and N. T. Wright, 3–18. New York: Oxford University Press, 1987.

Barr, William R., ed. *Constructive Christian Theology in the Worldwide Church*. Grand Rapids: Eerdmans, 1997.

Barreau, Jean-Claude. "Preface" to Olivier Clément, *The Roots of Christian Mysticism: Text and Commentary*, translated by Theodore Berkeley, 7–8. London: New City, 1993.

Barrett, C. K. "Faith and Eschatology in Acts 3." In *Glaube und Eschatologie: Festschrift für Werner Georg Kummel zum 80 Geburtstag*, edited by Erich Grasser and Otto Merk, 1–17. Tübingen: J. C. B. Mohr, 1985.

Barth, Karl. *The Holy Spirit and the Christian Life: The Theological Basis of Ethics*. Edited by Robin W. Lovin. Louisville: Westminster/John Knox, 1993.

———. "The Revelation of God as the Abolition of Religion." In *Church Dogmatics*, vol. 1.2, The Doctrine of God. Translated by G. T. Thomson and Harold Knight, 280–361. Edinburgh: T&T Clark, 1956.

Bartleman, Frank. *Azusa Street, 1925*. Reprint. Plainfield, NJ: Logos International, 1980.

Barton, Ruth Haley. *Life Together in Christ: Experiencing Transformation in Community*. Downers Grove, IL: InterVarsity, 2014.

Bauckham, Richard, and Benjamin Drewery, eds. *Scripture, Tradition, and Reason: A Study in the Criteria of Christian Doctrine*. Edinburgh: T&T Clark, 1988.

Becker, J. O. *Deep Listening: Music, Emotion, Trancing*. Bloomington, IN: Indiana University Press, 2004.

Beckford, Robert. *Dread and Pentecostal: A Political Theology for the Black Church in Britain*. London: SPCK, 2000.

Berryhill, Carisse Mickey. "From Dreaded Guest to Welcoming Host: Hospitality and Paul in Acts." In *Restoring the First-Century Church in the Twenty-First Century: Essays on the Stone-Campbell Restoration Movement*, edited by Warren Lewis and Hans Rollmann, 71–86. Eugene, OR: Wipf & Stock, 2005.

Betcher, Sharon V. "Grounding the Spirit: An Ecofeminist Pneumatology." In *Ecospirit: Religions and Philosophies for the Earth*, edited by Laurel Kearns and Catherine Keller, 315–36. New York: Fordham University Press, 2007.

———. *Spirit and the Politics of Disablement*. Minneapolis: Fortress, 2007.

Bollinger, Gary. "Pannenberg's Theology of the Religions and the Claim to Christian Superiority." *Encounter* 43 (1982) 273–85.

Boyd, James W. *Satan and Mara: Christian and Buddhist Symbols of Evil*. Studies in the History of Religions (Supplements to Numen) 27. Leiden: Brill, 1975.

Braatan, Carl E. "The Place of Christianity among the World Religions: Wolfhart Pannenberg's Theology of Religion and the History of Religions." In *The Theology of Wolfhart Pannenberg: Twelve American Critiques, with an Autobiographical Essay and Response*, edited by Carl E. Braatan and Philip Clayton, 287–312. Minneapolis: Augsburg, 1988.

Brathwaite, Renea. "The Azusa Street Revival and Racial Reconciliation: An Afro-Pentecostal Perspective." In *Forgiveness, Reconciliation, and Restoration:*

Multidisciplinary Studies from a Pentecostal Perspective, edited by Martin William Mittelstadt and Geoffrey William Sutton, 65–87. Eugene, OR: Pickwick, 2010.

Brock, B., and J. Swinton, eds. *Disability in the Christian Tradition: A Reader*. Grand Rapids: Eerdmans, 2012.

Bruce, F. F. "Eschatology in Acts." In *Eschatology and the New Testament: Essays in Honor of George Raymond Beasley-Murray*, edited by W. Hulitt Gloer, 51–63. Peabody, MA: Hendrickson, 1988.

Bruner, Frederick Dale, and William Hordern. *The Holy Spirit: Shy Member of the Trinity*. Minneapolis: Augsburg, 1984.

Buckley, James J., and David S. Yeago, eds. *Knowing the Triune God: The Work of the Spirit in the Practices of the Church*. Grand Rapids: Eerdmans, 2001.

Budziszewski, J., et al. *Evangelicals in the Public Square: Four Formative Voices on Political Thought and Action*. Grand Rapids: Baker Academic, 2006.

Bulgakov, Sergius. *The Bride of the Lamb*. Translated by Boris Jakim. Grand Rapids: Eerdmans, 2002.

———. *Relics and Miracles: Two Theological Essays*. Translated by Boris Jakim. Grand Rapids: Eerdmans, 2011.

Bundy, David. "The Genre of Systematic Theology in Pentecostalism." *PNEUMA: The Journal of the Society for Pentecostal Studies* 15 (1993) 89–108.

Burgess, Stanley M. "Implications of Eastern Christian Pneumatology for Western Pentecostal Doctrine and Practice." In *Experiences of the Spirit: Conference on Pentecostal and Charismatic Research in Europe at Utrecht University, 1989*. Studies in the Intercultural History of Christianity 68. Edited by Jan A. B. Jongeneel, 23–34. Frankfurt: Peter Lang, 1991.

Burrows, Mark S. "The Hospitality of Christ and the Church's Resurrection: A 'Performed' Christology as Social Reformation." In *In Essentials Unity: Reflections on the Nature and Purpose of the Church*, edited by Frederick R. Trost, M. Douglas Meeks, and Robert D. Mutton, 282–92. Minneapolis: Kirk, 2001.

Burton, Thomas G. *Serpent-Handling Believers*. Knoxville, TN: University of Tennessee Press, 1993.

Busto, R. V. *King Tiger: The Religious Vision of Reies Lopez Tijerina*. Albuquerque, NM: University of New Mexico Press, 2005.

Buxton, Graham. *The Trinity, Creation, and Pastoral Ministry: Imaging the Perichoretic God*. Milton Keynes: Paternoster, 2005.

Byrne, Brendan. *The Hospitality of God: A Reading of Luke's Gospel*. Collegeville, MN: Liturgical, 2000.

Cadbury, Henry J. "Acts and Eschatology." In *The Background of the New Testament and Its Eschatology: In Honour of Charles Harold Dodd*, edited by W. D. Davies and D. Daube, 300–21. Cambridge: Cambridge University Press, 1964.

Cantalamessa, Raniero. *Come, Creator Spirit: Meditations on the Veni Creator*. Translated by Denis and Marlene Barrett. Collegeville, MN: Liturgical, 2003.

Capper, Brian. "Reciprocity and the Ethic of Acts." In *Witness to the Gospel: The Theology of Acts*, edited by I. Howard Marshall and David Peterson, 499–518. Grand Rapids: Eerdmans, 1998.

Cardenal, Ernesto. *The Gospel in Solentiname*. 4 vols. Translated by Donald D. Walsh. Maryknoll, NY: Orbis, 1976–1979.

Carroll, John T. *Response to the End of History: Eschatology and Situation in Luke-Acts*. SBL Dissertation Series 92. Atlanta: Scholars, 1988.

Carson, D. A. *Showing the Spirit: A Theological Exposition of 1 Corinthians 12–14*. Grand Rapids: Baker, 1987.
Carter, Timothy L. "Looking at the Metaphor of Christ's Body in 1 Corinthians 12." In *Paul: Jew, Greek, and Roman*. Pauline Studies 5. Edited by Stanley E. Porter, 93–115. Leiden: Brill, 2008.
Cartledge, Mark J. "The Early Pentecostal Theology of Confidence Magazine (1908–1926): A Version of the Five-Fold Gospel?" *The Journal of the European Pentecostal Theological Association* 28, no. 2 (2008) 117–30.
———. *Practical Theology: Charismatic and Empirical Perspectives*. Waynesboro, GA: Paternoster, 2003.
Cassidy, Richard J. *Jesus, Politics, and Society: A Study of Luke's Gospel*. Maryknoll, NY: Orbis, 1978.
Castelein, John Donald. "Glossolalia and the Psychology of the Self and Narcissism." *Journal of Religion and Health* 23, no. 1 (1984) 47–62.
Castelo, Daniel. "Tarrying on the Lord: Affections, Virtues, and Theological Ethics in Pentecostal Perspective." *Journal of Pentecostal Theology* 13, no. 1 (2004) 31–56.
Chance, J. Bradley. *Jerusalem, the Temple, and the New Age in Luke-Acts*. Macon, GA: Mercer University Press, 1988.
Chester, Tim. *Mission and the Coming of God: Eschatology, the Trinity, and Mission in the Theology of Jürgen Moltmann and Contemporary Evangelicalism*. Milton Keynes: Paternoster, 2006.
Chung, Paul. *Spirituality and Social Ethics in John Calvin: A Pneumatological Perspective*. Lanham, MD: University Press of America, 2000.
Clayton, Philip. *Adventures in the Spirit: God, World, Divine Action*. Minneapolis: Fortress, 2008.
Clayton, Philip, and Paul Davies, eds. *The Re-Emergence of Emergence: The Emergentist Hypothesis from Science to Religion*. Oxford: Oxford University Press, 2006.
Cleary, Edward L. "Introduction: Pentecostals, Prominence, and Politics." In *Power, Politics, and Pentecostals in Latin America*, edited by Edward L. Cleary and W. Stewart-Gambino, 1–24. Boulder, CO: Westview, 1997.
Clemmons, Ithiel C. *Bishop C. H. Mason and the Roots of the Church of God in Christ*. Bakersfield, CA: Pneuma Life, 1996.
Cobb, John B., Jr. *Beyond Dialogue: Toward a Mutual Transformation of Christianity and Buddhism*. Philadelphia: Fortress, 1982.
———. "Global Theology in a Pluralistic Age." *Dharma World* 14 (1987) 31–37.
Collins, Raymond F. *First Corinthians*. Sacra Pagina 7. Collegeville, MN: Liturgical/Michael Glazier, 1999.
Conzelmann, Hans. *The Theology of St. Luke*. Translated by Geoffrey Buswell, 1961. Reprint. Philadelphia: Fortress, 1982.
Coppedge, Allan. "How Wesleyans Do Theology." In *Doing Theology in Today's World: Essays in Honor of Kenneth Kantzer*, edited by John Woodbridge and Thomas McComiskey, 267–90. Grand Rapids: Zondervan, 1991.
Corey, Michael A. *Evolution and the Problem of Natural Evil*. Lanham, MD: University Press of America, 2000.
Cornille, Catherine, and Valeer Neckebrouck, eds. *A Universal Faith?: Peoples, Cultures, Religions, and the Christ*. Louvain Theological and Pastoral Monographs 9. Louvain: Peeters, 1992.

Corten, André. *Pentecostalism in Brazil: Emotion of the Poor and Theological Romanticism*. Translated by Arianne Dorval. London: Macmillan, 1999.
Covington, Dennis. *Salvation on Sand Mountain: Snake Handling and Redemption in Southern Appalachia*. Reading, MA: Addison-Wesley, 1995.
Cox, Harvey G. *Fire from Heaven: The Rise of Pentecostal Spirituality and the Reshaping of Religion in the Twenty-First Century*. Reading, MA: Addison-Wesley, 1995.
Creamer, Deborah Beth. *Disability and Christian Theology: Embodied Limits and Constructive Possibilities*. Oxford: Oxford University Press, 2009.
Cruz, S. *Masked Africanisms: Puerto Rican Pentecostalism*. Dubuque, IA: Kendall/Hunt, 2005.
Csordas, Thomas J. *Body/Meaning/Healing*. New York: Palgrave Macmillan, 2002.
———. *The Sacred Self: A Cultural Phenomenology of Charismatic Healing*. Berkeley, CA: University of California Press, 1994.
Cunningham, David S. *These Three Are One: The Practice of Trinitarian Theology*. Malden, MA: Blackwell, 1998.
Cyril of Alexandria. "Sermon 127." In *A Commentary upon the Gospel according to Saint Luke*, part II, translated by R. Payne Smith, 587–90. Oxford: Oxford University Press, 1859.
Dabney, D. Lyle. "Otherwise Engaged in the Spirit: A First Theology for the Twenty-First Century." In *The Future of Theology: Essays in Honor of Jürgen Moltmann*, edited by Miroslav Volf, Carmen Krieg, and Thomas Kucharz, 154–63. Grand Rapids: Eerdmans, 1996.
———. "Starting with the Spirit: Why the Last Should Now be First." In *Starting with the Spirit: Task of Theology Today II*, edited by Gordon Preece and Stephen Pickard, 3–27. Adelaide: Australia Theological Forum, and Openbook, 2001.
———. "Why Should the Last Be First?: The Priority of Pneumatology in Recent Theological Discussion." In *Advents of the Spirit: An Introduction to the Current Study of Pneumatology*, edited by Bradford E. Hinze and D. Lyle Dabney, 238–61. Milwaukee: Marquette University Press, 2001.
Daniels, David D. "Charles Harrison Mason: The Interracial Impulse of Early Pentecostalism." In *Portraits of a Generation: Early Pentecostal Leaders*, edited by James R. Goff, Jr. and Grant Wacker, 255–70. Fayetteville, AR: University of Arkansas Press, 2002.
———. "The Color of Charismatic Leadership: William Joseph Seymour and Martin Luther King, Jr. as Champions of Interracialism." In *We've Come This Far: Reflections on the Pentecostal Tradition and Racial Reconciliation*. Encounter: The Pentecostal Ministry Series 2. Edited by Byron D. Klaus, 66–87. Springfield, MO: Assemblies of God Theological Seminary, 2006.
———. "Gotta Moan Sometime: A Sonic Exploration of Earwitnesses to Early Pentecostal Sound in North America." *PNEUMA: The Journal of the Society for Pentecostal Studies* 30, no. 1 (2008) 5–32.
Dasen, Véronique. *Dwarfs in Ancient Egypt and Greece*. Oxford: Clarendon, 1993.
Davidson, Donald. *Inquiries into Truth and Interpretation*. Oxford: Clarendon, 1984.
Dawn, Marva J. *Being Well When We're Ill: Wholeness and Hope in Spite of Infirmity*. Minneapolis: Augsburg, 2008.
———. *In the Beginning God: Creation, Culture, and the Spiritual Life*. Downers Grove, IL: InterVarsity, 2009.

Dayton, Donald W. *Theological Roots of Pentecostalism*. Peabody, MA: Hendrickson, 1987.
D'Costa, Gavin. "Revelation and Revelations: Discerning God in Other Religions Beyond a Static Valuation." *Modern Theology* 10 (1994) 165–83.
Del Colle, Ralph. "Incarnation and the Holy Spirit." *Spirit and the Church* 2, no. 2 (2000) 199–229.
Dempster, M. W. "Paradigm Shifts and Hermeneutics: Confronting Issues Old and New." *PNEUMA: The Journal of the Society for Pentecostal Studies* 15, no. 2 (1999) 129–35.
Dempster, Murray W., Byron D. Klaus, and Douglas Petersen, eds. *The Globalization of Pentecostalism: A Religion Made to Travel*. Oxford: Regnum, 1999.
De Vries, Hent, and Lawrence E. Sullivan, eds. *Political Theologies: Public Religions in a Post-Secular World*. New York: Fordham University Press, 2006.
Di Noia, J. A. *The Diversity of Religions: A Christian Perspective*. Washington, DC: Catholic University Press of America, 1992.
———. "Varieties of Religious Aims: Beyond Exclusivism, Inclusivism, and Pluralism." In *Theology and Dialogue: Essays in Conversation with George Lindbeck*, edited by Bruce D. Marshall, 249–74. Notre Dame, IN: University of Notre Dame Press, 1990.
Dollar, Harold E. *A Biblical-Missiological Exploration of the Cross-Cultural Dimensions in Luke-Acts*. San Francisco: Edwin Mellen, 1993.
Dumas, André. *Political Theology and the Life of the Church*. Translated by John Bowden. Philadelphia: Westminster, 1978.
Dunne, John S. *The Way of All the Earth: Experiments in Truth and Religion*. London: Collier Macmillan, 1972.
Dunning, Stephen. *Dialectical Readings: Three Types of Interpretations*. University Park, PA: Penn State University Press, 1997.
Dupuis, Jacques. *Jesus Christ and His Spirit: Theological Approaches*. Bangalore: Theological Publications in India, 1977.
Edwards, Denis. *Breath of Life: A Theology of the Creator Spirit*. Maryknoll, NY: Orbis, 2004.
Engelke, Matthew. *A Problem of Presence: Beyond Scripture in an African Church*. Berkeley, CA: University of California Press, 2007.
England, John C., and Alan J. Torrance, eds. *Doing Theology with the Spirit's Movement in Asia*. Singapore: ATESEA, 1991.
Ervin, Howard M. *Healing: Sign of the Kingdom*. Peabody, MA: Hendrickson, 2002.
Espinosa, Gastón. "Ordinary Prophet: William J. Seymour and the Azusa Street Revival." In *Azusa Street Revival and Its Legacy*, edited by Harold D. Hunter and Cecil M. Robeck, Jr., 29–60. Cleveland, TN: Pathway, 2006.
Evans, Donald D. *The Logic of Self-Involvement: A Philosophical Study of Everyday Language with Special Reference to the Christian Use of Language about God as Creator*. London: SCM, 1963.
Eyler, J. R., ed. *Disability in the Middle Ages: Reconsiderations and Reverberations*. Burlington, VT: Ashgate, 2010.
Faricy, Robert. *Wind and Sea Obey Him: Approaches to a Theology of Nature*. Westminster, MD: Christian Classics, 1988.
Farley, Edward. *Ecclesial Reflection: An Anatomy of Theological Method*. Minneapolis: Fortress, 1982.

Fee, Gordon D. *God's Empowering Presence: The Holy Spirit in the Letters of Paul.* Peabody, MA: Hendrickson, 1994.

Fehribach, Adeline. *The Women in the Life of the Bridegroom: A Feminist Historical-Literary Analysis of the Female Characters in the Fourth Gospel.* Collegeville, MN: Liturgical, 1998.

Fernando, Ajith. *The NIV Application Commentary: Acts.* Grand Rapids: Zondervan, 1998.

Feyerabend, Paul. *Against Method.* Rev. ed. London and New York: Verso, 1990.

Finger, Reta Halteman. *Of Widows and Meals: Communal Meals in the Book of Acts.* Grand Rapids: Eerdmans, 2007.

Finnegan, Gerald F. "Jesus as Savior of the World." In *Pluralism and Oppression: Theology in World Perspective*, edited by Paul F. Knitter, 141–50. Lanham, MD: University Press of America, 1991.

Fiorenza, Francis Schüssler. *Foundational Theology: Jesus and the Church.* New York: Crossroad, 1984.

Ford, J. Massyngbaerde. *My Enemy Is My Guest: Jesus and Violence in Luke.* Maryknoll, NY: Orbis, 1984.

Fredericks, James L. *Faith among Faiths: Christian Theology and Non-Christian Religions.* New York: Paulist, 1999.

Freeman, Dena, ed. *Pentecostalism and Development: Churches, NGOs, and Social Change in Africa.* New York: Palgrave Macmillan, 2012.

Fretheim, Terence E. *Creation Untamed: The Bible, God, and Natural Disasters.* Grand Rapids: Baker Academic, 2010.

Fulljames, Peter. *God and Creation in Intercultural Perspective: Dialogue between the Theologies of Barth, Dickson, Pobee, Nyamiti, and Pannenberg.* New York: Peter Lang, 1993.

Furnish, Victor Paul. *The Love Command in the New Testament.* Nashville: Abingdon, 1972.

Gadamer, Hans-Georg. *Truth and Method.* 2d rev. ed. Translated by Joel Weinsheimer and Donald G. Marshall. New York: Continuum, 1994.

Galileo. *Discoveries and Opinions of Galileo.* Translated by Stillman Drake. Garden City, NY: Doubleday Anchor, 1957.

Garrett, Susan R. *The Demise of the Devil: Magic and the Demonic in Luke's Writings.* Minneapolis: Fortress, 1989.

Geertz, Clifford. *The Interpretation of Cultures.* New York: Basic, 1973.

Geitz, Elizabeth Rankin. *Entertaining Angels: Hospitality Programs for the Caring Church.* Harrisburg, PA: Morehouse, 1993.

Gelpi, Donald L. *The Conversion Experience: A Reflective Process for RCIA Participants and Others.* New York: Paulist, 1998.

———. *The Divine Mother: A Trinitarian Theology of the Holy Spirit.* Lanham, MD: University Press of America, 1984.

———. *The Gracing of Human Experience: Rethinking the Relationship between Nature and Grace.* Collegeville, MN: Liturgical, 2001.

———. *The Turn to Experience in Contemporary Theology.* New York: Paulist, 1994.

———. *Varieties of Transcendental Experience: A Study in Constructive Postmodernism.* Collegeville, MN: Liturgical, 2000.

George, K. M. *The Silent Roots: Orthodox Perspectives on Christian Spirituality.* Risk Book Series 63. Geneva: World Council of Churches, 1994.

Gillman, John. "Hospitality in Acts 16." In *Sharper Than a Two-Edged Sword: Essays in Honor of Professor Dr. Jan Lambrecht, S.J.*, edited by Veronica Koperski and Reimund Bieringer, 181–96. Louvain: Faculty of Theology Katholieke Universiteit Leuven, 1992.

Giovanni, Zevola. "What Are You Talking About to Each Other, as You Walk Along? (Lk 24:17): Migration in the Bible and Our Journey of Faith." In *Faith on the Move: Toward a Theology of Migration in Asia*, edited by Fabio Baggio and Agnes M. Brazal, 93–117. Manila: Ateneo de Manila University Press, 2008.

Goette, Robert D., and Mae Pyen Hong. "A Theological Reflection on the Cultural Tensions Between First-Century Hebraic and Hellenistic Jewish Christians and Between Twentieth-Century First- and Second-Generation Korean American Christians." In *Korean Americans and Their Religions: Pilgrims and Missionaries from a Different Shore*, edited by Ho-Young Kwon, Kwang Chung Kim, and R. Stephen Warner, 115–23. University Park, PA: The Pennsylvania State University Press, 2001.

Goh, Jeffrey C. K. *Christian Tradition Today: A Postliberal Vision of Church and World*. Louvain Theological and Pastoral Monographs 28. Louvain: Peeters, 2000.

González, Justo L. "Reading from My Bicultural Place: Acts 6:1–7." In *Reading from This Place*, vol. 1: *Social Location and Biblical Interpretation in the United States*, edited by Fernando F. Segovia and Mary Ann Tolbert, 189–247. Minneapolis: Fortress, 1995.

Gorringe, T. J. *The Education of Desire: Towards a Theology of the Senses*. Harrisburg, PA: Trinity Press International, 2001.

Gort, Jerald, et al., eds. *Dialogue and Syncretism: An Interdisciplinary Approach*. Grand Rapids: Eerdmans, 1989.

Gould, Stephen Jay. *Rocks of Ages: Science and Religion in the Fullness of Life*. New York: Ballantine, 1999.

Gowler, David B. "Hospitality and Characterization in Luke 11:37–54: A Socio-Narratological Approach." *Semeia* 64, no. 1 (1993) 213–51.

Graham, Helen R. *There Shall be No Poor among You: Essays in Lukan Theology*. Quezon City, Philippines: JMC, 1978.

Green, Joel B. "Witnesses to His Resurrection: Resurrection, Salvation, Discipleship, and Mission in the Acts of the Apostles." In *Life in the Face of Death: The Resurrection Message of the New Testament*, edited by Richard N. Longenecker, 227–46. Grand Rapids: Eerdmans, 1998.

Greene, John C. *The Death of Adam: Evolution and Its Impact on Western Thought*. Ames, IA: Iowa State University Press, 1959.

Gregory, Peter N. "The Problem of Theodicy in the Awakening of Faith." *Religious Studies* 22 (1986) 63–78.

Grenz, Stanley J. "Commitment and Dialogue: Pannenberg on Christianity and the Religions." *Journal of Ecumenical Studies* 26 (1989) 196–210.

Grenz, Stanley J., and John R. Franke. *Beyond Foundationalism: Shaping Theology in a Postmodern Context*. Louisville: Westminster John Knox, 2001.

Griffith, R. M., and D. G. Roebuck. "Women, Role of." In *The New International Dictionary of Pentecostal and Charismatic Movements*, rev. and ex. ed., edited by S. M. Burgess and E. M. van der Mass, 1203–09. Grand Rapids: Zondervan, 2002.

Griffiths, Bede. *The New Creation in Christ: Christian Meditation and Community*. Springfield, IL: Templegate, 1994.

Griffiths, Paul J. *An Apology for Apologetics: A Study in the Logic of Interreligious Dialogue*. Maryknoll, NY: Orbis, 1991.

Griffiths, Paul J., ed. *Christianity through Non-Christian Eyes*. Maryknoll, NY: Orbis, 1990.

Grinnell, Frederick. *Everyday Practice of Science: Where Intuition and Passion Meet Objectivity and Logic*. Oxford: Oxford University Press, 2009.

Gritzmacher, Steven A., Brian Bolton, and Richard H. Dana. "Psychological Characteristics of Pentecostals: A Literature Review and Psychodynamic Synthesis." *Journal of Psychology and Theology* 16, no. 3 (1988) 233–45.

Grogan, Geoffrey W. "Isaiah." In *The Expositor's Bible Commentary*, 12 vols., edited by Frank E. Gaebelein, 1–354. Grand Rapids: Zondervan, 1985.

Gunter, W. Stephen, et al. *Wesley and the Quadrilateral: Renewing the Conversation*. Nashville: Abingdon, 1997.

Habito, Ruben L. F. *Healing Breath: Zen Spirituality for a Wounded Earth*. Maryknoll, NY: Orbis, 1993.

———. *Total Liberation: Zen Spirituality and the Social Dimension*. Maryknoll, NY: Orbis, 1989.

Hamm, Dennis. "Acts 3,1–10: The Healing of the Temple Beggar as Lucan Theology." *Biblica* 67, no. 3 (1986) 305–19.

———. "Acts 3:12–26: Peter's Speech and the Healing of the Man Born Lame." *Perspectives in Religious Studies* 11, no. 3 (1984) 199–217.

Hanciles, Jehu J. *Beyond Christendom: Globalization, African Migration, and the Transformation of the West*. Maryknoll, NY: Orbis, 2008.

———. "Migration and Mission: The Religious Significance of the North-South Divide." In *Mission in the Twenty-First Century: Exploring the Five Marks of Global Mission*, edited by Andrew Walls and Cathy Ross, 118–29. Maryknoll, NY: Orbis, 2008.

Hanh, Nhat. *Living Buddha, Living Christ*. New York: Riverhead, 1995.

Harrison, Nonna Verna. *God's Many-Splendored Image: Theological Anthropology for Christian Formation*. Grand Rapids: Baker Academic, 2010.

Harrison, Peter. *The Bible, Protestantism, and the Rise of Natural Science*. Cambridge: Cambridge University Press, 1998.

———. "Reinterpreting Nature in Early Modern Europe: Natural Philosophy, Biblical Exegesis, and the Contemplative Life." In *The Word and the World: Biblical Exegesis and Early Modern Science*, edited by Kevin Killeen and Peter J. Forshaw, 25–44. New York: Palgrave Macmillan, 2007.

Hauer, Christian E., and William A. Young. *An Introduction to the Bible: A Journey into Three Worlds*. 5th ed. Upper Saddle River, NJ: Prentice-Hall, 2001.

Hauerwas, Stanley, and Jean Vanier. *Living Gently in a Violent World: The Prophetic Witness of Weakness*. Downers Grove, IL: InterVarsity, 2008.

Hawthorne, Gerald F. *The Presence and the Power: The Significance of the Holy Spirit in the Life of Jesus*. Dallas: Word, 1991.

Hays, Richard B. *The Moral Vision of the New Testament: A Contemporary Introduction to New Testament Ethics*. San Francisco: HarperSanFrancisco, 1996.

Hefner, Philip. *The Human Factor: Evolution, Culture, and Religion*. Minneapolis: Fortress, 2000.

Heil, John Paul. *The Meal Scenes in Luke-Acts: An Audience-Oriented Approach*. SBL Monograph Series 52. Atlanta: Scholars, 1999.

Heim, S. Mark. "Elements of a Conversation." In *Grounds for Understanding: Ecumenical Resources for Responses to Religious Pluralism*, edited by S. Mark Heim, 208–23. Grand Rapids: Eerdmans, 1998.

Hensman, C. R. *Agenda for the Poor—Claiming Their Inheritance: A Third World People's Reading of Luke*. Quest 109. Colombo, Sri Lanka: Center for Society and Religion, 1990.

Hertig, Young Lee. "Cross-Cultural Mediation: From Exclusion to Inclusion—Acts 6:1–7; also 5:33–42." In *Mission in Acts: Ancient Narratives in Contemporary Context*, edited by Robert L. Gallagher and Paul Hertig, 59–72. Maryknoll, NY: Orbis, 2004.

Heyduck, Richard. *The Recovery of Doctrine in the Contemporary Church: An Essay in Philosophical Ecclesiology*. Waco, TX: Baylor University Press, 2002.

Hick, John. *An Interpretation of Religion: Human Responses to the Transcendent*. New Haven, CT: Yale University Press, 1991.

Hierotheos, Bishop of Nafpaktos. *Orthodox Spirituality: A Brief Introduction*. Translated by Effie Mavromichali. Greece: Birth of the Theotokos Monastery, 1996.

Hitching, Roger. *The Church and Deaf People: A Study of Identity, Communication, and Relationships with Special Reference to the Ecclesiology of Jürgen Moltmann*. Carlisle: Paternoster, 2003.

Hodges, M. L. *Build My Church*. Springfield, MO: Gospel, 1957.

Hodgson, Peter C. *Australasian Winds of the Spirit: A Constructive Christian Theology*. Louisville: Westminster John Knox, 1994.

Hollenweger, Walter J. *Pentecostalism: Its Origin and Development Worldwide*. Peabody, MA: Hendrickson, 1997.

———. *The Pentecostals: The Charismatic Movement in the Churches*. Minneapolis: Augsburg, 1972.

Homrighausen, Elmer G. "Who Is My Neighbor?: The Christian and the Non-Christian." *Interpretation* 4, no. 4 (1950) 401–15.

Hood, Ralph W., Jr., and W. Paul Williamson. *Them That Believe: The Power and Meaning of the Christian Serpent-Handling Tradition*. Berkeley, CA: University of California Press, 2008.

Hordern, William, and Frederick Dale Bruner. *The Holy Spirit—Shy Member of the Trinity*. Minneapolis: Augsburg Fortress, 1984.

Horgan, John. *The End of Science: Facing the Limits of Knowledge in the Twilight of a Scientific Age*. Boston: Little Brown, 1997.

Horton, Michael S. *Covenant and Eschatology: The Divine Drama*. Louisville: Westminster John Knox, 2002.

Howell, Kenneth J. *God's Two Books: Copernican Cosmology and Biblical Interpretation in Early Modern Science*. Notre Dame, IN: University of Notre Dame Press, 2002.

Hulswit, Menno. *From Cause to Causation: A Peircean Perspective*. Dordrecht: Kluwer Academic, 2002.

Hultgren, Arland J. "The Johannine Footwashing (13.1–11) as a Symbol of Eschatological Hospitality." *New Testament Studies* 28 (1982) 539–46.

Hunter, Harold D. "A Journey toward Racial Reconciliation: Race Mixing in the Church of God of Prophecy." In *Azusa Street Revival and Its Legacy*, edited by Harold D. Hunter and Cecil M. Robeck, Jr., 277–96. Cleveland, TN: Pathway, 2006.

Hurtado, Larry W. *Lord Jesus Christ: Devotion to Jesus in Earliest Christianity*. Grand Rapids: Eerdmans, 2003.

Hütter, Reinhard. *Suffering Divine Things: Theology as Church Practice*, translated by Doug Scott. Grand Rapids: Eerdmans, 2000.
Im, Chandler, and Amos Yong, eds. *Global Diasporas and Mission*. Regnum Edinburgh Centenary Series. Oxford: Regnum, 2013.
Irvin, Dale T. *Christian Histories, Christian Traditioning: Rendering Accounts*. Maryknoll, NY: Orbis, 1998.
———. "Drawing All Together in One Bond of Love: The Ecumenical Vision of William J. Seymour and the Azusa Street Revival." *Journal of Pentecostal Theology* 3, no. 6 (1995) 25–53.
Jenkins, Philip. *The New Faces of Christianity: Believing the Bible in the Global South*. Oxford: Oxford University Press, 2006.
Jensen, David H. *In the Company of Others: A Dialogical Christology*. Cleveland, OH: Pilgrim, 2001.
Johnson, Alonzo. *Good News for the Disinherited: Howard Thurman on Jesus of Nazareth and Human Liberation*. Lanham, MD: University Press of America, 1997.
Juel, Donald H. "Hearing Peter's Speech in Acts 3: Meaning and Truth in Interpretation." *Word and World* 12 (1992) 43–50.
Kalu, Ogbu U. *African Pentecostalism: An Introduction*. Oxford: Oxford University Press, 2008.
Kärkkäinen, Veli-Matti. *Toward a Pneumatological Theology: Pentecostal and Ecumenical Perspectives on Ecclesiology, Soteriology, and Theology of Mission*, edited by Amos Yong. Lanham, MD: University Press of America, 2002.
Kauffman, Stuart A. *Reinventing the Sacred: A New View of Science, Reason, and Religion*. New York: Basic, 2008.
Keck, Leander E., ed. *The New Interpreter's Bible*. Volume IX: *Luke, John*. Nashville: Abingdon, 1995.
Keener, Craig S. *Gift and Giver: The Holy Spirit for Today*. Grand Rapids: Baker Academic, 2001.
Kertson, Brandon, Thomas J. Oord, Craig A. Boyd, Joshua M. Moritz, and F. LeRon Shults. "Pentecostal Theology and Science: Spirit and Science Panel." *Canadian Journal of Pentecostal-Charismatic Christianity* 3, no. 1 (2012) 89–129.
Kim, Kyoung Jae. *Christianity and the Encounter of Asian Religions*. Zoetermeer, Netherlands: Uitgeverij Boekencentrum, 1994.
Kistler, Don, ed. *Sola Scriptura! The Protestant Position on the Bible*. Morgan, PA: Soli Deo Gloria, 1995.
Kloppenburg, Bonaventure. *Christian Salvation and Human Temporal Progress*. Translated by Paul Burns. Chicago: Franciscan Herald, 1979.
Knight, Henry H. *A Future for Truth: Evangelical Theology in a Postmodern World*. Nashville: Abingdon, 1997.
Knitter, Paul F. *Jesus and the Other Names: Christian Mission and Global Responsibility*. Maryknoll, NY: Orbis, 1995.
———. *One Earth Many Religions: Multifaith Dialogue and Global Responsibility*. Maryknoll, NY: Orbis, 1995.
Koenig, John. *New Testament Hospitality: Partnership with Strangers as Promise and Mission*. Overtures to Biblical Hospitality 17. Philadelphia: Fortress, 1985.
Koyama, Kosuke. "Observation and Revelation: A Global Dialogue with Buddhism." In *God and Globalization*, vol. 3: *Christ and the Dominions of Civilization*, edited

by Max L. Stackhouse and Diane B. Obenchain, 239-71. Harrisburg, PA: Trinity, 2002.

Krieger, David J. "Methodological Foundations for Interreligious Dialogue." In *The Intercultural Challenge of Raimon Panikkar*, edited by Joseph Prabhu, 201-23. Maryknoll, NY: Orbis, 1996.

———. *The New Universalism: Foundations for a Global Theology*. Maryknoll: Orbis, 1991.

Kydd, Ronald A. N. *Healing through the Centuries: Models for Understanding*. Peabody, MA: Hendrickson, 1998.

Lalive d'Epinay, Christian. *Haven of the Masses: A Study of the Pentecostal Movement in Chile*. Translated by Marjorie Sandle. London: Lutterworth, 1969.

Land, Steven J. *Pentecostal Spirituality: A Passion for the Kingdom*. Sheffield: Sheffield Academic, 1993.

———. "William J. Seymour: The Father of the Holiness-Pentecostal Movement." In *From Aldersgate to Azusa Street: Wesleyan, Holiness, and Pentecostal Visions of the New Creation*, edited by Henry H. Knight III, 218-26. Eugene, OR: Pickwick, 2010.

Lane, Anthony N. S. "Sola Scriptura?: Making Sense of a Post-Reformation Slogan." In *A Pathway into the Holy Scripture*, edited by Philip E. Satterthwaite and David F. Wright, 297-327. Grand Rapids: Eerdmans, 1994.

Lane, Thomas J. *Luke and the Gentile Mission: Gospel Anticipates Acts*. European University Studies Series 23. New York: Peter Lang, 1996.

Lash, Nicholas. "Performing the Scriptures." In *Theology on the Way to Emmaus*, 37-46. London: SCM, 1986.

LaVerdiere, Eugene. *The Breaking of the Bread: The Development of the Eucharist according to the Acts of the Apostles*. Chicago: Liturgy Training Publications, 1998.

———. *Dining in the Kingdom of God: The Origins of the Eucharist in the Gospel of Luke*. Chicago: Liturgy Training Publications, 1994.

Lederle, Henry I., and Mathew Clark. *What is Distinctive About Pentecostal Theology?* Pretoria: University of South Africa, 1983.

Lee, Chwen Jiuan A., and Thomas G. Hand. *A Taste of Water: Christianity through Taoist-Buddhist Eyes*. New York: Paulist, 1990.

Lee, Matthew T., and Among Yong, eds. *The Science and Theology of Godly Love*. DeKalb, IL: Northern Illinois University Press, 2012.

Lehmann, David. *Struggle for the Spirit: Religious Transformation and Popular Culture in Brazil and Latin America*. Cambridge, MA: Polity, 1996.

Lennartsson, Goran. *Refreshing and Restoration: Two Eschatological Motifs in Acts 3:19-21*. Lund: Lund University Centre for Theology and Religious Studies, 2007.

Lewis, Hannah. *Deaf Liberation Theology*. Aldershot: Ashgate, 2007.

Liefeld, Walter L. *Luke*. Expositors Bible Commentary 8. Edited by Frank E. Gaebelein, 797-1059. Grand Rapids: Regency Reference Library, 1984.

Lindbeck, George A. "The Church as Israel: Ecclesiology and Ecumenism." In *Jews and Christians: People of God*, edited by Carl E. Braaten and Robert W. Jenson, 78-94. Grand Rapids: Eerdmans, 2003.

———. "The Gospel's Uniqueness: Election and Untranslatability." In *The Church in a Postliberal Age*, edited by James J. Buckley, 223-52. Grand Rapids: Eerdmans, 2002.

———. *The Nature of Doctrine: Religion and Theology in a Postliberal Age*. Philadelphia: Westminster, 1984.

Linskens, John. *Christ Liberator of the Poor: Secularity, Wealth, and Poverty in the Gospel of Luke*. San Antonio, TX: Mexican American Cultural Center, 1976.

Lodahl, Michael E. "*Una Natura Divina, Tres Nescio Quid*: What Sorts of *Personae* are Divine *Personae*?" *Wesleyan Theological Journal* 36, no. 1 (2001) 218–30.

Loder, James E., and W. Jim Neidhardt. *The Knight's Move: The Relational Logic of the Spirit in Theology and Science*. Colorado Springs, CO: Helmers and Howard, 1992.

Lonergan, Bernard. *Method in Theology*. 2d ed. Toronto: University of Toronto Press, 1990.

Löning, Karl, and Erich Zenger. *To Begin with, God Created . . . : Biblical Theologies of Creation*. Translated by Omar Kaste. Collegeville, MN: Liturgical, 2000.

Macchia, Frank D. "From Azusa to Memphis: Evaluating the Racial Reconciliation Dialogue among Pentecostals." *PNEUMA: The Journal of the Society for Pentecostal Studies* 17, no. 2 (1995) 203–18.

———. *Justified in the Spirit: Creation, Redemption, and the Triune God*. Grand Rapids: Eerdmans, 2010.

———. "Roundtable: Racial Reconciliation." *PNEUMA: The Journal of the Society for Pentecostal Studies* 18, no. 1 (1996) 113–40.

———. *Spirituality and Social Liberation: The Message of the Blumhardts in the Light of Wuerttemberg Pietism*. Metuchen, NJ: Scarecrow, 1993.

———. "The Tongues of Pentecost: A Pentecostal Perspective on the Promise and Challenge of Pentecostal/Roman Catholic Dialogue." *Journal of Ecumenical Studies* 35, no.1 (1998) 1–18.

Mackinnnon, Edward. "Complementarity." In *Religion and Science: History, Method, Dialogue*, edited by W. Mark Richardson and Wesley J. Wildman, 255–70. New York: Routledge, 1996.

Maier, Gerhard. *Biblical Hermeneutics*. Translated by Robert W. Yarbrough. Wheaton, IL: Crossway, 1994.

Mananzan, Mary-John. *The Language Game of Confessing One's Belief: A Wittgensteinian-Austinian Approach to the Linguistic Analysis of Creedal Statements*. Linguistische Arbeiten 16. Tübingen: Max Niemeyer Verlag, 1974.

Marshall, Bruce D., ed. *Theology and Dialogue: Essays in Conversation with George Lindbeck*. Notre Dame, IN: University of Notre Dame Press, 1990.

Martin, David. "The Political Oeconomy of the Holy Ghost." In *Strange Gifts?: A Guide to Charismatic Renewal*, edited by David Martin and Peter Mullen, 54–71. Oxford: Basil Blackwell, 1984.

Martinson, Paul Varo. *A Theology of World Religions: Interpreting God, Self and World in Semitic, Indian, and Chinese Thought*. Minneapolis: Augsburg, 1987.

Matthews, Steven. "Reading the Two Books with Francis Bacon: Interpreting God's Will and Power." In *The Word and the World: Biblical Exegesis and Early Modern Science*, edited by Kevin Killeen and Peter J. Forshaw, 61–77. New York: Palgrave Macmillan, 2007.

May, John D' Arcy. *Transcendence and Violence: The Encounter of Buddhist, Christian, and Primal Traditions*. London: Continuum, 2003.

McClendon, James William, Jr. *Biography as Theology: How Life Stories Can Remake Today's Theology*. Nashville: Abingdon, 1974.

———. *Systematic Theology*. 3 vols. Nashville: Abingdon, 1986–2000.

McCutcheon, Russell T., ed. *The Insider/Outsider Problem in the Study of Religion: A Reader*. London: Cassell, 1998.
McDermott, Gerald. "What If Paul Had Been from China?: Reflections on the Possibility of Revelation in Non-Christian Religions." In *No Other God's Before Me?: Evangelicals and the Challenge of World Religions*, edited by John G. Stackhouse, Jr., 17–36. Grand Rapids: Baker, 2001.
McFarland, Ian A. "Who Is My Neighbor?: The Good Samaritan as a Source for Theological Anthropology." *Modern Theology* 17, no. 1 (2001) 57–66.
McGee, Gary B. *Miracles, Missions, and American Pentecostalism*. Maryknoll, NY: Orbis, 2010.
McGrath, Alister E. *Science and Religion: An Introduction*. Malden, MA: Blackwell, 2010.
———. *The Science of God*. Grand Rapids: Eerdmans, 2004.
———. *A Scientific Theology*, vol. 2: *Reality*. Grand Rapids: Eerdmans, 2002.
McIntyre, P. *Black Pentecostal Music in Windsor*. Ottowa: National Museums of Canada, 1976.
McQueen, Larry R. *Joel and the Spirit: The Cry of a Prophetic Hermeneutic*. Sheffield: Sheffield Academic, 1995.
Menuge, Angus J. L. "Interpreting the Book of Nature." *Perspectives on Science and Christian Faith* 55, no. 2 (2003) 88–98.
Menzies, William R. "Synoptic Theology: An Essay in Pentecostal Hermeneutics." *Paraclete* 13, no. 1 (1979) 14–21.
Merton, Thomas. *Contemplation in a World of Action*. New York: Doubleday, 1965.
Metzler, Irina. *Disability in Medieval Europe: Thinking about Physical Impairment during the High Middle Ages, c.1100–1400*. Routledge Studies in Medieval Religion & Culture 5. London: Routledge, 2006.
Mews, Constant J. "The World as Text: The Bible and the Book of Nature in Twelfth-Century Theology." In *Scripture and Pluralism: Reading the Bible in the Religiously Plural Worlds of the Middle Ages and Renaissance*. Studies in the History of Christian Traditions 123. Edited by Thomas J. Heffernan and Thomas E. Burman, 95–122. Leiden: Brill, 2005.
Meynell, Hugo. "The Idea of a World Theology." *Modern Theology* 1, no. 2 (1985) 149–61.
Miller, Albert G. "Pentecostalism as a Social Movement: Beyond the Theory of Deprivation." *Journal of Pentecostal Theology* 4, no. 9 (1996) 97–114.
Moessner, David P. *Lord of the Banquet: The Literary and Theological Significance of the Lukan Travel Narrative*. Minneapolis: Fortress, 1989.
Moltmann, Jürgen. *The Coming of God: Christian Eschatology*, translated by Margaret Kohl. Minneapolis: Fortress, 1996.
———. *The Spirit of Life: A Universal Affirmation*, translated by Margaret Kohl. Minneapolis: Fortress, 1992.
———. *The Way of Jesus Christ: Christology in Messianic Dimensions*, translated by Margaret Kohl. New York: HarperSanFrancisco, 1990.
Monteith, Graham W. *Epistles of Inclusion: St. Paul's Inspired Attitudes*. Guildford: Grosvenor, 2010.
Morris, Leon. *Testaments of Love: A Study of Love in the Bible*. Grand Rapids: Eerdmans, 1981.

Morris, Wayne. *Theology without Words: Theology in the Deaf Community*. Aldershot: Ashgate, 2008.
Moss, C. R., and J. Schipper, eds. *Disability Studies and Biblical Literature*. New York: Palgrave Macmillan, 2011.
Mostert, Johan. "Lessons from Our Struggle to Overcome Racial Segregation: A Brief History of the Apostolic Faith Mission of South Africa." In *We've Come This Far: Reflections on the Pentecostal Tradition and Racial Reconciliation*. Encounter: The Pentecostal Ministry Series 2. Edited by Byron D. Klaus, 153–62. Springfield, MO: Assemblies of God Theological Seminary, 2006.
Moulaison, Jane Barter. *Lord, Giver of Life: Toward a Pneumatological Complement to George Lindbeck's Theory of Doctrine*. Editions SR 32. Waterloo, ON: Wilfrid Laurier University Press, 2007.
Mullins, Ryan. "Some Difficulties for Amos Yong's Disability Theology of the Resurrection." *Ars Disputandi: The Online Journal for Philosophy of Religion* 11 (2011) 24–32.
Mundhenk, Norm. "The Invisible Man (Acts 4.9–10)." *The Bible Translator* 57, no. 4 (2006) 203–06.
Murphy, George L. "Reading God's Two Books." *Perspectives on Science and Christian Faith* 58, no. 1 (2006) 64–67.
Murphy, Nancey. *Anglo-Saxon Postmodernity: Philosophical Perspectives on Science, Religion, and Ethics*. Boulder, CO: Westview, 1997.
Murphy, Nancey, and W. J. Stoeger, eds. *Evolution and Emergence: Systems, Organisms, Persons*. Oxford: Oxford University Press, 2007.
Nagel, Thomas. *The View from Nowhere*. Oxford: Oxford University Press, 1986.
Neville, Robert Cummings. *Recovery of the Measure: Interpretation and Nature*. Albany, NY: SUNY, 1989.
———. "Sketch of a System." In *New Essays in Metaphysics*, edited by R. C. Neville, 253–74. Albany, NY: SUNY, 1987.
Newberg, Andrew, et al. "Cerebral Blood Flow during Meditative Prayer: Preliminary Findings and Methodological Issues." *Perceptual and Motor Skills* 97, no. 2 (2003) 625–30.
Newman, Joe. *Race and the Assemblies of God Church: The Journey from Azusa Street to the Miracle of Memphis*. Youngstown, NY: Cambria, 2007.
Nielsen, Anders E. *Until It Is Fulfilled: Lukan Eschatology according to Luke 22 and Acts 20*. Tübingen: Mohr Siebeck, 2000.
Nkulu-N'Sengha, Mutombo. "Interreligious Dialogue in Black Africa among Christianity, Islam, and African Traditional Religion." *Journal of Ecumenical Studies* 33 (1996) 528–56.
O'Collins, Gerald, and Daniel Kendall. *The Bible for Theology: Ten Principles for the Theological Use of Scripture*. New York: Paulist, 1997.
Oden, Thomas C. "Without Excuse: Classical Christian Exegesis of General Revelation." *Journal of the Evangelical Theological Society* 41 (1998) 69–84.
Olena, Lois. "I'm Sorry, My Brother." In *We've Come This Far: Reflections on Pentecostal Tradition and Racial Reconciliation*, edited by Byron D. Klaus, 130–52. Springfield: Assemblies of God Theological Seminary, 2007.
Orton, David E. "We Felt Like Grasshoppers: The Little Ones in Biblical Interpretation." *Biblical Interpretation* 11, nos. 3–4 (2003) 488–502.

Osborne, G. R. *The Hermeneutical Spiral: A Comprehensive Introduction to Biblical Interpretation*. Downers Grove, IL: InterVarsity, 1991.
Panikkar, Raimon. *The Intra-Religious Dialogue*. New York: Paulist, 1978.
Pannenberg, Wolfhart. *Basic Questions in Theology: Collected Essays*, vol. 2, translated by George Kehm. Philadelphia: Fortress, 1971.
———. "The Doctrine of the Spirit and the Task of a Theology of Nature." In *Toward a Theology of Nature: Essays on Science and Faith*, edited by Ted Peters, 123–37. Louisville: Westminster John Knox, 1993.
———. "Religious Pluralism and Conflicting Truth Claims: The Problem of a Theology of the World Religions." In *Christian Uniqueness Reconsidered: The Myth of a Pluralistic Theology of Religions*, edited by Gavin D' Costa, 96–106. Maryknoll, NY: Orbis, 1990.
———. *Systematic Theology*. 3 vols, translated by Geoffrey W. Bromiley. Grand Rapids: Eerdmans, 1991–1997.
Park, Andrew Sung. "A Theology of Transmutation." In *A Dream Unfinished: Theological Reflections on America from the Margins*, edited by Eleazer S. Fernandez and Fernando F. Segovia, 152–66. Maryknoll, NY: Orbis, 2001.
———. *Triune Atonement: Christ's Healing for Sinners, Victims, and the Whole Creation*. Louisville: Westminster John Knox, 2009.
Park, Sung Bae. *Buddhist Faith and Sudden Enlightenment*. Albany, NY: State University of New York Press, 1983.
Parry, Robin, and Chris Partridge, eds. *Universal Salvation?: The Current Debate*. Grand Rapids: Eerdmans, 2003.
Parsons, Mikeal C. *Body and Character in Luke and Acts: The Subversion of Physiognomy in Early Christianity*. Grand Rapids: Baker Academic, 2006.
Percy, Martyn. *Power and the Church: Ecclesiology in an Age of Transition*. Washington, DC: Cassell, 1998.
Peter Chrysologus. "Sermon 54, On Zacchaeus the Tax Collector." In *Selected Sermons*, volume 2, The Fathers of the Church: A New Translation, 109. Translated by William B. Palardy, 206–12. Washington, DC: The Catholic University of America Press, 2004.
Peters, Ted, and Martinez Hewlett. *Evolution from Creation to New Creation: Conflict, Conversation, and Convergence*. Nashville: Abingdon, 2003.
Petersen, Douglas. *Not by Might, Nor by Power: A Pentecostal Theology of Social Concern in Latin America*. Oxford: Regnum, 1996.
Phillips, Timothy R., and Dennis L. Okholm, eds. *The Nature of Confession: Evangelicals and Postliberals in Conversation*. Downers Grove, IL: InterVarsity, 1996.
Pilgrim, Walter E. *Good News to the Poor: Wealth and Poverty in Luke-Acts*. Minneapolis: Augsburg, 1981.
Pinnock, Clark H. *Flame of Love: A Theology of the Holy Spirit*. Downers Grove, IL: InterVarsity, 1996.
Pinnock, Sarah Katherine. *Beyond Theodicy: Jewish and Christian Continental Thinkers Respond to the Holocaust*. Albany, NY: State University of New York Press, 2002.
Pittman, Don A., et al., eds. *Ministry and Theology in Global Perspective*. Grand Rapids: Eerdmans, 1996.
Preus, Klemet. "Tongues: An Evaluation from a Scientific Perspective." *Concordia Theological Quarterly* 46, no. 4 (1982) 277–93.

Prior, Michael. *Jesus the Liberator: Nazareth Liberation Theology (Luke 4.16–30)*. The Biblical Seminar 26. Sheffield: Sheffield Academic, 1995.
Rahner, Karl. "Aspects of European Theology." In *Theological Investigations* 21, 78–98. New York: Crossroad, 1988.
Rambo, Lewis. *Understanding Religious Conversion*. New Haven, CT: Yale University Press, 1993.
Ratnayaka, Shanta. *Two Ways of Perfection: Buddhist and Christian*. Colombo: Lake House Investments, 1978.
Reat, Ross N., and Edmund Perry. *A World Theology: The Central Spiritual Reality of Humankind*. Cambridge: Cambridge University Press, 1991.
Reed, David A. *"In Jesus' Name": The History and Beliefs of Oneness Pentecostals*. Blandford Forum: Deo, 2008.
Resseguie, James L. *Spiritual Landscape: Images of the Spiritual Life in the Gospel of Luke*. Peabody, MA: Hendrickson, 2004.
Reynolds, T. E. *Vulnerable Communion: A Theology of Disability and Hospitality*. Grand Rapids: Brazos, 2008.
Richie, Tony. *Speaking by the Spirit: A Pentecostal Model for Interreligious Encounter and Dialogue*. Asbury Theological Seminary Series in World Christian Revitalization Movements in Pentecostal/Charismatic Studies 6. Wilmore, KY: Emeth, 2011.
Ricoeur, Paul. *The Conflict of Interpretations*, edited by Paul Ricoeur and Don Ihde. Evanston, IL: Northwestern University Press, 2000.
Riddle, Donald Wayne. "Early Christian Hospitality: A Factor in the Gospel Transmission." *Journal of Biblical Literature* 62, no. 2 (1938) 141–54.
Riggins, John R. "God's Inspired Word." In *Systematic Theology*, rev. ed., edited by Stanley M. Horton, 61–115. Springfield, MO: Gospel, 1995.
Robeck, Cecil M., Jr. "Historical Roots of Racial Unity and Disunity in American Pentecostalism." *Cyberjournal for Pentecostal-Charismatic Research* 14 (2005).
Rodgers, Darrin J. "The Assemblies of God and the Long Journey toward Racial Reconciliation." *Assemblies of God Heritage* 28 (2008) 50–66.
Rogich, Daniel M., ed. *St. Gregory Palamas: Treatise on the Spiritual Life*. Minneapolis: Light and Life, 1995.
Roloff, Matt, and Tracy Sumner. *Against Tall Odds: Being a David in a Goliath World*. Sisters, OR: Multnomah, 1999.
Rosato, Philip J. "Called by God, in the Holy Spirit: Pneumatological Insights into Ecumenism." *Ecumenical Review* 30 (1978) 110–26.
Rosenior, Derrick R. "The Rhetoric of Pentecostal Racial Reconciliation: Looking Back to Move Forward." In *A Liberating Spirit: Pentecostals and Social Action in North America*. Pentecostals, Peacemaking, and Social Justice Series 2. Edited by Michael Wilkinson and Steven M. Studebaker, 53–84. Eugene, OR: Pickwick, 2010.
———. "Toward Racial Reconciliation: Collective Memory, Myth, and Nostalgia in American Pentecostalism." PhD diss., Howard University, 2005.
Roth, S. John. *The Blind, the Lame, and the Poor: Character Types in Luke-Acts*. Sheffield: Sheffield Academic, 1997.
Ruether, R. R., and D. Ruether. *Many Forms of Madness: A Family's Struggle with Mental Illness and the Mental Health System*. Minneapolis: Fortress, 2010.
Rusch, William G. "The Theology of the Holy Spirit and Pentecostal Churches in the Ecumenical Movement." *PNEUMA: The Journal of the Society for Pentecostal Studies* 9 (1987) 17–30.

Rush, Ormond. *The Reception of Doctrine: An Appropriation of Hans Robert Jauss' Reception Aesthetics and Literary Hermeneutics.* Rome: Gregorian University Press, 1997.
Russell, Marta. *Beyond Ramps: Disability at the End of the Social Contract.* Monroe, ME: Common Courage, 1998.
Russell, Robert John. *Cosmology from Alpha to Omega: The Creative Mutual Interaction of Theology and Science.* Minneapolis: Fortress, 2008.
Ruthven, Jon. *On the Cessation of the Charismata: The Protestant Polemic on Postbiblical Miracles.* Sheffield: Sheffield Academic, 1993.
Ryan, Thomas. "Sharing Spiritual Gifts at the Dawn of the Third Millennium." *Ecumenism* 132 (December 1998) 8–12.
Saarinen, Risto. *God and the Gift: An Ecumenical Theology of Giving.* Collegeville, MN: Liturgical, 2005.
Sanneh, L. *Translating the Message: The Missionary Impact on Culture.* Maryknoll, NY: Orbis, 1989.
Satyavrata, Ivan. *God Has Not Left Himself Without Witness.* Oxford: Regnum, 2011.
Schipper, Jeremy. *Disability and Isaiah's Suffering Servant.* New York: Oxford University Press, 2011.
Schreiter, Robert John. *Eschatology as a Grammar of Transformation: A Study in Speech Act Theory and Structural Semantics and Their Application to Some Problems in Eschatology.* Oxford: Parchment, 1974.
Seccombe, D. P. "Possessions and the Poor in Luke-Acts." PhD diss., University of Cambridge, 1978.
Self, Charlie. *Flourishing Churches and Communities: Pentecostal Primer on Faith, Work, and Economics for Spirit-Empowered Discipleship.* Grand Rapids: Christian Library, 2012.
Sepulveda, J. "To Overcome the Fear of Syncretism: A Latin American Perspective." In *Mission Matters,* edited by L. Price, J. Sepulveda, and G. Smith, 157–68. Frankfurt: Peter Lang, 1997.
Seymour, William J. *The Doctrines and Discipline of the Azusa Street Apostolic Faith Mission of Los Angeles, California.* Joplin, MO: Christian Life Books, 2000.
———. "The Same Old Way." *Apostolic Faith* 1, no. 1 (1906) 3.
Shade, W. Robert. "The Restoration of Israel in Acts 3:12–26 and Lukan Eschatology." PhD diss., Trinity Evangelical Divinity School, 1994.
Sharpe, Kevin. *Sleuthing the Divine: The Nexus of Science and Spirit.* Minneapolis: Fortress, 2000.
Shaull, Richard, and Waldo Cesar. *Pentecostalism and the Future of the Christian Churches: Promises, Limitations, Challenges.* Grand Rapids: Eerdmans, 2000.
Sherry, Patrick. *Religion, Truth, and Language-Games.* New York: Barnes & Noble, 1977.
———. *Spirit and Beauty: An Introduction to Theological Aesthetics.* Oxford: Clarendon, 1992.
Shuman, J. "Pentecost and the End of Patriotism: A Call for the Restoration of Pacifism among Pentecostal Christians." *Journal of Pentecostal Theology* 9 (1996) 70–96.
Simon, Marcel. *St. Stephen and the Hellenists in the Primitive Church.* London: Longmans, Green, 1958.
Sloan, Robert B., Jr. *The Favorable Year of the Lord: A Study of Jubilary Theology in the Gospel of Luke.* Austin, TX: Scholars, 1977.

Smart, Ninian, and Steven Konstantine. *Christian Systematic Theology in a World Context*. Minneapolis: Fortress, 1996.
Smith, James K. A. *Thinking in Tongues: Pentecostal Contributions to Christian Philosophy*. Grand Rapids: Eerdmans, 2010.
Smith, Wilfred Cantwell. *The Meaning and End of Religion*. New York: Macmillan, 1962.
———. *Towards a World Theology: Faith and the Comparative History of Religion*. Philadelphia: Westminster, 1981.
Solivan, Samuel. *The Spirit, Pathos, and Liberation: Toward an Hispanic Pentecostal Theology*. Sheffield, UK: Sheffield Academic, 1998.
Spicq, Ceslaus. *Agape in the New Testament*. 3 vols, translated by Marie Aquinas McNamara and Mary Honoria Richter. St. Louis: Herder, 1963–1966.
Spittler, R. S. "Glossolalia." In *The New International Dictionary of Pentecostal and Charismatic Movements*, rev. and ex. ed., edited by Stanley M. Burgess and Eduard M. van der Maas, 670–76. Grand Rapids: Zondervan, 2002.
Sproul, R. C. *Scripture Alone: The Evangelical Doctrine*. Phillipsburg, NJ: P & R, 2005.
Stackhouse, John G., Jr. *Evangelical Landscapes: Facing Critical Issues of the Day*. Grand Rapids: Baker Academic, 2002.
Stackhouse, Max L. *Apologia: Contextualization, Globalization, and Mission in Theological Education*. Grand Rapids: Eerdmans, 1988.
Stephenson, Christopher A. "Reality, Knowledge, and Life in Community: The Metaphysical, Epistemological, and Hermeneutical Bases of Amos Yong's Theology." In *The Theology of Amos Yong and the New Face of Pentecostal Scholarship: Passion for the Spirit*, edited by Wolfgang Vondey and Martin Mittelstadt, 63–81. Leiden: Brill, 2013.
———. *Types of Pentecostal Theology: Method, System, Spirit*. Oxford: Oxford University Press, 2013.
Stronstad, Roger. *The Prophethood of All Believers: A Study in Luke's Charismatic Theology*. Sheffield: Sheffield Academic, 1999.
———. "Review Essay on Amos Yong, Who is the Holy Spirit?: A Walk with the Apostles." *Journal of Pentecostal Theology* 22, no. 2 (2013) 295–300.
Surin, Kenneth. "Revelation, Salvation, the Uniqueness of Christ, and Other Religions." *Religious Studies* 19 (1983) 323–43.
Suurmond, Jean-Jacques. *Word and Spirit at Play: Towards a Charismatic Theology*, translated by John Bowden. Grand Rapids: Eerdmans, 1995.
Swidler, Leonard. *After the Absolute: The Dialogical Future of Religious Reflection*. Minneapolis: Fortress, 1990.
———. *Toward a Universal Theology of Religion*. Maryknoll, NY: Orbis, 1987.
Swinton, John. *Raging with Compassion: Pastoral Responses to the Problem of Evil*. Grand Rapids: Eerdmans, 2007.
Swoboda, A. J. *Tongues and Trees: Towards a Pentecostal Ecological Theology*. Blandford Forum: Deo, 2013.
Tanzella-Nitti, G. "The Two Books Prior to the Scientific Revolution." *Perspectives on Science and Christian Faith* 57, no. 3 (2005) 235–48.
Tarr, D. *Double Image: Biblical Insights from African Parables*. New York: Paulist, 1994.
Tate, W. R. *Biblical Interpretation: An Integrated Approach*. Peabody, MA: Hendrickson, 1991.
Teasdale, Wayne. *The Mystic Heart: Discovering a Universal Spirituality in the World's Religions*. Novato, CA: New World Library, 1999.

Theissen, Gerd. "The Strong and the Weak in Corinth: A Sociological Analysis of a Theological Quarrel." In *Understanding Paul's Ethics: Twentieth-Century Approaches*, edited by Brian S. Rosner, 107–28. Grand Rapids: Eerdmans, 1995.

Thiselton, Anthony C. "Christology in Luke, Speech-Act Theory, and the Problem of Dualism in Christology after Kant." In *Jesus of Nazareth: Lord and Christ—Essays on the Historical Jesus and New Testament Christology*, edited by Joel B. Green and Max Turner, 453–72. Grand Rapids: Eerdmans, 1994.

Thomas, John Christopher. *The Devil, Disease, and Deliverance: Origins of Illness in New Testament Thought*. Sheffield: Sheffield Academic, 1998.

———. "Pentecostal Theology in the Twenty-First Century." *PNEUMA: The Journal of the Society for Pentecostal Studies* 20, no. 1 (1998): 3–19.

Thomas, Norman E. "The Church at Antioch: Crossing Racial, Cultural, and Class Barriers." In *Mission in Acts: Ancient Narratives in Contemporary Context*, edited by Robert L. Gallagher and Paul Hertig, 144–56. Maryknoll, NY: Orbis, 2004.

Thompson, H. Paul, Jr. "On Account of Conditions that Seem Unbearable: A Proposal about Race Relations in the Church of God (Cleveland, TN) 1909–1929." *PNEUMA: The Journal of the Society for Pentecostal Studies* 25, no. 2 (2003) 240–64.

Thorsen, Donald A. *The Wesleyan Quadrilateral: Scripture, Tradition, Reason, and Experience as a Model for Evangelical Theology*. Grand Rapids: Zondervan, 1990.

Thorson, Walter R. "Hermeneutics for Reading the Book of Nature: A Response to Angus Menuge." *Perspectives on Science and Christian Faith* 55, no. 2 (2003) 99–101.

Tilley, Terrence W. *The Evils of Theodicy*. Washington, DC: Georgetown University Press, 1991.

Tillich, Paul. *The Future of Religions*. New York: Harper & Row, 1966.

Tracy, David. *The Analogical Imagination: Christian Theology and the Culture of Pluralism*. New York: Crossroad, 1982.

———. *Blessed Rage for Order: The New Pluralism in Theology*. Chicago: University of Chicago Press, 1996.

———. *Plurality and Ambiguity: Hermeneutics, Religion, Hope*. Chicago: University of Chicago Press, 1987.

Tremain, S. L., ed. *Foucault and the Government of Disability*. Ann Arbor, MI: University of Michigan Press, 2005.

Turner, W. J., and T. V. Pearman, eds. *The Treatment of Disabled Persons in Medieval Europe: Examining Disability in the Historical, Legal, Literary, Medical, and Religious Discourses of the Middle Ages*. Lewiston, NY: Edwin Mellen, 2010.

Twelftree, Graham H. *Jesus the Exorcist: A Contribution to the Study of the Historical Jesus*. Tübingen: J. C. B. Mohr, 1993.

———. *Jesus the Miracle Worker: A Historical and Theological Study*. Downers Grove, IL: InterVarsity, 1999.

Unnamed. "Beginning of a World Wide Revival." *Apostolic Faith* 1, no. 5 (1907) 1.

———. "The Old Time Pentecost." *Apostolic Faith* 1, no. 1 (1906) 1.

van der Meer, Jitse M., and Scott Mandelbrote, eds. *Nature and Scripture in the Abrahamic Religions: Up to 1700*. Brill's Series in Church History 36. Leiden: Brill, 2008.

———. *Nature and Scripture in the Abrahamic Religions: 1700–Present*. Brill's Series in Church History 37. Leiden: Brill, 2008.

Van Dusen, Henry Pitt. *Spirit, Son, and Father: Christian Faith in the Light of the Holy Spirit*. New York: Charles Scribner's Sons, 1958.

Vanhoozer, Kevin J. *Biblical Narrative in the Philosophy of Paul Ricoeur: A Study in Hermeneutics and Theology*. Cambridge: Cambridge University Press, 1990.

———. "Discourse on Matter: Hermeneutics and the 'Miracle' of Understanding." In *Hermeneutics at the Crossroads*, edited by Kevin J. Vanhoozer, James K. A. Smith, and Bruce Ellis Benson, 3–34. Bloomington: Indiana University Press, 2006.

———. *The Drama of Doctrine: A Canonical-Linguistic Approach to Christian Theology*. Louisville: Westminster John Knox, 2005.

———. *First Theology: God, Scripture, and Hermeneutics*. Downers Grove, IL: InterVarsity, 2002.

———. *Is There a Meaning in This Text?: The Bible, the Reader, and the Morality of Literary Knowledge*. Grand Rapids: Zondervan, 1998.

———. "The Voice and the Actor: A Dramatic Proposal about the Ministry and Minstrelsy of Theology." In *Evangelical Futures: A Conversation on Theological Method*, edited by John G. Stackhouse, 61–106. Grand Rapids: Baker, 2000.

Vidu, Adonis. *Postliberal Theological Method: A Critical Study*. Milton Keynes: Paternoster, 2005.

Villafañe, Eldin. *The Liberating Spirit: Toward an Hispanic American Pentecostal Social Ethic*. Grand Rapids: Eerdmans, 1993.

Volf, Miroslav. *Exclusion and Embrace: A Theological Exploration of Identity, Otherness, and Reconciliation*. Nashville: Abingdon, 1996.

———. "The Final Reconciliation: Reflections on a Social Dimension of the Eschatological Transition." *Modern Theology* 16, no. 1 (2000) 91–113.

———. "Materiality of Salvation: An Investigation in the Soteriologies of Liberation and Pentecostal Theologies." *Journal of Ecumenical Studies* 26, no. 3 (1989) 447–67.

———. "A Study in Provisional Certitude." In *The Unique Christ in Our Pluralistic World*, edited by Bruce J. Nicholls, 96–106. Grand Rapids: Baker, 1994.

———. *Work in the Spirit: Toward a Theology of Work*. New York: Oxford University Press, 1991.

Volf, Miroslav, and Dorothy C. Bass, eds. *Practicing Theology: Beliefs and Practices in Christian Life*. Grand Rapids: Eerdmans, 2002.

Walls, Andrew F. "Toward a Theology of Migration." In *African Christian Presence in the West: New Immigrant Congregations and Transnational Networks in North America and Europe*, edited by Frieder Ludwig and J. Kwabena Asamoah-Gyadu, 407–17. Trenton, NJ: Africa World, 2011.

Walton, John H. *The Lost World of Genesis One: Ancient Cosmology and the Origins Debate*. Downers Grove: IVP Academic, 2009.

Ward, Keith. *Religion and Revelation: A Theology of Revelation in the World's Religions*. Oxford: Clarendon, 1994.

———. "Truth and the Diversity of Religions." In *The Philosophical Challenge of Religious Diversity*, edited by Philip L. Quinn and Kevin Meeker, 109–25. Oxford: Oxford University Press, 2000.

Ware, Frederick L. "The Church of God in Christ and the Azusa Street Revival." In *The Azusa Street Revival and Its Legacy*, edited by Harold D. Hunter and Cecil M. Robeck, Jr., 243–57. Cleveland, TN: Pathway, 2006.

Warren, E. Janet. *Cleansing the Cosmos: A Biblical Model for Conceptualizing and Counteracting Evil.* Eugene, OR: Pickwick, 2012.

Wayman, Alex. "Eschatology in Buddhism." In *Eschatology in Christianity and Other Religions.* Studia Missionalia 32, 71-94. Rome: Gregorian University Press, 1983.

Welker, Michael, ed. *The Spirit in Creation and New Creation: Science and Theology in Western and Orthodox Realms.* Grand Rapids: Eerdmans, 2012.

Wenk, Matthias. *Community-Forming Power: The Socio-Ethical Role of the Spirit in Luke-Acts.* Sheffield: Sheffield Academic, 2000.

Wesley, John. "The Use of Money." In *John Wesley's Sermons: An Anthology,* edited by Albert Cook Outler and Richard P. Heitzenrater, 347-58. Nashville: Abingdon, 1991.

Westhelle, Vítor. "Liberation Theology: A Latitudinal Perspective." In *The Oxford Handbook of Eschatology,* edited by Jerry L. Walls, 311-27. New York: Oxford University Press, 2008.

Williams, Demetrius K. "Upon All Flesh: Acts 2, African Americans, and Intersectional Realities." In *They Were All Together in One Place?: Toward Minority Biblical Criticism.* SBL Semeia Studies 57. Edited by Randall C. Bailey, Tat-siong Benny Liew, and Fernando F. Segovia, 289-310. Leiden: Brill, 2009.

Williams, D. H. *Retrieving the Tradition and Renewing Evangelicalism: A Primer for Suspicious Protestants.* Grand Rapids: Eerdmans, 1999.

Wilson, Stephen G. *The Gentiles and the Gentile Mission in Luke-Acts.* Society for New Testament Studies Monograph Series 23. Cambridge: Cambridge University Press, 1973.

Wink, Walter. *Engaging the Powers: Discernment and Resistance in a World of Domination.* Philadelphia: Fortress, 1992.

———. *Naming the Powers: The Language of Power in the New Testament.* Philadelphia: Fortress, 1984.

———. *Unmasking the Powers: The Invisible Forces that Determine Human Existence.* Philadelphia: Fortress, 1986.

Witherington, Ben. *The Acts of the Apostles: A Socio-Rhetorical Commentary.* Grand Rapids: Eerdmans, 1998.

Wong, David B. "Three Kinds of Incommensurability." In *Relativism: Interpretation and Confrontation,* edited by Michael Krausz, 140-58. Notre Dame, IN: University of Notre Dame Press, 1989.

Woods, Edward J. *The Finger of God and Pneumatology in Luke-Acts.* Sheffield, England: Sheffield Academic, 2001.

Work, Telford. *Living and Active: Scripture in the Economy of Salvation.* Grand Rapids: Eerdmans, 2001.

Wright, N. T. *Jesus and the Victory of God.* Minneapolis: Fortress, 1996.

———. *The New Testament and the People of God.* Minneapolis: Fortress, 1992.

Wright, Terry J. *Providence Made Flesh: Divine Presence as a Framework for a Theology of Providence.* Milton Keynes: Paternoster, 2009.

Yong, Amos. "Academic Glossolalia?: Pentecostal Scholarship, Multi-Disciplinarity, and the Science-Religion Conversation." *Journal of Pentecostal Theology* 14, no. 1 (2005) 61-80.

———. "As the Spirit Gives Utterance: Pentecost, Intra-Christian Ecumenism, and the Wider *Oekumene.*" *International Review of Mission* 92, no. 366 (2003) 299-314.

———. "The 'Baptist Vision' of James William McClendon, Jr.: A Wesleyan-Pentecostal Response." *Wesleyan Theological Journal* 37, no. 2 (2002) 32–57.

———. *Beyond the Impasse: Toward a Pneumatological Theology of Religions*. Grand Rapids: Baker Academic, 2003.

———. *The Bible, Disability, and the Church: A New Vision of the People of God*. Grand Rapids: Eerdmans, 2011.

———. "Conclusion—From Demonization to Kin-domization: The Witness of the Spirit and the Renewal of Missions in a Pluralistic World." In *Global Renewal, Religious Pluralism, and the Great Commission: Toward a Renewal Theology of Mission and Interreligious Encounter*. Asbury Theological Seminary Series in World Christian Revitalization Movements in Pentecostal/Charismatic Studies 4, edited by Amos Yong and Clifton Clarke, 157–74. Lexington, KY: Emeth, 2011.

———. *The Cosmic Breath: Spirit and Nature in the Christianity-Buddhism-Science Trialogue*. Philosophical Studies in Science and Religion 4. Leiden: Brill, 2012.

———. "The Demise of Foundationalism and the Retention of Truth: What Evangelicals Can Learn from C. S. Peirce." *Christian Scholar's Review* 29, no. 3 (2000) 563–88.

———. "The Demonic in Pentecostal-Charismatic Christianity and in the Religious Consciousness of Asia." In *Asian and Pentecostal: The Charismatic Face of Christianity in Asia*, edited by Allan Anderson and Edmond Tang, 93–127. Baguio City, Philippines: Asia Pacific Theological Seminary Press, 2005.

———. *The Dialogical Spirit: Christian Reason and Theological Method for the Third Millennium*. Eugene, OR: Cascade, 2014.

———. "Disability and the Gifts of the Spirit: Pentecost and the Renewal of the Church." *Journal of Pentecostal Theology*, 19, no. 1 (2010) 76–93.

———. "Disability and the Renewal of Theological Education: Beyond Ableism." In *Theology and the Experience of Disability: Interdisciplinary Perspectives from Voices Down Under*, edited by Andrew Picard and Myk Habets, 250–63. London: Routledge, 2016.

———. "*Disability in the Christian Tradition*: An Overview and Historiographical Reflection." *Journal of Religion, Disability, and Health* 17, no. 3 (2013) 236–43.

———. "Disability, the Human Condition, and the Spirit of the Eschatological Long Run: Toward a Pneumatological Theology of Disability." *Journal of Religion, Disability, and Health* 11, no. 1 (2007) 5–25.

———. "Disability Theology of the Resurrection: Persisting Questions and Additional Considerations—A Response to Ryan Mullins." *Ars Disputandi* 12 (2012) 4–10.

———. *Discerning the Spirit(s): A Pentecostal-Charismatic Contribution to Christian Theology of Religions*. Sheffield: Sheffield Academic, 2000.

———. "Faith and Science: Friend or Foe?" *Enrichment Journal* 17, no. 4 (2012) 46–51.

———. "The Future of Asian Pentecostal Theology: An Asian American Assessment." *Asian Journal of Pentecostal Studies* 10, no. 1 (2007) 22–41.

———. *The Future of Evangelical Theology: Soundings from the Asian American Diaspora*. Downers Grove, IL: IVP Academic, 2014.

———. "Global Pentecostalisms and the Public Sphere." In *The Oxford Handbook of Political Theology*, edited by Shaun Casey and Michael Kessler. Oxford: Oxford University Press, forthcoming.

———. "Globalizing Christology: Anglo-American Perspectives in World Religious Context." *Religious Studies Review* 30, no. 4 (2004) 259–66.

———. "Guests, Hosts, and the Holy Ghost: Pneumatological Theology and Christian Practices in a World of Many Faiths." In *Lord and Giver of Life: Perspectives on Constructive Pneumatology*, edited by David H. Jensen, 71–86. Louisville: Westminster John Knox, 2008.

———. "The Hermeneutical Trialectic: Notes Toward a Consensual Hermeneutic and Theological Method." *Heythrop Journal* 45, no. 1 (2004) 22–39.

———. *Hospitality and the Other: Pentecost, Christian Practices, and the Neighbor.* Maryknoll, NY: Orbis, 2008.

———. "In Search of Foundations: The *Oeuvre* of Donald L. Gelpi, S.J., and Its Significance for Pentecostal Theology and Philosophy." *Journal of Pentecostal Theology* 11, no. 1 (2002) 3–26.

———. *In the Days of Caesar: Pentecostalism and Political Theology.* Grand Rapids: Eerdmans, 2010.

———. "The Inviting Spirit: Pentecostal Beliefs and Practices Regarding the Religions Today." In *Defining Issues in Pentecostalism: Classical and Emergent*, edited by Steven Studebaker, 29–44. Eugene, OR: Wipf & Stock, 2008.

———. "Justice Deprived, Justice Demanded: Afropentecostalisms and the Task of World Pentecostal Theology Today." *Journal of Pentecostal Theology* 15, no. 1 (2006) 127–47.

———. "Many Tongues, Many Practices: Pentecost and Theology of Mission at 2010." In *Mission After Christendom: Emergent Themes in Contemporary Mission*, edited by Ogbu U. Kalu, Edmund Kee-Fook Chia, and Peter Vethanayagamony, 43–58. Louisville: Westminster John Knox, 2010.

———. "Mind and Life, Religion and Science: The Dalai Lama and the Buddhist-Christian-Science Trilogue." *Buddhist-Christian Studies* 28 (2008) 43–63.

———. "The Missiology of Jamestown: 1607–2007 and Beyond—Toward a Postcolonial Theology of Mission in North America." In *Remembering Jamestown: Hard Questions About Christian Mission*, edited by Amos Yong and Barbara Brown Zikmund, 157–67. Eugene, OR: Pickwick, 2010.

———. "On Divine Presence and Divine Agency: Toward a Foundational Pneumatology." *Asian Journal of Pentecostal Studies* 3, no. 2 (2000) 167–88.

———. "Performing Global Pentecostal Theology: A Response to Wolfgang Vondey." *PNEUMA: The Journal of the Society for Pentecostal Studies* 28, no. 2 (2006) 313–21.

———. *Pneumatology and the Christian-Buddhist Dialogue: Does the Wind Blow through the Middle Way?* Studies in Systematic Theology 11. Leiden: Brill, 2012.

———. "A P(new)matological Paradigm for Christian Mission in a Religiously Plural World." *Missiology: An International Review* 33, no. 2 (2005) 175–91.

———. "Poured Out on All Flesh: The Spirit, World Pentecostalism, and the Performance of Renewal Theology." *PentecoStudies* 6, no. 1 (2007) 16–46.

———. "Reading Scripture and Nature: Pentecostal Hermeneutics and Their Implications for the Contemporary Evangelical Theology and Science Conversation." *Perspectives on Science and Christian Faith* 63, no. 1 (2011) 1–13.

———. "Ruach, the Primordial Waters, and the Breath of Life: Emergence Theory and the Creation Narratives in Pneumatological Perspective." In *The Work of the Holy Spirit: Pneumatology and Pentecostalism*, edited by Michael Welker, 183–204. Grand Rapids: Eerdmans, 2006.

———. "Running the (Special) Race: New (Pauline) Perspectives on Theology of Sport." *Journal of Religion, Disability, and Health* 15, no. 4 (2013) 339–50.

———. "Speaking in Scientific Tongues: Which Spirit/s, What Interpretations?." *Canadian Journal of Pentecostal-Charismatic Christianity* 3, no. 1 (2012) 130–39.

———. "The Spirit Bears Witness: Pneumatology, Truth, and the Religions." *Scottish Journal of Theology* 57, no. 1 (2004) 14–38.

———. *The Spirit of Creation: Modern Science and Divine Action in the Pentecostal-Charismatic Imagination.* Grand Rapids: Eerdmans, 2011.

———. "The Spirit of Hospitality: Pentecostal Perspectives toward a Performative Theology of the Interreligious Encounter." *Missiology: An International Review* 35, no. 1 (2007) 55–73.

———. *Spirit of Love: A Trinitarian Theology of Grace.* Waco, TX: Baylor University Press, 2012.

———. "Spirit Possession, the Living, and the Dead: A Review Essay and Response from a Pentecostal Perspective." *Dharma Deepika: A South Asian Journal of Missiological Research* 8, no. 2 (2004) 77–88.

———. *The Spirit Poured Out on All Flesh: Pentecostalism and the Possibility of Global Theology.* Grand Rapids: Baker Academic, 2005.

———. "Spiritual Discernment: A Biblical-Theological Reconsideration." In *The Spirit and Spirituality: Essays in Honor of Russell P. Spittler*, edited by Wonsuk Ma and Robert P. Menzies, 83–104. New York: T &T Clark, 2004.

———. *Spirit-Word-Community: Theological Hermeneutics in Trinitarian Perspective.* Aldershot: Ashgate, 2002.

———. "Technologies of Liberation: A Comparative Soteriology of Eastern Orthodoxy and Theravada Buddhism." *Dharma Deepika: A South Asian Journal of Missiological Research* 7, no. 1 (2003) 17–60.

———. *Theology and Down Syndrome: Reimagining Disability in Late Modernity.* Waco, TX: Baylor University Press, 2007.

———. "A Theology of the Third Article?: Hegel and the Contemporary Enterprise in First Philosophy and First Theology." In *Semper Reformandum: Studies in Honour of Clark H. Pinnock*, edited by Stanley E. Porter and Anthony R. Cross, 208–31. Carlisle: Paternoster, 2003.

———. "Tongues of Fire in the Pentecostal Imagination: The Truth of Glossolalia in Light of R. C. Neville's Theory of Religious Symbolism." *Journal of Pentecostal Theology* 12 (1998) 39–65.

———. "Tongues, Theology, and the Social Sciences: A Pentecostal-Theological Reading of Geertz's Interpretive Theory of Religion." *Cyberjournal for Pentecostal/Charismatic Research* 1 (1997).

———. "A Typology of Prosperity Theology: A Religious Economy of Global Renewal or a Renewal Economics?" In *Pentecostalism and Prosperity: The Socioeconomics of the Global Charismatic Movement.* Christianities of the World 1. Edited by Amos Yong and Katherine Attanasi, 15–33. New York: Palgrave Macmillan, 2012.

———. "What Spirit(s), Which Public(s)?: The Pneumatologies of Global Pentecostal-Charismatic Christianity." *International Journal of Public Theology* 7 (2013) 241–59.

———. "Whither Systematic Theology?: A Systematician Chimes in on a Scandalous Conversation." *PNEUMA: The Journal of the Society for Pentecostal Studies* 20, no. 1 (1998) 85–93.

———. *Who is the Holy Spirit?: A Walk with the Apostles*. Brewster, MA: Paraclete, 2011.

———. "Zacchaeus: Short and Unseen." In *Disability*, edited by Robert B. Kruschwitz, 11–17. Waco, TX: The Center for Christian Ethics at Baylor University, 2012.

Yong, Amos, and Christian T. Collins Winn. "The Apocalypse of Colonialism, Colonialism as Apocalyptic Mission; Or, Notes Toward a Postcolonial Eschatology." In *Evangelical Postcolonial Conversations: Global Awakenings in Theology and Praxis*, edited by Kay Higuera Smith, Jayachitra Lalitha, and L. Daniel Hawk, 139–51. Downers Grove: IVP Academic, 2014.

Yong, Amos, Frank D. Macchia, Ralph Del Colle, and Dale T. Irvin. "Christ and Spirit: Dogma, Discernment, and Dialogical Theology in a Religiously Plural World." *Journal of Pentecostal Theology* 12, no. 1 (2003) 15–83.

Yong, Amos, and Jonathan A. Anderson. *Renewing Christian Theology: Systematics for a Global Christianity*. Waco, TX: Baylor University Press, 2014.

Yong, Amos, ed. "Pentecostalism, Science, and Creation: New Voices in the Theology-Science Conversation." A collection of six articles in *Zygon: Journal of Science and Religion* 43, no. 4 (2008) 875–989.

Yong, Amos, ed. *The Spirit Renews the Face of the Earth: Pentecostal Forays in Science and Theology of Creation*. Eugene, OR: Pickwick, 2009.

Yong, Amos, and Estrelda Alexander, eds. *Afro-Pentecostalism: Black Pentecostal and Charismatic Christianity in History and Culture*. New York: New York University Press, 2011.

Yong, Amos, and Estrelda Alexander, eds. *Philip's Daughters: Women in Pentecostal-Charismatic Leadership*. Princeton Theological Monographs Series 104. Eugene, OR: Pickwick, 2009.

Yong, Amos, and James K. A. Smith, eds. *Science and the Spirit: A Pentecostal Engagement with the Sciences*. Bloomington, IN: Indiana University Press, 2010.

Yong, Amos, and Katherine Attanasi, eds. *Pentecostalism and Prosperity: The Socioeconomics of the Global Charismatic Movement*. Christianities of the World 1. New York: Palgrave Macmillan, 2012.

Yong, Amos, Veli-Matti Kärkkäinen, and Kirsteen Kim, eds. *Interdisciplinary and Religio-Cultural Discourse on a Spirit-Filled World: Loosing the Spirits*. New York: Palgrave Macmillan, 2013.

Young, Frances. *The Art of Performance: Towards a Theology of Holy Scripture*. London: Darton, Longman, & Todd, 1990.

Zalanga, Samuel. "What Empire? Which Multitude?: Pentecostalism and Social Liberation in North America and Sub-Saharan Africa." In *Evangelicals and Empire: Christian Alternatives to the Political Status Quo*, edited by Bruce Ellis Benson and Peter Goodwin Heltzel, 237–51. Grand Rapids: Brazos, 2008.

Zehnle, Richard F. *Peter's Pentecost Discourse: Tradition and Lukan Reinterpretation in Peter's Speeches of Acts 2 and 3*. Nashville: Abingdon, 1971.

Index of Scripture

GENESIS

1–3	92
1	93–94
1:2–3	75
1:2	77, 95
1:7	76
1:9–10	76
1:11	76
1:16	76
1:20	76
1:21	76
1:24	76
1:25	76
1:26	76, 115
1:27	76
2:7	75, 248
4:11	114
11	64
12:1–3	223

EXODUS

4:10–12	226

LEVITICUS

19:18	114
21:16–24	134
21:17–23	130
28:15–68	130

DEUTERONOMY

23:1	129

EZRA

1	47

JOB

34:14–15	75, 95

PSALMS

19:1	84, 86
22:3	115
33:6	75
34:8	40
50:6	115
68:31	129
104:29–30	75, 95
110:1	178
139:7–12	46

ISAIAH

11:2	200
11:6–9	167
32:15–17	109
32:15–16	167
32:15	75, 95
34:4	86
35:6–7	212
35:6	212
40:1–2	179n2
43:25–44:3	179n2
45:1	47
45:14	129
52:13–53:12	133
56:3–5	130

ISAIAH (continued)

61:1–12	199, 201
65:25	167

JEREMIAH

31:8–9	131
31:31–34	179n2
33:4–11	179n2

LAMENTATIONS

4:22	179n2

EZEKIEL

1	102
36:24–33	179n2
37:1–14	178

JOEL

2:28–32	219

MICAH

4:6–7	131

ZEPHANIAH

3:9–10	129
3:19	131

MATTHEW

1:18	44, 200
5:3	165
7:21–23	44
7:21	286
7:23	286
9:10	205n4
10:40–42	44
12:28	202, 202n12
17:25	205n4
18:23–27	202
19:19	114
22:29	87
25:31–46	114, 160, 165
26:6	205n4
26:18	205n4

MARK

3:20	205n4
3:31–35	164
7:17	205n4
7:24	205n4
9:28	205n4
10:10	205n4
12:31	114
14:3	205n4

LUKE

1:17	215
1:22	226
1:32	216
1:32–33	214
1:35	200
1:40	167
1:46–55	214, 214n1
1:52–53	165, 214
1:55–56	223
1:55	214
1:62–63	226
1:67–79	214n1
1:67	215
1:68–71	215
1:68	223
1:71	178
1:78–79	215
1:80	200
2:11	216
2:20	228
2:22–38	214n1
2:25–32	200
2:25	215, 223
2:30–32	215
2:30	228
2:31–32	220
2:36–38	167
2:38	215, 223
2:52	200
3:6	228
3:16	223
3:21–22	200

4:1	200, 204	14:23	131
4:14	200, 204	17:11–19	202
4:18–19	170, 199–201, 204	17:21	203
4:18	211, 268	18:27	213
4:19	167, 203, 211	18:35–43	201, 229
4:32–34	201	19	138
4:38–39	205	19:1–10	134–35, 201
5:12–14	202	19:1–9	205n4
5:17	205	19:3	134–35
5:29	205	19:4	136
6:20–21	165	19:5	205
6:24–25	165	19:7	136
7:11–17	201	19:8	134
7:21–22	201	19:9	130, 135, 137
7:36	205	19:10	135
7:47–50	201	22:10–14	205
8:1–4	167	23:34	221
8:1–3	201	23:46	200
8:19–21	164	24:13	23n2
8:26–40	201	24:29	205
9:1–2	202	24:30	205
9:37–43	201	24:47	202, 220
9:42	202	24:49	179, 190, 201, 220
9:48	203		
9:51–56	206	## JOHN	
9:58	205		
10:5–7	205	1:9	44, 280
10:17	202	1:14	36
10:24	228	5:14	130
10:25–37	206	7:39	29
10:25	206	8:32	42
10:27	96, 114	9:2–3	130
10:38–42	201	9:3	158
10:38	205	10:16	44
11:13–15	201	14	4
11:13	219	14:6	42
11:14–26	202n12	14:12	170
11:20	202	14:17	42
11:27–28	167	14:26	43
11:37	205	15:26	42
12:11–12	268	16:13–15	43
13:10–17	135	16:13	42, 52
14	130	17:17–19	43
14:1–24	129n1	20:22–23	202
14:1	205		
14:3–5	130	## ACTS	
14:13	131		
14:21	131, 206	1:3	216

ACTS (continued)

1:5	223
1:6–7	210
1:6	223
1:8	42, 64, 180, 207, 220, 221n8, 267, 287
1:11	203
2	63, 65, 166, 175, 225n3
2:1–5:11	220
2:2–3	226
2:2–4	190
2:4–11	120, 193
2:4	84, 223, 264
2:5–11	231
2:5	231
2:6	226, 264
2:7–11	227
2:7	264
2:9–11	166
2:11	42, 64, 70, 83, 89, 95, 226, 233, 264, 287
2:12–13	43
2:13–15	266
2:14–20	219
2:17–18	43, 167, 208, 264
2:17	10, 36, 42, 44, 64, 107, 203, 228, 280, 287
2:19–20	43, 167
2:19	287
2:20	211
2:21	43, 178, 209, 219, 287
2:22–40	178n1
2:22–38	43
2:22–23	200
2:22	178
2:23	179
2:24	200
2:32	200
2:33	179, 190, 226
2:36	178–79, 200, 221, 287
2:37	179
2:38–39	43, 179
2:38	163, 202, 211, 219–21
2:39	164, 180, 221
2:40–47	166
2:40	179
2:41	231
2:42–47	43, 222, 268
2:42	222
2:44	203, 208
2:45	232
2:46	208
2:47	208
3–4	135
3:1–10	202
3:1	211
3:6	211
3:8	212
3:10	210
3:11–12	211
3:13	211
3:14–15	211
3:16	210
3:17	228
3:19–21	168, 210
3:19	202, 211, 221
3:20	221
3:21	203, 221
3:22	211
3:23	211
3:25	64, 223, 287
4:4	231
4:8	223
4:9–12	210
4:13	166, 203
4:20	228
4:27	200
4:31	223
4:32–37	166, 208
4:34–37	268
4:34–35	222
4:34	232
5:12–7:60	220
5:16	202, 231
5:31	202, 221
5:42	208
6	208n22
6:1–16	165
6:1–6	203
6:1–3	268
6:1	208, 232
6:2–4	233
6:5	232
7	233
7:44–53	233
7:44–50	210n5, 211n9

7:55	223	13:52	223
8	166	14:8–10	202
8:1–25	220	15	51n10
8:6–7	202	15:25	219
8:6	228	15:28	266
8:12	164	16:14–15	164
8:15	223	16:15	207
8:18–20	219	16:16–18	202
8:22	221	16:31–33	164
8:26–40	129n1, 135, 166	16:32–34	207
8:32–33	130	17:2	269
8:36–38	164	17:6	180
8:38	130	17:7	207
9–28	220	17:15	207
9–10	51n10	17:28	44
9:8	207	18:3	207
9:11	207	18:4	269
9:17	223	18:7	207
9:17–19	207	18:8	164, 166
9:17–18	163	18:17	166
9:25	207	18:24	166
9:27	207	19:2	223
9:30	207	19:8–10	269
9:32–35	202	20:8	207
9:36	208n22	20:35	208n22
10	27, 166	21:4	207
10:2	208n22	21:7	207
10:4	208n22	21:8	207
10:6	207n18	21:8–9	203
10:23	207n18	21:16	207
10:34	43, 265	22:15	228
10:31	208n22	22:16	163, 221
10:38	200	23:23–24	207
10:43	202, 221	24:17	208n22
10:45	219	24:23	207
10:47–48	164	24:26	207
10:47	223	26:18	202, 221
10:48	204, 207n18	27:3	207
11:14	164	27:33–37	207
11:16	223	28:2–10	208
11:17	219	28:7–10	166
11:25–26	207	28:8–9	202
11:27–30	208n22	28:14	208
12:12–17	207n18	28:23–30	208
13:6–12	202		
13:7–12	166	**ROMANS**	
13:9	223		
13:38–39	202, 221	1:3–4	200

ROMANS (continued)

1:20	30n11, 86
2:12–16	114
5:5	47, 190, 280
5:9	203
6–8	61
6:3–4	164
8:18–27	44, 107
8:19–23	167
8:22–23	75
8:29–30	61
8:39	47
12:1–2	61
12:6–8	54
12:13–21	54
13:1	47
13:9	114
13:11	158, 203

1 CORINTHIANS

1	4
1:12	124
2:9–16	61
2:10–16	249
3:4	124
3:11	245
3:12–15	114
7:14	164
11	124
12	123, 159
12:3	286
12:4–7	126
12:4	265
12:7	53
12:11–13	126
12:12	53
12:13	164, 265
12:14–26	265
12:14	127
12:15–17	125
12:21–26	124
12:21	125
12:22–23	125
12:22	125, 127
12:23	125, 127
12:26	127
12:27	265
12:29–30	53
13:12	89, 94, 285
13:8	245
14	124
14:22–24	54
14:29	95
15:20–23	44–45
15:28	169, 286

2 CORINTHIANS

11:14	283
13:14	222

GALATIANS

3:28	165, 203
5	43
5:14	114
5:19–23	61
5:22–24	285

EPHESIANS

1:13–14	44
4:15–16	164
6:12	167

PHILIPPIANS

2:5–8	50
2:9–11	169
2:12–13	106
2:12	286

COLOSSIANS

1:16–17	95
3:11	203

1 TIMOTHY

2:4	221n9
3:16	200
5:19	45

2 TIMOTHY

3:16	266

| 4:20 | 142 | 3:10 | 114 |

TITUS

| 1:12 | 165 |

HEBREWS

1:2	95
1:3	271
2:17	200
5:7–8	200
9:14	200
11:17	279

JAMES

1:27	165
2:8–17	61
2:8	114
2:14–26	44

1 PETER

2:11	279
2:12	54n2
2:15–17	54n2
2:24	156
3:18	200

2 PETER

| 1:21 | 266 |

1 JOHN

2:27	43, 52
3:2	245
3:11–24	61
4:20–21	44
5:6	42

2 JOHN

| 2 | 43 |

3 JOHN

| 3–4 | 43 |

REVELATION

5:9	166, 279
6:14	86
7:9	65, 166, 279
13:7	166
14:6	279
21:22–26	166
21:24–26	193
21:24	279
21:26	172, 279
22:2	157
22:17	168

Index of Subjects and Names

Augustine, 86, 140, 142, 148, 152, 153

Bacon, Francis, 87
Buddhism, 37, 40, 51, 57–62, 66, 105, 106, 108, 255

Colonialism, 121, 187–88, 256, 268, 273–75
Complementarity, 84, 85–90, 101, 154, 165, 199, 278, 286

Dabney, D. Lyle, 53, 264n19

Ecclesiology, 13–14, 33, 51, 123–28, 149, 156, 160, 164, 239
Eiesland, Nancy, 145, 148, 153
Emergence, 17–18, 75–78, 79–84, 98–103, 106–07, 143–45, 244–52, 282–91
Epistemology, 4–6, 17, 25, 36, 38–45, 52, 57, 63–71, 88n12, 121–22, 152, 227–30, 237–43, 244–52, 260, 283
Eschatology, 14–16, 44–45, 75–78, 104–11, 129–31, 139–46, 155–60, 167–69, 190–91, 202–03, 209–13, 244–52, 285–91
Evolution, 48, 68, 77, 83, 90n17, 94, 102, 112–15, 121

Feyerabend, Paul, 237–38
Foundationalism, 245, 260–61, 282–84

Foundational Pneumatology, 1, 2–4, 5, 8, 10–11, 12–13, 15, 16, 17, 46n2, 246–47

Gelpi, Donald, 78, 246n6, 262
Glossolalia, 79–84

Hauerwas, Stanley, 139–46, 150, 153, 255n7
Hegel, G. W. F., 36, 42, 148, 149, 152, 153
Hermeneutics, 1, 6–10, 11, 17, 30, 56, 62, 63, 66, 85–90, 124–25, 133, 154, 173, 199, 225–27, 237–43, 244–52, 260–63, 287–89

(In)commensurability, 9, 40–41, 58, 69, 254
Interdisciplinarity, 64, 79–84, 85–90, 110
Irenaeus, 32

Lindbeck, George, 7–10, 39, 58, 121n8, 247n8, 253–59

Metaphysics, 1, 2–4, 6, 24, 26–28, 37, 68–69, 78, 108, 237, 244–52
Migration, 187–91, 231–33

Oneness Pentecostalism, 24, 263, 277–78
Ontology, 1, 2–4, 8, 11, 37, 41, 87, 101, 237, 245–47

Panikkar, Raimon, 34
Parsons, Mikeal, 135, 137
Peirce, C. S., 40n6, 78, 101, 102, 243, 245, 246, 248n7
Pinnock, Clark, 28, 105n3, 264n21
Pneumatological Imagination, 1, 4–6, 8, 9, 10, 13, 15–16, 17, 24–25, 28, 50, 88, 119–22, 123, 237–43, 248, 285–86, 287–91

Rahner, Karl, 28

Reuther, Rosemary Radford, 148

Thomas Aquinas, 102, 144n12, 148, 152, 153, 223
Tracy, David, 7–10, 251

Vanhoozer, Kevin, 257–59
Vanier, Jean, 148, 150, 152, 153

Wink, Walter, 48n5, 165, 246n5

www.ingramcontent.com/pod-product-compliance
Lightning Source LLC
Chambersburg PA
CBHW030433300426
44112CB00009B/975